ADVANCES IN
INDUSTRIAL AND
LABOR RELATIONS

Volume 5 • 1991

ADVANCES IN INDUSTRIAL AND LABOR RELATIONS

A Research Annual

Editors: DONNA SOCKELL
Institute of Labor-Management Relations
Rutgers University

DAVID LEWIN
Graduate School of Business
Columbia University

DAVID B. LIPSKY
New York State School of
Industrial and Labor Relations
Cornell University

VOLUME 5 • 1991

JAI PRESS INC.

Greenwich, Connecticut   *London, England*

CONTENTS

LIST OF CONTRIBUTORS

Karen E. Boroff

Stillman School of Business
Seton Hall University

Renae F. Broderick

Center for Advanced Human Resource
  Studies
Cornell University

Gary N. Chaison

Graduate School of Management
Clark University

Richard P. Chaykowski

Department of Economics
School of Industrial Relations
Queen's University

James R. Chelius

Institute of Management and
  Labor Relations
Rutgers University

Joel Cutcher-Gershenfeld

School of Labor and Industrial Relations
Michigan State University

Edward M. Davis

Graduate School of Management
Macquarie University

Morley Gunderson

Centre for Industrial Relations
University of Toronto

Thomas Kochan

Sloan School of Management
Massachusetts Institute of Technology

Russell Lansbury

Department of Industrial Relations
University of Sydney

Barbara A. Lee   Department of Industrial Relations
                                            and Human Resources
                                          Rutgers University

Daniel J.B. Mitchell   Institute of Industrial Relations
                                          University of California, Los Angeles

Allen Ponak   Industrial Relations Research Group
                                          University of Calgary

Roberta Edgecomb Robb   Department of Economics
                                          Brock University

Joseph B. Rose   Faculty of Business
                                          McMaster University

Mark Thompson   Faculty of Commerce
                                          University of British Columbia

Anil Verma   Industrial Relations Centre
                                          University of Toronto

ADVANCES IN INDUSTRIAL AND LABOR RELATIONS

Editorial Board and Submissions Information

Professor Fiorito has kindly served as a member of our board since its establishment, but he was inadvertently left out of the listing in Volume 4 of AILR.

AILR is a refereed research volume published annually or biannually. Although the series is designed to focus on industrial relations issues, the editors welcome articles from scholars in diverse disciplines, such as economics, law, history, organizational behavior, psychology, and sociology. Independent of discipline, scholars interested in submitting papers for publications on any aspect of industrial relations should send three copies of their manuscript, entirely double spaced, to:

Jane Wildhorn
Institute of Industrial Relations
UCLA
1001 Gayley Ave.
Los Angeles, CA 90024
Tel: (213) 825-9192; Fax: (213) 825-0023

GUEST EDITOR'S INTRODUCTION

The first five papers of this volume originated in the Pacific Rim Labour Policy Conference in Vancouver, Canada in 1987, sponsored by the Asia Pacific Business Institute and The Bureau of National Affairs, and organized by Profs. Joseph M. Weiler, W. Craig Riddell, and Mark Thompson, all from the University of British Columbia. The conference featured papers from Australia, Canada, Japan, and the United States on four themes: employee involvement, public sector labor relations, wage flexibility/gain-sharing compensation arrangements, and comparable worth. Due to competing demands on the authors' time and data, plus the editorial requirements of the *Advances* series, only a sample of the papers presented at the conference were available for this volume. Taken together, however, they provide comparative perspective on major issues in industrial and labor relations.

EMPLOYEE INVOLVEMENT (EI)

The two papers on EI discuss a variety of issues of interest to scholars in many countries. Lansbury and Davis, drawing upon the Australian experience, identify a fundamental distinction among EI plans. Employers generally tend to favor programs at the level of the workplace designed to improve productivity or implement technological or organizational change. However, Australian employers oppose statutory requirements for such programs. The

Australian labor movement and its political allies have favored industrial democracy, by which they mean an employee voice at higher organizational levels, normally involving unions already established in the firm.

This theme is echoed by Cutcher-Gershenfeld, Kochan, and Verma, who discuss the American experience with EI. They divide EI programs into two categories: self-contained and integrated. Self-contained programs do not involve any change in other aspects of organizational structures and are initiated by management, presumably for the reasons identified by Lansbury and Davis. Integrated programs are more likely to involve union participation and entail a redistribution of power in the organization. In the United States, the authors find that there has been a high attrition rate in EI programs, and they hypothesize that self-contained programs will survive longer than integrated programs, although the former are easier for employers to start than the latter.

Both papers address the issue of institutionalized opposition to EI. Employers are unwilling to yield authority over their workforces and thus oppose many types of EI. Unions in both systems exist to offset management power, so they have little interest in supporting what is essentially a competing forum for representing employee interests. In addition, the respective legal systems in the two countries are not receptive to EI initiatives.

The two papers also identify possible sources of support for EI programs. Australian unions have supported industrial democracy principally in the areas of wages and working conditions, traditional fields for trade union action. In the United States, the highest probability of success occurs where both technology and business strategy stress flexibility, participation is associated with changes in the organization of work, and labor leaders take on new roles which presumably involve them in major management decisions outside the traditional scope of collective bargaining.

The Australian paper points out the political dimension of EI in that country. There have been short-lived government initiatives to encourage participation in Australia (such initiatives have never really been raised seriously in the United States), and the paper concludes with suggestions for the role of public policy. Given the emphasis of both these papers on the barriers to participation and on the relationship between changes in managerial authority and the success of EI, it is difficult to be optimistic about the possibility for major change in work organization without government action.

PUBLIC SECTOR INDUSTRIAL RELATIONS

For a predominantly American audience, the Thompson-Ponak paper presents both similarities and differences in public sector industrial relations in the United States and Canada. The contrasts suggest a number of areas for research in these and other countries.

Because all Canadian jurisdictions permit strikes by at least some public sector employees, experience with legal public sector strikes offers opportunities for research on the outcomes of strikes by different employee groups, the effectiveness of partial strikes by essential employees, and the testing of models of strike behavior that incorporate the noneconomic variables that are so important in Canada. Canadian legislation permits bargaining over wages and salaries, although not always over pensions and civil service personnel functions. Because research has concentrated on public sector wages, data are lacking on the ways in which public sector unions influence decisions on issues excluded from bargaining or the impact of restrictions on bargaining scope on the outcome of negotiations over bargainable issues.

These subjects also raise fundamental questions about the role of politics in public sector industrial relations. At one extreme, it can be claimed that all industrial relations in the public sector is political. The U.S. literature of the 1970s put considerable emphasis on multilateral bargaining, a subject identified by Thompson and Ponak as having little importance in Canada. They end their paper by attacking the politicization of industrial relations by Canadian governments. In general, however, industrial relations research has neglected the linkages between politics and industrial relations processes.

FLEXIBLE COMPENSATION

Mitchell and Broderick examine a fragmented body of literature on flexible compensation in the United States. Compensation specialists have traditionally espoused such plans to promote productivity, and in the 1980s economists raised the possibility that these systems could reduce unemployment without stimulating inflation. The authors identify four types of flexible pay plans: simple incentives, profit sharing, gain sharing, and employee stock ownership plans (ESOPs). Profit sharing seems to be the most common of the types, while simple incentives are declining in importance. Seldom are the effects of these systems analyzed objectively, but there is a large body of literature written by advocates touting their successes and neglecting their failures.

Academic research indicates that there are weak links between productivity improvements and flexible pay plans. However, managers in organizations which have these systems are generally supportive of them. Despite the favorable publicity and generous tax treatment for ESOPs in the 1980s, a sample of managers surveyed seem reluctant to promote these plans. The authors suggest that tax exemptions might be better directed toward profit sharing.

There is an air of frustration in the authors' conclusions. Despite the theoretical appeal of flexible pay plans, data on their incidence are inadequate, proof of their impact is lacking, and the viewpoints of practitioners and researchers are still too diverse to give direction to public policy.

COMPARABLE WORTH

Gunderson and Robb discuss the Canadian experience with comparable worth from the economist's perspective. They find that a portion of male-female wage differentials can be attributed to discrimination, and equal pay legislation has existed for a considerable period in Canada without affecting differentials substantially. Therefore, there is a justification for comparable worth programs, which address both wage discrimination and occupational segregation. However, their paper concentrates on difficulties in implementing these policies.

The design of effective comparable worth programs has proven to be complex. There are technical problems in constructing estimates of the weights given to factors in predominantly male and female jobs. The question of functional form arises in the estimation of male and female pay lines, and several different regression techniques have been used to analyze such data. When differentials have been identified, Canadian enforcement agencies have tried several ways of adjusting female rates to male rates. Two enforcement systems are used in Canadian comparable worth plans; these are known as complaints-based and system-wide proactive. Complaints-based systems generate a small number of cases, presumably because of the burden they place on employees. Proactive plans allow cases to be opened based on job evaluation information. Finally, enforcement procedures can take several forms, although there is still too little information to permit identification of the optimum system.

Based on very limited empirical evidence, the impact of comparable worth programs has been modest in both the United States and Canada. The more significant question then is the impact of such policies when applied more broadly. The Gunderson and Robb paper clearly shows that achieving consensus on the need for a comparable worth program, difficult though that task may be, is really only the beginning. Implementation of these policies raises major problems for both scholars and practitioners.

Mark Thompson
Guest Editor

SERIES EDITORS' INTRODUCTION

This volume of *Advances in Industrial and Labor Relations* (AILR) includes nine papers, five of which were originally presented at the Pacific Rim Labour Policy Conference and which are introduced above by Guest Editor, Professor Mark Thompson, one of that conference's organizers. We are indebted to Professor Thompson for his efforts in this regard and wish explicitly to acknowledge those efforts here. This Series Editors' Introduction will briefly preview and summarize the four remaining papers in this volume.

The first of these papers, by Professors Gary Chaison and Joseph Rose, addresses the factors accounting for the divergent trends between Canada and the United States with respect to union membership in the work forces of these North American countries. As is well-known, union membership in Canada has risen dramatically in recent years, while at the same time, union membership has declined markedly (even dramatically) in the United States. What factors account for these strikingly contrasting experiences?

Foremost, in this regard, according to Chaison and Rose, are the different legal frameworks for and treatments of union organizing in Canada and in the United States. The Canadian approach to this issue features a reliance on authorization card counts and expedited union representation elections, which combine to produce relatively swift election outcomes. In the United States, by contrast, authorization cards mark the beginning, not the end, of a representation election, and delay rather than expeditiousness characterizes the representation election process. Conditioned by these respective legal environments, employer opposition to union organizing and election-related activity is far greater in the United States than in Canada—though, as Chaison and Rose note, latent employer opposition to unionism in Canada could be much more overt if that country operated under United States-style labor law.

The aforementioned legal environments also stimulate different union behaviors in the two countries. In Canada, according to Chaison and Rose, labor unions have adopted an aggressive posture whereby they actively seek out organizing targets, whereas United States unions have followed a defensive, hold the line posture in terms of organizing efforts. Chaison and Rose go on to speculate that the very "success" of Canadian unions may spur the tendency toward severance and autonomy of certain international unions, especially those beset by financial difficulties. Though they do not say so, Chaison and Rose's interpretation of the "Continental Divide" thesis might perhaps be strengthened by an analysis of the stance of public-sector employers toward employee unionism, which in the United States, at least, is generally believed to be far less hostile than that of private-sector employers.

The seventh paper in this volume, by Professor Karen Boroff, examines the perceived effectiveness of a workplace grievance procedure in one nonunion company. Grievance procedures and research about them in unionized settings are well-known, but hardly the same can be said of such procedures and research in nonunion settings. Further, most grievance procedure research has not incorporated the perceived fairness of these procedures by employees (to say nothing of managers), so that in this respect Professor Boroff breaks new ground.

Her multivariate analyses show that employees and managers who use a grievance procedure (certain managerial employees are generally eligible to use such procedures in nonunion companies) assess effectiveness along different dimensions than "nonusers." Moreover, nonunion employees judge grievance procedure effectiveness to be enhanced when an adversarial, factfinding component is included in such a procedure. This finding is important because nonunion grievance procedures apparently vary considerably along this dimension, and because a third-party component is more typically associated with the exercise of collective voice than individual voice. Professor Boroff also shows that research on grievance procedures must distinguish between employees who (perceive that they) experience unfair treatment in the employment relationship and those who do not; aggregating these experiences, she tells us, is very likely to lead to invalid conclusions about grievance procedure effectiveness, even, and perhaps especially, when investigated within a quantitative, multivariate framework of analysis. Finally, Professor Boroff alerts us to the relevance of reference groups in assessing nonunion (and, by inference, unionized) employees' perceptions of grievance procedure effectiveness.

The paper by Professor Richard Chaykowski expands on recent research into the nonwage outcomes of collective bargaining by his use of Canadian data and by the exhaustive nature of his analysis, portions of which include the disaggregation of a data set encompassing 2,000 bargaining units covering one million workers. Professor Chaykowski finds that disaggregated analyses do matter in that the statistical significance of independent variables which influence bargaining outcomes—for example, bargaining unit size, size of the parent union, the presence of an employer association, and union affiliation—varies markedly when an aggregate data base is decomposed. In particular, the effect of union characteristics on the "demand" for alternative nonwage bargaining outcomes varies by categories of contract clauses which, in turn, influences the tradeoffs that occur in these differing bargaining contexts. This conclusion from a collective bargaining study supports Boroff's findings from a nonunion study, namely, that there are risks and costs associated with strictly aggregate analyses of industrial relations data bases, both at the macro and micro levels.

Professor Chaykowski also contributes to research on nonwage bargaining outcomes by providing a new comprehensive coding scheme that assesses each contract clause on the bases of its "favorableness" to the union, and by testing the data based on this coding scheme along both ordinal and dichotomous dimensions. Among specific empirical results, Chaykowski finds that percent female (among union members) and the presence of an employer association have strong influences on the substitution between pecuniary and nonpecuniary bargaining outcomes. These and the many other findings reported in his study are offered by Professor Chaykowski, in part, to inform the making of public policy toward unionism and collective bargaining in Canada—especially because such policy-making often assumes certain "central" outcomes to flow from collective bargaining when, in fact, such outcomes vary markedly among collective bargaining relationships.

In the final paper in this volume, Professors Barbara Lee and James Chelius examine the criteria used by state and federal courts to evaluate the constitutionality of New Jersey's Casino Control Act in terms of its restrictions on union officers' "freedom to associate." The authors begin by reviewing the doctrine of freedom of association, relying heavily on decisions of the U.S. Supreme Court in this regard, and then apply this doctrine and these decisions to the activities of Local #54 of the Hotel and Restaurant Employees and Bartenders International Union. Certain officers of this union were required in 1983 to resign their positions as a condition of Local #54's continued representation of members in the New Jersey casino industry, on the ground that they had knowingly associated with organized crime figures. As Lee and Chelius note, the outcome of this case is probably attractive to those who want to reduce the influence of organized crime generally and on unions in particular, but "it has troubling implications for individual liberty"—which is, to say, freedom of association.

The authors then go on to assess both the specific and the broader implications of the decision in the Local #54 case. They observe that the legal proceedings in this case took stronger note of the "social" and "political" associations among certain of Local #54's leaders and organized crime figures than of the "economic" and intimate" associations among them. The authors propose that each of these four associational dimensions be carefully assessed before union officers are judicially separated from their union(s). More broadly, the authors express concern that the Federal Racketeer Influenced and Corrupt Organizations (Rico) statute and comparable state laws may sweep with too broad a brush and unnecessarily assume that, in the context of union activity, the mere association of union officials with (alleged) organized crime figures compromises a union's independent and effective functioning. A showing that criminal offenders actually wielded influence in union affairs, say Lee and Chelius, would provide more judicial specificity in this area as well as a better balance between restrictions on criminal activity and the freedom to associate in a union context. Readers should note that this is one of the few scholarly articles to have emerged on this industrial relations topic.

We believe that Volume 5 of AILR offers a rich and interesting mix of articles on contemporary and comparative industrial relations. We trust that readers of this annual series will share our belief.

David Lewin
Donna Sockell
David B. Lipsky
Series Editors

ACKNOWLEDGMENTS

The editors of AILR wish to thank the following individuals who served as referees for manuscripts submitted for publication consideration in this volume.

Steven Allen	Thomas Knight
Richard Arvey	Thomas Kochan
George Bain	Thomas Kohler
Phillip Beaumont	John Lawler
James Begin	Peter B. Levy
Fran Blau	James Martin
Richard Block	Marick Masters
Peter Cappelli	Daniel J.B. Mitchell
Dan Cornfield	Olivia Mitchell
Joel Cutcher-Gershenfeld	Edward Montgomery
John T. Delaney	Robert McKersie
Peter Feuille	Charles O'Reilly
Jack Fiorito	Craig Olson
Daniel Gallagher	Paul Osterman
John Godard	Solomon Polachek
Michael Gold	Allen Ponak
Charles R. Greer	Joseph Rose
Morley Gunderson	Susan Schowhau
Wallace Hendricks	Michael Schuster
Casey Ichniowski	Robert Smith
Sandy Jacoby	Lloyd Ulman
Bruce Kaufman	Anil Verma
Jeffrey Keefe	Hoyt Wheeler
Morris Kleiner	Mahmood Zaidi

The editors also wish to thank Ms. Drew Claxton, Senior Research Assistant of the Industrial Relations Research Center, for her invaluable help in the administrative matters associated with the preparation of the volume.

Finally, this fifth volume is the final volume of which Professor David B. Lipsky will serve as editor. Involved with AILR since its inception, Professor Lipsky has made invaluable contributions to the development of AILR as a quality series. We will miss Professor Lipsky's help and guidance and hope that he will return to the series after he completes his time as Dean of the New York State School of Industrial and Labor Relations, Cornell University. Until that time, we hope to carry on the fine tradition he has established.

RECENT DEVELOPMENTS IN U.S. EMPLOYEE INVOLVEMENT INITIATIVES:
EROSION OR DIFFUSION

Joel Cutcher-Gershenfeld, Thomas Kochan, and

Anil Verma

INTRODUCTION

A visitor from abroad making inquiries about the recent U.S. developments in increased employee participation (or involvement)[1] in workplace decisions will readily make three observations. First, after two decades of slow experimentation with participation programs, U.S. firms began to rapidly adopt a variety of participative forms in the early 1980s. Writing of conditions leading up to 1980, one researcher compared innovations in participative structure in the United States with those in Japan and Sweden and concluded that for a number of reasons, the United States had largely lagged behind (Cole 1982). However, by 1985 a number of surveys reported that between one-third to one-half of U.S. firms had adopted some form of direct employee participation in workplace affairs.[2] Such rapid diffusion has led some experts

Advances in Industrial and Labor Relations, volume 5, pages 1-32.
Copyright © 1991 by JAI Press Inc.
All rights of reproduction in any form reserved.
ISBN: 0-89232-940-8

to warn managers to look beyond the "fad" and to carefully examine the true potential of such innovations (Lawler and Mohrman 1985). Second, although no precise estimates are available, first-hand information provided by consultants and managers suggests that there is a high rate of attrition in adopted participation programs. By one estimate, roughly 40 percent of such initiatives last only for two or three years or less (Rankin 1986). Moreover, while participative programs appear to be more frequently initiated in nonunion establishments than in unionized ones (Freedman 1985; Verma 1983), there is also some evidence to suggest that the presence of a union increases the probability that, once initiated, participation will survive over time.

In this paper, we attempt to develop a theoretical framework in which all of these related but separate developments can be understood. In other words, we pose the following questions: Why have certain forms of employee participation diffused more rapidly in the 1980s than previously? Equal, why are some of them so short-lived? What are the impediments to diffusing and sustaining these programs in unionized settings? While some of these questions have been considered separately by other studies in the past, the literature lacks a comprehensive treatement of how the employee involvement (EI) processes are integrated with the rest of the organization. Our focus will be on the unionized sector since it is in these settings—with an institutionalized set of adversarial relations—that participation poses the deepest questions. This contrast is usually less salient in nonunion organizations but distinct implications for nonunion settings will be noted. In the first section of this paper, after reviewing highlights from the literature, a framework is developed to explain the organization. The second section identifies five critical issues that affect the diffusion and institutionalization of these processes and presents examples of pivotal events centered on each. Lastly, implications for research, policy, and practice are drawn.

THEORETICAL FRAMEWORK

To begin with, it is important to adopt a precise definition of what we mean by employee involvement or worker participation as it is variously called. In the literature, a large variety of forms—from suggestion schemes to autonomous work groups to joint labor-management committees—have been referred to as forms of worker participation. In this paper, we limit our definition to those forms that provide for *direct* employee input through a *formal* and *group* structure into decisions that directly affect their jobs. Thus, we exclude indirect representation, as well as programs that are informal or based only on individual rather than group effort. Further, we exclude programs that only provide for employee inputs into extra-mural activities such as sport clubs and Christmas dinners. This approach also differs from the common use of the term participation in much of the literature on industrial democracy, since it does not necessarily imply the existence of a legally mandated formal structure for participation, such as works councils. Our use obviously reflects current policy and practice in North America where there are no legal requirements for such structures. In the last section of the paper we explore policy options that we feel are appropriate to the U.S. context.

Our reasons for choosing this definition are two-fold. First, theoretical developments to date suggest that not all forms of participation are likely to have the same impact (Dachler and Wilpert 1978; Cotton, Vollrath, Froggartt, Legnick-Hall, and Jenniye 1988). Hence, there is a need for a parsimonious typology that can help researchers focus on each conceptually distinct form of participation. This adoption of a more precise definition is likely to bring greater conceptual clarity in contrast to grouping together all the different forms of participation in one classification. Second, while other forms of participation (e.g., individual effort, indirect, informal, etc.) have been around for many years now, it is those contained in our definition that are relatively "new" to the American workplace.[3] Moreover, these are the forms of participation that have been rapidly growing in recent years. Thus, more than other forms of participation, the type selected here is critical in terms of invested resources and their potential impact on the organization.

The major thrust in organization research on employee participation has been on examining its effects (e.g., job satisfaction, productivity, etc.) at the individual level. Since three comprehensive reviews of such studies are available (Cotton et al. 1988; Miller and Monge 1986; Locke and Schweiger 1979), we will refer only selectively to those studies in this paper. It should be noted, however, that our conclusions directly contradict one main finding of the Miller and Monge (1986) study, which found little support (via meta-analytic methods) for what they called "contingent" models of participation. This paper presents evidence from contingent institutional developments (which emerged, interestingly, in one case out of an individual-level attitude survey) and finds support for contingencies that were not addressed in any of the articles selected for the meta-analysis. This contrast is but one example of a gap in the literature around the issue of integrating employee involvement with *organizational* and *institutional* (e.g., collective bargaining) structures and processes. Of course, some studies do touch on organizational issues and our attempt is to build upon this theoretical foundation.

TWO APPROACHES TO IMPLEMENTATION OF EMPLOYEE PARTICIPATION

The substantive content of any participation form or scheme is a good point of departure in building a theoretical framework. Sifting through the large case study literature (and our own cases described later), it is not difficult to recognize the two polarized types of participative structure that vary by the extent to which they are integrated with the rest of the organization. The first type is characterized by its *self-contained* nature, that is, the participative structure is not accompanied by any corresponding changes in organizational structure, procedures, and other subsystems. What are often referred to as Japanese Quality Control Circles (QC) is a good example of this form of participation. (In fact, other forms of participation can be found in Japan, but it is the narrow form that is best known.) This narrow form is notable because it does not threaten or require a change in the traditional hierarchical structure of authority (Cole 1982). Because of their self-contained nature, such forms can be seen as an add-on feature which requires relatively less effort to implement. Perhaps for this reason, quality circles have become the single most popular form of employee participation in the United States (see note 2). One distinction among the narrowly focused efforts that has proven to be of great consequences is the extent to which it begins as a unilateral management program or as a joint initiative. We return to this distinction later in the paper.

The second type of employee participation is characterized by its high degree of *integration* with and impact on the rest of the organization. Such forms require a host of changes in organizational structures, procedures, and other subsystems. Typical examples of this type of participation are autonomous work groups (*sjalvstyrand grupper*) in Sweden which have been, by their very design, intended to challenge and alter the traditional hierarchical structure of authority (Aguren, Hansson, and Karlsson 1976; Trist 1981). Because of their substantial impact on other organization subsystems, such forms require a large investment in terms of cost and effort and, hence, are more difficult to implement. This partially explains why only a handful of U.S. firms have adopted this form for introducing employee involvement to their organizations.

The main thesis of this paper is that the self-contained type of participative structure may be easier to implement, but its ability to sustain itself in the long run is limited—at least in the American setting.[4] Because of the relatively low start-up costs, these forms can serve as useful *starting points* for introducing greater employee involvement in a traditional hierarchical organization. However, the self-contained and narrowly-focused form is unstable in the long run because it cannot meet the conditions necessary for institutionalizing employee involvement in decision making (which will be discussed shortly). Conversely, the more participative principles become employed in addressing a wider scope of issues, the more likely that they will sustain over time and, thereby, become institutionalized within the formal organization. Indeed, we will argue that the reasons for instability, on the one hand, and integration, on the other, are linked. Before turning to our case study evidence on this point, however, it will be helpful to review findings in the literature on the stability of participation efforts.

AN OVERVIEW OF THE LITERATURE

There are two major streams of research findings that suggest that narrowly focused, self-contained participative forms are likely to be unstable in the long run. First, a number of studies by behavioral scientists on the participative process indicate that participation is never very effective in increasing morale and productivity when used in isolation from other organizational subsystems (Cotton et al. 1988; Miller and Monge 1986; Locke and Schweiger 1979). For example, the critical role of a contingent reward system in mediating the effect of participation on behavioral and attitudinal outcomes has been well documented (see, for example, Neider 1980; Rosenberg and Rosenstein 1980). Another set of studies has demonstrated that narrowly focused participation in work decision is not as effective as when participation in work decisions has a broader mandate such as in planning the work itself and setting objectives for what is to be accomplished (see, for example, Peterson, Peterson, and Macy 1982; Lee and Schuler 1982). Lastly, some studies have found that while self-contained types of participative programs have enhanced employee perceptions of their own influence, perceptions of the influence and control wielded by upper management (and hence their lack of integration with the organization) have remained unchanged (Dickson 1982).

The second stream of research comes from the industrial relations tradition which generally holds that, in order for an industrial relations system to be stable, the system must continually meet the goals and aspiration of each of the parties in the system (Kochan 1980; Dunlop 1958). In the case of employee involvement, this means that adopted participative forms must meet the goals of employers, employees, and, in unionized settings, of the union.[5] As an overview of this literature, we will consider the goals of employers, employees, and unions in turn.

Employers' Interest and Participation

Even though the question of whether participation per se improves productivity has not been definitively answered (Katz, Kochan, and Gobeille 1983; Miller and Monge 1986; Cotton et al. 1988), employee involvement has been frequently associated with several positive outcomes for employers. There is some indication that membership in employee involvement programs increases workers' identification with employer-defined goals of the organization (Verma and McKersie 1987). Another study reported improved employee perceptions of the management and its performance (Lischerson and Wall 1975). Such participative forms have also been found to increase workers' acceptance of the need to upgrade technology (Verma and Zerbe 1989). Finally, our research group has concluded elsewhere on the basis of earlier case studies that participation has often served as a necessary first step in building trust and opening up the parties to broadening the scope of their change efforts to address larger problems affecting organizational performance (Kochan, Katz, and Mower 1984). It is perhaps for these reasons that American management has been an enthusiastic promoter of at least self-contained and narrowly focused forms of participation (see, for example, Orr and Blumberg 1977). However, a key caveat to note concerns middle- and lower-level managers, who often see participation programs as limiting their managerial activity and possibly even threatening their job security (Klein 1986). The response to employee participation has been less enthusiastic among these managers.

Employees' Interests and Participation

For employees, positive outcomes such as higher job satisfaction (Miller and Monge 1986; Locke and Schweiger 1979) and increased communication (Harrison 1985) have been indicated. While the issue of job security under participative forms has not been fully investigated, workers surveyed in at least one firm indicated no perceived loss of job security due to the employee involvement program (Verma and McKersie 1987). On the negative side, the research to date suggests that self-contained and narrowly focused forms of participation have failed to address a number of employee concerns. For employees, such programs typically raise expectations of a more consultative and democratic workplace. In several studies, workers enrolled in participative programs have reported a higher need for "say" and influence in decision compared to workers who are not enrolled (Rafaeli 1985). Meanwhile, given the self-contained nature of many of these programs, a number of studies have found little change in the organization either in substantive terms or in terms of management style to meet those raised expectations (Witte 1980; Kochan, Katz, and Mower 1984). In one study of failure in several quality circle programs, Frazer and Dale (1986) reported perceived lack of management support as one of the key causes of the programs' demise.[6] Although failures have not been systematically examined in any large sample, case study research has identified numerous other causes relating to organizational inability to make corresponding changes in its subsystems. For example, several researchers have pointed to the need for developing a compensation policy designed to reward extra effort expended by employees in participative decision making (Kanter 1986; Sell 1986).

Union Interests and Participation

Next, we must examine if the union's goals are met in participative form of workplace organization. Most American unions have either remained cool or opposed to employee involvement, some in principle while others for reasons involving the manner in which participation has been implemented (Kochan 1985; Kochan, Katz, and Mower 1984). Management's position in many cases had been one of "going it alone" on employee involvement with no attempt to solicit union's participation (Verma and McKersie 1986). For both union and managment the underlying belief for unions' noninvolvement is that narrow forms of employee involvement and collective bargaining (the main forum for union-management relations) are ideally kept mutually exclusive—ostensibly, the better the separation, the greater the chance of success in each arena. Such ideas also appeared in the early writings of theorists (Kochan and Dyer 1976) and practitioners (Bluestone 1981), but were later modified through both empirical and conceptual reexamination (Schuster 1985; Rankin 1986; Kochan, Katz, and McKersie 1986). A number of studies show that in cases where collective bargaining and employee involvement were strictly separated, the participative forms were by necessity, very narrow in their scope. This finding is amply supported by the case examples presented below. With a strict separation, participation groups cannot reexamine or redesign jobs or wage payments systems, they cannot alter schedules and work assignment patterns, and they are restricted in changing many other aspects of the workplace—all of which have significant effects on productivity, but all of which are governed by the collective agreement. It follows then that the more separated employee involvement is from collective bargaining, the more narrowly focused the program will be. It is ironic, given the insistence by so many unions on this separation, that it leaves the efforts less likely to meet any of the union's goals or the employees' goals in making meaningful changes in the workplace. The employee involvement process under these conditions is likely to stagnate and eventually decline.

Another link between unions and participation has been articulated by Kochan, Katz and Mower (1984), who have argued that unions' endorsement of and involvement in the participation program has major consequences for the type of worker that the program is likely to attract. If the union is involved in the program, workers would perceive the program as a part of the union's overall plan. Workers who are more active in the union and also those who think more favorably of the union are likely to volunteer for joining the EI program, workers active in the union would be unlikely to join if EI is not part of the overall plan. Thus, a narrowly focused program which does not have the support of the union is more likely to create a schism among the workers unfriendly to the union. In one organization where the union was uninvolved in the participation program, it was found that the workers less interested in union activities were more likely to volunteer for the program (Verma and McKersie 1987). Thus, a union's lack of involvement may lead to adverse outcomes for the union. It is less likely that such a program would last over time, given that the union's goals will not be met under such conditions.

A DYNAMIC MODEL OF PARTICIPATION IN THE ORGANIZATIONAL CONTEXT

Based on the discussion so far, we can now develop a set of propositions about the conditions under which the employee involvement process is likely to take root and become integrated into the organization. At this point it is important to note that the process of institutionalizing participative forms is composed of two complementary parts—the motivating pressures and the attitudinal and behavioral changes in union-management relations required to initiate change, on one hand, and the structural changes in the organization through which institutionalization takes form, on the other. In this paper we focus only on the latter since we see the institutionalization of change as the central challenge facing labor and management today and the pivotal determinant of the extent to which innovations in industrial relations will diffuse to a broader set of relationships.[7] Also, in some of the propositions we emphasize what we term an iterative process involving a sequence of pivotal events. This formulation has emerged in an inductive manner from our field research, which is discussed in some detail in the body of this paper. It rests, however, on a long tradition of viewing social relations from a dynamic perspective. It is a stance reflected in the work of one of the founding U.S. industrial relations theorists, John R. Commons (1918), as well as in the work of other leading social theorists (see, for example, Lewin 1951; Trist 1981). Briefly, the view that we have developed may be summarized in terms of the following propositions.

Proposition 1.   Self-contained and narrowly focused participative forms are most likely to be selected as starting points because of the low level of investment required and the relatively lower political risks they pose for union-management relations.

Proposition 2.   However, if the participative process is strictly separated from collective bargaining and other aspects of the employment relationship, the employee involvement initiative is likely to remain narrowly focused. This will lead to stagnation and demise because a narrowly focused program cannot meet the goals of all parties over time.

Proposition 3.   Participative programs that are jointly sponsored by union and management are likely to survive longer than unilateral programs in unionized settings because joint sponsorship makes it more likely that the self-contained participative form can be broadened in scope and gradually integrated into the organization.

Proposition 4.   Participative forms that come to be broadened in scope are likely to make changes in information flow, access to decision makers, how work is organized on the shop-floor, employment security, the content and process of collective bargaining, and even strategic decisions around resource allocation. These changes, in turn, can reinforce and even transform the participative process insofar as the changes help attain the goals of all parties involved. This symbiosis will increase the probability that employee involvement will take root and survive in the long run.

Proposition 5. The process by which this broadening in scope occurs is not a smooth continuous evolution or in any sense inevitable. Rather, the parties confront a series of pivotal events associated with the issues mentioned in the previous point. Some of these events represent major joint opportunities and others reveal areas of potentially deep conflict (both reflecting what is inherently a mixed motive relationship). These pivotal events serve to illuminate the extent to which participative initiatives are, or are not meeting the parties' needs. As such, it is expected that these events will mark the steps toward or away from deeper integration in the organization. Thus, each of these pivotal events can be seen as having a double-edged potential either to undercut or reinforce and transform the participative efforts.

These propositions should serve to focus and expand on themes initially developed in the Kochan, Katz, and McKersie study of *The Transformation of American Industrial Relations* (1986). The propositions are principally concerned with the staying power of participative initiatives that are, at the outset, narrowly focused. In fact, most programs begin this way. Accordingly, this will be the main focus of the following examples. However, towards the end of this paper consideration will be given to efforts designed from the outset to be broader in scope.

CASE STUDY EVIDENCE

As a preliminary test of the viability of the above hypotheses, we will turn to detailed case study data drawn from nine field sites that were the subject of a three-year study conducted under the auspices of MIT's Industrial Relations Section with support from the U.S. Department of Labor. The cases are part of a panel of nine firms and fifteen local or national unions that were selected as having at least two or three years experience with new patterns of industrial relations. Thus, we use these cases to illustrate the dynamics associated with the diffusion and institutionalization of the new patterns. They are not, however, necessarily representative of all developments in the United States. At the conclusion of this paper, we explicitly discuss the extent to which these findings are suggestive, but not conclusive, in pointing new directions for policy and practice.

Although the cases and the research methodology have been discussed in more detail elsewhere (Kochan and Cutcher-Gershenfeld 1988), it should be noted that at least twenty-five interviews (and in some cases over 100) were conducted with union and management leaders, and workers in each site over a three-year period of time. Key individuals were interviewed a number of times over the three years. As well, in some cases attitude surveys were conducted and performance data were examined. A brief description of each case is included below.

The United Automobile Workers Union (UAW) and General Motors (GM)

Our focus in this case was on the Fiero and Lake Orion assembly plants, both of which feature a fundamental reorganization of work design. The roles of labor and management have been significantly modified to afford employees greater autonomy, less supervision, and, in the case of Fiero, union representation in all plant-level strategic and administrative decisions. During our research the joint design and creation of the Saturn Corporation was also solidified and the GM plant in Fremont, California, was re-opened (after a two year shutdown) as a joint venture with Toyota. We followed some aspects of both of these developments as well. Also, following the completion of the research, the idling of the Fiero plant was announced. At one point below, some of the implications of this recent development are noted.

The Amalgamated Clothing and Textile Workers Union (ACTWU) and Xerox

The seven plants in Xerox's home manufacturing complex (near Rochester, New York) show how narrowly focused quality circles can evolve to encompass multiple forms of employee participation and innovation in the organization of work, all of which is reinforced via contractual language including a no-layoff guarantee, joint decision making regarding outsourcing, and gainsharing. Further, the parties have built on a history of informal consultation about strategic issues with the establishment of joint "horizon" planning committees on human resource management and other issues, the joint design of a new manufacturing facility, and union involvement in new product development.

The Air Line Pilots Association (ALPA), the International Brotherhood of Teamsters (IBT), the Association of Flight Attendants (AFA), and the Air Transport Employees (ATE) Western Airlines

A financial crisis brought on by industry deregulation led Western to pose concession demands to all four unions. Though each of the negotiations was different, all four unions ultimately emerged with significant minority stock ownership for the members, a seat on the board of directors, and, in one case, an agreement to pursue greater employee participation in daily decisions. Of particular interest is the great variation in the strategies selected by the four unions.

The International Association of Machinists (IAM) and the Boeing Corporation

Rapid advances in manufacturing technology led the union to push for joint roles in the exploration, selection, and implementation of new technology. The operation of the joint structure that evolved over the course of two contract cycles in Boeing's Seattle, Washington, facility and a parallel quality circle effort were the focus of this research.

The Aluminum, Brick and Glass Workers Union (ABGWU) and Alcoa

A rolling mill, in a highly competitive portion of the aluminum industry, was the setting in which these parties attempted to guide employee involvement activities and work re-organization through a period of major wage and benefit concessions. The concessions also reflect decentralization of bargaining in the industry. We explore the consequences within the local union and in a range of joint activities.

The United Automobile Workers (UAW) and the Budd Company

These parties have sought to sustain employee involvement initiatives, limited just-in-time delivery, and quality control improvement. These changes have been prompted by customer pressure in the context of the highly competitive auto supply industry. During our research, efforts were initiated to link plant-level participative activities to cooperation at the corporate/international union level. Also, one local negotiated an agreement to accept significant work rule changes and the use of a team concept approach to work organization in return for reinvestment in its facilities.

The Diesel Workers Union (DWU) and the Officer and Clerical Unit (OCU) and Cummins Engine

After nearly a decade of experimentation with the design of nonunion facilities based on sociotechnical principles, the parties are now trying to integrate these innovations into the company's unionized home manufacturing complex. We have followed the diffusion of new systems for the organization of work, as well as related changes in collective bargaining as they have evolved during a period of layoffs and management turnover at the corporate level.

The Paperworkers Union and Boise Cascade Corporation

Two decades of low performance in the company's newest and largest facility—partly connected with an increasingly complex set of work rules—led to company bargaining demands for a sweeping revision of the contract and hundreds of attached memorandums of agreement. After a lengthy strike, the company prevailed, and imposed a contract with only four job classifications, a team-based, flexible work organization, a no lay-off pledge covering current employees and substantial wage increases for those affected by the job classification changes. Critical questions in this case concern the implementation and evolution of such changes when they are imposed by hard bargaining.

The United Rubber Workers Union (URW) and Goodyear Corporation

Gradually, over about ten years, the parties have made a series of incremental changes in the organization of work and the structure of union-management relations in their Lincoln, Nebraska, facility. We were interested in the process and results of these changes.

In addition to drawing on data from these nine research sites, we will also highlight aspects of a handful of other current labor-management initiatives that either we or others have studied. Although some examples and cases are drawn from nonmanufacturing settings (e.g., Western Airlines), it should be noted that our data are largely drawn from experiences in medium-sized and large manufacturing facilities. This increases our confidence in the applicability of our conclusions to similar manufacturing settings, but may limit the broader generalizability of these findings.

The case data will be organized around some of the most common and most important issues that participative initiatives confront over time and that either help institutionalize or erode participation in an organization. These issues are: (1) access to information and organization decision makers, (2) employment security, (3) variation in worker preferences, (4) work organization reforms, (5) collective bargaining shocks, and (6) strategic shocks.

Access to Information and Organization Decision Makers

Even a narrowly focused quality circle requires more than just regular time off the job, training, and facilitation if it is to effectively solve problems of importance to either the employees or the firm. Innumerable problems require access to information previously not available to these employees. Furthermore, once a proposed solution is offered by the group, a response is required from the organization—often creating new demands on organizational decision makers and changes in the distribution of power within the management structure. These two issues, access to information and access to decision makers, are among the first points of tension to emerge in a narrowly focused participative initiative.

The double-edged quality of the first issue, access to information, is clear. Without information on costs, layout, procedures, and a host of other matters not normally shared with employees, problem solving is constrained. With such information, a rich bank of ideas—informed by extensive experiences—can be brought to bear on various problems. Interviews with over a dozen employee problem solving groups in Xerox, Alcoa, Budd, and General Motors facilities confirmed the importance of this issue. Each group indicated that one of the first and most significant barriers to their effectiveness was withholding of information and mistrust by managers, engineers, and even co-workers.

The question of information sharing goes beyond the body of information specifically required for a given problem. For example, at Alcoa's Lebanon, Pennsylvania, aluminum rolling mill—which is organized by the Aluminum, Brick, and Glass Workers Union (ABGWU)—management has found it important to buttress the problem-solving efforts with regular performance feedback for work areas and biannual plant-wide reports by the works manager and union leaders. Indeed, given this plant's experience with two concessionary agreements in the first half of the 1980s (which will be discussed in the section on collective bargaining), the absence of this broader information would have undercut any ability for management to assert a common interest with employees in addressing a highly competitive marketplace. Thus, even this more diffuse aspect of information sharing can be understood as having a double-edged potential to either reinforce or undercut participation.

Issues regarding organizational decision making are often interwoven with the issue of information sharing. For example, the manager of engineering in one medium-sized manufacturing plant commented that the major consequence of employee involvement for him was a doubling in the amount of work that comes across his desk. Although an organizational change to address this bottleneck was being discussed at the time of the interview, this was only after a period of almost two years of increased delays for both the EI groups and the set of technical and supervisory employees that always required decisions from him. In essence, the decision of this manager represented critical information for EI groups and for other constituencies. The consequence of delays in sharing this information was three-fold in this plant. First, they undercut the enthusiasm of the EI groups. Second, and it turns out more damaging, they heightened the skepticism of employees not involved with the voluntary EI effort. This skepticism contributed to a tension between the employees who were and were not involved in the process. Finally, the bottleneck in the flow of information undercut support from technical and supervisory employees who previously had less competition for access to the manager.

While delays or other difficulties with access to decision makers can undercut an employee involvement effort, the speedy resolution of group proposals will have the opposite effect. Indeed, a close look at the EI effort in a Ford Motor Company plant, which was organized by the United Automobile Workers Union (UAW), revealed that the EI process was so expeditious in generating answers to proposals from EI groups, that middle managers had developed a habit of channelling their own ideas through the groups. They found that this was quicker and resulted in more favorable decisions than occurred when issues were sent up the normal chain of command. In this way, the successful resolution of the issue of access to decision makers led to an informal broadening of the focus of the EI effort.

At the Xerox Corporation the experiences with employee involvement in the unionized home manufacturing complex—in Webster, New York—are a major factor in an effort intended to fundamentally transform organizational decision making. Referred to as Leadership Through Quality (LTQ) this is a process for regular dialogue across levels in Xerox that began with the top officer of the corporation and, in their terms, and cascaded down the organization. It involves an assessment by each individual of their own capabilities and of the requirements of all the customers—internal and external—for their output. Among the most important customers for managers at each level are, of course, their subordinates and superiors. The process is structured around regular face-to-face meetings with the internal and external customers. The result, at least ideally, is an ongoing process of negotiations that can go well beyond ensuring appropriate responses to problem-solving group suggestions. In fact, it is intended to build internal responsiveness as a part of everyday operations. Though it is too soon to assess this change effort, it reveals the transformational implications of participative principles.

Ultimately, giving greater influence to employees redistributes power and status within the managerial structure by breaking down traditional patterns of control. Supervisors, middle-managers, and staff experts who controlled information and resources under traditional management systems experience the largest losses. Thus, it is not surprising that these groups resist the expansion of participative efforts at precisely the point that the process infringes on previous domains of managerial control (Klein and Posey 1986). It is partly in response to these points of resistance that we see the emergence of both narrow supervisory training programs and comprehensive efforts to change organizational "culture" such as the Leadership Through Quality program at Xerox. Failure to deal with middle-management and first-line supervisor resistance can severely reduce the probability of success of any participative effort while addressing their concerns can enhance the participation of effort and, in the process, transform aspects of organizational information handling and decision making.

It should be noted that the pivotal nature of information and decision making issues is not any less salient *within* a union structure. It is manifest, for example, in tensions between appointees helping facilitate Quality of Work Life (QWL) problem solving and those elected representatives who view this activity as a threat to the status of the grievance procedure as the principal vehicle for addressing members' concerns. This sort of internal tension surfaced in basic questions over the respective roles of local union officers, stewards, and appointees in most of the research sites examined. Formal or informal resolution of such tensions was critical if EI groups were to have access to the full information needed to be effective. In the case of Xerox, for example, there had not been a formal redefinition of union roles, but high levels of informal communications and trust between stewards and EI coordinators facilitated access to information. On the one hand, the coordinators were given sufficient freedom to advocate for groups on matters that might traditionally be channelled through stewards and, on the other hand, the stewards were quickly apprised of core contractual issues that had surfaced in EI group discussions. At Fiero there was a formal redefinition of roles that expanded the problem-solving responsibilities of elected committeemen. While these changing union roles are discussed in more detail elsewhere (McKersie, Cutcher-Gershenfeld, and Wever 1988), they help to illustrate how both union and management structure intresect with the increasing need for EI groups to have access to information and organizational decision makers.

Employment Security

Employment security is an issue that arises in different forms at various stages of a participative effort. Even at the early stages of a narrowly focused effort, employees will express concern that neither they nor their co-workers lose their jobs as a direct result of suggestions submitted by a problem-solving group. A majority of unionized efforts and many nonunion efforts will state this explicitly as a ground rule prior to beginning the initiative. Without this assurance the consequence is clear; suggestions that would otherwise lead to improvements in productivity will not be submitted. With the assurance, management has committed itself to a form of workforce allocation that, even in this limited form, represents a significant departure from patterns of unilateral managerial control of these issues.

Over time, the issue of employment security often arises again, but in a much broader form. Even layoffs that are market driven or otherwise unrelated to the efforts of problem-solving groups have the effect of undercutting the sense of common purposes that is supposed to motivate employee involvement efforts. This was the case in Xerox's main manufacturing complex in Webster, New York, which is organized by the Amalgamated Clothing and Textile Workers Union (ACTWU). Increasing world competition became manifest throughout the Xerox Corporation in 1981 and 1982 in a series of unprecedented layoffs of exempt and nonexempt employees. Though technically not in violation of the ground rules specified for Quality of Work Life efforts that were initiated in 1980, these layoffs had the unintended consequence of slowing down the rate at which employees were volunteering for QWL groups. Although 90 problem-solving groups had been established in the first year of the QWL effort and 150 in the second, very few were established in the third year—partly as a result of the layoffs.

Thus, the parties' 1983 negotiation of a no-layoff guarantee for the ACTWU members in the Webster area had significant implications for the participative efforts. If the guarantee had not been made, it was clear that a limit would have been imposed on the diffusion of the participative effort. As it was, the company agreed to provide such a guarantee for the three-year term of the agreement and this has since been extended in the recent 1986 collective bargaining agreement. In the process, however, a link was forged between QWL and collective bargaining—two processes that the parties had originally intended to keep separate.

As we will see in the next section, which examines variation in worker-preferences, the provision of the no-layoff guarantee was a necessary but not a sufficient condition for a broader diffusion of participation principles. Before turning to the next section, however, a caveat is in order regarding questions of employment security. Many firms find themselves unable to offer such assurances for reasons of cyclical hiring and layoff patterns or for reason of product-market uncertainty. The Budd Company, for example, has indicated its recognition of the damaging consequences that layoffs have for cooperative efforts, but has also felt unable to make such explicit guarantees given the highly competitive and uncertain nature of the auto supply industry. Even so, a number of Budd plants in the United States and Canada have worked closely with union leaders on an informal basis to minimize layoffs and to develop creative approaches that at least increase the degree of employment stabilization.

Variations in Worker Preferences

Numerous surveys have shown that a high proportion of blue- and white-collar workers express an interest in participation in decisions involving how to perform their jobs. Surveys conducted in large plants at Xerox and Boeing, and across a carrier-wide sample of Western Airlines employees supported this finding. Between 80 and 95 percent of workers indicated an interest in participating in decisions involving their jobs. Yet these surveys also found mixed reactions to the specific forms of participation embodied in QWL or related problem solving, team activities. For example, 88 percent of the surveyed employees in one plant at Xerox reported they liked the idea of employee involvement, 85 percent wanting more say in their job, and 88 percent reported wanting management to share more business information. Yet, at the time of this survey (three years after the beginning of the QWL effort) only about 30 percent of the employees had volunteered for QWL teams, and only about 11 percent of those not currently participating in an EI team indicated they would be interested in joining a team.[8] A similar set of results was found in a survey of nonparticipants in Boeing's quality circles. At Boeing less than 20 percent of employees were in QCs at the time of the survey, and less than one-half of the remaining nonparticipants expressed any interest in joining a QC. Furthermore, nonparticipants in both settings gave less favorable evaluations of the contributions of the QWL process to improving plant operations, quality, and labor-management relations, then did participants.

A close analysis of the variations in employee preferences regarding participation suggests that a self-selection process was at work in both organizations (Cutcher-Gershenfeld 1987; Verma and McKersie 1987), which was then further exacerbated by experience. Those workers with high preferences for teamwork and group problem-solving activities were the first to volunteer to participate in QWL activity. Those with positive experiences with the process strengthened their commitment to the process over time. However, some became disenchanted or lost interest as the process began to plateau, and discounted the achievements of the groups. Nonparticipants had lower preferences for regular group involvement to begin with, and also devalued the achievements of the groups. Thus, while many of the nonparticipants endorsed involvement in workplace-level decision making and problem solving *in principle*, a significant proportion of them did not see formal, weekly problem-solving meetings (as practiced by QWL teams) as their preferred means of participation. Based on these survey findings and our field interviews, we conclude that more varied options for involvement may be necessary to match the interest in participation of different employees. The case of Xerox and the Amalgamated Clothing and Textile Workers Union (ACTWU) provides one example of how this can be done.

The above survey results prompted Xerox and ACTWU to allow the parties in different work units to adapt the participation process to the particular needs and preferences of each group of employees. One plant, for example, is divided into approximately forty different Business Area Work Groups (BAWG) which meet on a biweekly basis for feedback on performance, safety, and other factors. This is a mandatory, minimum level of participation. It involves workers, supervisors, engineers and union officials. Beyond this level, individual group members have the option to form formal problem-solving teams, temporary task forces to solve specific problems, autonomous working groups (operating without a supervisor), or to serve as "individual contributors." This flexible form of participation allows each BAWG to take into account the varied preferences for involvement found within the work unit. The key constant, however, is a commitment to a participatory decision-making mode of interaction. In other parts of Xerox autonomous working groups, temporary task forces, and joint planning teams are used in various combinations, reflecting the same contingent principle that underlies the BAWG concept. Thus, what started out as a narrow but standardized EI process has evolved into multiple modes of applying the principles and techniques of participation to a range of temporary and recurrent problems and issues, using a variety of different methods and personnel.

This experience illustrates how a naturally occurring crisis (namely, the decline in interest in problem-solving groups) became the vehicle for reinforcing and substantially extending participative activities. In the process, however, the nature of employee participation was transformed.

Work Organization Reforms

Recent efforts by employers to negotiate greater flexibility in the application of work rules largely reflect an interest in cutting costs through the shedding of labor (Capelli and McKersie 1986). Sometimes, however, the goal has also been to introduce new forms of work organization that included among their attributes high levels of employee autonomy and participation. These new work systems seek to tap the motivational advantages of broad task designs (Hackman and Oldham 1980; Walton 1980). Furthermore, these work systems aim to better match human resource allocation to the flexible capabilities of new technologies and to competitive pressures for higher quality, improved delivery, and lower cost (Piore and Sabel 1984; Shimada and MacDuffie 1986). Thus, work organization reforms can either serve as an opportunity to broaden and extend participative principles or as a threat to cooperation that is imposed unilaterally by an employer as a device to cut costs or to undermine the union or to subvert the collective bargaining process. In this sense, work organization reform often serves as another pivotal issue encountered by participative initiatives.

The most successful introduction of these flexible forms of work organization has been in new ("greenfield") worksites or in facilities that have been closed and completely retro-fitted. Most of these facilities operate on a nonunion basis and place a great emphasis on the recruitment of a workforce with a high teamwork orientation. Even in a unionized setting such as the Pontiac Fiero plant—which was completely redesigned to emphasize flexible, highly participative forms of work organization—there was an extensive orientation to ensure that employees with contractual transfer rights exercised some self-selection over whether they wanted to work under the new system. Without this process it is possible that fundamental disagreements over the new system would emerge. In fact, this is precisely what occurred in General Motors' Lake Orion plant (located within twenty miles of the Fiero plant and opened at about the same time), which was designed to be even more team-work oriented but did not feature the initial orientation and self-selection. In local negotiations the union leaders at Lake Orion reflected the sentiments of a workforce with a wide range of attitudes, including many who sought to completely eliminate the new system. The parties' first contract represented a substantial modification of the structure—allowing employees to choose whether or not to work under the team system. In both the Fiero and Lake Orion cases, the resulting arrangements can be understood, at least in part, as a reflection of the prior selection of the workforce.

General Motors' new Saturn Division, which features joint roles for the union at all levels, is the best known example of a unionized work setting that contemplates high levels of flexibility and participation. Although it is too soon to assess this initiative, parallels can be found in the experiences of Fiero; in

GM's joint venture with Toyota in Fremont, California—New United Motors Manufacturing, Inc. (NUMMI); and in the experience of Xerox and ACTWU with the joint design and start-up of a new toner plant. We discuss each of these examples below.

Xerox had initially decided unilaterally to build a new toner plant in the South, principally to take advantage of lower energy costs. It took a confrontation on the part of the union to assert its legitimacy and its capacity to contribute to this sort of capital investment issue, which was then followed by a fruitful collaboration that ultimately led to the construction of a plant in Webster, New York (the union's goal), that had a simplified and more efficient layout and design. Favorable energy and local tax rates were also negotiated for the facility via a joint lobbying effort. Thus, previous patterns of managerial decision making posed an initial hurdle to collaboration on a new plant design that, once overcome, then led to quite extensive collaboration.

At Fiero, after about three years' experience with this new form of work organization, the parties began to discuss the need for a fundamental self-assesment. Initially, they had assumed that the new design represented a coherent institutionalized (that is, fully integrated) structure. While it indeed features joint decision making that extends to permanent union membership on the plant management team and an open invitation for the plant manager to attend local union meetings, the layoff of the second shift in the third year of operations led both labor and management to re-evaluate the structure. While they have kept its main features, the parties have formalized and distinguished some union and management roles, on the one hand, but have also expanded the scope of their joint decision making. Moreover, they concluded that a continual adaptive capacity was required in even this most advanced setting.

Collective Bargaining Shocks

Variation in worker preferences are often hidden or opaque until they are thrown into sharp relief by a shock or crisis event. Collective bargaining is one such event, and can potentially bolster or cripple participative efforts. The strong impact of collective bargaining on these efforts follows from the fact that such negotiations remain the central forum in which employers and unions confront the issues over which they have some of their most significant differences. Sustaining QWL and other forms of cooperative problem solving at the workplace requires a particular way of managing the conflicts that are channeled through the negotiations process. Walton and McKersie (1965) described this challenge as one of resolving the behavioral dilemmas required for engaging in both distributive and integrative bargaining.

Acrimonious negotiations and contract changes that employees believe to be inconsistent with the trust and commitment involved in workplace participation are often followed by a halt and even an erosion of the diffusion of QWL processes. In some cases these are temporary setbacks; in others the climate becomes so chilled that participative efforts are disbanded. At the same time, collective bargaining agreements on employment security, gainsharing, and other issues have provided essential reinforcements to QWL efforts. It is in this sense that the collective bargaining process can both undercut *and* reinforce participative efforts. Either consequence, it should be noted, reveals the limitations of a ground rule common to many efforts in unionized settings, which is a stated intention of maintaining a complete separation between participative efforts and collective bargaining. While it is important that neither process supplant the other, one of our conclusions is that it is no less important to attend to the interconnections between the two.

As was discussed earlier, the 1983 negotiations at Xerox contained a no-layoff guarantee that reflected, in part, a recognition of the way bargaining outcomes can reinforce participative efforts. A second set of contract provisions negotiated in 1983 had a similar effect. These concerned the establishment of a company commitment to extend the principle of joint decision making to issues of subcontracting or outsourcing. Two other provisions of this agreement had an opposite effect. They were, first, the establishment of a highly restrictive absenteeism control program and, second, a set of unpopular modifications to the health insurance package. For those employees who were skeptical of QWL, the absenteeism control program and healthy benefit changes were seen as inconsistent and cause for giving even less support to joint efforts. For employees who valued the QWL process, the no-layoff guarantee and outsourcing language were more salient and served as reinforcement and validation. Thus, collective bargaining amplified employee responses to QWL. A single agreement served *both* to reinforce and undercut participative efforts.

At Alcoa's Lebanon, Pennsylvania, aluminum rolling mill, changes in absenteeism policies, similar to those at Xerox, along with deep wage concessions, led to the disbanding of the plant union-management steering committee that oversaw a participation process that had been underway for two years. The concessions demanded of the Aluminum Brick and Glass Workers Union (ABGWU) also led to a significant decline in volunteers for the training needed to join a participative group. After approximately a six-month hiatus, however, a new steering committee was formed and the participation process was revitalized. The revitalized process reflected important learning about employee preferences, and was less constrained to a single form of group problem solving. Instead, the new efforts focused more directly on quality and productivity problems by embracing a variety of different processes including statistical process control training and methods, semi-autonomous work groups for selected operations, sociotechnical planning process for designing and installing a new cold mill operation in the plant, an expanded joint apprenticeship program, and expanded joint information sharing programs.

While these more focused participative efforts have gained momentum in the Alcoa plant over the past several years, the legacy of employee discontent with the concessions continues to divide the local union. Employees and union leaders are strongly interested in negotiating a form of gain-sharing or other compensation arrangement that allows them to recoup their wage concessions and to be rewarded for their contributions to the plant's competitiveness. Although these efforts have not yet been successful, they reveal the way collective bargaining can reinforce or set back workplace level participation efforts. The success of these efforts may well depend on whether or not a gain-sharing or other compensation arrangement is negotiated, which employees perceive as an equitable response to their flexibility and participation in work improvement and redesign.

This issue of gain-sharing is deserving of a special note before concluding this discussion of the relationship between collective bargaining and employee participation. Evidence from Scanlon plans initiated over three decades ago (Lesieur 1959) and more recently from Scanlon and other forms of gain-sharing or profit sharing (Metzger 1980; Zager and Rosow 1982; Cohen-Rosenthal and Burton 1987) clearly indicates the importance of having a participative component for any such plan to be viable. The current interest in gain-sharing on the part of many companies and unions with participative experience suggests an obverse implication. That is, it may be that some form of gain-sharing or profit sharing represents a critical complement to a participative initiative.

Many of our research sites are in the process of exploring and/or experimenting with gain-sharing options. The evidence from these explorations and experiments suggests that there are a host of potentially contentious issues raised by the gain-sharing concept. In one facility that operates largely on a piece rate, the addition of gain-sharing would exacerbate a set of already thorny piece-rate-related inequities. In another facility, the concept has encountered fierce resistance from middle-level managers that suggests the persistence of a zero-sum mindset. These managers are vociferous in arguing: "The employees are already paid quite well to give their best effort—why pay them more on top of that?" At the same time, work groups have been unambiguous in calling for some form of gain-sharing as the next step in their participative activities. Yet, for almost two years, the strength of the middle-level managers' feelings limited follow-through on a top level union-management commitment to establish experimental, pilot gain-sharing initiatives. Clearly, this is an arena with great collaborative potential, but there are a set of contentious issues that must be addressed in order for this potential to be realized.

While the links between collective bargaining and employee participation raise many thorny issues for companies and unions, our conclusion is that the linkage is inevitable. Collective bargaining issues such as the structure of compensation or work rules are pivotal for participative efforts—serving either to reinforce or undercut the efforts. Equally, the experiences with participation can serve to improve or destroy the potential for integrative problem solving at the bargaining table.

Strategic Shocks

Although distant from workplace participation activities, top-level decisions by managers and labor leaders about broad strategic direction, resource allocation, and basic organizational structure are pivotal. They can thoroughly undercut or completely transform participative activities. Similar to collective bargaining in effect, the potential impact of such top-level decisions can reach much further. In particular, the relationship between participative activities and top-level strategic decision making raises fundamental questions about management's willingness to share power and a union's approach toward the very real risks associated with participating in such decisions.

At the unionized main manufacturing facilities of Cummins Engine, for example, the imposition of a major layoff by management in a unilateral fashion, without consulting the union, or using the QWL process to explore alternatives, dealt a severe blow to the commitment of union officials and workers to the QWL activities initiated in the Columbus, Indiana, facilities. The layoff represents a top-level cost-cutting initiative aimed at reducing the risk of a hostile takeover. In this case, QWL efforts had been reinforced by negotiated language in the contract giving management and union representatives at the plant level the right to increase flexibility by reducing job classifications. In another situation, Cummins sought and received simplified work rules in a new parts distribution center in exchange for union recognition in this new facility. Specific joint union-management efforts and discussions continue to focus on job preservation and creation, but the layoff of approximately 10 percent of the blue- and white-collar workforce in 1986 brought union and worker support for formal QWL activities to a halt. Not only is a massive layoff almost always a shock to a participative initiative, but the unilateral nature of this management decision and its inconsistency with the principles of participation and consultation even more deeply undercut the QWL process in this case.

In other settings, crisis events involving strategic decisions have been handled differently and ended up reinforcing participative activities. At Xerox, the first such crisis involved the threat of subcontracting the work of a group of people making and assembling wire harnesses. If the corporation had decided unilaterally to subcontract, the union indicated that it might well have to withdraw from QWL. When it was decided, instead, to examine the issue with a joint study team, the principle of participation was significantly extended. By expanding the scope of participation to include this set of strategic resource allocation decisions, a threat to employee involvement is transformed into a reinforcer of the process.

At Budd, management had to decide whether or not to reinvest in an old plant by changing the layout and flow of materials, thereby changing the job structure and organization of work. Because the union was willing to engage these new issues, the investment served to reinforce and expand the collaborative decision-making process.

The case of Alcoa involved a decision about how to organize the work system in a new cold roll mill. Here again, the parties followed a highly participative design process where employees were involved in the engineering planning process at the earliest stages. The experience had the additional benefit of complementing other forms of employee involvement and legitimizing their extension into issues of work organization and design.

For all the complexities of a new plant design, it is even more difficult to fully retro-fit an organization "on-line"—that is, without the luxury of building a new facility in an empty field (which is usually the case) or even without a plant shutdown for a period of one or two years (which was the case at Fiero and NUMMI). Wholesale changes are rarely welcomed by employees, unions, or middle- and lower-managers.

Thus, a more common "on-line" retro-fit strategy involves the complete restructuring of work in one portion of a facility. These changes are typically the result of a pivotal event around the threat of job loss, the prospect of new investment, or turnover in management or union leadership. In each case, the new form of work organization is precisely the sort of transformation of participative efforts discussed earlier in this paper. The changes build on prior collaborative experiences, as well as some degree of demonstrated management commitment on issues of employment security. Yet, these efforts then become subject to their own set of pivotal events around their integration or differentiation from the rest of the organization. Each of these events carries its own double-edged potential, suggesting the far-reaching nature of this dynamic. In each of these cases the participation process and other aspect of the labor-management relationship were addressed so as to complement one another.

In each case, the situation could have deteriorated and the change become a point of controversy. Successfully attending to these issues not only reinforced, but extended and transformed participation.

A recent strategic shock at Fiero has posed a harsh test for labor and management in this plant. General Motors announced in early 1988 that, because of poor sales performance, the Fiero product line would be discontinued and, since no replacement product had yet been scheduled for the Fiero plant, the plant would be idled in 1989. For both labor and management at the plant, the announcement came as a shock. Moreover, given the sudden unilateral nature of the corporate decision, many other union and management leaders within and outside of General Motors see the event as undercutting other participative initiatives. As of this writing, alternative uses for the Fiero plant are under discussion. The fate of the participative and work organization innovations at Fiero, and perhaps in other parts of General Motors, rests in the outcome of these strategic level discussions. This development illustrates that ultimately the durability of plant level innovations will depend on the extent to which they are integrated into or ignored in corporate level strategic decisions.

One particular domain of strategic decision making—the introduction of new technology—is especially pivotal. The introduction of new technology is one of the most pervasive events occurring in organizations today and it is important to both employees and employers. It is often seen as a key domain of competitive advantage for management, while employees find new technology to be a source of profound and often threatening change for employees. Employee participation is commonly recognized as a critical requirement of success in settings where the parties adopt a technology strategy that emphasized flexibility, continuous learning and improvement, and high levels of interdependence between the hardware and human resource dimensions of the technology. Conversely, where technology is viewed in the narrow technical sense as a set of labor saving and/or controlling machines independent of worker input, the introduction of new technology can serve to undercut any concurrent efforts to promote employee participation.

This basic proposition is most clearly developed in the current work of our colleagues studying the use of new technology in U.S. auto plants. Shimada and MacDuffie (1987) have described how the production systems used by Toyota, Honda, and most other Japanese manufacturing firms emphasize the interdependence between the hardware and the "humanware" elements of production. In another study, Krafcik (1987) has shown how those auto plants that integrated their technology and human resource strategies have achieved higher levels of productivity and product quality ratings than more highly automated auto plants that have failed to achieve this integration. While the basic lesson here is becoming quite clear and, in fact, is now rather widely accepted by top executives in American auto companies, there still are great variations in how technology is being introduced and the extent to which employee participation and other human resource issues are considered in specific implementation processes. Boeing and the IAM have been able to agree, for example, to innovative contract language concerning union involvement in the implementation of new technology, but have learned that giving life to such language adds a union role to an already complex internal organizational decision-making process.

In all areas of broad strategic decision making, the key determinant of whether or not the successful extension of participation to larger aspects of the relationship is made appears to be the willingness of top-level management and union leaders to assert their commitment to the principles of problem solving and participation in the face of new, potentially contentious situations. Often this extension of participative principles does not happen of its own accord, but only after a union confrontation aimed at establishing its legitimacy to be involved in such strategic decisions. This suggests a potential limitation on the capacity of nonunion organizations to foster participation at this level. It also can only be understood as a set of activities that will almost inevitably transform what was an incremental program for diffusing QWL teams. While this does not ensure that a set of participative principles will be applied to every crisis or opportunity that might benefit by problem-solving processes, each time it does occur the transformation becomes more distinct.

SUMMARY AND CONCLUSIONS

The overriding conclusion we draw from these cases is that stand-alone employee involvement processes have a low probability of being sustained over time in organizations. We have observed few examples where participation has been sustained and diffused in collective bargaining relationships without leading to or being associated with more fundamental structural changes in the labor-management relationship. Thus, if employee participation is to become a lasting feature of the U.S. industrial relations system, it will do so as part of a more fundamental restructuring of labor-management relations, not as an independent or isolated pehnomenon. More specifically, we expect employee participation to have the highest probability of being institutionalized as a lasting feature of industrial relations in settings where:

1. Participation leads to or is associated with changes in the organization of work that allow for and reinforce decentralization of decision-making responsibility, flexibility in task assignment, and reward (pay and promotion) systems that encourage learning new skills and participation in group problem solving.
2. Business strategies are adopted that place a strong emphasis on product and/or service quality, flexibility, and innovation rather than on labor cost minimization.
3. Technology strategies are followed that emphasize or perhaps even require high levels of skill, flexibility, and employee commitment.
4. Labor union leaders take on new and broader roles in the governance process of the labor-management relationship that facilitate both joint problem solving and the resolution of conflicts.

Our analysis has stressed that the broadening and integration of participation processes that is required occurs through an interactive process or set of pivotal events in which the cooperative features of participation confront the conflictual features of employment relationships. Such events or moments of choice should be seen as inevitable since employment relations are inherently mixed motive in nature. Participation, even accompanied by the types of structural changes suggested above, does not eliminate these points of conflict. For specific participative initiatives (such as employee involvement) to be sustained, however, the emergent conflicts must not only be addressed, but they must be addressed in ways that are consistent with participative principles. If they are not, the periodic emergence of conflict episodes can impede the continuity of the participative effort. That is why we stress the dual edged nature of these pivotal events.

Implications for Research

To date, most research on employee participation programs and processes in the United States has taken one of three forms: (1) tests of models of participation in laboratory or field settings that fail to fully consider the institutional contexts in which participation occurs, (2) cross-sectional surveys or snapshots of individuals or establishments involved in what we have described above as highly dynamic and evolving processes, or (3) case study histories of particular projects that lack quantitative measures of the projects' effects on the outcomes of critical concern to the parties involved. While each of these approaches can provide useful information, they are all somewhat limited as research designs for drawing causal inferences or firm conclusions. Thus, what has been presented in this paper should be treated as, at best, a set of interim summary statements or working hypotheses drawn from the cumulative results of these studies. Future research on this topic needs to pay considerably more attention to designing studies that can test these and other critical hypotheses. In doing so, however, care must be taken to cast tests to specific hypotheses within a robust model of organizational change and with explicit attention to the institutional contexts in which the processes occur.

Implications for Public Policy

To date, employee participation has evolved in the United States as a set of private experiments largely independent of public policy. Indeed, this is a development pattern followed by other features of U.S. industrial relations that are now deeply embedded in our system. Collective bargaining, grievance arbitration, union security agreements, fringe benefit negotiations, advance notice of plant closings, and other innovations were all introduced and served as private experiments of labor and management before being endorsed, adopted, and integrated into the public policies governing industrial relations. Yet the critical role played by public policy in these historic patterns should also be noted. Each of these earlier innovations only diffused widely over time after they were integrated into state and national labor and employement policies.

In a similar fashion, significant private experimentation and yet limited diffusion of employee participation has now occurred in the United States.

Active support of public policy may, therefore, be needed to encourage further diffusion and eventual institutionalization of participatory principles in the U.S. industrial relations system. While we are not prepared at this point to make specific policy proposals, we can suggest three broad principles that might serve as a foundation for policy in this area.

The first principle would be that barriers in current labor law that inhibit various forms of employee participation at the workplace or in strategic decision making should be removed. A number of such barriers have been discussed elsewhere (Kochan, Katz, and McKersie 1986; Schlossberg and Fetter 1986) such as the outmoded distinction or line of demarcation between workers and supervisors, restrictions on the scope of bargaining, constraints on the use of employer technical and financial resources to support employee or union activities in participation efforts, the ability of management to withhold financial information in bargaining (unless management chooses to raise an inability to pay argument), the ambiguous status of worker representatives on boards of directors or employee representatives who otherwise receive confidential information from management, and so forth. These constraints probably do not deter firms and unions that are already committed to participation. These rules are more likely to be a barrier where *one* party is tentatively interested but is deterred by the legal obstacles or arguments relied upon by the other, less interested party to the relationship.

An indirect but perhaps equally important constraint on participation comes from the failure of current law and/or enforcement procedures to cope with increased employer resistance and illegal conduct in representation election procedures. Union leaders see the current law and enforcement efforts as providing employers unfair advantages. This in turn makes it politically difficult for union leaders to support cooperative efforts at the workplace. Thus, putting these fundamental aspects of our labor law in good working order should be viewed as a necessary, but not sufficient step in updating our labor policies.

A second principle would be to more fully integrate labor policies designed to promote innovation and industrial relations reform with the broad array of other employment and economic policies that are aimed at improving the performance of the U.S. economy. Taking this step would amount to a more active and explicit endorsement of participation and consultation than has heretofore been the case. For example, it would stand in marked contrast to the experiences with deregulation of the airline and trucking industry—an economic policy enacted in the late 1970s without any significant consideration for its effects on employment standards. Only now with hindsight can we see that a policy designed to foster greater competition and efficiency has led to deep wage concessions, intensified adversarial labor relations, an escalation in managerial resistance to unionization, and substantial consumer externalities.

Finally, a third principle would be for national policy makers to take a more active leadership role in encouraging growth and development of professionals and intermediary institutions that can help to diffuse greater understanding and expertise with participation. Experience has shown, however, that such intermediary institutions cannot stand alone. Rather, they must be linked into broader economic and policy making. The National Center on Productivity and Quality of Working Life (which emerged out of earlier presidential commissions) never succeeded in elevating these issues into broad policy debates. Indeed, the fate of many national and regional initiatives in the United States has been analogous in many ways to the fate of narrowly focused EI initiatives in organizations. This stands in contrast, for example, with the experiences of the National War Labor Board, which was instrumental in helping to establish practical solutions to collective bargaining problems and then link these developments to national income policy debates. In this way the War Labor Board helped to institutionalize collective bargaining in American industry in the 1940s. Third party organizations and professionals may help facilitate the diffusion and institutionalization of forms of employee participation, provided they are responsive to the diverse contexts and problems encountered in contemporary employment relationships and provided their efforts rest on a public mandate that allows for their integration into policy making.

While these are only very general and broad principles, they may serve as a basis for initiating the debate needed to establish a more supportive policy environment for employee participation. If history is any guide, the outcome of these debates will have an important effect on the extent to which participation diffuses and becomes a lasting feature of the U.S. industrial relations system.

ACKNOWLEDGMENTS

The authors' names are listed in alphabetical order to reflect the equal contributions made by all three authors. The analysis and data presented here are derived in large part from a study conducted by the MIT Industrial Relations Section under a grant from the U.S. Department of Labor, Bureau of Labor Management Relations and Cooperative Programs (Contract No. J 9-P-4-0021). Supplementary support was provided by several of the companies and unions included in the study. This paper was first drafted and presented in 1988 in Vancouver, B.C., at the Pacific Rim Labor Policy Conference sponsored by the Asia Pacific Business Institute and the Bureau of National Affairs. While the views expressed are solely those of the authors, we wish to thank Russell Lansbury, Robert McKersie, and two anonymous reviewers for their comments on an earlier draft.

NOTES

1. Throughout this paper, the terms "employee participation," "worker participation," and "employee involvement" are used interchangeably.

2. Three separate surveys commissioned by the New York Stock Exchange, Business Week, and the American Management Association all indicate that about 35-50 percent of U.S. firms report the use of some form of employee participation programs. See Verma and McKersie (1987, footnote 1) for details.

3. In fact, there is a long and little studied history of employee participation including extensive shop floor committees in the 1920s in the railroad and apparel industries, as well as various collaborative efforts during both World War I and World War II (Gomberg 1967; Jacoby 1983; Mitchell 1984; Cutcher-Gershenfeld 1985). However, these experiences, though highly similar in form to current efforts, are rarely linked via any direct lineage. Thus, we refer to today's efforts as "new."

4. It is pointed out by some that the self-contained quality circle type of employee participation has proven to be durable in Japan. Our view is that this is because workplace participation in Japanese organizations is reinforced by other important support systems (easy flow of information, greater job security for a core workforce, and a consultative decision-making style) which explain the long-run success of participation. As we will discuss later in this paper, adoption of these same organizational support systems increases the probability of successfully institutionalizing participative processes in American firms as well.

5. Although both the government and the public are important actors in any industrial relations system, we exclude these parties from our discussion in this portion of the paper in order to confine our treatment to the plant or facility level of the organization. The broader public interest is addressed in the last section of the paper.

6. Given the apparent benefits of participation for management, this finding suggests divergent interests within the management structure—a thesis supported by Klein's (Klein and Posey 1986) research on first-line supervisors.

7. In another paper that we and others have written on this subject, our focus is on both these dimensions and on a wider range of issues (Kochan and Cutcher-Gershenfeld 1988). In contrast, this paper presents a more detailed treatment of the structural issues.

8. Note that this was *after* the parties had negotiated collective bargaining language providing a no-layoff guarantee. As will be discussed below, we conclude that the limits on employee interest in joining a QWL group were not just a function of the prior uncertainty over layoffs.

REFERENCES

Aguren, S., R. Hansson, and K.G. Karlsson. 1976. *The Impact of New Design on Work Organization.* Stockholm: The Rationalization Council, SAF-LO.

Bluestone, I. 1981. Quality-of-Work-Life Goals Fulfill Union Objectives. *World of Work Report* 6(12).

Capelli, P. and R.B. McKersie. 1986. *Strategic Choice and the Control of Labor Costs.* Working paper ν1855-87, Alfred P. Sloan School of Management.

Cohen-Rosenthal, E. and C.E. Burton. 1987. *Mutual Gains: A Guide to Union-Management Cooperation.* New York: Praeger.

Cole, R.E. 1982. Diffusion of Participatory Work Structures in Japan, Sweden and the United States. In *Change in Organizations,* edited by P.S. Goodman et al. San Francisco, CA: Jossey-Bass.

Commons, J.R. et al. 1918. *History of Labor in the United States.* New York: Macmillan.

Cotton, J.L., D.A. Vollrath, K.L. Froggartt, M.L. Legnick-Hall, and K.R. Jenniye. 1988. Employee Participation: Diverse Forms and Different Outcomes. *Academy of Management Review* 13(1):8-22.

Cutcher-Gershenfeld, J. 1985. Reconceiving the Web of Labor-Management Relations. *Labor Law Journal* 36(8):637-645.

_____ 1987. *A Workforce Divided: Theoretical and Practical Implications of In-Groups in QWL Initiatives.* Sloan School of Management, MIT. Mimeo.

Dachler, H.P. and B. Wilpert. 1978. Conceptual Dimensions and Boundaries of Participation in Organizations: A Critical Evaluation. *Administrative Science Quarterly* 23:1-39.

Dickson, J.W. 1982. Participatory Forums and Influence. *Academy of Management Journal* 25(4):915-920.

Dunlop, J.T. 1958. *Industrial Relations Systems.* New York: Holt, Rinehart & Winston.

Frazer, V.C.M. and B.G. Dale. 1986. U.K. Quality Circle Failures—The Latest Picture. *Omega* 14(1):23-33.

Freedman, A. 1985. *The New Look in Wage Policy and Employee Relations.* New York: The Conference Board, Inc.

Gomberg, W. 1967. Special Study Committees. Pp. 235-251 in *Frontiers of Collective Bargaining,* edited by J.T. Dunlop and N.W. Chamberlain. New York: Harper and Row.

Hackman, J.R. and G.R. Oldham. 1980. *Work Redesign.* Reading, MA: Addison-Wesley.

Harrison, T.M. 1985. Communication and Participative Decision Making: An Exploratory Study. *Personnel Psychology* 38(1):93-116.

Jacoby, S.M. 1983. Union-Management Cooperation in the United States: Lessons from the 1920s. *Industrial and Labor Relations Review* 37(1):18-33.

Kanter, R.M. 1986. The New Workforce Meets the Changing Workplace. *Human Resource Management* (Winter):515-537.

Katz, H., T.A. Kochan, and K.R. Gobeille. 1983. Industrial Relations Performance, Economic Performance, and QWL Programs: An Interplant Analysis. *Industrial and Labor Relations Review* 37(1):3-17.

Klein, J.A. and P.A. Posey. 1986. A Good Supervisor is a Good Supervisor—Anywhere. *Harvard Business Review* (November-December).

Kochan, T.A. 1980. *Collective Bargaining and Industrial Relations.* Homewood, IL: Irwin.

_____ ed. 1985. *Challenges and Choices Facing American Labor.* Cambridge, MA: MIT Press.

Kochan, T.A. and L. Dyer. 1976. A Model of Organizational Change in the Context of Union-Management Relations. *Journal of Applied Behavioral Science* 12:59-78.

Kochan, T.A., and J. Cutcher-Gershenfeld. 1988. *Institutionalizing and Diffusing Innovations in Industrial Relations.* Washington, DC: U.S. Department of Labor.

Kochan, T.A., H.C. Katz, and R.B. McKersie. 1986. *The Transformation of American Industrial Relations.* New York: Basic.

Kochan, T.A., H.C. Katz, and N.R. Mower. 1984. *Worker Participation and American Unions.* Kalamazoo, MI: Upjohn Institute.

Krafcik, J. 1986. *Learning from NUMMI.* International Motor Vehicle Program, MIT. Mimeo.

Lawler, E.E., III and S.A. Mohrman. 1985. Quality Circles After the Fad. *Harvard Business Review* 63(1):64-71.

Lewin, K. 1951. *Field Theory in Social Science.* New York: Harper and Row.

Lee, C. and R.S. Schuler. 1982. A Constructive Replication and Extension of a Role and Expectancy Perception Model of Participation in Decision-Making. *Journal of Occupational Psychology* 55(2): 109-118.

Lesieur, F.G. 1959. *The Scanlon Plan: A Frontier in Labor-Management Cooperation.* Cambridge, MA: MIT Press.

Lischerson, J.A. and T.D. Wall. 1975. Employee Participation—An Experimental Field Study. *Human Relations* 28(9):863-884.

Locke, E.A. and D.M. Schweiger. 1979. Participation in Decision-Making: One More Look. In *Research in Organizational Behavior*, vol. 1, edited by B.M. Staw. Greenwich, CT: JAI Press.

McKersie, R.B., J. Cutcher-Gershenfeld, and K.R. Wever. 1988. *The Changing Role of Union Leaders.* Washington, DC: U.S. Department of Labor.

Metzger, B.L. 1980. *Increasing Productivity Through Profit Sharing.* Evanston, IL: Profit Sharing Research Foundation.

Miller, K.I. and P.R. Monge. 1986. Participation, Satisfaction and Productivity: A Meta-Analytic Review. *Academy of Management Review* 29(4):727-753.

Mitchell, R. 1984. *Rediscovering Our Roots: A History of Quality Circle Activities in the United States from 1918 to 1948.* Paper presented at the IAQC Annual Conference, April.

Neider, L.L. 1980. An Experimental Field Investigation Utilizing and Expectancy Theory View of Participation. *Organizational Behavior and Human Performance* 26(3):425-442.

Orr, D. and P.I. Blumberg. 1977. Employee Representation and Cooperation. *Harvard Business Review* (January-February):36-38.

Peterson, M.F., S.M. Peterson, and B.A. Macy. 1982. Study of a Quality of Worklife Program: Organizational Control, Experienced Influence and Objective Involvement. *Group and Organizational Studies* 74(4):476-484.

Piore, M. and C. Sabel. 1984. *The Second Industrial Divide.* New York: Basic.

Rafaeli, A. 1985. Quality Circles and Employee Attitudes. *Personnel Psychology* 38:603-615.

Rankin, T. 1986. Integrating QWL and Collective Bargaining. *Worklife Review* 5(3).

Rosenberg, R.D. and E. Rosenstein. 1980. Participation and Productivity: An Empirical Study. *Industrial and Labor Relations Review* 33(3):355-367.

Schlossberg, S.I. and S.M. Fetter. 1986. *U.S. Labor Law and the Future of Labor Management Cooperation.* Washington, DC: U.S. Department of Labor.

Schuster, M. 1985. A Re-examination of Model of Cooperation and Change in Union Settings. *Industrial Relations* 24(2):382-394.

Shimada, H. and J.P. MacDuffie. 1986. *Industrial Relations and "Humanware."* Working paper *v*1855-87, Alfred P. Sloan School of Management.

Sell, R. 1986. The Politics of Workplace Participation. *Personnel Management* 18(6):34-37.

Thacker, J.W. and M.W. Fields. 1987. Union Involvement in Quality-of-Worklife Efforts: A Longitudinal Investigation. *Personnel Psychology* 40:97-111.

Trist, E. 1981. *The Evolution of Socio-Technical Systems.* Toronto: Ontario Ministry of Labor, Ontario Quality of Working Life Centre.

U.S. Department of Labor. 1987. *Institutionalizing and Diffusing Innovations in Industrial Relations.* Report prepared by Industrial Relations Section, Sloan School of Management, MIT.

Verma, A. 1983. *Union and Nonunion Industrial Relations Systems at the Plant Level.* Ph.D. dissertation, Sloan School of Management, MIT.

————. 1987. Employee Involvement Programs: Do They Alter Worker Affinity Towards Unions? *Proceedings of the Thirty-Ninth Annual Meeting, Industrial Relations Research Association,* Madison, Wisconsin.

Verma, A. and R.B. McKersie. 1986. *Industrial Relations at the Boeing Company.* Working paper, Faculty of Commerce and Business Administration, University of British Columbia.

————. 1987. Employee Involvement: The Implications of Non-Involvement by Unions. *Industrial and Labor Relations Review* 40(4):556-568.

Verma, A. and W. Zerbe. 1989. Employee Involvement Programs and Worker Perceptions of New Technology. Pp. 117-134 in *New Technology: International Perspectives on Human Resources and Industrial Relations,* edited by R. Lansbury and G. Bamber. London: Unwin and Hyman.

Walton, R.E. 1980. Establishing and Maintaining High Commitment Work Systems. Pp. 208-290 in *The Organizational Life Cycle*, edited by J.R. Kimberly and R.H. Miles. San Francisco, CA: Jossey-Bass.

Walton, R. and R.B. McKersie. 1965. *A Behavioral Theory of Labor Negotiations*. New York: McGraw-Hill.

Witte, J. 1980. *Democracy, Authority, and Alienation in Work*. Chicago: University of Chicago Press.

Zager, R. and M. Rosow. eds. 1982. *The Innovative Organization: Productivity Programs in Action*. New York: Pergamon Press.

EMPLOYEE INVOLVEMENT AND WORKERS' PARTICIPATION IN MANAGEMENT:

THE AUSTRALIAN EXPERIENCE

Russell D. Lansbury and Edward M. Davis

INTRODUCTION

Before the 1970s, the concept of employee involvement or workers' participation in management had attracted little interest in Australia. During the 1970s, there were a number of significant experiments in both the private and public sectors; policy statements in employee participation and industrial democracy were announced by the major political parties, and the confederations of both the trade union movement and employers' organizations formulated policies in this area (see Lansbury and Prideaux 1984). However, as one commentator noted, "the rapidity with which this new thinking, debate and experimentation occurred inevitably created confusion" Derber 1979). By the end of the 1970s, discussions of the topic had waned. Yet the 1980s have witnessed a resurgence of interest, especially after the

Advances in Industrial and Labor Relations, volume 5, pages 33-57.
Copyright © 1991 by JAI Press Inc.
All rights of reproduction in any form reserved.
ISBN: 0-89232-940-8

election of the federal labor government (led by R.J. Hawke) in 1983. In order
to explain this ebb and flow of interest in employee involvement and industrial
democracy, attention must be paid to changes in the economic, political, legal,
and social environment which have helped to shape policies and experience
in this field.

As in several other countries, no single term has been accepted by
governments, unions, and employers. Unions have tended to employ the term
"industrial democracy" and have stressed the importance of rights to participate
in management decision making. Employers, on the other hand, have preferred
to talk about employee involvement or participation; they have commonly
envisaged employees being more interested and involved in the performance
of their particular work tasks. The distinction between union and employer
approaches is that unions believe that greater industrial democracy inevitably
involves a redistribution of decision-making power in their favor. This outcome
is not welcomed by employers who have stated that they will resist industrial
democracy but will foster those forms of employee involvement which pose
no threat to their traditional prerogatives (Davis and Lansbury 1987). The
approach preferred by the authors is to see industrial democracy as the
significant involvement of workers, for the most part through their unions,
in the important decisions that affect their work life (Davis and Lansbury 1986,
Ch.1).

Various theories have been advanced in order to explain the reason why
forms of industrial democracy or employee participation flourish or wither
away. Cutcher-Gershenfeld, Kochan, and Verma (1987) distinguish between
two types of employee participation: those which are *self-contained* and are
not accompanied by any major changes in organizational structure, and those
which are highly *integrated* with the rest of the organization. They conclude
that the former type of "stand alone" employee participation processes have
a low probability of being sustained over time, while the "integrated" approach
is more likely to survive because it is not an independent or isolated
phenomenon. As Cutcher-Gershenfeld et al. point out, however, employee
participation in the United States has evolved to date as a set of private
experiments largely independent of public policy. By contrast, in countries such
as Sweden and West Germany, the introduction of forms of employee
participation or industrial democracy has followed considerable public debate
and has been based on a legal framework, thus ensuring a more comprehensive
and integrated approach to the subject.

The Australian experience tends to fall somewhere between the U.S. and
Swedish experience. While conservative governments have been in power, there
have been few public policy initiatives on employee participation and most
activities in this area have been of a "stand alone" variety. Nevertheless, support
for limited forms of participation, designed to raise productivity, has been
forthcoming from many employers. During periods of labor government,

especially since 1983, the environment for public policy initiatives on the issue of industrial democracy has been more positive. Unions have pressed for more integrated and far-reaching programs of change, yet the labor government has been hesitant about undertaking radical measures which would meet opposition from employers.

This paper seeks to examine why integrated forms of employee participation have not been more common in Australia, despite the existence of supportive policies in recent years from both the federal Labor government and the trade union movement. The Australian situation is very different from that of the United States due to the existence of a well-organized labor movement and a reformist federal Labor government since 1983. It should, in many respects, provide an ideal situation in which to test the propositions advanced by Cutcher-Gershenfeld et al. about the requirements for sustainable reforms which would encourage the diffusion and eventual institutionalization of participatory principles. The explanation of why such a transformation has failed to occur, it may be hypothesized, is to be found in the turbulent economic and social context of the 1980s, the lack of political support which the Labor government has perceived for reforms in industrial democracy, strong employer antipathy to changes which would challenge the rights of management in the workplace, and uncertainty within sections of the labor movement about the benefits to be gained from industrial democracy. Notwithstanding these factors, support for various forms of employee participation and industrial democracy has steadily increased.

AN OVERVIEW OF THE LITERATURE

The popularity of employee participation and industrial democracy as a field of interest is illustrated by the growing number of publications under one or another title. An annotated bibliography of Australian publications, for example, listed 366 entries for the period 1970-1978, and this figure had grown to 857 by 1982 (Jones 1978, 1982). It should be noted that the bibliography was selective and described only a small part of the literature on the subject. The vast majority of publications, however, have been of a descriptive rather than analytical nature and very few rigorous surveys have been conducted of employee participation or industrial democracy in practice. Furthermore, according to Vaughan (1986), the case for industrial democracy has not had much effect on the realities of industrial relations and corporate practices. Ordinary workers, he argues, are no closer now to participating in the management of organizations than they were before the subject of industrial democracy became popular.

The limited survey research which does exist reveals a wide range of attitudes among employees, managers, union officials, and employers toward employee participation (see, for example, Milton 1977; Bull and Barton 1978; Frenkel 1986; Plowman, Adams, and Burke 1986). It is difficult to gauge precisely the views of the various parties due to the diverse range of questions asked in surveys and the variety of methods used to collect data. Nevertheless, Spillane, Findlay, and Borthwick (1982) argue that it has generally been shown that Australian employers prefer "immediate" forms of participation, such as job enrichment or redesign, whereby employees are involved in lower-level decisions within the organization. By contrast, workers tend to favor "intermediate" forms of participation which require the acquisition of greater skills through training and the provision of more extensive information by management. Neither employees nor management give much support to "distant" forms of participation in which workers are involved in corporate-level decisions through representation on the board of directors.

One of the most extensive surveys of employee attitudes to participation was conducted by the Metal Trades Industry Association (MTIA) during the mid-1980s (see Frenkel 1986). The fourteen varieties of employee participation covered in the survey were grouped into three broad types: (1) *participative*, which involve direct contact between management and employees; (2) *representative*, where employee representatives consult or negotiate with management; and (3) *financial*, which involve share-owning or profit sharing plans. Among the 30 percent of organizations in the survey that had used some form of employee participation during the past decade, participative schemes were the most popular (45 percent), followed by representative schemes (40 percent) and financial schemes (15 percent). The main reasons given by employers for introducing such schemes were improving management and employee relationships (67 percent), raising productivity (50 percent), and improving the working environment (45 percent). Almost 87 percent of managers reported that their participative schemes were effective, although they did not support schemes which involved any substantial power sharing with their employees. Frenkel (1986) concluded that schemes that were most likely to gain support from management were those which resulted in fewer workplace disputes and higher productivity.

A cross-industry study by Carlin and Cannon (1981) found that interest in employee participation was greatest among mining companies (87 percent of whom reported the existence of some form of scheme), followed by manufacturing (65 percent), construction, transport, and storage (64 percent), wholesale and retail (62 percent), recreational, personnel and other services (50 percent), while finance, property, and business services showed the least interest (43 percent). It is interesting to note that there appeared to be a positive correlation between the degree of unionization and the level of reported participation. The industries with the highest level of unionization (such as mining and manufacturing) reported far more participative schemes in operation than those with lower levels of unionization (such as finance and related areas). In a pilot survey of union experience with employee participation, Tilley (1986) reported that approximately two-thirds responded positively. Unions with the least involvement in participative schemes tended to be those which covered unskilled occupations with high levels of casual and part-time employment, had a geographically dispersed membership, lacked workplace organization, and were industrially weak.

Data on employee attitudes to employee participation and industrial democracy, drawing upon a broad cross-section of the labor force, are rare. In one large-scale official survey of working conditions, however, employees were asked what changes they most desired at work (Australian Bureau of Statistics 1979). Among manual workers, employed mainly in manufacturing, the issues in descending order of importance were: greater job security, higher pay, and more influence in decision making. Among clerical workers (employed across all industries), influence in decision making was ranked first. In a study of metal workers, Frenkel and Coolican (1984) reported widespread concern for more job control, particularly in the way in which work was performed, and a willingness to assume more responsibility for decision making.

As noted in Frenkel's (1986) study, the results of surveys in Australia have tended to reveal a fairly consistent pattern; each group tends to look to employee participation or industrial democracy to achieve different objectives. Management views participation as a means of lowering unit labor costs and increasing profits, while employees look to it as a vehicle for enhancing job control and improving work satisfaction. While union leaders endorse the latter view, they also seek to safeguard their institutional interests by demanding that union involvement (if not control) be a central feature of any initiatives in this field. These findings suggest that for any scheme to succeed it must not significantly increase the power of any single group at the expense of another. Thus, if employee participation is to gain the support of all parties it must provide sufficient incentives (or rewards) for all those who are involved. To understand the way in which the Australian debate has been conducted, it is useful to examine the economic and social contexts, the views of the parties and examples which have gained the support of both management and the unions.

THE ECONOMIC AND SOCIAL CONTEXT

Australia is a mixed economy in which there is a heavy concentration of power in a small number of large enterprises. The largest 200 firms employ about one-half of the labor force and account for 60 percent of fixed capital expenditure. Yet there are also vast numbers of small enterprises.

Approximately 95 percent of the 30,000 or more firms engaged in manufacturing employ less than 100 people. The 1950s and 1960s were decades of steady economic growth, low inflation, and full employment. Conservative political parties, which have dominated the federal government since the turn of the century, made little attempt to develop comprehensive planning of either a compulsory or indicative nature. Protectionist economic policies resulted in the creation of a manufacturing sector that produced goods for a small domestic market behind high tariff barriers. In such a climate, neither management nor unions sought to explore the possibilities of major changes to the customary style of work and to the traditional pattern of authority within the workplace.

Significant changes occurred in the early 1970s. The level of inflation moved up sharply from an average of 2.5 percent per annum for 1960-1970 to 6.7 percent per annum for 1970-1973. It gathered pace, reaching an average of 15.1 percent for 1973-1975. While the rate of inflation declined in 1977 and 1978, this deceleration was not sustained and inflation remained at relatively high levels in the 1980s. The problem was not simply one of high inflation and the usual dislocation as groups within society sought to protect their standard of living; it was compounded by the fact that Australian inflation exceeded that of its major trading partners. This was a major blow to Australian competitiveness on both domestic and international markets.

The economic difficulties of the late 1970s were also reflected in problems which beset the manufacturing industry (and later the agricultural and mining sectors). High tariff barriers did not prevent the decline of manufacturing employment which resulted from a combination of structural and technological changes in the Australian economy. During the decade 1973-1983, the proportion of the Australian labor force employed in manufacturing declined from 24 percent to 18 percent. The general level of unemployment also increased from the early 1970s, when it was around 2 percent, and by 1983 some 10 percent of the Australian labor force were registered as unemployed. The deteriorating economic situation forced both unions and the Australian Labor Party (ALP) to seek an agreed approach to achieve "national reconciliation and reconstruction" through the establishment of an *Accord on Prices and Incomes* (ALP-ACTU 1983). The "Accord" also included reference to the need for industry development and "continuous consultation and cooperation between the parties involved." The "Accord" committed the Labor government to implement a more expansionary economic policy, to consult with unions over various reforms, and to support union proposals that employees be notified and consulted by employers about technological and other changes (Lansbury 1985).

The 1970s were also conspicuous for the speed and breadth of technological change. Development in microelectronics, particularly the application of microcomputers, ensured that change extended across many sectors of the economy. Previous conceptions of technological change as largely confined to increased automation in manufacturing were overturned as the organization of work within offices, factories, and ships was transformed. The issue of employee and union participation in decision making at work became more critical as traditional patterns of work and employment were radically changed by new technology. As outlined later in this paper, the Australian Council of Trade Unions (ACTU) successfully mounted a case before the Australian Industrial Relations Commission during the early 1980s seeking information and consultation rights for employees in the face of employer proposals to introduce technological change.

It should be noted that some serious economic problems emerged in the mid-1980s. These included an extraodinarily volatile exchange rate, chronic balance of payments deficits, high interest rates, high inflation, and signs of increasing unemployment. These problems initially tended to deflect interest and attention away from industrial democracy. They also put the "Accord" under pressure as the Hawke government found itself unable to honor former commitments such as the maintenance of real wage levels (Davis 1987).

Nonetheless, current government thinking is that greater employee participation is essential as a means to improve organizational efficiency, productivity and, hence, competitiveness (Department of Employment and Industrial Relations 1986). This view is mirrored in the ACTU/Trade Development Council's (TDC) important paper, *Australia Reconstructed* (ACTU/TDC 1987). This emphasizes that industrial democracy, together with greater attention to the implementation of appropriate technologies, improved forms of work organization and higher levels of training, should be "harnessed as a force in production." Recent national wage decisions by the Australian Industrial Relations Commission have also encouraged greater employee involvement in decision making. In March 1987 the Commission introduced a two-tier wage fixing system in which wage increases of up to 4 percent could be gained by negotiations over "restructuring and efficiency." Although much attention has been focused on reforms in work practices achieved under the new system, the means by which these changes were introduced was through the establishment of consultative procedures. In August 1988, the wage fixing system underwent further changes with the introduction of the "structural efficiency principle." This further extended the process of reform and required unions and employers to undertake a fundamental review of their award structures to achieve greater flexibility and efficiency. A key requirement of the new system was consultation between the parties in order to eliminate impediments to multiskilling and to establish career paths for workers (see Rimmer and Zappala 1988).

THE POLITICAL CONTEXT

The political initiative on industrial democracy was first taken during the early 1970s by the South Australian Labor government. It instigated a major inquiry into worker participation and then established an Industrial Democracy Unit within the Department of Industrial Relations to advise and assist in the development of industrial democracy (Anderson 1976). After focusing initially on the promotion of job enrichment and quality of work life activities, the unit switched its emphasis toward the establishment of representative structures designed to enhance worker participation in decision making at the enterprise level. The South Australian Labor government also organized a major international conference on industrial democracy in 1978 which helped to raise consciousness among both Australian businesses and unions. However, when the government lost office in the late 1970s, it had not secured legislation in this field and the influence of its Industrial Democracy Unit had been mainly confined to the public sector. Nevertheless, the government's initiatives did stimulate debate and interest in the area of employee participation and industrial democracy throughout Australia during the decade of the 1970s.

On the conservative side of politics, the Liberal Party ignored the issue of industrial democracy throughout most of the 1970s, preferring to leave it to employers and unions to develop their own strategies. In 1978, however, the federal Liberal-National Party government enunciated a policy on "employee participation" which encouraged direct participation by employees through changes in work organization at the enterprise level and the establishment of representative systems to facilitate joint decision making on a voluntary basis. The government also argued that "prescriptive" legislation was neither an appropriate nor practical means of introducing employee participation since no single system should be imposed. The policy stressed that, while trade unions should be involved in the introduction of employee participation schemes, nonunionists must not be excluded. A National Employee Participation Steering Committee was set up with representatives of trade unions, professional associations, employers, and employers' organizations to establish a national strategy for the implementation of employee participation. However, the government's policy allowed a wide variety of interpretation and this discouraged a joint approach. No significant government initiatives were achieved during the period of the Fraser government between 1975 and 1983.

A small political party which has held the balance of power at various times in the Australian Senate, the Australian Democrats, has taken a keen interest in the issue of industrial democracy. In November 1981, an Industrial Democracy Bill, sponsored by the Democrats, was introduced into the Senate. The stated objective of the bill was to encourage industrial democracy through reduction of company tax for those enterprises that met certain specified criteria. However, the bill ultimately failed to gain sufficient support from the major parties to be passed as an Act of Parliament.

The Hawke Labor government, through the "Accord," has been formally committed to the pursuit of increased industrial democracy as part of its general strategy on industrial relations. At a major government-sponsored seminar on Industrial Democracy and Employee Participation held in mid-1984, Prime Minister Hawke drew attention to the operation of tripartite consultative processes foreshadowed in the "Accord," such as the Economic Planning Advisory Council (EPAC) and the Advisory Committee on Prices and Incomes (ACPI). On this basis, he claimed that "industrial democracy at the macro or national level" had been established (Hawke 1985). Employers were exhorted to follow the federal government's example and, where appropriate, to provide information to employees and the unions representing them and to involve employees and unions in the discussion and analysis of policy (see also *Guidelines on Information Sharing* drawn up by the tripartite National Labour Consultative Council). The government also commissioned a Green Paper, subsequently retitled a "Policy Discussion Paper," on industrial democracy.

When it was released in December 1986, the Policy Discussion Paper proposed a number of measures to encourage the introduction of more employee participation and, therefore, higher levels of industrial democracy (Department of Employment and Industrial Relations 1986). Although it did not exclude the possibility of legislative guidelines for information sharing, the paper warned that "legislation setting out a rigid prescription for all organizations is not an appropriate option. If legislation is considered it must take into account the need for local flexibility and responsibility." The paper recommended that the government consider a variety of "facilitative measures" including financial incentives, such as taxation benefits, to organizations which introduced participative practices. It also urged the provision of education and training, advice, and assistance to both employers and unions to encourage initiatives at the enterprise level.

The Hawke government introduced a number of changes in the public sector. In a policy paper, *Reforming the Australian Public Service* (1984), it was stated that:

> A more participative approach to management will improve decision-making by ensuring full opportunities for the staff who will be affected to make their views known and to have them properly considered. An administration more responsive to the needs of staff will enjoy improved morale and performance, while at the same time enriching the working lives of men and women who are part of the Government's workforce (Stanton 1984, p. 173).

The areas tackled have included work organization, financial and staff planning, occupational health and safety, and the introduction of new technologies. In addition, and as detailed in the *Public Sector Reform Act 1984,* each department and prescribed authority has been required to develop and implement an "industrial democracy plan." The federal government thus appears to be using the public sector as a "pace setter" for industrial democracy, hoping that the private sector will follow its example.

While the Hawke government has taken a rather cautious approach on industrial democracy, some of the state labor governments have been more adventurous. This has been most notable in Victoria where the Labor Party won office in 1982 after twenty-seven years in opposition. The new government moved quickly to establish a more consultative style of operation than embraced by its conservative predecessors. Legislation was enacted which set in place structures for greater worker participation in decision making on occupational health and safety (although not without considerable opposition) and within the transport sector (see Sonder 1983; Hartnett 1986). In addition, the Victorian government has stated that it "encourages the introduction of industrial democracy and is keen to see that all Victorians are aware of the alternate strategies, processes and advantages to be gained." Issues such as organizational and technological change, health and safety, industrial relations procedures, and training and development are identified as suited to the process of industrial democracy. Recent progress has been slower in the other states currently administered by the Labor Party (New South Wales, South Australia, and Western Australia), and there has been a marked lack of interest in the two states under conservative governments (Queensland and Tasmania).

THE LEGAL CONTEXT

The development of employee involvement and industrial democracy in Australia has been greatly influenced by the practice of conciliation and arbitration both at the federal level and within the states. The Australian Industrial Relations Act, enacted in 1904 (but replaced by a new act in 1988), obliged employers to recognize trade unions registered under the act and empowered unions to make claims on behalf of all employees within an industry. Under this act, unions are required to register with the arbitration authorities (the Industrial Registrar) in order to obtain full corporate status under the law. Unions must meet certain requirements in regard to their constitutions to qualify for registration. Once registered, however, unions can compel employers to go before the Australian Industrial Relations Commission and have an award (covering wages and other terms of employment) legally enforced. On the other hand, unions have largely been restricted to negotiation on "industrial matters" and excluded from matters judged to be "managerial rights." Dr. J.E. Isaac, a former Deputy President of the federal Commission, has argued that the practice of conciliation and arbitration, federally and within states, has tended to restrict employee involvement and industrial democracy (Isaac 1980). It has commonly buttressed the notion of managerial prerogative and, thereby, limited the opportunities for workers and their unions to be involved in the planning and organization of work. Isaac (1980) has commented that the federal commission has tended to take a narrow view of the kinds of matters over which it should adjudicate. In this respect, it has been influenced by the High Court. Isaac quotes a former Chief Justice, Sir Garfield Barwick, who stated that the management of an enterprise should not be a subject matter for industrial dispute. Because the Industrial Relations Commission is permitted by the constitution to be involved only in the prevention and settlement of *industrial disputes*, it has not generally been able to make rulings about the process of management.

Recent developments have ushered in some important changes. In the Social Welfare Union case (1983), the High Court's decision indicated that it was ready to take a much broader view of what constituted an "industrial dispute" (Smith 1985). A major implication of this decision was that matters previously regarded as managerial prerogative might now be determined by the federal commission. This impression was reinforced in the High Court's decision in late 1984 to uphold a ruling of the Victorian Industrial Relations Commission. The Victorian body had been challenged on its decision to ratify the insertion of a clause in the Commercial Clerks' Award requiring extensive consultation between employers and employees *before* the introduction of technological change in the workplace. The new clause required employers to notify the Federated Clerks Union and employees of any decision to begin feasibility studies on technological change, to consult with the union and employees during the feasibility study, and to advise these groups as soon as any decision was made. Furthermore, the employer was also obliged to consult on the issue of alternative proposals. One judge, in his summing up, commented that the workers' claim:

> is a demand to be treated as more than wage-hands—to be treated as men and women who should be informed about decisions which might materially affect their future, and to be consulted on them. It is a demand . . . to be treated with respect and dignity.

Other decisions have also been important. Most notably a Full Bench of the federal commission heard a lengthy test case on the issue of job protection. The ACTU, supported by the Hawke government, sought the establishment of rights for employees to be notified and consulted by employers about the proposed introduction of technological change. In its *Termination, Change and Redundancy Decision* (1984), the commission granted workers' rights, to be set down in their awards, to information and to consultation with employers over their plans for technological change and organizational restructure. The decision which preceded the High Court's ruling on the Commercial Clerks'

Award was hailed as a landmark in Australian industrial relations. Taken together with the rulings of the High Court, it has suggested an erosion of managerial prerogative (Deery 1986; Davis and Lansbury 1987).

The Committee of Review into Australian Industrial Relations Law and Systems, chaired by Professor Keith Hancock, also gave strong support to broadening the jurisdiction of the federal tribunal (Committee of Review 1985). It argued that government should legislate to remove "artificial limitations" on the ability of the federal tribunal to deal with workplace matters. It also gave strong encouragement to employers to provide relevant information to, and consult with, employees and the unions representing them and to pursue industrial democracy. Such behavior was believed to be particularly appropriate in the case of proposals for technological change (Lansbury and Davis 1985).

TRADE UNION ATTITUDES AND POLICIES

Unions have long sought to influence management decision making. For the most part, however, union efforts have been restricted to issues connected with wages and conditions. During the 1970s, many unions indicated a desire to participate in a broader range of issues. This, among other things, encouraged debate and the formulation of explicit policy on industrial democracy within the Australian Council of Trade Unions (ACTU). Policy on this was passed at the 1977 Biennial Congress of the ACTU and has been revised at subsequent congresses. Current policy declares that democracy in the workplace is a fundamental democratic right which should be enshrined in legislation. Furthermore, it should be channelled through unions, and education courses are desirable to prepare members for increased participation in decision making. The point is also made that the implementation of industrial democracy will lead to a more equal distribution of power within the enterprise; traditional patterns of ownership, organization, and control will inevitably be challenged.

Two developments have been of particular interest. First, ACTU officials have argued that the "Accord" represents a blueprint for industrial democracy. It is seen to encourage greater employee participation, through unions, in the determination of the critical matters affecting worklife. Moreover, this participation takes place at national, industry, enterprise, and workplace levels. Second, unions have been encouraged to play an active part in the drive for industrial democracy. Following policy revisions made at the 1985 ACTU Congress, they were urged to draw up logs of claims which identified those issues of greatest importance to workers (such as employment security, work organization, technological change, and occupational health and safety) and then to seek rights to information, to consultation, and to decision-making influence on these matters. In other words, unions have been encouraged to negotiate on industrial democracy in the same way that they have conducted negotiations on wages and conditions.

The growth of explicit interest in industrial democracy at the peak council level has been reflected in the policies and experience of several unions. Two prominent examples are the Public Service Union (PSU), which covers clerical and other staff within the federal public service, and the Amalgamated Metal Workers Union (AMWU), which covers maintenance and other metal workers. Of interest, both organizations have benefitted from government industrial democracy subsidies in the last three years.

The PSU has welcomed government interest in the development of more participative management' styles. However, it has insisted that government policy on this will not be translated into practice unless union workplace representatives are given the time, training, and facilities to prepare for joint consultative meetings. To date, the PSU's view is that the establishment of consultative councils has increased the flow of information to union members. In addition, the union, through consultation and negotiation, has been able to exercise a greater influence over a broader range of matters than formerly possible (Robson 1986).

Problems, however, have been encountered. First, so many initiatives for union-management consultation have flourished that the union has not been able to offer an adequate response. Put simply, it has lacked the resources to train and assist its members to assume a more participative role in management. Second, in many sections of the public sector, management has shown little willingness to consult with worker representatives and has been reluctant to provide information resources and facilities to union representatives.

Industrial democracy has been a topic on the AMWU's agenda since the mid-1970s (Ruskin 1986). For most full-time officials and active shop stewards, it has meant the pursuit of greater rights and influence within the workplace. This was set out in the AMWU's *Shop Stewards' Charter* which listed union claims for rights to information, facilities, and influence within the workplace. Of interest, the term "industrial democracy" was regarded with some suspicion by many within the union. This was on two counts. First, many stewards reported that managements were reorganizing methods of work in ways which often increased workers' influence over the immediate aspects of their job. Workers were exhorted to support the revised approach on the basis that it was "industrial democracy." Stewards objected to the fact that they had not been consulted about the reorganization; they pointed to the limited nature of decision-making opportunities granted to workers and were generally cynical of management intentions to implement industrial democracy. Second, many full-time officials and stewards felt uncomfortable with the orientation to consensus that appeared, according to conventional wisdom, to be an ingredient in industrial democracy. This did not sit easily with the union's traditional emphasis on militant struggle for improved wages and conditions.

Current AMWU approaches to industrial democracy emphasize the importance of negotiations over increased rights for workers; the *Shop Stewards' Charter* remains the appropriate vehicle for workplace democracy. But, at the same time, in line with sentiments expressed in the "Accord," union officials have appeared less reserved about entering into more consultative and cooperative arrangements with employers.

ATTITUDES AND POLICIES
OF EMPLOYERS' ORGANIZATIONS

The early growth of unions in Australia, fostered by the establishment of conciliation and arbitration systems at both state and federal levels, also led to the establishment of employers' associations. Unlike the unions, however, the employers have not succeeded in establishing a single national body. The largest employers' group, the Confederation of Australian Industry (CAI) was formed in 1977 and is represented on the tripartite National Labour Consultative Council (NLCC). The Hawke Labor government has sought to forge a consensus between the CAI, ACTU, and itself through the NLCC on industrial democracy and employee participation, but has so far only achieved agreement on the broadest principles. At the conference on Employee Participation/Industrial Democracy, organized by the NLCC in 1984, the Director-General of the CAI emphasized that although his member organizations favored employee participation in relevant aspects of decision making, it should be left to individual enterprises to devise their own mutually accepted approaches. He also stressed that "employers and managers will resist the implementation of theories of industrial democracy which seek to bring about fundamental change in society to their disadvantage" (Noakes 1985).

The Australian Chamber of Manufacturers, a major constituent of the CAI, has also indicated that while it is in favor of greater involvement in the workplace it opposes industrial democracy programs—which it views as merely devices to increase union power. Furthermore, when employers support employee participation, this means *all* employees and not just union members. Management must be able to devise and develop appropriate styles of work with all their employees. The chamber has also counselled against the enactment of specific prescriptions for worker participation and argued that legislation of this kind would be unacceptable.

The Business Council of Australia (BCA) was formed in 1983 to represent the views of large employers. It sees little merit in industrial democracy, which it believes poses a critical threat to the operation of management. However, the BCA does favor employee involvement as an integral component of a new management style, fashioned by the rigors of a rapidly changing international market and fierce competitive pressure. It is anticipated that such an approach will help to break down long-standing worker-management divisions and so contribute to a better climate of enterprise relations, encourage greater productivity, and improve organizational effectiveness. The stress is on relations involving employees in the workplace and line management, rather than management (or unions) at higher levels. The BCA sums up its position as follows:

> Employee participation with its primary focus on the individual employee, would contribute significantly to personal development, attitudinal change, healthy relationships at work, increased productivity and economic revitalisation. Industrial democracy, based on trade unions operating as the single channel of employee representation and communication and contractual or award-based rights and entitlements, increases the risk of further rigidities, conflicts and anti-productive behaviour (BCA 1986).

UNION-INITIATED APPROACHES TOWARD INDUSTRIAL DEMOCRACY

Until recently, few unions had initiated explicit programs of involvement or participation by workers in decision making and certainly few unions had devised plans for an alternative structure of management based on workers' participation. An exception was an initiative taken by the Victorian branch of the Australian Railways Union (ARU) which investigated the perceived crisis facing the Victorian railways, developed a plan to revive the railways, and sought to have this acted upon by management (Alford 1986). The issue was particularly pressing for the union since employment in the industry had been in steady decline for a number of years. A key feature of the ARU's approach was the formulation of an alternative plan; the union did not simply wait for management to act. Moreover, new consultative mechanisms were designed which led to unions in the railways becoming better informed about their industry and more closely involved in the decision-making process.

In the telecommunications industry, technological change acted as a catalyst to unions to seek more direct participation and involvement by employees in decision making. In 1977, Telecom management proposed to introduce new computer-controlled technology that would have the effect of centralizing the work of engineers in the organization. The Australian Telecommunications Employees Association (ATEA), which covered these workers, objected to the fact that there had been minimal consultation with the union over this plan and articulated members' fears for their jobs, career opportunities, and job satisfaction (Musumeci 1984; Matthews 1985). The ATEA imposed bans in support of the demand to have alternative proposals for change considered by management. The ATEA stated that their objection was not the technology chosen by management, but to their plans to reorganize the workforce.

Telecom refused to adopt the ATEA's counter-proposals and a strike ensued. The member of the Industrial Relations Commission who heard the matter determined that the alternative system proposed should be allowed to operate for a trial period, and then be evaluated. The criteria for judgment were efficiency of operation, standard of service, job satisfaction, career opportunities, maintenance of technical standards, and retention of expertise and the public interest. The trials and further commission hearings paved the way for a technology agreement between Telecom and relevant unions. Importantly, the agreement specified the principles to be applied in the process of technological change. These included joint management-union consideration of proposals for change (including those submitted by unions) *before* a firm decision had been made and employer provision of information and resources to unions to enable them to make accurate assessments of the implications of the proposals being considered.

The Victorian government's desire to implement a more participative management style in the public sector was noted previously. This was evident in the *Victorian Public Sector Technological Change Agreement* (1985), which was the result of negotiations between the government and the Victorian Trades Hall Council (VTHC), the state peak union council. The agreement recognized that the process of technological change usually involves six stages:

1. the "concept stage" at which discussion first takes place of a proposal for change;
2. the "contemplative stage" at which resources are committed to study proposals for change;
3. the "development stage" which involves detailed investigation of the proposals and the forming of recommendations;
4. the "approval stage" at which a proposal is adopted and tenders sought;
5. the "implementation stage" at which change is actually introduced; and
6. the "post-implementation stage" at which the operation and repercussions of changes are monitored.

The agreement determined that a Joint Public Sector Technological Change Committee and Joint Technological Change Standing Committee be established. The former comprises representatives from public sector organizations, the VTHC, and government. It is charged with the task of monitoring technological change in the public sector and making policy recommendations to the Minister. It also provides advice to the Standing Committees, which operate within government departments or organizations and which involve representatives from management and unions. Their task is to advise management on how best to introduce technological change, and to oversee the implementation of consultative practices.

A key feature of the agreement is that workers and their unions are to be notified of proposals for change at the "contemplative stage," thereby enabling them to be involved at an early stage in discussions of change and of alternative approaches. Furthermore, the government will provide resources, through a Technological Change Unit, to assist both management and union representatives in their efforts to understand and deal with issues. Finally, the government has drawn attention to "basic principles" which should be taken into account in proposals for change. These emphasize the importance of the repercussions from changes on employment, the relevance of workers' skills, the need for training and retraining, job satisfaction, and occupational health and safety.

MANAGEMENT-INITIATED APPROACHES TO EMPLOYEE PARTICIPATION

Management-initiated approaches to employee participation have increased during the past decade. They have been extremely varied, including such examples as the introduction of semi-autonomous work groups, joint consultation, co-determination, and issues-based approaches.

Co-determination and Board Level Representation

There are some examples of employee representation at the board of directors' level within the public sector in Australia. The Whitlam Labor government (1972-1975) appointed several trade union officials to the boards of statutory authorities and nationalized corporations such as Australia Post, Telecom Australia, Qantas Airways, and the Reserve Bank. In most cases, the board members were appointed rather than elected and were not directly responsible to the employees. One interesting exception was in the Australian Broadcasting Commission (ABC) where staff were given the opportunity to elect one of the commissioners. After the defeat of the Whitlam Labor government in 1975, the incoming coalition government of Liberal and National Country Parties reverted to the previous system of appointing all commissioners to the ABC. Some of the unions with coverage of employees in the ABC took industrial action in an attempt to restore the system of staff-elected commissioners, but to no avail. The NSW Labor government also appointed "worker directors" to the boards of state-owned enterprises although only on a rather limited scale. To establish a system of co-determination along West German lines, which also involves the private sector, would require extensive changes in company law at both the state and federal levels (see Pritchard 1976). So far neither major political party is seeking to introduce reforms of this kind.

Examples of co-determination in the private sector are comparatively rare. One Australian example which does involve some broad aspects of co-determination is provided by Fletcher Jones and Staff Pty. Ltd., a major clothing manufacturer with factories and retail stores throughout Australia. Employees at Fletcher Jones hold two-thirds of the shares and have the right to vote for representatives on the board of directors. In each subsidiary company, there is a junior board of directors whose members are elected for a two-year term of office. Nine of the directors are elected by employees and nine are nominated by management. The junior boards meet at monthly intervals to help determine retail sales targets, hear any appeals from employees regarding promotion, and make recommendations to the central board of directors. Management is not obliged to implement the recommendations of the junior board, although reasons must be given for their rejection. Furthermore, management nominates the central board of directors who must then be ratified by the shareholders.

Some observers of the system practiced by Fletcher Jones claim that the junior boards of directors have little power in running the enterprise and attract minimal interest among the employees. The central board of directors, it is argued, takes a paternalistic approach to the employees and can veto junior board decisions with which it disagrees. Nevertheless, the Fletcher Jones system has persisted for many years and appears to have general employee support. It is important to note the strong influence on the development of the system by the original owner of Fletcher Jones, who was well known for his philanthropic and reformist attitudes. Furthermore, the main factory in which the ideas of Fletcher Jones were initially practiced is located in a small country town where it is the major employer. These unique features may limit the degree to which the Fletcher Jones example could be applied elsewhere.

Joint Consultation

One of the most prevalent forms of employee participation in Australia during past decades has been joint consultation. This has mainly involved employee representatives and management meeting together to discuss issues related to amenities, working conditions, and other enterprise-level matters. A survey of the growth of joint consultative schemes in Australia during the 1950s attributed their development to three main factors (see Wall and Butler 1959): (1) reports of successful overseas experience such as the Glacier Metal Company and others in Britain, (2) a wider acceptance by management of employee participation as a means of achieving greater cooperation and productivity, and (3) recognition by management of the potential among employees to contribute to more efficient methods and increased production. However, many employees, unions, and management have been disillusioned with joint consultation. Employees have tended to see consultation as a means of fostering greater employee motivation without infringing managerial prerogatives. Employees have generally been restricted to discussing matters of relatively minor importance. Not surprisingly, many unions have become critical of the consultative process. Nevertheless, there are some successful cases of joint consultation in both the private and public sectors.

Semi-Autonomous Work Groups

Some notable advances in participation and involvement by employees have been made at the shopfloor or workplace level. These developments include the election by groups of their own supervisor or foreman, the restructuring of jobs to provide workers with greater opportunities to exercise choice and initiative, and the creation of semi-autonomous work groups which manage their own work schedules and decide the way in which tasks should be shared and performed. The underlying objective of many of these initiatives is to introduce "management from below" to replace the traditional approach of "rule from above." Fred Emery's experience at the Tavistock Institute of Human Relations in England, as well as his role in Norwegian and other Scandinavian industrial democracy projects, has influenced much Australian activity (see Emery and Thorsrud 1976; Emery 1978). In a few instances, provision for semi-autonomous work groups has been incorporated into some federal and state arbitration awards (this is equivalent to union-management contracts in other countries; see Isaac 1980). The introduction of semi-autonomous work groups in certain areas of manual work at CSR Limited, for example, required an increase in the range of skills on the part of workers concerned. In some other cases, employers and unions have achieved agreements on the introduction and operation of semi-autonomous work groups, which they have registered with the appropriate tribunal. The Pacific Can Company introduced semi-autonomous work groups in some areas of its operation. A registered agreement was concluded between Pacific Can and several metal unions that contained a provision enabling workers whose skills were enlarged to be considered for regrading.

An interesting experiment with semi-autonomous work groups and other alternative methods of work organizations was undertaken by the Woodlawn Mining Company. This was a joint venture between three parent organizations, one Australian and two American, and is involved in mining a complex ore body of copper, lead, and zinc. An open-cut mine began operating in 1978 (see Gilmour and Lansbury 1984).

Two main goals were stated by the general manager of Woodlawn when the venture was established: (1) to create a corporate structure that would enable responsibility for many operating decisions to be devolved to relatively low levels within the organization, and (2) to provide opportunities for employees to develop through multiskilling and to pay them according to their skill levels. Every task in the four main sections of Woodlawn Mines (the open-cut, the mill, engineering, and the warehouse) was carefully defined and groups of related tasks were combined into what became known as operating areas.

Out of the concept of multiskilling there arose agreements with unions that prevented potential industrial relations problems. On a typical Australian mining site, there can be more than 70 job classifications covered by a range of unions, each of which seeks to protect the domain of jobs performed by its members. This situation is the cause of many demarcation (jurisdictional) disputes between unions. In order to minimize these problems, Woodlawn negotiated a collective agreement which gave three unions exclusive coverage of employees at Woodlawn.

Another important innovation at Woodlawn was the replacement of the traditional "foreman" or "supervisor" by a "shift coordinator" and "technical adviser." The objective was to facilitate the development of semi-autonomous work groups that would be less reliant on the traditional "shift boss" for direction. The "technical advisers" operated in the engineering department while the "shift coordinators" functioned in both the mine and the mill. All of the coordinators at Woodlawn were recruited on the basis of both technical competence and ability to facilitate the development of semi-autonomous work groups.

Although Woodlawn encountered financial difficulties due to problems in mining the complex ore body, it provided a model for other organizations to follow. Concepts of multiskilling, payment according to skill, and reductions in the number of job classifications became key elements embodied in the "restructuring and efficiency" principle of the 1988 National Wage Case. Several companies within the mining, ship building, and manufacturing industries have incorporated a number of the principles of work organization and employee participation pioneered at Woodlawn.

Issues-Based Approaches

Many of the developments in Australian enterprises during the last few years have concentrated on attempts to set up various types of structures that have incorporated particular principles of industrial democracy and have frequently mirrored overseas forms. One aspect of these developments has been a concern for how such structures should be designed. For example, there has been controversy over the distribution of membership on joint consultative committees between various employee, union, and management groups. Often there has been such preoccupation with structural issues, that such bodies have not achieved effective operation. Similarly, questions of what type of decisions should be the subject of participation, and at what levels, often dominated discussions.

Currently, however, there is less concern with structure and more with making employee involvement in management a part of accepted organizational practice. This has sometimes been referred to as an "issues-based" approach, in that it gives priority to increasing, by various means, the involvement of employees in issues of joint concern to management and employees. Employees are involved both in the identification of issues and the determination of action to be taken.

Caltex Oil introduced an issues-based approach as an outcome of a quality of work life program. The program initially involved a senior management review of the state of employee relations and the consideration of possible action which could be taken. There followed a series of management seminars that raised management awareness of employee needs and of quality of work life issues. This, in turn, led to a formal company-wide attitude survey which sought to ascertain employee attitudes to work and to highlight major areas where change was required to achieve better quality of work life. Results of the survey were fed back to employees, but no opportunity was given for them to provide information other than that which was sought in the survey. Furthermore, employees were not invited to participate in bringing about changes in the workplace.

It was evident that employees had a genuine desire to become involved in improving work life. After much deliberation it was decided to conduct "Participative Action Study Workshops." The title was chosen to highlight two important points: (1) participation by employees in identifying issues requiring attention and (2) an action orientation toward the development of solutions. An important principle that evolved from the workshops was the need to involve employees in the problem-solving process.

Commenting on this type of approach, Ken Wang (1980) stated:

> In comparison to workshops which concentrate on industrial democracy matters, the Participative Action Study Workshops certainly produced quite a different result. Industrial democracy workshops that I have been involved with in the past generally ended in proposals which were heavily structure-and-form oriented. Often, industrial democracy as an end-product has been seen by the participants as the way to achieve a better work environment. This is not so with Participative Action Study Workshops which usually treat industrial democracy as a means of resolving and handling issues.

CONCLUSION

The 1980s have witnessed steady, although not spectacular, development in employee participation and industrial democracy. Since the mid-1970s, the Australian trade union movement has favored a policy of industrial democracy with unions acting as the sole channel of representation, while employers have preferred the alternative of employee participation with less emphasis on union involvement. The election of the Hawke Labor government in 1983 strengthened the trend toward industrial democracy although, of note, its 1986 Policy Discussion Paper indicated preference for a voluntarist approach to employee participation. Employers have also supported a nonregulated approach which emphasizes direct participation by employees in job-related decisions, such as quality control. Employers have generally sought to discourage the establishment of representative structures in which the role of unions would be enhanced.

The expansionary economic conditions in 1983-1985 created a relatively favorable environment for the development of industrial democracy during the initial period of the Hawke Labor Government. The "Accord" between the ACTU and the government also provided a framework which supported union initiatives. Many new tripartite bodies were established, such as the Economic Planning Advisory Council (EPAC) and the Advisory Committee on Prices and Incomes (ACPI). But these provided involvement for very few union members and participation at this level was necessarily at a considerable distance from the membership in the workplace. Progress toward greater industrial democracy was hampered by the deterioration in Australia's economic fortunes in 1985 and 1986, mounting strain on the "Accord," and increasingly strident opposition to industrial democracy on the part of some major employers. Current government and union thinking, however, appears to view greater industrial democracy as an important ingredient in moves to improve the competitiveness of Australian industry.

Employer-initiated schemes of employee participation and involvement have tended to play down the role of unions. Nevertheless, many of these schemes have proven to be popular with employees and have some relevance for industrial democracy. For example, semi-autonomous work groups can lead to workers having a greater degree of influence over their own work tasks, although more significant decisions about their work will be made elsewhere. Participation of workers at board level is also rare and most board-level worker representatives are commonly in a minority and unable to influence the decision-making process. Joint consultative committees are becoming more prevalent; but while these usually provide opportunities for employee representatives to obtain work-related information, they rarely act as decision-making forums on critical issues affecting the workplace. Finally, a wide variety of issues-based approaches to employee involvement are being initiated by employers, some of which involve workers and their representatives deciding important issues. However, their contribution to the extension of industrial democracy is often limited by the fact that management has initiated the exercise and determined the agenda.

The Australian case provides partial support for the thesis of Cutcher-Gershenfeld et al. (1987) that employee participation programs that are not accompanied by major changes in organizational structure, or integrated with other far-reaching changes, are unlikely to be sustained over time. Unlike the United States, however, both the union movement and the federal government in Australia are now acknowledging industrial democracy/employee participation as important ingredients in significant economic and structural change. Furthermore, recent changes to the system of wage determination are likely to act as a catalyst to greater employee participation in decision making within the enterprise.

The main barrier to more rapid change along these lines, however, remains opposition among employers, especially to changes that could enhance the influence of trade unions in decision making at the enterprise level. The uncertain economic situation, especially following the stock market crash of 1987, has also made the federal government reluctant to introduce measures which could disturb confidence in the economy. Moreover, many unions remain poorly equipped to increase their involvement in management decision making.

REFERENCES

Alford, J. 1986. Changing Power Relations in the Victorian Railways. Pp. 73-91 in *Democracy and Control in the Work Place,* edited by E.M. Davis and R.D. Lansbury. Melbourne: Longman Cheshire.

Anderson, G. 1977. The South Australian Initiative. In *Industrial Democracy in Australia,* edited by R.L. Pritchard. Sydney: CCH Ltd.

Australian Bureau of Statistics (ABS). 1979. *Working Conditions: Australia* (February-May, Catalogue No. 6335.0). Canberra: Australian Government Publishing Service.

Australian Council of Trade Unions (ACTU). 1985. Policy on Industrial Democracy. Pp. 332-339 in *Democracy and Control in the Work Place,* edited by E.M. Davis and R.D. Lansbury. Melbourne: Longman Cheshire.

Australian Council of Trade Unions/Trade Development Council (ACTU/TDC). 1987. *Australia Reconstructed.* Canberra: Australian Government Publishing Service.

Australian Labor Party and Australian Council of Trade Unions (ALP-ACTU). 1983. *Statement of Accord.* Melbourne: ACTU.

Bull, P. and G.A. Barton. 1978. Attitudes to Worker Participation. *Journal of Industrial Relations* 20:303-316.

Business Council of Australia (BCA). 1986. Policy on Employee Participation. Pp. 340-357 in *Democracy and Control in the Work Place,* edited by E.M. Davis and R.D. Lansbury. Melbourne: Longman Cheshire.

Carlin, L. and P. Cannon. 1981. Employee Participation: Experiences and Attitudes of Managers in Western Australia. *Work and People* 7(2).

Committee of Review into Australian Industrial Relations Law and Systems. 1985. *Report,* vols. 1-3. Canberra: Australian Government Publishing Service.

Cutcher-Gershenfeld, J., T. Kochan, and A. Verma. 1987. *Recent Developments in U.S. Employee Involvement Initiatives.* Pacific Rim Labor Policy Conference, Asia Pacific Business Institute/Bureau of National Affairs, Vancouver.

Davis, E.M. 1987. Unions and Wages: ACTU Federal Conference November 1986. *Australian Quarterly* 59(1):4-14.

Davis, E.M. and R.D. Lansbury. eds. 1986. *Democracy and Control in the Work Place.* Melbourne: Longman Cheshire.

_____. 1987. Worker Participation in Decisions on Technological Change in Australia. *Labour and Society* 12(2):217-234.

Deery, S. 1986. New Technology, Union Rights and Management Prerogatives: The Australian Experience. *Labour and Society* 11(1):67-81.

Derber, M. 1979. "Advancing Australian Industrial Democracy. *Industrial Relations* 17(1):112-116.

Department of Employment and Industrial Relations. 1986. *Industrial Democracy and Employee Participation: A Policy Discussion Paper.* Canberra: Australian Government Publishing Service.

Emery, F.E. 1978. *The Emergence of a New Paradigm of Work.* Canberra: Centre for Continuing Education, Australian National University.

Emery, F.E. and E. Thorsrud. 1976. *Democracy at Work.* Leiden: Martinus Nijhoff.

Frenkel, S.J. 1986. *Employee Participation in Decision Making in the Metal and Engineering Industry.* Canberra: Australian Government Publishing Service.

Frenkel, S.J. and A. Coolican. 1984. *Unions Against Capitalism?* Sydney: Allen and Unwin.

Gilmour, P. and R.D. Lansbury. 1984. *Marginal Manager: The Changing Role of Supervisors in Australia.* St. Lucia: University of Queensland Press.

Hartnett, B.C. 1986. Trade Unions and the Cain Government. Pp. 45-55 in *How Labor Governs in Victoria,* edited by M. Richards and M. Henry. Melbourne: Australian Fabian Society Pamphlet No. 45.

Hawke, R.J. 1985. Industrial Democracy within the Context of National Economic and Social Planning. *Proceedings of a Conference on Industrial Democracy and Employee Participation.* Canberra: Australian Government Publishing Service.

Isaac, J.E. 1980. Industrial Democracy in the Context of Conciliation and Arbitration. Pp. 34-53 in *Democracy in the Work Place,* edited by R.D. Lansbury. Melbourne: Longman Cheshire.

Jones, G.P. ed. 1978. *Worker Participation in Management,* 1st ed. Canberra: College of Advanced Education.

_____. ed. 1982. *Worker Participation in Management,* 2nd ed. Canberra: College of Advanced Education.

Lansbury, R.D. 1985. The Accord Between the Unions and Government in Australia: A New Experiment in Industrial Relations. *Labour and Society* 19(2):223-234.

Lansbury, R.D. and E.M. Davis. eds. 1984. *Technology, Work and Industrial Relations.* Melbourne: Longman Cheshire.

_____. 1985. The Hancock Report and Industrial Democracy. *Journal of Industrial Relations* 27(4):544-554.

Lansbury, R.D. and G.J. Prideaux. 1984. Industrial and Organisational Democracy: The Australian Experience. Pp. 495-511 in *International Perspectives on Organisational Democracy,* edited by B. Wilpert and A. Sorge. New York: Wiley.

Matthews, J. 1985. *Technology, Trade Unions and the Labour Process.* Working paper, School of Humanities, Deakin University, Geelong.

Milton, P. 1977. Employee Participation: A Survey of Views in Queensland. *Work and People* 8(2):14-20.

Musumeci, M. 1985. Industrial Democracy and Technological Change: A Union View of the Telecom Experience. *Proceedings of a Conference on Industrial Democracy and Employee Participation.* Canberra: Australian Government Publishing Service.

Noakes, B. 1985. An Employer Perspective on Industrial Democracy. *Proceedings of a Conference on Industrial Democracy and Employee Participation.* Canberra: Australian Government Publishing Service.

Oakshott, R. 1978. *The Case for Worker Co-ops.* London: Routledge and Kegan Paul.

Plowman, D., J. Adams, and C. Burke. 1986. *Employer Associations, Industrial Democracy and Employee Participation.* Canberra: Australian Government Publishing Service.

Powell, B. 1985. Employer Concerns Relating to Industrial Democracy. *Proceedings of a Conference on Industrial Democracy and Employee Participation.* Canberra: Australian Government Publishing Service.

Pritchard, R.D. ed. 1976. *Industrial Democracy in Australia.* Sydney: CCH Ltd.

Rimmer, M. and J. Zappala. 1988. Labour Market Flexibility and the Second Tier. *Australian Bulletin of Labour* 14(4):564-591.

Robson, P. 1986. Public Service Reform and Employee Relations. *Proceedings of a Conference on Industrial Relations in the Public Sector.* Canberra: Centre for Continuing Education, Australian National University.

Ruskin, N. 1986. Union Policies on Industrial Democracy: The Case of the AMWU. Pp. 176-191 in *Democracy and Control in the Work Place,* edited by E.M. Davis and R.D. Lansbury. Melbourne: Longman Cheshire.

Smith, G.F. 1985. The High Court and Industrial Relations in the 1980s. *Australian Bulletin of Labour* 11(2):82-101.

Sonder, L. 1983. Labor and the Unions. Pp. 238-249 in *Labor to Office,* edited by B.J. Costar and C.A. Hughes. Melbourne: Drummond.

Spillane, R.M., A.W. Findlay, and K. Borthwick. 1982. Perceptions of Worker Participation: The Influence of Job Status and Political Affiliation. *Journal of Industrial Relations* 24(1):19-32.

Stanton, M. 1984. Industrial Democracy in the Australian Public Service. *Canberra Bulletin of Public Administration* 11(3):170-176.

Tilley, L. 1986. Unions and Industrial Democracy: A Survey. In *Diversity, Change and Tradition,* edited by B. Ford and L. Tilley. Canberra: Australian Government Publishing Service.

Vaughan, E. 1986. Industrial Democracy in Australia: Some Day Still Far Away. Pp. 30-51 in *Democracy and Control in the Work Place,* edited by E.M. Davis and R.D. Lansbury. Melbourne: Longman Cheshire.

Wall, L.R. and W.P. Butler. 1959. Management-Employee Committees: The Results of Australian Research. *Personnel Bulletin* 15(1):38-44.

Wang, K. 1980. Issues Based Industrial Democracy Programmes: A Case Study. *Work and People* 5(2):11-17.

Willis, R. 1984. Industrial Democracy: The Government Commitment. *Work and People* 10(3):3-5.

CANADIAN PUBLIC SECTOR INDUSTRIAL RELATIONS:
POLICY AND PRACTICE

Mark Thompson and Allen Ponak

In 1967, the federal government of Canada enacted the Public Service Staff Relations Act, which introduced collective bargaining for 150,000 federal civil servants. While two provinces, Saskatchewan and Quebec, had previously passed public sector collective bargaining legislation, this action of the federal government conferred legitimacy on the concept of unionism and collective bargaining in the Canadian public sector.

The two decades that followed saw the virtually universal adoption of collective bargaining by public employees throughout the country. In many cases, this meant abandoning traditional civil service and professional models of employee relations based on consultation which had existed for decades. In 1956, there were less than 200,000 public sector union members (a large percentage in municipal government); by 1984 more than 1.5 million employees belonged to public sector labor organizations, and a larger number were covered by collective agreements.

Advances in Industrial and Labor Relations, volume 5, pages 59-93.
Copyright © 1991 by JAI Press Inc.
All rights of reproduction in any form reserved.
ISBN: 0-89232-940-8

Because Canada has a federal system of government, it was inevitable that many different arrangements for bargaining would emerge. Ultimately, each province and the federal government established its own legal regime for bargaining in various parts of the public sector. Like Australia, Canada moved closer to the private sector model of industrial relations than most other industrialized nations, in keeping with a relatively liberal public policy toward labor (Lipset 1986). Employees generally are free to join the union of their choice and bargain over a range of issues. The largest public sector unions affiliated with national labor centers previously dominated by private sector unions. Every jurisdiction granted at least some public employees the right to strike, and grievances were handled through bilateral systems or special tribunals that resemble the private sector grievance machinery.

From the outset, three issues were central to discussions of public sector collective bargaining. Perhaps the most emotional was the debate over the right to strike. Traditionally, North American unionists have regarded the right to strike as an essential element to any bargaining regime.[1] While most Canadian public sector union leaders adopted that view wholeheartedly, legislators, business interests, and the public often feared the disruption of normal life or even public safety that strikes by public employees might cause. As well, some observers argued that the power of public sector unions with access to the strike weapon was so great that normal governmental processes in a democratic society would be subverted, especially the allocation of budgets among various governmental functions (Christensen, 1980).

The second issue to emerge in the debate about public sector labor relations concerned the sovereignty of government. When bargaining rights were granted to public employees, governments seldom gave unions the same latitude to negotiate over the full range of terms and conditions of employment that prevails in the private sector. In addition, governments have exerted their sovereign powers to impose unilateral controls on public sector wages and to end legal strikes.

The third issue to dominate discussion of public sector industrial relations was compensation. Initially, debate on this point was limited, as many public sector positions for a long time had been paid less than corresponding work in the private sector. But public sector workers, clearly dissatisfied with this state of affairs, quickly seized the initiative in bargaining. At the extreme, some occupations rose from minimum wage levels to average labor market compensation levels within a few years. The ability of public sector workers to extract sharp wage increases was enhanced by a growing demand for many government services, especially health and education and accelerating rates of inflation (Gunderson 1982). Full of enthusiasm after their initial successes at the bargaining table, public sector unions called upon government to be a "model employer." Inevitably, perhaps, a public perception developed that government wages were outstripping those in the private sector. Compensation

Table 1.   Public Sector Paid Employment—1986
(000s)

Education	863
Medicine and Health	564
Local Government	294
Provincial Government	480
Federal Government	369
Government Enterprises	465
Total	3,035
Total paid employment	11,474
Public sector proportion of total employment	26.5%

Source: Statistics Canada, Provincial Government Employment, Federal Government Employment, Local Government Employment, Labour Forces Survey (1986); Sutherland and Doern (1985).

levels, as opposed to the cost of government, became a political and bargaining issue.

Experience with public sector industrial relations has demonstrated that these issues form the core of controversy and change in public policy in the field. Accordingly, after a survey of the institutional context, this paper will focus on the three central issues in the continuing development of Canadian public sector industrial relations—dispute procedures, sovereignty, and compensation.

INSTITUTIONAL CONTEXT

For purposes of this discussion, the public sector is defined to include the following: (1) federal, provincial, and local government, (2) health care, (3) education, and (4) government enterprises. Employment in the Canadian public sector stood at slightly under three million in 1984, representing almost one-third of paid employment in the overall economy (Table 1). This proportion is similar to that of Australia and Western Europe (Rawson 1987). Education and health care accounted for almost one-half of the public employment total.

Union Development

Over two-thirds of all public sector employees belonged to unions in 1985 (Table 2), a rate substantially greater than in other high union density sectors of the Canadian economy such as construction, manufacturing, mining, and forestry. Growth in public sector unionism has been a recent phenomenon. Public sector union membership more than doubled between 1965 and 1970 and then doubled again in the next five years (Table 3), a rate of growth much

Table 2.   Union Members as a Percentage of Paid Employees,
By Sector—1985

Forestry	45.7
Mines, Quarries, Oil Wells	26.3
Manufacturing	37.9
Construction	47.8
Transportation, Communication, Utilities	53.1
Trade	9.9
Finance, Insurance, Real Estate	2.7
Service	36.2
Public Administration	70.8
Overall Economy	34.4

Source: Statistics Canada, Corporations and Labour Unions Returns Act, *Annual Report* (1985).

Table 3.   Public Sector* Union Membership Growth, 1965-1984

	Union Membership (000s)			
Sector	1965	1970	1975	1984
Education	14	36	313	535
Health and Welfare	64	121	232	500
Local Government	75	86	107	153
Provincial Government	16	116	150	174
Federal Government	3	125	176	188
Total	172	484	978	1,550
Overall Economy	1,589	2,173	2,884	3,651
Public Sector as Proportion of Total	10.8%	22.3%	33.9%	42.5%

Note: * Figures were not available for public enterprises which generally are highly unionized. With public enterprises included, it is likely that public sector unionism would have accounted for half the Canadian union total in 1984.

Sources: Figures for the overall economy were obtained from Labour Canada, *Directory of Labour Organization in Canada* (various issues). Public sector union membership figures obtained as follows: 1965—Canada Department of Labour, Economics and Research Branch, *Industrial and Geographic Distribution of Union Membership in Canada,* 1965; 1970—Industrial and Geographic Distribution of Union Membership Canada in 1970, *The Labour Gazette,* August 1971, pp. 557-562; 1975—Industrial and Geographic Distribution of Union Membership in Canada, 1975, *The Labour Gazette,* May 1977, pp. 224-226; 1984—Statistics Canada, *Survey of Union Membership.*

greater than that of the rest of the labor movement (Rose 1984). By 1984, public sector union members accounted for over 40 percent of all union members in Canada. These growth patterns have been reflected in the dramatic expansion of the three largest public sector unions, which have become the three largest unions in Canada (Table 4).

Many explanations have been offered for the rapid transition of public employees from nonunion to union status (Goldenberg, 1987; Ponak, 1982; Rose, 1984). Certainly, favorable legislation enacted in the 1960s and 1970s

Table 4. Public Sector Unions

Union	Level of Government	Members 1985	Percent Increase in Members since 1974
Canadian Union of Public Employees (CUPE)	Local/Health	295,961	61.3
National Union of Provincial Government Employees (NUPGE)	Provincial	244,992	56.9
Public Service Alliance of Canada (PSAC)	Federal	181,460	43.3

Source: M. Thompson, *From Compromise to Resistance: Public Sector Industrial Relations in Canada* (paper delivered at Seventh World Congress of the International Industrial Relations Research Association, Hamburg, Germany, September, 1986), p. 5.

was a powerful influence promoting unionization. An important element in the growth process was the history of employee organization in the public sector. Although government employees did not become *unionized* until the mid-1960s, they had long been *organized* into employee and professional associations. Dating in some cases to World War I, these associations engaged in consultation with public sector employees on subjects as diverse as training, educational opportunities, social functions, and compensation.

Unionism in most of the public sector emerged when these organizations transformed themselves from associations into unions and exchanged consultation for collective bargaining. Important factors in this transformation included: (1) rising employee expectations and militancy which characterized society in general during the 1960s, (2) the demonstration effect of successful action by existing public sector unions, (3) increasing evidence of the inadequacies of traditional consultation mechanisms (Frankel 1960), and (4) a shift in public policy from a position of hostility toward public sector unions to one of positive support.

This pattern of union development (i.e., transition from association to union), largely unique to the public sector, has certain implications. Growth in public sector union membership came relatively easily. In contrast to the usual model of "organizing the unorganized," Canadian public sector union growth occurred through "organizing the already organized." Employers rarely mounted opposition to certification campaigns and in some cases were openly supportive of collective bargaining initiatives. Large association membership bases, complete with mailing lists, staff, and funds already existed. One obvious consequence was the ability of public sector unions to achieve very high rates of representation in short periods of time.

Some less obvious consequences also emerged. "Instant" growth meant that many public sector unions had never been through the crucible of a fiercely contested organizing campaign. As the saturation point for traditional membership bases is reached, the absence of previous organizing experience or a militant past diminishes the prospect of future expansion. Private sector unions were not always enthusiastic about the appearance of large organizations of public employees claiming the right of full participation in labor centrals. Tensions between the two groups of unions contributed to splits in the Canadian Labour Congress and the Quebec Federation of Labour (Rose 1983; Thwaites 1984).

Rapid growth also gave rise to structural problems. Organizations designed for consultation activities were not necessarily well adapted to collective bargaining. Large increases in membership and numerous new locals were difficult for most organizations to digest. Analyzing a strike conducted by Canada's largest public sector union (Canadian Union of Public Employees), one observer pointed to:

> (a) a multiplicity of elected positions barren of power, (b) powerful staff positions, notably the regional directors, unaccountable to an electorate, (c) dues paid to locals and rebated to the central organization, leaving it preoccupied with fiscal survival and debt collection rather than policy and leadership functions, and (d) in the hospital sector, a national servicing staff stretched very thinly, unsupported by any locally paid officers (Deverell 1982, p. 181).

Looking at the Public Service Alliance of Canada, the country's third largest union, another observer commented that the union "continues to cling to an antiquated structure ... incompatible with the occupational bargaining units which cut across government departments" (Rose 1984, p. 110).

In short, the large size achieved by Canada's public sector unions should not necessarily be interpreted as a sign of strength and internal cohesion. The special circumstances of the growth have produced organizational tensions which have yet to be effectively resolved.

Management and Politics

Less spectacular than union growth, although equally important, has been the development of management structures for public sector collective bargaining. In the initial rounds of bargaining, unions, whatever their own organizational difficulties, frequently proved to be better prepared and more capable negotiators than their management counterparts. As the complexities of collective bargaining became apparent, public sector employers devoted additional resources to the labor relations function, recruiting experienced staff and developing more effective decision-making mechanisms.

In the federal and provincial governments, specialized agencies were established when collective bargaining first appeared. The most common model was to place industrial relations responsibilities under a "Treasury Board," a senior cabinet committee responsible for overall control of government expenditures (Sutherland and Doern 1985). Representatives of both line and staff management typically sit on negotiating committees under the general authority of Treasury Board officials (Feuille and Anderson 1980).

Practices vary widely among municipalities, school boards, hospitals, and local government employers. Most large public employers have an industrial relations staff. Elected officials often take an active part in bargaining for smaller organizations (House 1980; Anderson 1977). In several provinces, local governments rely on employer associations with responsibilities ranging from coordination of bargaining positions to negotiation of common collective agreements. Employer associations often are the bargaining agents for hospitals and school boards in Western provinces (Wetzel and Gallagher 1984).

Quebec is an exception to the national pattern. In that province, a highly centralized system of bargaining covering most of the major parts of the public sector has evolved. Employers and labor organizations negotiate over economic matters on a province-wide basis. Because the consequences of these negotiations for the provincial budget and the provision of public services are substantial, senior government officials, especially the Minister of Finance, are personally involved in bargaining. Each round of public sector bargaining in Quebec has become a major political event in the life of the province, and virtually every set of negotiations has entailed the passage of at least one piece of special legislation (Hebert 1984).

Outside of Quebec, however, a notable feature of management's role in public sector industrial relations is the apparent lack of direct involvement by politicians in routine labor relations activities. In the United States, "multilateral" or "end run" bargaining appears to be common (Freeman 1986). Unions bargain not only with their managerial counterparts, but with other interested public parties. Such activities have been documented at the municipal level in the United States (Kochan 1974), but empirical evidence in Canada indicates that unions rarely deal directly with elected officials or outside interest groups beyond the bargaining table (Anderson 1977; Goldenberg 1987).

Given the importance of the outcomes of collective bargaining and a tradition of interest group representation in Canadian politics, the low incidence of direct political involvement in bargaining (Quebec excepted) is initially surprising. One explanation clearly is the relatively broad extension of bargaining rights in the Canadian public sector. Despite some restrictions on the scope of bargaining, the central subjects in most negotiations, wages, fringe benefits, and working conditions, typically are negotiable. On such items, unions have recourse to either a work stoppage or binding arbitration should an impasse occur. Consequently, public sector unions are not normally forced into the political arena to deal with the central issues in an employment relationship. Subjects excluded from the bargaining table are usually covered by comprehensive civil service or pension legislation not susceptible to easy amendment.

The removal of bargaining from politics is reinforced by the management structures established for bargaining. Treasury boards wield substantial authority free from day-to-day scrutiny by junior politicians. Government members can question cabinet members only in confidential caucus sessions, and the opposition is seldom able to make the results of negotiations a political issue. Employer associations and professional managers also dilute the authority of individually elected officials so that individual politicians have little immediate influence on negotiations. In addition, provincial governments have been reluctant to undermine the authority of elected representatives of hospitals or school boards by attempting to dominate bargaining, even when the senior level of government is responsible for a major share of the employer's funding (Wetzel and Gallagher 1984).

In federal and provincial governments, the parliamentary system limits the utility of lobbying individual legislators. Party solidarity ensures that individual legislators have virtually no opportunity to influence government decisions on labor relations issues. In general, lobbying by private interest groups is most profitably directed to senior civil servants (Thompson and Stanbury 1979). In the labor relations context, however, it is the senior civil servants who, in effect, are management, and they are unlikely to be persuaded by lobbying by their erstwhile opponents in bargaining.

Finally, the existence of a labor-backed social democratic party in Canada, the New Democratic Party (NDP), gives labor a focus for political activity. In some jurisdictions, the NDP granted bargaining rights to public sector unions. Generally, it has avoided involvement in public sector bargaining, preferring to emphasize its appeal to broader political interests. In turn, the Canadian labor movement has concentrated its activities, within both the NDP and the wider political system, on broad social and economic issues.

The absence of multilateral bargaining does not mean that public sector bargaining is completely apolitical, however. Political considerations are significant in major negotiations, especially when a strike is imminent or occurs. Senior politicians become involved in labor relations when the issues are sufficiently important. When broad government initiatives, such as the sale of public corporations, changes in funding levels, or arrangements for social services affect the underlying bases of public sector employment, the unions involved are active participants in the political decisions.

Public Policy Framework

Under the *Constitution Act, 1981* labor relations are a provincial responsibility. The federal government's role is restricted to its own civil servants and certain specified sectors such as banking, telecommunications, and air, rail, and sea transportation. In practice this means that each province plus the federal government has the responsibility for devising its own labor legislation. Thus, there are eleven different legislative regimes governing labor-management relations across Canada.

Further complicating the issue is the decision of most jurisdictions to have separate statutes for its public and private employees. The federal government, for instance, has enacted the Canada Labour Code to cover the private sector (e.g., bank employees) and the Public Service Staff Relations Act to govern its civil servants and employees of certain crown agencies (e.g., National Film Board). In addition, many jurisdictions have multiple statutes for the various components of the public sector. The province of Ontario, for example, has separate legislation for the private sector, school teachers, hospital workers, police, firefighters, college teachers, and civil servants.

The multiplicity of statutes reflects an absence of consensus on important aspects of public sector labor policy. Whereas private sector legislation is guided by a generally accepted underlying set of policy considerations derived from the U.S. Wagner Act of 1935, no such model exists for the public sector. As in the United States, each jurisdiction has experimented and devised its own solutions to the issues posed by public employee unionism.

Not surprisingly, this has produced considerable variation, both within jurisdictions and across jurisdictions. In Alberta, for example, teachers, municipal employees, and liquor board workers have the right to strike, while hospital workers, police and firefighters, college and university staff, and civil servants do not. Civil servants, hospital employees, police and fire personnel in Ontario cannot strike; teachers from elementary school through university and some liquor distribution employees have the right to strike. Police in several provinces are prohibited from joining associations affiliated with the general labor movement; no such restrictions are in place elsewhere. Six jurisdictions place government enterprises under general private sector statutes; in the remaining five, regulations for the civil service govern. These are also notable public and private sector differences with respect to bargaining unit determination and union recognition (Ponak 1982).

The evident diversity of approach should not obscure, however, some important commonalities between the private and public sectors and across jurisdictions. The freedom of employees to engage in union activity without employer interference is well-entrenched in the public sector as in the private. Employers are obliged to recognize and engage in meaningful, or "good faith," negotiations with a union enjoying majority support, much as in the private sector. Grievance procedures for the resolution of rights disputes through binding arbitration are provided almost universally whatever the statutory framework (Swinton 1984). In all jurisdictions, municipal workers (police and firefighters excepted) are governed by the general private sector legislation and enjoy the same rights as private sector workers.

Taken as a whole, the public sector statutory system (if it can be characterized as a system) reflects a combination of influences that includes historical arrangements, the power of particular interest groups, short-run political considerations, and private sector practices. In some cases, these factors have been unique to a specific jurisdiction (e.g., the Quebec government's concern with central budget control produced extreme politicization). Elsewhere several factors were responsible for a system (e.g., historical arrangements with municipal employees). Policies covering interest dispute resolution, compensation, and sovereignty have remained the most controversial and have received the most diverse treatment. It is to these specific issues that the discussion now turns.

STRIKES AND DISPUTE PROCEDURES

Canadian labor policy has historically displayed an almost obsessive concern with the prevention of work stoppages. This concern was exemplified by the 1907 Industrial Disputes Investigation Act introduced by the country's first labor minister. Among other things, the act obliged labor and management to utilize a two-stage conciliation process and imposed a mandatory cooling-off period as preconditions to a legal work stoppage. Applicable originally to essential services, this approach was later extended to all industries and remained a hallmark of Canadian private sector dispute procedures until the early 1970s (Woods 1973; Weiler 1986).

Canadian policy has not been notably successful, however. Since World War II Canada has had relatively high strike rates compared to other democratic, industrial nations (Adams 1987). It is hardly surprising, therefore, that the right of public employees to strike should have become one of the most controversial aspects in the enactment of collective bargaining legislation for the public sector. Canada already had an unenviable record with respect to work stoppages; policy makers had demonstrated an historic concern with the issue; and government workers provided a variety of sensitive, and in some cases, irreplaceable services. On the other hand, union leaders argued vigorously for strike rights and backed up their demands with a combination of political pressure and direct (albeit illegal) action.

Government response has varied (see Table 5). In some jurisdictions, Quebec for example, most public employees have been provided the right to strike; in Ontario, at the other extreme, only teachers and municipal employees can legally withdraw their services. Where the right to strike has been removed, it has been replaced by compulsory arbitration. As well, a hybrid approach, known as "choice of procedures," has been introduced in the federal civil service, British Columbia, and Saskatchewan. Under this procedure, one of the parties can choose between the right to strike or arbitration, forcing its choice on the other party (Ponak and Wheeler 1980).

Table 5. Dispute Procedures[a] by Jurisdiction, 1986

Jurisdiction	General Municipal	Police	Firefighters	Hospitals	Teachers	Civil Service
British Columbia	RTS	C-O-P	C-O-P	C-O-P	ARB	RTS
Alberta	RTS	ARB	ARB	ARB	RTS	ARB
Saskatchewan	RTS	C-O-P	C-O-P	RTS	C-O-P	RTS
Manitoba	RTS	RTS	ARB	RTS	ARB	RTS
Ontario	RTS	ARB	ARB	ARB	RTS	ARB
Quebec	RTS	ARB	ARB	RTS	RTS	RTS
New Brunswick	RTS	RTS	ARB	RTS	RTS	RTS
Nova Scotia	RTS	RTS	RTS	RTS	RTS	ARB
Prince Edward Island	RTS	ARB	ARB	ARB	ARB	ARB
Newfoundland	RTS	RTS	RTS[b] or ARB	RTS	RTS	RTS
Federal[c]	n.a.	n.a.	C-O-P	C-O-P	C-O-P	C-O-P

Notes: [a] RTS—Right-to-Strike; C-O-P—Choice-of-procedures; ARB—Compulsory Arbitration

[b] Firefighters in St. John's, the provincial capital, must submit disputes to arbitration.

[c] Choice-of-procedures under the P.S.S.R.A. (e.g., national Film Board); right-to-strike under the Canada Labour Code (e.g., Air Canada).

Source: Table compiled as of September 1986 through a statutory review of each jurisdiction.

69

Municipal employees can strike in all provinces, as can employees of government enterprises except in Ontario and Prince Edward Island. For other groups, the situation varies greatly. For example, police have the right to strike in four jurisdictions, fall under choice-of-procedure frameworks in two others, and use arbitration in the remaining four provinces. Hospital workers, teachers, and civil servants each have the right to strike in six provinces (not necessarily the same ones) and are governed by a combination of arbitration or choice-of-procedures in the remaining five jurisdictions. Overall, the right-to-strike is the most commonly used dispute resolution procedure. However, general municipal employees excepted, all groups are prohibited from striking in at least some jurisdictions.

An important restriction on the right-to-strike in several jurisdictions is the designation of members of the bargaining unit as essential and thus legally barred from striking. Originally, the designation approach was seen as a variation on the "nonstoppage strike," a way to balance the interests of the public, the union, and the employer. In a 1976 hospital strike in Vancouver, approximately 10 percent of the striking nonprofessional hospital staff was designated as essential. The remaining employees were allowed to withdraw their services, a situation which placed pressure on both the union and the employer, while still protecting public safety (Weiler 1980).

To work effectively, designation requires that a "correct" number of employees be deemed essential. Too high a number and the right-to-strike becomes illusory; too low a number and public welfare may be jeopardized. For instance, the federal government has deemed virtually all air traffic controllers essential, meaning that the right of controllers to strike exists in theory only (Subbarao 1986). Quebec has employed similar tactics with respect to social service employees, including hospital and transit workers. As a result, the designation approach, designed to protect the right-to-strike in sensitive public services, has become another restrictive element in public policy in several jurisdictions.

Strike Experience

One measure of the effectiveness of Canadian public sector dispute resolution policy can be seen in Tables 6-8 which summarize time lost due to strikes.[2] Annual totals of public sector working days lost due to work stoppages are presented in Table 6. There is substantial annual fluctuation both with respect to total time lost and the public sector proportion of overall strike activity in the economy. In any given year, one or two disputes account for a significant proportion of the time lost. This pattern is normal for all Canadian strike activity; usually six to eight large strikes of long duration account for one-half of the total working days lost in any year. It is apparent that this pattern holds for the public sector. Large work stoppages in Quebec and in the postal service have contributed disproportionately to national totals.

Table 6.   Public Sector Strike Loss, Annual Totals, 1973-1985

Year	Working Days Lost (000s)	As Percentage of Overall Economy	Comments
1973	773	13.4	Nationwide CN rail strike accounts for one-half of the total
1974	631	6.8	Nationwide postal strike accounts for one-quarter of the total
1975	1,873	17.2	Nationwide postal strike, Toronto teachers strike
1973-1975 (Mean)	1,092	12.6	
1976	2,226	19.2	Major Quebec public sector strikes
1977	428	12.9	Anti-inflation guidelines reduced total
1978	849	11.5	Nationwide postal strike
1979	1,801	23.0	Quebec public sector, Saskatchewan civil service
1980	2,426	27.0	Quebec teachers strike accounts for 40 percent of the total
1976-1980 (Mean)	1,546	19.8	
1981	2,657	29.9	Nova Scotia health care, B.C. municipalities, postal disputes account for two-thirds of the total
1982	823	14.2	Alberta nurses, B.C. civil service account for 40 percent of the total
1983	2,072	46.6	Quebec teachers, B.C. general strike account for two-thirds of the total
1984	638	16.5	Recession and public sector wage controls reduced total
1985	531	16.7	Ontario Hydro and Air Canada flight attendants account for one-half of the total
1981-1985 (Mean)	1,344	25.7	

Source: Labour Canada, *Strikes and Lockouts in Canada,* 1973-1985. (Note that because of definitional differences, the totals in this table are not identical to totals calculated by Labour Canada.)

A second attribute of the strike data is that the total time lost annually appears to have decreased slightly in the most recent time period. Between 1981 and 1985, public sector work stoppages averaged 1.3 million working days lost annually, whereas in the previous five-year period the annual average was 1.5 million working days. Thus, on an absolute basis, the public sector strike situation has stabilized or even fallen marginally. On a proportional basis, however, it is clear that over time the public sector accounts for a growing share of total working days lost. Until 1975, the public sector share of total

Table 7.   Public Sector Strike Loss, By Jurisdiction, 1973-1985

Jurisdiction	Percentage of Public Sector Total Working Days Lost 1973-1985	Percentage of Total Public Employment[a]
British Columbia	13.4	10
Alberta	4.9	7
Saskatchewan	3.3	3
Manitoba	1.0	5
Ontario	12.3	29
Quebec	38.9	21
New Brunswick	0.9	2
Nova Scotia	5.1	3
Prince Edward Island	0.0	1
Newfoundland	1.7	2
Federal	18.5	17
Total	100.0	100

Note: [a] Estimate for 1975 (see Ponak 1982).
Source: Labour Canada, *Strikes and Lockouts in Canada,* 1973-1985.

time lost was slightly over 10 percent. By 1980, the share of overall strike activity was 20 percent and between 1981 and 1985 the public sector contributed more than one-quarter of working days lost due to work stoppages in the overall economy.

A breakdown of public sector time lost by jurisdiction between 1973 and 1985 reveals that the Quebec public sector, accounting for about one-fifth of Canada-wide public employment, was responsible for 40 percent of all time lost (Table 7). In contrast, Ontario's share of strike time is only 12 percent, substantially less than its 30 percent proportion of public employees. Such differences partially reflect variation in strike restrictions among jurisdictions. The Quebec situation, however, is in many respects a unique one and is embedded in broader social, political, and cultural forces peculiar to that province (Boivin 1982; Hebert 1984). Elsewhere in Canada, public sector disputes have been less common.

On a sectoral basis, time lost in education, health care, local government, and provincial government service is roughly proportional to the respective shares of total government employment (Table 8). The federal government, however, is greatly under-represented. Accounting for 15 percent of all employees, the federal government contributed only 3 percent of total time lost. This fact is especially noteworthy because most federal government employees have the access to the right-to-strike. Employees of government enterprises, on the other hand, who also widely enjoy the right to withdraw their services, are somewhat over-represented in terms of their share of working days lost.

There has only been one study which systematically examined factors that might be associated with Canadian public sector strike variation. Smith (1984)

Table 8. Public Sector Strike Loss, By Component, 1973-1985

Component	Percentage of Public Sector Total Working Days 1973-1985	Percentage of Total Government Employment[b]
Education	29.8	24.6
Health Care	16.5	17.8
Local Government	14.7	11.5
Provincial Government	12.5	16.4
Federal Government	2.8	15.2
Government Enterprises[a]	23.7	14.5
Total	100.0	100.0

Notes: [a] Government enterprises mainly comprise provincially and federally owned railways, airlines, and utilities. Privately owned telephone companies are not included. For consistency, Canada Post is counted as a government enterprise for the entire period even though postal workers were part of the federal civil service until 1981.

[b] Estimate for 1975; see Ponak (1982).

Source: Labour Canada, *Strikes and Lockouts in Canada,* 1973-1985.

tested a model in which strike activity was posited as a function of unanticipated inflation, unemployment levels, wage guidelines, contract expirations, and a time trend line. Dependent variables were strike frequency, working days lost, and workers involved, each measured on a quarterly basis from 1972 to 1980, inclusive. The only dependent variable that was statistically significant in any of the equations was the time trend variable (i.e., strike activity in the public sector increased over time). None of the other variables was significant, regardless of the dependent variable, and signs were often in opposite directions from the hypotheses. The explanatory power of the equations was weak, particularly when working days lost and workers involved were used as dependent variables. The results were similar when Quebec data were treated separately.

Two comments can be made about Smith's findings. First, the data end at the fourth quarter of 1980. The data in this paper show (Table 6) that strike activity (expressed as working days lost) decreased slightly after 1980. Thus, extending Smith's analysis through 1985 might produce somewhat different results with respect to the time trend line, the only statistically significant variable in his model. Second, the model that Smith used in his study was developed largely on the basis of private sector models, an explicit and deliberate aspect of the research. An important objective was to determine whether factors which had been found to account for private sector strike variation could also explain public sector strike activity. The answer appears to be "no." Smith's model provided adequate results for the private sector, but not for the public sector.

These results reinforce what most observers of the public sector have long suggested—namely, that the underlying dynamics of collective bargaining and dispute resolution is different between the two sectors. In particular, there exists a political dimension to decision making and the costs of agreement and disagreement in the public sector which is largely absent in the private sector. Models of public sector strike activity which fail to adequately capture such forces will, in all likelihood, continue to produce disappointing results.

Interest Arbitration

The most common substitute for the right-to-strike in the Canadian public sector is compulsory interest arbitration (see Table 5). It is used where work stoppages are statutorily prohibited and has almost completely eliminated strikes among employees covered by it. Traditional or conventional arbitration procedures usually prevail; that is, the arbitration board is free within certain statutory guidelines, to fashion its own solution to the issues in dispute. Unlike the United States, final offer selection is rarely used.

Much has been written about the impact of compulsory arbitration on the negotiation process (Downie 1979; Feuille 1979; Kochan 1979; Thompson 1981; Ponak and Falkenberg 1987). Early statements by practitioners and academics predicted that the presence of arbitration would severely reduce the likelihood of negotiated settlements, perhaps to the point of eliminating serious bargaining.

The evidence in Canada (and the United States) clearly shows that bargaining can and does survive under a regime of compulsory arbitration, although the settlement rate is lower than in situations when a strike is possible. Table 9 compares the settlement rates of parties in the Canadian public sector under both strike-based and arbitration-based systems. Settlement rate is defined as the proportion of negotiations where agreement is reached prior to utilizing the ultimate impasse resolution device, be it arbitration or a work stoppage. Under arbitration, the parties are able to negotiate their own collective agreements between 65 and 82 percent of the time. With strike-based procedures, settlement rates go up to the 90 percent range. The average gap between the two systems is in the order of 15 percent.

Canadian policy makers in most jurisdictions have obviously concluded that a trade-off of lower settlement rates for the prevention of strikes is warranted. Arbitration is most often imposed in situations where it is believed the consequences of a strike are too high—firefighters and police are situations where such sentiments most often prevail. Furthermore, even under the least productive arbitration systems, negotiators still manage to settle two-thirds of their disputes without arbitration. The trade-offs are much more difficult to justify in situations where the settlement rate is much lower or where the groups involved are arguably less essential. For example, clerks at government-owned liquor stores in Alberta were prohibited from striking for many years—a restriction that was lifted in 1983.

Table 9.   Settlement Rates[a]: Arbitration vs. Strike-Based Systems

Study	Settlement Rate (%)	Total Number of Negotiations	Time Period	Type of Employee	Jurisdiction
Arbitration					
Hines (1972)	81	565	1966-1970	Hospital	Ontario
Thompson (1981)	65	1,660	1960-1980	Teachers	British Columbia
Mitchell (1982)	82	1,035	1969-1982	Federal Civil Service	Canada
Blouin (1982)	73	1,054	1973-1981	Firefighters, Police	Quebec
Swimmer and MacDonald (1985)	70	979	1979-1982	Firefighters, Police, Hospital, Public Service	Ontario
Right-To-Strike					
Swimmer and MacDonald (1985)	93	611	1979-1982	Teachers, Hydro, Municipal	Ontario
Ponak and Wheeler (1980)	88	137	1967-1979	Federal Civil Service	Canada
Anderson (1977)	93	58	1976-1977	Inside and Outside Workers	Various Provinces

Note: Settlement rate is defined as the proportion of negotiations where settlement was reached without a work stoppage or resorting to arbitration, as the case may be.

Another issue that arises from compulsory arbitration is the strong union opposition to strike restrictions. Almost unanimously, labor leaders have denounced the widespread prohibitions against strikes by public employees (Werlin 1984), citing the right-to-strike as an integral element of freedom of association. The courts have rejected that argument so far,[3] and it is not even clear that the rank and file union members, especially white-collar employees, object to the absence of the right-to-strike. Surveys of university faculty (Ponak and Thompson 1985) and registered nurses (Ponak and Haridas 1978) have shown strong preferences for compulsory arbitration settlement of interest disputes. Swimmer (1984) found that an overwhelming majority of nonprofessional white-collar workers had doubts about the effectiveness of strikes, although more than one-half had actually been on strike. Furthermore, research into choice-of-procedure systems, under which unions can actually choose between a strike or arbitration, has indicated a four-to-one preference for arbitration (Ponak and Wheeler 1980). In other words, public rhetoric to the contrary, many in the public sector are not unhappy with arbitration.

The degree of acceptance could change, however, if arbitration is subject to government control. The acceptability of arbitration rests on its perceived fairness. Indeed, the most publicized illegal strike against an arbitration award, a 1969 Montreal police strike, was the result of suspected bias in the arbitration process. Traditionally, most arbitration systems have relied on a corps of ad hoc arbitrators, typically lawyers or university professors. Statutory guidelines usually exist, but have usually allowed for significant arbitral discretion (i.e., guidelines such as comparable wage rates, internal salary equity, any other factors considered relevant). Basically, arbitrators have been able to make decisions based on what they believe most appropriate under all the circumstances of a case.

Developments in Alberta and British Columbia threaten to undermine this tradition of arbitral independence. Alberta has mandated that arbitration boards must consider the written fiscal policy on public sector compensation of the Provincial Treasurer (Dubensky 1984; Mason 1985). Because the Provincial Treasurer is a member of the cabinet, he or she is hardly a disinterested party in the outcome of public sector arbitration cases.

In British Columbia, the government went a step further by appointing a special tribunal to oversee public sector wage movements (Peck 1985). The tribunal was given special powers to assess an employer's ability to pay, replacing arbitral discretion in such matters (Thompson 1985). Arbitration awards subsequently were overturned by the tribunal and some arbitrators, fearing loss of independence, refused to participate in the arbitration system. In 1987, the tribunal was abolished, but arbitrators were required to give paramount consideration to the employer's ability to pay, thereby undermining the force of other (more conventional) arbitral guidelines.

To date, such experiments have been restricted to only two provinces. Should such approaches spread and should they lead to a perception of bias on the part of labor organizations, the consequences could well be seen in an increase in illegal strike activity. This would result in erosion of one of the major attributes of Canadian arbitration policy—the elimination of strikes in sensitive parts of the public sector.

Choice of Procedures

In addition to wide usage of compulsory arbitration, several Canadian jurisdictions have developed a dispute resolution system known as choice-of-procedures (see Table 5). Under choice-of-procedures, the union determines whether an interest dispute is to be resolved through arbitration or a work stoppage. This choice may be altered each round of bargaining and, depending on the jurisdiction, may be made at the point of impasse (British Columbia) or prior to the commencement of negotiations (federal government). The employer is obliged to abide by the impasse procedures choice made by the union.

The experience under this dispute resolution system was examined in a study by Ponak and Wheeler (1980). Over 3,000 sets of negotiations were analyzed, including those from two American states, Minnesota and Wisconsin, which had adopted similar approaches. The findings showed that the arbitration option was chosen far more frequently than was the strike option (79 percent chose arbitration). Once arbitration was chosen, settlement occurred in 62 percent of the cases prior to an arbitration award actually being issued. By contrast, the settlement rate when the strike option was chosen was 82 percent. Overall, it was found that strikes occurred in less than 2 percent of the total negotiations in the four jurisdictions which were reviewed.

Choice-of-procedures has not become widely used, partly because of its potential to significantly tip the scale of bargaining power in favor of the party with discretion to specify the impasse process. In addition, no data have been collected since 1979. Nevertheless, available evidence suggests that the arbitration/strike choice system has several positive attributes. First, it provides a right-to-strike to public employees, a right of considerable ideological and philosophical importance to organized labor. Second, choice-of-procedures systems produce higher overall settlement rates than do pure compulsory arbitration systems. Settlement rates under choice of procedures ranged from 78 percent (federal) to 94 percent (Minnesota). Third, although unions with strong economic power tend to choose the strike option, stoppages are rare (2 percent of negotiations) under choice-of-procedures systems.

GOVERNMENT SOVEREIGNTY

One of the most fundamental issues in public sector industrial relations is the appropriate relationship between employment decisions and broader public policies. This question was originally posed as the challenge of collective bargaining to government sovereignty (i.e., government bodies and agencies enjoy and need basic powers that cannot be shared with or delegated to other private groups). The outcomes of collective bargaining affect both the budgets of public sector employers and their ability to deliver services to clients. For instance, if teachers negotiate higher salaries, school boards may be forced to increase class size, to the detriment of the educational quality. Alternatively, a public sector police union might seek to negotiate the number of personnel in patrol cars, a condition of employment that affects the safety of the public. Consequently, the argument went, it is necessary to restrict either the power of public sector unions or the scope of bargaining to protect democracy (Cohen 1979).

In its extreme form, this position denies the very existence of collective bargaining in the public sector. Indeed, as late as 1964, the Premier of Quebec proclaimed, "The Queen does not negotiate with her subjects" (Goldenberg 1973). Obviously that view ceased to command widespread support in Canada shortly after it was expressed. When collective bargaining rights were granted, governments implicitly decided to separate political decisions about levels of service from the determination of wages and conditions of employment for public sector workers. The latter decisions would be the result of negotiation and arbitration, and government budgets would incorporate wages as one of several costs of providing a public service.

Although granting public employee bargaining rights removed the most basic claim of sovereignty, debate on the issue continued. As the systems of public sector industrial relations developed, several aspects of the sovereignty issue have continued to provoke controversy: the appropriate scope of bargaining, public sector age controls, and back-to-work legislation.

Scope of Bargaining

Canadian labor legislation imposes virtually no restrictions on the scope of bargaining in the private sector, but almost every public sector bargaining statute limits the subjects open to negotiation. There is no dichotomy between "mandatory" and "permissive" subjects of bargaining found in American labor law, or the "management rights" jurisprudence that exists in the Australian arbitration system. Instead, arbitrators and the courts have fashioned a doctrine of "residual rights" for management which holds that rights not specifically abridged by the collective agreement are vested in management. In the public sector, this doctrine prevails, and statutes also entrench management rights by excluding several subjects from the scope of bargaining, especially personnel matters and pensions.

Restrictions on personnel issues are pervasive. Early in the twentieth century, central controls over appointments, promotions, and staffing were instituted in the public service to remove these subjects from political influence (Sutherland and Doern 1985). With the adoption of collective bargaining, the restrictions remained, either to protect the tradition of political neutrality or to preserve management rights. Depending on the statute, subjects such as promotion criteria, seniority rights, personnel transfers, technological change, staffing levels, and hiring procedures are vested exclusively with the employer.

The implications of these restrictions for bargaining are substantial. Such routine issues as proposals for flexible working hours, the use of seniority as a criterion for promotions, performance appraisals, and educational leaves have been held to be outside the scope of bargaining or arbitration. Bargaining agents have also been precluded from negotiating provisions calling for consultation on subjects outside of the scope of bargaining (Finkelman and Goldenberg 1983, vol. 1).

These exclusions have been the subject of extensive litigation and have not entirely prevented determined public sector unions from raising demands that were clearly outside of the legally permissable bargaining arena. The Canadian Air Traffic Controllers Association struck over the issue of the use of the French language in air traffic control in Quebec in violation of the law (Swan 1983). British Columbia teachers negotiated agreements (presumably legally unenforceable) on working conditions that went far beyond "salaries and bonuses," the only topics for which the law required negotiations prior to 1987. Many public sector unions appear to have a long-term agenda to expand the scope of bargaining over personnel issues, although they have seldom attempted to circumvent the bargaining process.

In extreme cases, restrictions on the scope of bargaining have proven so onerous that the parties have agreed to change the legislative regime under which they operated. Although both management and the Canadian Union of Postal Workers recognized the importance of technological change and wished to negotiate the subject, provisions of the Public Service Staff Relations Act precluded formal bargaining (Swan 1984). Ultimately, frustration over this restriction was a major factor in causing both parties to approach the government and request that the postal service be converted from the public service to a public enterprise, thereby placing negotiations under less restrictive legislation.

As in most countries, public sector pension plans generally predated the appearance of collective bargaining. At the outset, benefits were considered relatively liberal, creating few pressures from employees to place pensions on the bargaining table. For their part, governments preferred to maintain the freedom to control capital reserves in public pension plans. There seems to have been an additional fear that labor leaders would seek to restrict eligibility or to use pension reserves for their own political ends.

Despite the generous terms of most public sector pensions (Gunderson 1984), disputes have arisen from time to time. Because normal collective bargaining was not possible, the issues have been raised in the political arena, including an illegal strike by teachers in British Columbia and threatened job action by provincial government employees there. In a few cases, public sector pensions were perceived as being inadequate, at least in part because governments have used them as low-cost sources of capital. Public employees have also pressed for the inclusion of social criteria in investment decisions, a subject remote from the scope of bargaining, but have been satisfied by the appointment of representatives to pension boards.

Taken together, these exclusions from the scope of bargaining represent a substantial deviation from the private sector model of industrial relations. The exclusions constitute an entrenchment of management rights stronger than other employers enjoy.

Table 10. Public Sector Compensation Control Programs*

Jurisdiction	Statute	Type	Effective Dates	Comments
British Columbia	Compensation Stabilization Act	Statutory controls	February 1982-October 1983	Commissioner set guidelines as limits; 2-year term
	Compensation Stabilization Amendment Act	Statutory controls	October 1983-Summer 1987	Controls became permanent
	Industrial Relations Act	Statutory control of arbitration	Summer 1987	Permanent requirement that arbitrators consider ability to pay, with enforcement procedure; guidelines abolished
Alberta	Labour Statutes	Criteria for arbitrators	June 1983	Permanent—hospital employees lost right to strike
Saskatchewan	—	Cash limits	August 1982-August 1984	Guidelines of CPI minus 1 in Economic Recovery Program
Manitoba	—	Cash limits	November 1983	Restrictions on funding of all public institutions
Ontario	Act respecting the Restraint of Compensation in the Public Sector of Ontario	Statutory limits on compensation increases	October 1983-October 1984	Collective agreement extended one year
	Public Sector Prices and Compensation Act	Statutory limits on transfer payments	October 1984-October 1985	
Quebec	Act concerning wages in the public sector	Statutory reduction in compensation	May 1982-April 1983	
	Act concerning working conditions in the public sector	Statutory limits on increases	May 1982-December 1985	Annual increases of CPI minus 1.5 percent—a few groups excluded

New Brunswick	—	Voluntary wage freeze	May 1983-April 1984	Guarantees against layoffs
Nova Scotia	An Act Respecting Compensation in the Public Sector	Collective agreements extended one year	September 1982-March 1985	6 percent increase in one-year extension
Prince Edward Island	Compensation Review Act	Statutory limits on compensation increases	April 1983-March 1986	Coverage commenced with expiry of collective agreements, 2-year program
Newfoundland	—	Cash limits	November 1983-1986	Limits on health care compensation in 1984 and 1985, 2-year wage freeze in 1984, commencing with expiry of collective agreements
Federal	Public Sector Compensation	Statutory limits	June 1984-1985-1986	Initial limits of 6 percent and 5 percent for two years
				1984 budget speech reduced a wideline from 5 to 4 percent program expired with collective agreements

Source: D.D. Carter and Pradeep Kumar. 1985. Public Sector Wage Restraint Programs: Two Views. *Proceedings of the 21st Annual Conference* of the Canadian Industrial Relations Association. Quebec: CIRA.

Public Sector Wage Controls

Beginning in 1982, wage controls specific to the public sector appeared in Canada for the first time. Between 1975 and 1978, the federal government had imposed the nation's first peacetime wage and price controls, covering both the public and private sectors. After these controls expired, there was little enthusiasm for reimposing a full-scale program covering wages and prices in the private sector. However, the experience of the 1970s taught government that restrictions on the compensation of its own employees were politically popular and offered the promise of restraining wages generally.

As the economy faltered in the early 1980s, governments declared their intention to reduce public spending. Every jurisdiction imposed limits on the level of increase in public sector compensation (Table 10). Five provinces and the federal government enacted legislation restricting public sector compensation. The remaining provinces adopted variations of the British "cash limits" system. Expenditure levels were specified in advance of bargaining with the intention that these limits would in turn be imposed on negotiated wage changes. Increases in excess of the overall limit were permitted as a result of increased productivity, reductions in levels of service, or (rarely) shifts in the allocation of resources.

The advent of these controls was attacked by some observers as a fundamental reversal in the direction of Canadian labor policy. Since the 1930s, public policy generally expanded the protection of workers. The hurried introduction of public sector wage controls was taken as the first step in the recision of labor's legal rights (Panitch and Swartz 1984).

In general, these programs accomplished their primary objective—reduction in the rate of increase of public sector compensation. Outside of British Columbia and Quebec, the labor movement was unable to mount any effective protests against these measures and labor's efforts in those two provinces failed (Thompson 1985; Hebert 1984; Palmer 1987).

However, by 1987 all jurisdictions had terminated statutory wage control programs, although two provinces restricted interest arbitration awards. Government spending rose steadily while compensation restraints were in place (Thompson 1988). In a more conciliatory approach, when the federal government established a task force to recommend spending reductions, participation by unions representing federal employees was sought and obtained. Consequently, the long-term impact on collective bargaining of the 1982 round of wage restrictions does not appear substantial.

Back-to-Work Legislation

A significant expression of government sovereignty is the passage of back-to-work legislation (i.e., special legislation enacted to end a particular strike

Table 11.   Back-to-Work Legislation, 1950-1986

Years	Federal Jurisdiction	Provincial Jurisdiction	Total
1950-1954	1	—	1
1955-1959	1	1	2
1960-1964	2	1	3
1965-1969	2	8	10
1970-1975	4	9	13
1975-1979	6	16	22
1980-1986	2	27	29
Total	18	62	80

Sources: 1950-1984—MacDonald (1985); 1985-1986—unpublished data from Labour Canada.

that is legal under existing labor relations statutes). (Illegal strikes normally are subject to court injunctions.) The incidence of such laws increased sharply in the late 1970s through the mid-1980s. These developments, when combined with public sector wage restraint programs, seemed to support the view that workers were being systematically stripped of their collective bargaining rights, beginning with the last group actually to obtain such rights, public employees (Panitch and Swartz 1984). To others, enactment of legislation to end public sector strikes represented a welcome relief from the permissive climate for government workers which had prevailed since the 1960s (MacDonald 1985).

The basic data on the incidence of back-to-work legislation seem to support the thesis that workers' rights were being seriously eroded. As Table 11 indicates, the absolute number of back-to-work laws rose sharply after 1975. While the exact form of these laws varied somewhat, the most common framework was to order the end to an existing strike together with arbitration to resolve the dispute. Although an increase from approximately 1.4 laws per year (the average 1966 and 1975) to 4.6 per year (the average for 1976-1986) is substantial, closer examination of the data casts doubt on the assertion that a general attack on workers' rights is underway.

To appreciate the significance of Canadian back-to-work legislation, it is necessary to disaggregate the data (Table 12). Between 1960 and 1986, the federal parliament enacted 16 pieces of back-to-work legislation, of which only 2 were directed at the public sector. By contrast, on 8 occasions, special legislation was used to end strikes in the ports of Vancouver or Montreal. In general, therefore, the federal government has avoided special legislation, especially in the public sector, a reflection of sophisticated dispute-settlement procedures and the relatively small size of the federal government.

Back-to-work legislation has been much more common at the provincial level. The rapid extension of bargaining into sensitive areas such as health care and education in the 1960s and 1970s virtually guaranteed some stoppages and

Table 12.   Back-to-Work Legislation, Public Sector, 1950-1986

Years	Federal Jurisdiction	Quebec	Ontario	British Columbia	Other Provinces	Total
1950-1954	—	—	—	—	—	0
1955-1959	—	—	—	—	—	0
1960-1964	—	—	—	—	—	0
1965-1969	—	5	1	—	—	6
1970-1974	—	2	2	—	—	4
1975-1979	2	5	6	3	1	17
1980-1986	—	9	4	2	6	21
Total	2	21	13	5	7	48

Source: Unpublished data, Labour Canada.

accompanying public pressure for a legislative response. Between 1961 and 1986, a total of 51 laws were passed to end public sector strikes, over 75 percent of them in the period 1976-1986. Initially, this trend seems to support the thesis that such legislation is becoming a significant aspect of public sector industrial relations. Closer scrutiny of the data suggests otherwise. Close to one-half of the back-to-work orders (40 percent) were enacted in Quebec, a proportion almost identical to its share of time lost in public sector strikes. One quarter of these statutes involved the Montreal Transit System, the latest being a law that requires drivers to provide rush-hour service in any future dispute. Moreover, the Quebec experience with back-to-work legislation should be viewed against the industrial relations climate in the province. Since the mid-1960s, several pieces of labor legislation have been passed each year, reaching a total of 84 labor bills for the period 1965-1983 (Morin and Leclerc 1986).

Ontario accounted for one-quarter (27 percent) of the provincial back-to-work laws. Over one-half of such statutes (8 to 13) were passed to end strikes in schools. Five of the laws were enacted in 1976, the first year of operation of a comprehensive statute to regulate bargaining and disputes by teachers. Since then, strikes have not been numerous, and one of the two additional back-to-work laws enacted to cover teachers was not proclaimed (i.e., never actually took effect) (Downie 1984).

COMPENSATION

The third contentious policy issue in public sector industrial relations involves the appropriate level of compensation. During the early years of public sector bargaining in the 1960s and 1970s, public sector settlements were high in absolute terms and often exceeded private sector levels, giving rise to fears that collective bargaining was causing excessive increases in public sector compensation (Christensen 1980). Early research reinforced these fears

(Cousineau and Lacroix 1977). Although the issue has been defined in several ways, four basic questions emerged: (1) comparison of levels of compensation in the public and private sectors, (2) comparison of the rates of change of public and private sector compensation, (3) the sensitivity of public and private sector compensation to changing economic conditions, and (4) spillover of public sector wage rates into the private sector.

On a normative level, the stated objective of compensation policy in most jurisdictions has been parity between the public and private sectors, at all levels in the organizational hierarchy. When a modern federal civil service system was established for the federal government in the 1940s, public policy declared that there should be equality between the public and private sectors. From time to time, independent bodies set up to review pay in the senior ranks have also recommended that compensation be competitive with the private sector (Advisory Group on Executive Compensation in the Public Service 1978). Finally, economists who frequently advise governments and write for academic journals also regard parity as the natural order for an effective compensation system.

These views, quite defensible on theoretical (and often political) grounds, tend to neglect the practical difficulties of comparing compensation for many public sector occupations with the private sector (Swan 1984). Moreover, the assumption of parity overlooks the existence of substantial interindustry wage differentials for the same occupations (Gunderson 1980b). Thus, on both theoretical and empirical grounds, it is possible to take the position that parity should be the exception, rather than the rule, in comparisons between the two sectors. Despite these difficulties, the assumption of parity prevails in Canada except for the stated positions of some public sector unions, who urge that such criteria as "social utility" of jobs should override private sector comparisons.

Direct occupational comparisons between the public and private sectors suffer from a number of methodological limitations, including the lack of comparable private sector occupations for many employees in the public sector, regional and industrial wage differentials, the absence of measurements for job security, and the like. Subject to these qualifications, data from the mid-1960s through 1980 demonstrate a public sector wage advantage of the magnitude of 1 to 15 percent, with a central tendency of approximately 10 percent, not controlling for union membership. Moreover, these data show that the gap between public and private sectors was greatest in the late 1970s and had already begun to stabilize when the first round of wage controls was implemented in 1975. The advantage was concentrated among lower-paid occupations and women, while high-level occupations had lower compensation in the public sector (Gunderson 1984). These results generally correspond with data from the United States and the United Kingdom (Ehrenberg and Schwarz 1986; Layard 1985; Mitchell 1987). Given the higher levels of union penetration in the public sector and evidence that union membership is associated with higher compensation, most of the public sector advantage seems to be accounted for by union membership levels (Wilton 1986).

Comparisons of rates of change of public and private sector wages are complicated by two periods of wage controls and the greater prevalence of cost of living allowance (COLA) clauses in the private sector. The 1975-1978 Anti-Inflation Program was most effective with public sector wages, although controls covered virtually all compensation. Only public sector wages were subject to regulation in the post-1982 period. During the inflationary period of the 1970s, private sector unions were frequently successful in negotiating COLA clauses into their collective agreements, a rare feature in the public sector. Thus, direct comparisons between negotiated settlements in the two sectors must be treated cautiously, because one would expect to find lower rate increases in negotiated settlements which also included COLA clauses.

After reviewing all data available through 1983 and controlling for COLA clauses, one scholar concluded:

> A review of the existing literature and empirical evidence on public sector wage settlements leads one to draw the following three conclusions concerning public sector wage compensation. First, over the 1967-1983 time period, wage settlements in the public sector have not exceeded settlements in the private sector ... Second the economic structure of wage settlements in the public sector (excluding arbitrated settlements) is not dissimilar to the structure of wage settlements in the private sector ... Finally, there is no empirical evidence that public sector wage settlements will, in general, spill over into the private sector and permeate throughout the entire economy (Wilton 1986, p. 281).

While aggregate data suggest that public sector compensation has not moved ahead of the private sector, the responsiveness of wages in the two sectors to economic variables is still of concern, given the impact of legislative control programs for part of the time period since 1977. In other words, how might public sector wages respond to changing economic conditions in the absence of controls? The earliest study (Cousineau and Lacroix 1977) indicated that public sector wages were less responsive to changes to economic variables than those in the private sector. Subsequent studies, incorporating the effects of the Anti-Inflation Program and more sophisticated methodologies failed to confirm this conclusion. This research found that the determinants of public and private sector wages were generally similar, excluding arbitrated settlements. Labor market conditions seem to affect wages in both sectors in similar ways, and in some cases public sector settlements are more sensitive to changes in the labor market than the private sector. Arbitration, however, seems to impart a slight upward bias to wage changes (Wilton 1986).

Finally, private sector commentators alleged that public sector wage settlements "spilled over" into the private sector, either by forcing the market rate for some occupations upward or setting off coercive comparisons between bargaining groups in the two sectors. Several studies were unable to verify that any such spillover occurred. In fact, the movement was in the opposite direction—private sector wage changes influenced movements in the public sector more than the reverse (Wilton 1986).

CONCLUSIONS

The past two decades have been eventful in Canadian public sector industrial relations. The transformation from a paternalistic and traditional system of employee relations to bilateral and occasionally adversarial labor-management relations has caused stress for all concerned—the parties, governments, and the public. For the first 10 years, the course of public policy was almost exclusively directed at the extension of rights to public employees. Since the late 1970s, however, employee gains have been more than offset by restrictions on bargaining imposed by governments. The fundamental question in 1987 is whether the third decade of public sector industrial relations will see a continuation of the retrenchment of the 1970s.

Policy developments in industrial relations usually reflect two broad sets of forces. The first is the performance of the system itself. Public policy may correct perceived malfunctions in the system, alter slightly the balance of power, or make minor changes based on political priorities. A second set of forces lies in the political system. An ideologically motivated government can change an industrial relations system to favor either party irrespective of the performance of the system. The liberalization of public sector industrial relations in Quebec in the 1960s was an integral part of a wholesale transformation of Quebec society in that era. The process of reform did not depend on a convincing demonstration that the existing system of employee relations was unworkable—rather it was politically driven. Whether future change in public sector industrial relations is based on the first set of forces or the second, the experience of the past two decades will prove instructive.

Looking first at strikes and dispute procedures, Canadian experience indicates that public employees are less strike-prone than their private sector counterparts. But strike activity by public employees is rising relative to the private sector and, given that one-half of all unionized employees work in the public sector, public employee strikes could eventually become predominant. Moreover, the relative public/private share of these totals says nothing about the impact of work stoppages. There is little doubt that a national postal strike, of which there have been seven since 1973, has far greater impact on public perceptions of strike propensities than major private sector stoppages. Thus, the objective reality of public sector strikes may be overwhelmed by the political realities.

Where public employees do not have the right to strike, compulsory arbitration is almost universally available. Canada data show that bargaining and compulsory arbitration can coexist, even over long periods of time, contrary to early assertions that the parties would avoid settling without the pressure of a strike. However, the rates at which arbitration is used are substantially higher than the incidence of strikes, a reflection of the relative costs of the two techniques of dispute resolution. Where utilized, compulsory interest arbitration has largely eliminated strikes. Its widespread acceptance is a function of attitudes of public sector workers, many of whom are fearful of strikes and are content to have wages and conditions established by neutral arbitrators, despite union rhetoric to the contrary.

In granting their employees bargaining rights, governments typically have reserved a number of subjects for unilateral determination. In addition, they have also changed the rules of bargaining to restrain compensation or, in rare cases, to force striking employees to return to work. Restrictions on the scope of bargaining have not eliminated disputes (or even bargaining) over these subjects.

Public sector wage controls appeared in 1982, four years after the end of a national wage and price controls program. The salient aspect of the second set of controls was that the most intrusive measures, statutorily imposed wage levels, were allowed to lapse after a relatively short life, with the exception of British Columbia. In retrospect, controls in most jurisdictions appear to have been based on government desires to limit or reduce public spending in the face of sharply declining revenues, not any fundamental dissatisfaction with the system of collective bargaining.

Similarly, back-to-work legislation has become much more common in the past 15 years, but is heavily concentrated in those jurisdictions and industries where stoppages are common and affect the public welfare directly and seriously. There is little evidence that governments have developed an appetite for such measures elsewhere.

Nowhere are the data on the results of public sector industrial relations more persuasive than in the area of compensation. Early fears that public employees would gain substantial advantages in compensation as a result of obtaining bargaining rights have been laid to rest. It is true that a combination of the adoption of bargaining, growth in the public sector, and the expansion of public funding in health services produced a temporary surge in public sector wage increases between 1967 and 1978. Since then, however, changes in compensation in the public and private sectors have been quite similar, with shifts in demand and legislative controls causing public sector compensation to revert to private sector averages.

Where do these conclusions leave the debate on the future of public sector industrial relations? The major changes of the 1980s—public sector wage controls or restrictions on interest arbitrators—appear to represent a political response to public issues of the day rather than an attempt to eliminate disfunctions or problems in the system. Perhaps this response could have been predicted. The dramatic changes which occurred in the public sector over twenty years may have made some backlash inevitable. A general swing to the right in several Canadian jurisdictions has made attacks on trade unions politically popular. Other changes, restrictions on the right-to-strike, back-to-work legislation, for instance, appear in retrospect to have been ad hoc responses to specific problems. Those responses were certainly conditioned by the political climate, but were related to economic conditions of concern to governments.

Based on a review of public sector industrial relations, one concludes that Canada has performed well. By any standards, profound change was accomplished in a relatively short time with minor disruptions. The democratic values of collective bargaining became available to thousands of employees. These groups, after initial hesitation, embraced collective (if not militant) action. Their employers, also after initial problems, proved equal to the tasks given them. A variety of systems evolved that reflected the basic elements of private sector labor relations—reliance on collective bargaining to determine wages and conditions of employment, the use of economic sanctions or arbitration to resolve disputes, and only moderate involvement by political institutions of the state in industrial relations issues.

The major risk for the future seems to be greater intrusion of political forces into labor-management relations, thereby undermining the major features of the industrial relations systems. By 1988 there were significant examples of political bargaining to determine wages and conditions of employment, complete with political sanctions exerted by both parties and substantial political intervention in industrial relations. The experience with politicized public sector industrial relations has been difficult for all parties concerned. Continuation of this trend will change the nature of employer-employee relations in the Canadian sector.

NOTES

1.   Strikes in the private sector are relatively common and unusually long by international standards (Lacroix 1986).

2.   It should be noted that the data in these tables differ from summary data compiled by Labour Canada and from similar analyses undertaken by Lacroix (1986) and Smith (1984). The difference lies in the definition of the public sector. Smith (1984), following Labour Canada definitions, includes telephone companies, many of which are privately owned, but excludes government enterprises such as Air Canada and Canadian National Railway and also appears to exclude urban transit. Lacroix (1986) excludes government enterprises, including major utilities such as B.C. Hydro. The definition used in this paper, on the other hand, includes government enterprises and urban transit and excludes private telephone companies. The resulting patterns obtained in this study are not markedly different compared to the earlier studies, but yearly variance does occur.

3.   Re: *Public Service Employee Relations Act* (*Alta*) (1987) S.C.C. No. 10.

REFERENCES

Adams, R. 1987. Industrial Relations Systems: An International Comparison. Pp. 437-464 in *Union-Management Relations in Canada,* edited by J. Anderson, M. Gunderson, and A. Ponak. Toronto: Addison-Wesley.

Advisory Group on Executive Compensation in the Public Service. 1978. *Report No. 6.* Ottawa. Mimeo.

Anderson, J.C. 1977. *Union Effectiveness: An Industrial Relations Systems Approach.* Unpublished doctoral dissertation, Cornell University, Ithaca, New York.

Blouin, R. 1982. Arbitration of Bargaining Disputes in Quebec. *Proceedings of the 19th Annual Meeting of the Canadian Industrial Relations Association,* pp. 209-238. University of Ottawa, Ontario.

Boivin, J. 1982. Labour Relations in Quebec. Pp. 422-456 in *Union-Management Relations in Canada,* edited by J. Anderson and M.Gunderson. Toronto: Addison-Wesley.

Christensen, S. 1980. *Unions and the Public Interest.* Vancouver: Fraser Institute.

Cohen, S. 1979. Does Public Employee Unionism Diminish Democracy? *Industrial and Labor Relations Review* 32:189-195.

Cousineau, J. and R. Lacroix. 1977. *Wage Determination in Major Collective Agreements in the Private and Public Sectors.* Ottawa: Economic Council of Canada.

Deverell, J. 1982. The Ontario Hospital Dispute 1980-81. *Studies in Political Economy* (Fall):179-190.

Downie, B. 1979. *The Behavioral, Economic and Institutional Effects of Substituting Compulsory Arbitration for the Right to Strike.* Ottawa: Economic Council of Canada.

_____. 1984. Collective Bargaining Under an Essential Services Commission. In *Conflict or Compromise,* edited by M. Thompson and G. Swimmer. Montreal: The Institute for Research on Public Policy.

Dubensky, A. 1984. Arbitration: Is the Process Working? Pp. 1-8 in *Labour Arbitration Conference Proceedings,* edited by C.L. Rigg and A. Ponak. Calgary, Alberta: The University of Calgary.

Ehrenberg. R. and J. Schwarz. 1986. Public-Sector Labor Markets. Pp. 1219-1268 in *Handbook of Labor Economics,* vol. 2, edited by O. Ashenfelter and R. Layard. Amsterdam: Elsevier.

Feuille, P. 1979. Selected Benefits and Costs of Compulsory Arbitration. *Industrial and Labor Relations Review* 33:64-76.

Feuille, P. and J.C. Anderson. 1980. Public Sector Bargaining Policy and Practice. *Industrial Relations* 19:309-324.

Finkelman, J. and S.B. Goldenberg. 1983. *Collective Bargaining in the Public Service: The Federal Experience in Canada,* vols. 1 and 2. Montreal: The Institute for Research on Public Policy.

Frankel, S. 1960. Staff Relations in the Canadian Federal Public Service: Experience with Joint Consultation. Pp. 370-385 in *Canadian Public Administration,* edited by J.E. Hodgetts and D.C. Corbett. Toronto: Macmillan.

Freeman, R. 1986. Unionism Comes to the Public Sector. *Journal of Economic Literature* 24:41-86.

Goldenberg, S. 1973. Collective Bargaining in the Provincial Public Services. Pp. 11-44 in *Collective Bargaining in the Public Service,* edited by J.F. O'Sullivan. Toronto: The Institute of Public Administration of Canada.

_____. 1987. Public Sector Labor Relations in Canada. Pp. 266-313 in *Public Sector Bargaining,* 2nd ed., edited by B. Aaron, J. Najita, and J. Stern. Washington, DC: The Bureau of National Affairs.

Gunderson, M. 1980a. *Labour Market Economics: Theory, Evidence and Policy in Canada.* Toronto: McGraw-Hill Ryerson.

_____. 1980b. Public Sector Compensation in Canada and the U.S. *Industrial Relations* 19:257-271.

_____. 1982. Union Impact on Wages, Fringe Benefits, and Productivity. Pp. 247-268 in *Union-Management Relations in Canada*, edited by J.C. Anderson and M. Gunderson. Toronto: Addison-Wesley.

_____. 1984. The Public/Private Sector Controversy. In *Conflict or Compromise*, edited by M. Thompson and G. Swimmer. Montreal: The Institute for Research on Public Policy.

Hebert, G. 1984. Public Sector Bargaining in Quebec: A Case of Hypercentralization. Pp. 229-282 in *Conflict or Compromise*, edited by M. Thompson and G. Swimmer. Montreal: The Institute for Research on Public Policy.

Hines, R.J. 1972. Mandatory Contract Arbitration—Is It a Viable Process? *Industrial and Labor Relations Review* 25:533-544.

House, J.H. 1980. *Organizational Structures for Collective Bargaining in Ontario Education.* Unpublished manuscript, Ontario Institute for Studies in Education, Department of Education Administration.

Kochan, T. 1974. A Theory of Multilateral Collective Bargaining in City Government. *Industrial and Labor Relations Review* 27:525-542.

_____. 1979. Dynamics of Dispute Resolution in the Public Sector. Pp. 150-190 in *Public Sector Bargaining*, edited by B. Aaron, J. Grodin and J. Stern. Madison, WI: Industrial Relations Research Association.

Lacroix, R. 1986. Strike Activity in Canada. Pp. 161-209 in *Canadian Labour Relations*, edited by W.C. Riddell. Toronto: University of Toronto Press.

Layard, R. 1985. Public Sector Pay: The British Perspective. Pp. 3-12 in *Public Sector Compensation*, edited by D. Conklin, T. Courchene, and W. Jones. Toronto: Ontario Economic Council.

Lipset, S.M. 1986. *Unions in Transition.* San Francisco: Institute for Contemporary Studies.

MacDonald, D. 1985. *Royal Commission on the Economic Union and Development Prospects for Canada.* Ottawa: Minister of Supply and Service.

Mason, D. 1985. Bill 44; What For and What Next. Pp. 1-12 in *Second Annual Labour Arbitration Conference Proceedings*, edited by A. Ponak and C. Rigg. Calgary: The University of Calgary.

Mitchell, D. 1987. Collective Bargaining and Compensation in the Public Sector. Pp. 124-149 in *Public Sector Bargaining*, 2nd ed., edited by B. Aaron, J. Najita, and J. Stern. Madison, WI: IRRA.

Mitchell, L. 1982. Interest Arbitration in the Federal Public Service. Pp. 239-258 in *Proceedings, 19th Annual Meeting of the Canadian Industrial Relations Association.* Quebec: CIRA.

Morin, F. and C. Leclerc. 1986. The Use of Legislation to Control Labour Relations: The Quebec Experience. Pp. 67-166 in *Labour Law and Urban Law in Canada*, edited by I. Bernier and A. Lajoie. Toronto: University of Toronto Press.

Palmer, B. 1987. *Solidarity: The Rise and Fall of an Opposition in British Columbia.* Vancouver: New Star Books.

Panitch, L. and D. Swartz. 1984. From Free Collective Bargaining to Permanent Exceptionalism: The Economic Crisis and the Transformation of Industrial Relations in Canada. Pp. 403-436 in *Conflict or Compromise*, edited by M. Thompson and G. Swimmer. Montreal: Institute for Research on Public Policy.

Peck, E. 1985. The British Columbia Compensation Stabilization Programme and the Interest Arbitration Process. Pp. 109-115 in *Proceedings of the 21st Annual Meeting of the Canadian Industrial Relations Association*, edited by B. Downie. Quebec: CIRA.

Ponak, A. 1982. Public-Sector Collective Bargaining. Pp. 343-378 in *Union Management Relations in Canada*, edited by J. Anderson and M. Gunderson. Toronto: Addison-Wesley.

Ponak, A. and L. Falkenberg. 1989. Interest Dispute Resolution. Pp. 260-290 in *Collective Bargaining in Canada,* edited by A. Sethi. Toronto: Nelson.

Ponak, A. and T.P. Haridas. 1979. Collective Bargaining Attitude of Registered Nurses in the United States and Canada. *Relations Industrielles* 34:576-590.

Ponak, A. and M. Thompson. 1985. Faculty Views of Collective Bargaining: The Voice of Experience. *Relations Industrielles* 39:449-465.

Ponak, A. and H.N. Wheeler. 1980. Choice of Procedures in Canada and the United States. *Industrial Relations* 19:292-308.

Rawson, D. 1987. *Public Sector Labour Relations in Australia.* Paper delivered to Pacific Rim Labour Policy Conference, Vancouver.

Rose, J. 1983. Some Notes on the Building Trades—Canadian Labour Congress Dispute. *Industrial Relations* 22:87-93.

————. 1984. Growth Patterns of Public Sector Unions. Pp. 83-120 in *Conflict or Compromise,* edited by M. Thompson and G. Swimmer. Montreal: The Institute for Research on Public Policy.

Smith, D. 1984. Strikes in the Canadian Public Sector. In *Conflict or Compromise,* edited by M. Thompson and G. Swimmer. Montreal: The Institute for Research on Public Policy.

Subbarao, A. 1986. Impasse Choice in the Canadian Federal Service: An Innovation and an Intrigue. *Relations Industrielles* 40:567-591.

Sutherland, S. and G. Doern. 1985. *Bureaucracy in Canada: Control and Reform.* Toronto: University of Toronto Press.

Swan, K. 1983. Safety Belt or Straight Jacket? Restrictions on the Scope of Public Sector Bargaining. Pp. 37-55 in *Essays on Collective Bargaining and Industrial Democracy,* edited by G. England. Toronto: CCH Canadian.

————. 1984. Grating Expectations: The Limitations in the Development of Normative Criteria in Interest Arbitration. In *Conflict or Compromise,* edited by M. Thompson and G. Swimmer. Montreal: The Institute for Research on Public Policy.

Swimmer, G. 1984. Militancy in Public Sector Unions. Pp. 147-228 in *Conflict or Compromise,* edited by M. Thompson and G. Swimmer. Montreal: The Institute for Research on Public Policy.

Swimmer, G. and A. MacDonald. 1985. Dispute Resolution in the Ontario Public Sector: What's So Wrong About the Right to Strike? Pp. 154-178 in *Public Sector Compensation,* edited by D. Conklin, T. Courchene, and W. Jones. Toronto: Ontario Economic Council.

Swinton, K. 1984. Grievance Arbitration in the Public Sector. Pp. 339-372 in *Conflict or Compromise,* edited by M. Thompson and G. Swimmer. Montreal: The Institute for Research on Public Policy.

Thompson, F. and W.T. Stanbury. 1979. The Political Economy of Interest Groups in the Legislative Process in Canada. Pp. 224-249 in *The Canadian Political Process,* 3rd ed., edited by R. Sebultz, O. Kruhlah and J. Terry. Toronto: Holt, Rinehart and Winston.

Thompson, M. 1981. Evaluation of Interest Arbitration: The Case of British Columbia Teachers. Pp. 79-97 in *Interest Arbitration,* edited by J.M. Weiler. Toronto: Carswell.

————. 1985. Restraint and Labour Relations: The Case of British Columbia. *Canadian Public Policy* 11(June):171-179.

————. 1988. Public Sector Industrial Relations in Canada: The Impact of Restraint. Pp. 502-508 in Industrial Relations Research Association, *Proceedings of the 1988 Spring Meeting,* edited by B. Dennis, Madison, WI: IRRA.

Thwaites, J. 1984. Tensions Within the Labour Movement in Quebec: Relations Between the Public and Private Sectors in Three Case Studies from 1972 to 1982. Pp. 121-146 in *Conflict or Compromise,* edited by M. Thompson and G. Swimmer. Montreal: The Institute for Research on Public Policy.

Weiler, J.M. 1986. The Role of Law in Labour Relations. Pp. 1-66 in *Labour Law and Urban Law in Canada,* edited by J. Bernier and A. Lajoie. Toronto: University of Toronto Press.

Weiler, P. 1980. *Reconcilable Differences.* Toronto: Carswell.

Wetzel, K. and D. Gallagher. 1984. Management Structures to Accommodate Multi-Employer Hospital Bargaining in Western Canada. Pp. 283-314 in *Conflict or Compromise,* edited by M. Thompson and G. Swimmer. Montreal: The Institute for Research on Public Policy.

Werlin, D. 1984. Labour's View of Arbitration. Pp. 9-17 in *Proceedings of the First Labour Arbitration Conference,* edited by C.I. Rigg and A. Ponak. Calgary, Alberta: University of Calgary.

Wilton, D. 1986. Public Sector Wage Compensation. Pp. 257-284 in *Canadian Labour Relations,* edited by C. Riddell. Toronto: University of Toronto Press.

Woods, H.D. 1973. *Labour Policy in Canada,* 2nd ed. Toronto: Macmillan of Canada.

FLEXIBLE PAY SYSTEMS IN
THE AMERICAN CONTEXT:
HISTORY, POLICY, RESEARCH, AND IMPLICATIONS

Daniel J.B. Mitchell and Renae F. Broderick

INTRODUCTION

In the past, American economists—like their counterparts in other countries—focused on the magnitude of pay, rather than on the way in which pay was determined. But this limited approach is changing (e.g., Ehrenberg and Milkovich 1987). Two macroeconomic disappointments initially accounted for the new interest in pay systems. First, particularly in the 1970s, the U.S. economy was at times characterized by both high unemployment and high inflation. A more satisfactory balance was not achieved until a severe recession in the early 1980s ushered in a period of declining unemployment and relatively low inflation. Second, productivity growth was disappointing, especially after 1973. With the exception of the hard-pressed manufacturing sector, even the recovery of the 1980s failed to restore the old 3 percent productivity improvement factor.

Advances in Industrial and Labor Relations, volume 5, pages 95-149.
Copyright © 1991 by JAI Press Inc.
All rights of reproduction in any form reserved.
ISBN: 0-89232-940-8

Alternative Perspectives

Economists and compensation specialists have different perspectives on the effects of pay systems. Compensation specialists have obviously been more concerned with the productivity aspects of pay than with general issues of economic stability. Unlike economists, they have seen productivity as an issue centered around individual worker performance and located at the level of the organization. In that regard, the perspectives of industrial psychologists and behavioral scientists have been closer to that of the compensation specialist than to the economic approach.

This paper, in its original version, was presented to an international conference of industrial relations researchers, economists, and practitioners in a section dealing with wage flexibility, largely from a macroeconomic perspective.[1] We have brought in other perspectives and have sought to add a micro as well as macro focus to the issue of pay flexibility. Nonetheless, it is likely that the various "interest groups" that have seen the topic of pay systems mainly from their own vantage points will each feel that we have omitted important points or oversimplified.

We suggest that the paper be viewed as an exercise in introducing the various interest groups—economists, psychologists, behavioral scientists, compensation consultants, and practitioners—to alternative approaches. In addition, those unfamiliar with American pay practices and institutions as they relate to pay flexibility will find this review to be a useful introduction. Our focus will be on nonsupervisory employees, although we will make some allusions to practices relating to managers and executives.

Outline of the Paper

Below we first examine the two concerns—macro performance and productivity trends—which have given rise to the new interest of economists in pay systems, especially flexible pay systems. The various forms of flexible pay systems which have received most attention (but not necessarily widespread use) are then defined. A history of flexible pay systems in the United States is briefly presented as a lead-in to a discussion of the current incidence of these compensation arrangements.

We then turn to prevailing views in the United States concerning the efficacy of flexible pay systems. Attitudes of managers on the effects of these systems ultimately determine their usage. We present some new evidence on these attitudes, based on a survey of American managers. The survey deals with management beliefs about the utility of the various plans taken alone and about the substitutability or complementarity of alternative forms of flexible pay. We end with a discussion of American public policy options, which might foster flexible compensation systems, and of the research issues that remain.

An American Approach to Pay Flexibility

In American economic literature, as in the literature of other countries, there is a tradition of puzzling about, and theorizing about, wage rigidity. Often such literature has been directed at union wage bargaining as a cause of the rigidity of wages, a tradition going back to Keynesian and pre-Keynesian debates of the 1930s and earlier.[2] In the context of the U.S. labor market of the 1980s, where the union representation rate in the private sector was about one-sixth and falling, a collective bargaining approach to the issue is not warranted. Most American wage determination is nonunion.

There have also been concerns in some countries about rigidity of wage structure rather than wage levels. But again, the U.S. economy lacks an obvious institutional arrangement (such as the Australian arbitration system) which determines and holds wage relativities.[3] At one time, it was believed by many that pattern bargaining in the union sector was such an arrangement. However, the force of pattern bargaining, even at its peak, tended to be exaggerated, and, in any case, such bargaining was substantially constrained in the 1980s. Absent an institution or a public policy which hardened the American wage structure, an essay on wage flexibility in the United States which focused mainly on structural matters would at best be aimed at a side issue.

In the contemporary U.S. environment, it is most reasonable to concentrate on the alternative pay systems which the myriad of decentralized wage decisions makers might adopt. Some of these systems can introduce flexibility into pay determination. It is on this potential that our paper is focused.

THE MACROECONOMIC BACKGROUND OF FLEXIBLE PAY

Figure 1 illustrates the U.S. macroeconomic dilemma using two measures of economic distress: unemployment and inflation. The figure shows peak and trough annual unemployment rates from the early 1960s to the mid-1980s and indicates the trend and magnitude of consumer price inflation. In general, when unemployment has hit a cyclical peak, inflation has been either trendless or decelerating. When unemployment has hit a trough, inflation has tended to accelerate.

Also apparent from the figure is a rising underlying trend in unemployment. The peak annual unemployment rates of the 1960s, 1970s, and 1980s were 6.7 percent, 8.3 percent, and 9.7 percent, respectively: the trough rates (through 1987) were 3.5 percent, 4.9 percent, 5.8 percent, and 6.2 percent. Although some analysts have attributed this upward drift to changing workforce composition (more young people and women), the compositional effects cannot be the sole source of the trend. For example, a similar pattern of upward creep will emerge even if the unemployment rate is narrowly confined to married males with

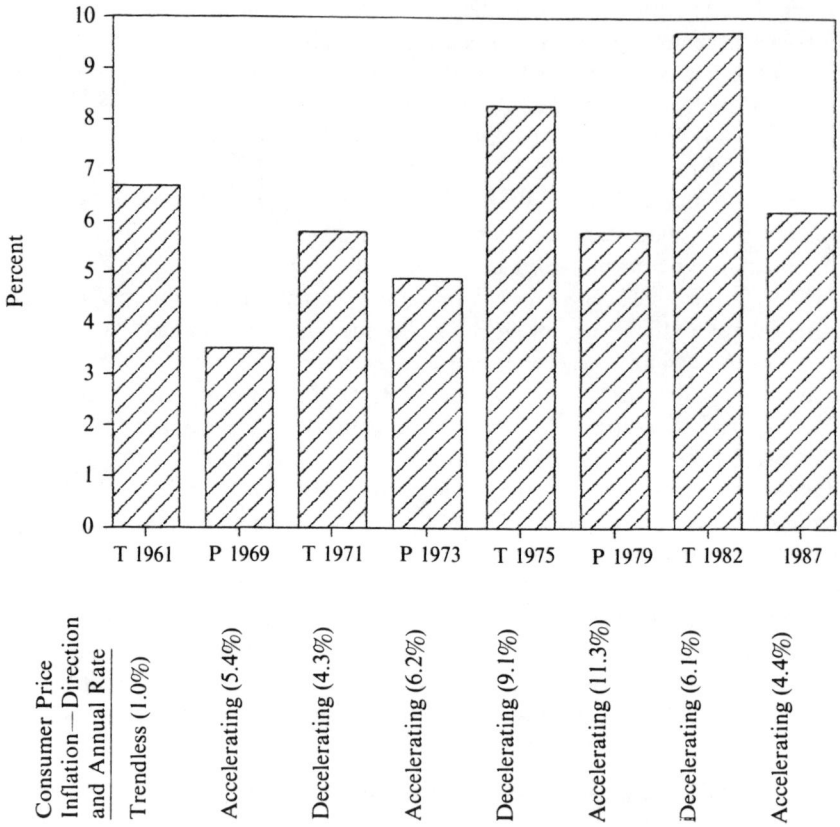

Note: Figure 1 shows the civilian unemployment rate (bars) during trough (T) and peak (P) years of the business
          cycle. Shown below the bars is the direction of consumer price inflation (accelerating or decelerating)
          and the annual rate of change of the Consumer Price Index (CPI-U).
Source: U.S. Bureau of Labor Statistics.

Figure 1.   Unemployment and Price Inflation

spouses present (a group weighted towards prime age males with strong labor
force attachments).

   From the viewpoint of economic policy, only two basic options emerge. One
is simply to assume that there is a need for relatively high unemployment and
slack labor markets to keep inflation in check. The conclusion would then be
that efforts to lower unemployment through expansionary demand policies risk
both inflation acceleration and a repeat of the stop/go policies of the 1970s

and early 1980s. An alternative approach is to analyze the economic system to see if some institution might be altered, thus making low unemployment and low, nonaccelerating inflation simultaneously compatible. It is the latter type of analysis which has led some economists to search for a remedy in the system of pay determination.

THE WEITZMAN PROPOSAL

Martin L. Weitzman of MIT has attracted considerable attention from American economists and editorial writers with his proposal concerning profit sharing. Yet his ideas have so far had their greatest effect in Britain (another economy where stagflation has been a problem); the British government enacted a system of tax incentives in 1987 to encourage profit sharing.[4] He argues that the institution which needs to be changed to improve macro performance is the formula for wage setting, essentially because the contemporary wage system lacks a significant share element (Weitzman 1983, 1984, 1985; *New York Times* 1985a, 1985b). He paints the modern wage system as rigidly based on protecting a wage rate, either real or nominal, regardless of the level of product demand.

The idea that profit sharing would add "flexibility" to the wage structure has a long history. It received renewed attention in the 1980s, due to the Japanese example of a bonus system with a profit sharing element (Hashimoto 1979; U.S. Bureau of International Labor Affairs 1985, pp. 77-78). Indeed, Weitzman himself uses the Japanese example in support of his proposal (Freeman and Weitzman 1987).

What Weitzman added to the previously vague idea that flexibility would be a "good thing" from a macro perspective, was a clear-cut supporting micro analysis (i.e., a theoretical justification). His analysis suggests that, with more profit sharing, firms would have a greater incentive both to hire more workers (thus reducing unemployment) and to avoid laying them off when demand fell (thus keeping unemployment at its low level). With the economy tending toward full employment, swings in demand would be largely nominal (i.e., affecting prices rather than real output). Monetary policy could then focus more easily (and less painfully) on maintaining price stability.

Unlike many clever economic schemes that have been proposed in the past, Weitzman's proposal does not require a new technology. Profit sharing has been around for a long time. But in the past, it has generally been seen by compensation analysts as a micro device aimed only at modifying employee behavior. Viewed that way, society as a whole could—and presumably should—leave it to firm-level decision makers to decide if profit sharing would be beneficial in their particular circumstances (Alchian and Demsetz 1972).

Profit sharing according to Weitzman, however, is more important as a device to modify employ*er* behavior. He argues that profit sharing has "externalities," creating a social interest in its propagation. He can point to evidence that, even viewed in the conventional way, use of a profit sharing bonus to reflect company "ability to pay" in wage compensation is likely to be seen as "fair" by the general population (Kahneman, Knetsch, and Thaler 1986).

AMERICAN PRODUCTIVITY TRENDS

There is little point in belaboring the well-known deterioration in U.S. productivity performance, which became apparent by the late 1970s. The 3 percent annual improvement in productivity, which had come to be expected by the early 1970s, seemed mysteriously to vanish. From the cyclical peak 1973 to cyclical peak 1979, measured nonfarm productivity hardly rose at all.

Careful analysis of the phenomenon initially suggested a variety of partial explanations, but none which either provided a large portion of the answer, nor which pointed to a solution (Denison 1979). Since 1979, there has been some improvement in productivity growth, when it is compared with trends of the late 1970s. However, there has been no resumption of the pre-1973 trend for the overall economy, despite the many press accounts of corporate reorganizations, reductions of overhead personnel, and plant closings. The deteriorating American trade balance in the 1980s, although mainly a function of U.S. dollar appreciation until early 1985, focused increased public attention on the question of international competitiveness and its relation to productivity growth. Evidence that the trend in U.S. productivity improvement was below that of most other industrialized countries reinforced this questioning.

In the past, suggestions among economists that workplace attitudes might play an important role in aggregate productivity developments have tended to be made by "radicals" (Weisskopf, Bowles, and Gordon 1983). More conventional economists probably will concede that the method of compensation could influence worker output, but have generally not devoted much thought to the topic. To the extent that arrangements such as profit sharing have been considered by contemporary economists, their existence would probably be explained by general references to principal/agent models. Under such models, the workers (agents) are viewed as being given a compensation incentive to identify their interests with the firm owners (principals). To the extent that there has been more detailed analysis by economists, it has until recently been largely confined to the rare cases of worker-owned firms (Vanek 1970).

In contrast, compensation specialists have placed much more substantial weight on concepts such as incentives and pay for performance, particularly during the 1980s (William M. Mercer, Inc. 1980, p. 11; 1983, p. 5). Moreover, at least on an intellectual level, human resource managers and union representatives are likely to believe that the workplace environment has an important role in determining productivity and quality.

DEFINITION OF FLEXIBLE PAY PLANS

"Flexible pay" has often been used loosely to refer to such systems as subjectively determined merit awards. In this paper, however, flexible pay is defined to mean compensation that is contingent on some measure of performance and that is not added to an individual's base salary (Lawler 1984). Even within that definition, however, there are four types of plans that are commonly lumped together: (1) simple incentives such as piece rate plans or commission plans,[5] (2) profit sharing plans, (3) gain sharing plans (such as Scanlon, Rucker, Improshare plans), and (4) Employee Stock Ownership Plans (ESOPs, tax-credit ESOPs).

Each plan can be distinguished by type, by its motivational impact on employee performance (including productivity), by its external economic impact, and by tax treatment. In principle, the many forms of executive compensation, such as stock options, could have been added to the four types of plans considered in this paper. However, the narrow range of employees potentially covered by executive pay, the complex tax issues entailed, and broad issues raised about the relations between owners and top managers preclude analysis of such pay plans here.

Flexible Pay Plan Types

Simple incentive plans began as piece rate plans in early manufacturing settings. Under such plans, each piece of work was priced and the worker's pay determined by the number of completed units. Both Adam Smith in his *Wealth of Nations* and Karl Marx in *Capital* referred to such plans. Smith (1937, pp. 81-82) thought that piece rates were so effective in stimulating worker effort that ill health would result from overexertion. Marx (1906, pp. 602-611) cited examples of piece rates going back to the fourteenth century and viewed such pay systems as both a way of determining "an exact measure for the intensity of labour" and a way of reducing the need for "superintendence" (supervision). He also cited the periodic cutting of piece rates as a source of labor-management friction.

The scientific management movement in the United States had its roots in the search for a better piece rate. Frederick Taylor—the father of the movement—believed it was important to pay for work accomplished rather than for time. Yet he recognized that the standard practice of setting piece rates perversely created incentives for workers to engage in "soldiering" (working below full capacity). Management casually set the price per piece based on observation of worker output and then cut the price when additional worker effort raised the average wage.

Taylor's (1914, p. 638) solution was to rely on scientific time and motion studies to obtain both the right price and to determine the correct sequence of worker motions. Worker and employer interests would be harmoniously directed toward increased output, workplace frictions would end, and unions and strikes would become "unnecessary." Rather than a simple piece rate, Taylor proposed a differential rate, that is, a kinked scale with a higher price for output above the scientifically-set standard.

As scientific management developed in the early part of this century, more elaborate systems evolved (Bedaux, Emerson, Halsey, Rowan, and Gantt plans). These plans, or variants, are still in use today. They also involve engineered, hourly or daily standards of production. Workers receive a base wage for production levels that meet the standard and incentive premiums for above-standard production. Such standard-based plans are also found in some service organizations (banks, insurance and travel companies, etc.).

A second example of a simple incentive plan is the commission plan used in sales work. Commission plans tie pay to individual achievement of specific revenue or sales objectives. Simple incentive plans, of the types described above, are distinguished from other flexible pay plans by their emphasis on linking pay to individual, quantitative measures of performance, and frequent payments (usually with each paycheck)[6] (Lawler 1981).

In contrast, *profit sharing plans* link pay or bonuses to company profits at longer intervals, often annual. Beyond this common linkage of pay to profit measures, profit sharing plans vary considerably. The actual measure of profit used, the portion of profits shared with employees, the rules governing distribution of profit shares to individual employees, and the extent to which the plan incentive formulas are formal versus discretionary are all plan design features that vary.

Like more complex piece rates and incentives, profit sharing has its modern roots in the nineteenth century. Profit sharing avoided the standard-setting problem addressed by Taylor, and was viewed as providing an incentive to avoid behaviors such as the wasting of materials or the substituting of quantity for quality which piece rates might induce. In addition, profit sharing was viewed as a way of solving the problem of antagonism between capital and labor by making workers into mini-capitalists (U.S. Commissioner of Labor 1886, pp. 279-293; Walker 1876, pp. 282-283; Gilman 1891, p. 416).

There are two major types of profit sharing plans in use today: cash and deferred. In addition, there are profit sharing plans with both cash and deferred elements. Under a cash plan, an employee's share is paid in cash when earned. Under a deferred plan, an employee's share is paid to a trust account maintained by the employer. Claims on the trust are distributed according to some specified vesting schedule (Profit Sharing Research Foundation 1984).

Gain sharing plans, like profit sharing plans, can come in various forms. In the nineteenth century, gain sharing was seen as a compromise between company-level profit sharing and individual-level piece rates. Profit sharing was seen as remote from the worker, whereas gain sharing was a kind of plant level (or work-group level) sharing (i.e., closer to home and thus a better incentive). Early gain sharing systems, such as that introduced in the 1880s by Henry R. Towne, did not have the elements of worker participation often associated with such plans today (Thompson 1949, p. 6).

In recent years, the gain sharing label has sometimes been applied to any plan that ties pay to group measures of performance (O'Dell 1981; Lawler 1981). In this paper we use the label in the narrower sense typified by the Scanlon, Rucker, and Improshare plans (Schuster 1984). These plans commonly provide a monthly bonus to the workers of a production line or plant. The bonus is based on value-added or cost savings, defined as the difference between present production or labor costs and the historical averages of these costs (as established by accounting data). Savings are split between employers and management (Freund and Epstein 1984; O'Dell 1981; Lesieur 1958).

Finally, Employee Stock Ownership Plans (ESOPs) represent a form of flexible pay plan which has been especially singled out for preferential tax treatment since the 1970s.[7] The modern ESOP movement has antecedents in the nineteenth century interest in worker cooperatives and worker-owned enterprises. As in the case of profit sharing, nineteenth century authors viewed worker ownership as a possible solution to the labor problem. Yet doubts about worker ability to manage enterprises often led to a preference by commentators of the period for profit sharing. Modern ESOPs, however, do not necessarily involve workers in management or the selection of management.

In an ESOP plan, employers purchase stock from their own shareholders or create new stock. These shares are contributed to employee accounts held in trust. Some plans are known as "leveraged" or leverageable ESOPs because the employer can borrow through the ESOP, issue stock to the ESOP trust fund in the amount of the loan, and then deduct repayment of principal as well as interest from corporate income taxes (Bureau of National Affairs, Inc. 1987; Marsh and McAllister 1981). Not all ESOPs are leveraged; some plans merely hold stock for workers.

A variant on an ESOP, known as a tax credit ESOP, involves special tax incentives given to employers as a reward for plan creation. The most recent type, so-called PAYSOPs, became available to any private employer in 1983 (Bureau of National Affairs, Inc. 1987). Under these plans, the employer received a tax credit for stock contributions up to 1.5 percent of the payroll. The tax subsidy for PAYSOPs ended with the 1986 Tax Reform Act.[8]

Motivational Impact of Flexible Pay Plans: Current Views

Flexible pay plans that tie money rewards to job or employee performance are believed to have an impact on employee work motivation (Lawler 1971; Locke 1982; Pinder 1984). Indeed, proponents of any one of the four types of plans discussed in this paper claim that organization implementation of the plan will have a positive effect on employee performance. The challenge in the design and implementation of such plans is to appropriately match them to the organization's performance requirements, environment or conditions, and workforce. A discussion of the literature on factors influencing such matches is beyond the scope of this paper (for such reviews, see Galbraith 1977; Freedman and Montanari 1980; Kerr 1982; Pinder 1984). In summary, however, it can simply be stated that flexible pay plans that tie appropriate performance measures to money rewards are more likely to lead to better performance than those that are not tied to appropriate performance measures. In addition, background organization conditions can either strengthen or weaken the pay-performance link (Kerr 1975; Lawler 1981).

Motivation theory predicts that simple incentive plans provide a potential for increasing employee work output (Yukl, Latham, and Pursell 1976; Lawler 1981; Locke 1982). Ideally, such plans tie pay to individual performance and payments are both discernable and frequent. However, the organization conditions needed for maximum impact of simple incentives are stringent: objective measures of output, employee control over performance, and relative stability of work design, methods, and technology (Galbraith 1977; Lawler 1981).

Tying pay to subjective measures of output, or to those over which employees have little control, often results in perverse work group norms, for example, the employee restrictions on output which worried Frederick Taylor (Whyte 1955). Frequent changes in work design, methods, or technology require continual changes in plan design and can lead to high administrative costs (Lawler 1981). Such conditions limit the number of work settings in which simple incentives can be used successfully.

The conceptual literature on gain sharing plans suggests that their potential for increasing work group (plant, division) output or productivity stems from an increase in work group cooperation, innovation, and commitment (Lawler 1981; O'Dell 1981; Schuster 1984). However, there is little behavioral theory developed to suggest why gain sharing plans increase worker cooperation, innovation, and commitment and, thus, productivity. Bullock and Lawler (1984, p. 36) speculate that increases in employee participation in work decisions and communications about the role of the work group in the overall success of the organization encourage employees to work harder, to think about how to improve work methods, and to care about the overall performance of their group. These behaviors, in turn, lead to higher productivity. Most proponents of gain sharing plans hold that a work environment that encourages such participation and communication is essential to plan success. (The exception is the Improshare plan [Fein 1981].) In addition, work should be designed, and workers should be trained, so as to foster teamwork.

If the success of gain sharing plans does depend on such a work environment, then their successful implementation may be limited to those organizations whose managements are committed to plan development. Employees will also be more likely to accept gain sharing if the employer has not only the historical accounting data needed to establish gain sharing formulas, but is also willing to share data with employees or their representatives (Schuster 1984). This information sharing is yet another condition that many organizations may not be willing to offer.

The links between pay and performance and their motivational impact on employee work behavior become tenuous in the case of profit sharing. Simple incentive plans tie compensation to individual performance and pay out as often as every week. In principle, workers should be aware of their individual contributions to group performance under gain sharing plans. The payout for gain sharing is often monthly, not as frequent as a simple incentive plan, but still a regular event.

However, profit sharing ties pay to organization performance measures over which individual workers have little control, the remoteness issue already recognized in nineteenth-century discussions.[9] Moreover, in large firms, the share of the worker in the fruits of his/her incremental contribution to profits is diluted by the division of the amount reserved for sharing between all workers. Thus, if the firm has 1,000 employees, each worker will receive at most only 1/1000 of his/her contribution to profits.[10]

The profit sharing payout is often annual, and in the case of deferred plans, can be put off until retirement. Compensation specialists and economists tend to diverge on the significance of this aspect of profit sharing. Economists, using a model of rational decision makers with good information, may not view the frequency of payment, or deferral of payment, as a major behavioral issue, since workers may be assumed to value bonuses appropriately, regardless of timing. But compensation specialists tend to assume a more limited version of rationality prevails; their view is more in keeping with the "bounded rationality" proposed by Herbert Simon (1957, p. 198) than the simple models of all-knowing economic man. In short, the bounded view is that bonuses may be a motivator but you have to see and feel them (often) to believe them.

Given the remoteness problem, there is no behavioral theory directly supporting the notion that profit sharing can increase employee productivity.[11] Proponents of profit sharing, however, maintain that it can increase employee commitment or loyalty to the firm by instilling a sense of involvement in the firm's fortunes. Commitment or loyalty can be defined as the desire to remain part of the organization, as an acceptance of organization goals, and as a willingness to exert effort for the organization (Pinder 1984, p. 103). Proponents of profit sharing plans believe that employee commitment is enhanced if the plan is made highly visible and if employees are educated about how business conditions, as well as their own performance, can influence profit measures (Profit Sharing Research Foundation 1985). Finally, ESOPs can lay even less claim on producing higher productivity than many profit sharing plans, for reasons discussed below. The exception here may be the 100 percent worker-owned firm in which individual employees would have the same interest as stockholders in firm productivity. However, such ESOPs are rare.[12]

Economic Impact and Tax Treatment of Flexible Pay Plans

As noted earlier, Weitzman has suggested that the external economic benefits of profit sharing create a social interest in its propagation. In the Weitzman view, neither simple incentive plans nor ESOPs foster external macroeconomic benefits. Whether or not gain sharing plans foster such benefits depends upon the cost savings formula used. If the Weitzman view is correct, then relative to the other plans, only profit sharing plans should receive preferred tax treatment.

In fact, there is no tax preference for simple incentive nor for gain sharing plans. Payments under both types of plans are taxed as ordinary income. Income from profit sharing plans that pay immediate cash bonuses does not receive any tax preference. But under deferred profit sharing plans, tax liability is also deferred. However, the implicit tax subsidy is no greater than provided under qualified pension plans or deferred savings arrangements such as 401(k) plans.[13] Thus, current tax law does not promote profit sharing. In sharp contrast to the other types of flexible pay plans, ESOPs have received increasingly favorable tax treatment since the mid-1970s. The tax preference issue is revisited in the concluding section of this paper.

HISTORY OF FLEXIBLE PAY IN THE UNITED STATES: THE TWENTIETH CENTURY

It would be pleasant to report that there were reliable statistics tracing usage of alternative forms of pay systems historically. Unfortunately, information on forms of pay—as opposed to magnitudes—has been collected only on an ad hoc basis, sometimes by the U.S. Bureau of Labor Statistics and sometimes by private organizations. As is usually the case with statistical information, the further back in time one goes, the more spotty are the data sources.

Piece Rates and Incentive Bonus Systems

Simple piece rates were common in factory work in the nineteenth century. Exactly how common, it is difficult to say. The only data source available is the 1890 Census of Manufactures which reported that 1 percent of factory production workers were on piece rates. However, the census questionnaire used probably resulted in a gross underestimate of actual piece work (Pencavel 1977, pp. 227-229).

It is safer to assume that, despite the census estimate, piece rates were the norm for production workers. Certainly, the discussion in the early literature on scientific management are predicated on the widespread use of piece rates. In many respects, piece rates bridged the transition between workers functioning as independent artisans and workers hired as paid employees. An independent shoemaker charging a price for a pair of shoes is effectively collecting a piece rate from his customers. Thus, paying an employee/ shoemaker a piece rate treats him as a quasi-contractor to the shoe factory.

As noted above, in the early twentieth century, the growing popularity of "scientific management" focused more attention on the details of the payment system. A wide variety of incentive and bonus systems were introduced and promoted. By the mid-1920s, roughly one-half of factory employees were covered by some kind of piece rate or incentive system (National Industrial Conference Board 1930).

Apart from simple piece rates, industry wage surveys by the U.S. Bureau of Labor Statistics (BLS) suggest that bonus arrangements were commonly found in manufacturing establishments in the 1920s and early 1930s, as can be seen from Table 1. Usage, however, varied substantially from industry to industry. Unfortunately, terminology regarding bonuses was loose. Some "bonuses" reported by BLS were actually wage premiums for overtime work, for night shifts, and so forth. Nevertheless, many of the bonuses were related to the achievement of production goals or to labor-cost or labor-time savings. Some bonuses were rewards for good attendance records or for the avoidance of accidents or damage to equipment. (Profit sharing plans were reported as bonus systems only in a handful of cases.)

The available evidence from BLS surveys indicates a substantial upward trend in the use of time rates rather than piece and incentive rates after the 1920s. The rise of unions in the 1930s appears to have played some role in this shift. Yet the change is more complex since union attitudes about piece rates vs. time rates were not uniform prior to the 1930s. To the extent that unions accepted piece rates, they tended to prefer simple plans as opposed to some of the more complex formulas which evolved out of scientific management (McCabe 1912, pp. 185-219; Jacoby 1985a, pp. 44-46). Some of the new industrial unions, such as the Auto Workers, generally opposed piece rates of any type.

Apart from the union factor, another climate shift had been occurring prior to the 1930s. Scientific management had long had critics who argued that its results in actual practice were less impressive than the "fakirs" and "industrial patent medicine men" who were selling it wanted management to believe (Hoxie

Table 1. Bonus System Usage in the 1920s and Early 1930s

Industry	Year	Surveyed Establishments with Bonuses (%)	Industry	Year	Surveyed Establishments with Bonuses (%)
Tires	1923	31	Silk and rayon goods	1931	16
Foundries	1923	15	Woolen and worsted goods	1926	61
	1927	14		1928	58
	1929	11		1930	42
	1931	9		1932	21
Machine shops	1923	19	Cotton goods	1926	17
	1927	22		1930	21
	1929	23			
	1931	24	Hosiery	1928	22
				1932	19
Paper and pulp	1923	11			
			Underwear	1928	17
Meatpacking	1927	42		1932	12
	1929	49			
	1931	49	Airplanes and aircraft engines	1929	5
Boot and shoe	1926	21			
	1930	11	Portland cement	1929	19
Men's clothing	1924	4	Furniture	1929	15
	1928	2			
	1929	0	Cigarettes	1930	23
Paper box-board	1925	16	Textile dyeing and finishing	1930	21
				1932	28
Lumber mills	1923	1			
			Cane sugar refining	1930	52
Motor vehicles	1925	38			
	1928	45	Bakeries	1931	3
Rayon and synthetic yarn	1930	57	Gas stations and garages	1931	6
			Metal mines	1931	37
Leather goods	1932	17			

Source: U.S. Bureau of Labor Statistics (various industry wage studies).

1916, p. 117). Moreover, the Taylor Society itself—a disparate group of reformers and efficiency experts—began moving away from the emphasis on piece rates to interests in other aspects of management. By 1929, the society set forward as key components of scientific management four elements:

management research, management standards, management control, and cooperation (with labor). Piece rate systems were not listed (Taylor Society 1929, pp. 10-11).

Still another factor was an upsurge in awareness in the widespread restriction of output by workers, even in the face of time and motion analysis. Research in the early part of the century had focused on restrictions by *union* workers (U.S. Commissioner of Labor 1904). But the famous Mathewson study of the early 1930s found that nonunion workers, and even foremen, were involved in restrictions. Moreover, fear of unemployment—the major economic problem facing workers in the 1930s—played an important role in fostering restrictions (Mathewson [1931] 1969, pp. 53-54, 86).

Finally, the rise of a human relations approach to management led to a playing down of economic incentives. While not advocating abolition of piece rates, personnel experts in the 1920s began advocating techniques such as job design to make work more interesting rather than use of pay systems "to bribe the worker into drudgery by a money stake in the outcome" (Tead 1929, p. 242). Texts of the period emphasized techniques other than pay incentives for increasing productivity, such as "mental testing" to put people in the right jobs (Scott and Hayes 1921).

The Hawthorne experiments at Western Electric, which suggested the importance of the human factor in employee relations, received much attention in the 1930s and thereafter (Roethlisberger and Dickson 1939). As one textbook author put it, "the new theory suggests that it is the emotional factor in human beings which makes for the greatest variation in success and failure" (Shepard 1938, p. 217). Had not World War II intervened, the shift in climate against incentive rates might have continued uninterrupted.

World War II created two incentives for a renewed interest in piece rates. First, there was great pressure to increase military production. Even leftist unions which might have opposed incentives previously were willing to accept them after Germany attacked the Soviet Union. Second, the war-related labor shortage put upward pressure on wages. Because incentive rates can involve frequent re-timing and re-pricing of jobs, such rates were sometimes seen as a way of evading wartime wage controls (Wolf 1957, p. 68).

After the war, there was some uncertainty over whether wartime incentive systems would be retained. Advocates of such pay systems saw the postwar period as an opportunity to recoup the losses of the 1930s. Some of the unions, which had acceded to incentives during the war, found that the constant changing of rates led to unwanted grievances and frictions (Van Dusen 1945, p. 63). But data collected a decade-and-a-half after the war's end revealed no negative union influence on the incidence of simple incentives (McKersie, Miller, and Quarterman 1964).

The intellectual tilt against incentives continued with academics proclaiming that what was needed was a "new model, socioeconomic man to replace the discredited economic man who has held sway in the incentive systems most common in industry today" (Whyte 1955, p. 2). But practitioner-oriented advocates of incentives fought back. As one put it: "Anyone who believes incentive systems... are basically unfair to employees and serve management no good purpose needs to start his business education over again" (Toedt et al. 1962, p. 719). A loose consensus view seemed to emerge by the 1960s that incentives might be effective in some circumstances for some people, but that the surrounding atmosphere of employee relations was very important (Gellerman 1963).

In any case, at the end of World War II, perhaps two-thirds of U.S. factory workers were on time rates. But by the late 1950s and early 1960s, the proportion had increased to three-fourths. All indications are that the upward trend in time-based wages continued into the 1970s, not only for factory workers but others as well (Lewis 1960; Cox 1971; Carlson 1982).

At the all-occupation level, one factor behind the decline in piece rates and related pay systems—apart from union, management, and academic attitudes—is clearly the shift in job mix to white-collar employment and, generally, to jobs where output measurement is difficult. Within manufacturing, there has been a secular decline in the proportion of production workers in total payroll employment.[14] Since the drop in incentive usage appears to have occurred even for production workers within manufacturing, other influences must also be present. That is, it would be difficult to make a case that production worker jobs have so changed in the postwar period that it would be technically impossible for management to use simple incentives for a rising percentage of them.

Use of time-based pay does not necessarily imply that employee performance has no effect on pay. Employers may set standards, measure output, and use performance appraisal techniques, even if they do not choose to link pay mechanically to production. Good supervision, although at a cost, may be a rational, cost-effective substitute for simple incentives. Despite the best efforts of Frederick Taylor and his descendants, simple incentives still have costs in terms of administration, employee dissatisfaction and grievances, and output restriction. These costs must be weighed against alternative managerial methods.

For a long period after the 1930s, however, use of incentives potentially conflicted with an appealing social norm. The notion that jobs should provide steady, guaranteed incomes is at odds with systems linking pay to production, efficiency, or other measures of performance. New Deal policies were focused on providing or encouraging income security and guarantees. Later, these ideas were reflected in union demands for guaranteed annual wages (GAW) in the 1940s and 1950s.

Income security goals were not fully achieved by New Deal policies, such as minimum wages and unemployment insurance, nor by the supplemental unemployment benefits plans negotiated by some unions as an outgrowth of the GAW agitation. However, such policies and programs did shift the climate of thinking about what kind of wage system was appropriate for a "progressive" employer to provide. There is evidence, for example, that increased wage rigidity developed in the post-World War II period, linked to these concepts (Mitchell 1985b, 1985c). Good employers were not supposed to vary the wage in response to labor demand or business conditions, as had been common practice before the New Deal (Shister 1943, p. 542).

Finally, as indicated earlier, simple piece rates and incentives receive no special preferential tax treatment, unlike many other forms of compensation. Congress has diverted the attention of compensation specialists toward keeping pace with the latest wrinkles in the tax code, and to complying with numerous regulatory requirements. Pensions, health insurance, and savings arrangements are thus kept at the center of compensation policy. Tinkering with piece rates and incentives is no longer the chief focus of managers charged with determining pay.

Performance Appraisal and Merit Plans as an Alternative to Simple Incentive Plans

Despite problems with the implementation of incentive pay plans, industrial psychologists continued to emphasize the beneficial effects of tying pay to performance (Campbell, Dunnette, Lawler, and Wieck 1970; Lawler 1981; Pinder 1984). They have warned that any increase in pay not related to performance would reward good and mediocre performers alike. As a result, the good performers might either leave the firm or restrict performance. In addition, attitude surveys of managers and white-collar workers have long indicated that these groups strongly believe pay and performance should be linked (Dyer, Schwab, and Theriault 1976; Opinion Research Corporation 1949).

Thus, psychologist warnings, combined with managerial and employee attitudes and the difficulty of developing performance standards for many workers, may have led many employers to develop performance appraisal and merit systems as alternatives to simple incentives. Recent surveys relating to salaried employees indicate that 57-72 percent of U.S. employers claim to use merit systems alone as a basis for pay increases. Another 20-28 percent report using merit in combination with across-the-board pay adjustments (Administrative Management Society 1984, p. 3; Wyatt Co. 1988).

There is a divergence in the use of merit across occupational groups, however. A 1980 survey of merit system use found that 80-90 percent of white-collar workers were covered by such systems. But for plant and service workers, the proportions were lower: 60 percent for nonunion workers and 16 percent for union workers (Bureau of National Affairs 1981, pp. 10, 13). The prevalence of the discretionary merit approach for salaried white-collar workers may have helped foster the declining use of simple incentives for production workers.[15]

Most employee performance appraisals link pay increases to relatively subjective performance indicators. The most common form requires an employee's supervisor to rank each of his or her subordinates as outstanding, good, satisfactory, or unsatisfactory on vaguely defined work dimensions (Laud 1984). The budgeted merit pay pool is then allocated to employees based on their performance ratings. Merit pay decisions are typically made annually, even if not all employees are eligible for merit awards.

The merit system is not flexible in the sense defined earlier because overall employee performance may not affect the size of the merit pool.[16] Generally, the merit pool is not linked by any formula to the firm's economic condition. Also, merit pay increases are added to base pay just as any across-the-board pay increase would be; they are "flexible" only in the determination of *which* workers benefit the most, but in the aggregate do not reduce wage rigidity. Indeed, there is evidence that both supervisors and their subordinates view merit increases in much the same way as general "cost of living" increases (Haire, Ghiselli, and Gorden 1967; Lawler 1971; Pearce 1986).

Performance appraisal and merit systems have also been associated with perverse incentives similar to those associated with simple incentive systems. Pearce (1986) found that supervisors try to "beat the system" by giving all subordinates a merit increase no matter what their performance. This behavior extends to giving promotions in order to assure that everyone receives an increase. Other studies have shown that even when supervisors do distinguish among performers, those employees who receive low performance ratings and merit pay increases do not subsequently improve their performance. These results persist despite improvements in the performance appraisal system and training for supervisors (Pearce, Stevenson, and Perry 1985).

However, there are those who argue that in some organizations—especially where work interdependencies and culture make it difficult to define individual performance standards objectively—merit systems can have positive incentive effects (Kopelman and Reinharth 1982). They argue that judgmental merit pay systems provide a tangible source of positive feedback that, at a minimum, helps to encourage and retain top performers. In short, there is a trade-off between a subjective merit approach and simple incentives and the evidence suggests a long-term decline in the use of simple incentives. Merit and/or other motivational tools have apparently been found the more cost-effective and administratively efficient device by a growing proportion of employers over the long haul.

Profit Sharing

It is pointless to attempt to pinpoint the first profit sharing plan in the United States. Some researchers have claimed to find examples as far back as the eighteenth century (Jeuck 1949; National Industrial Conference Board 1934). Others put the date later, and suggest the origins of profit sharing lie in Europe (Cooper 1934). However, profit sharing as a notable form of compensation in modern corporations dates from the late nineteenth century in the U.S. context (Metzger 1975, 1978). As already noted, some advocates of profit sharing in the nineteenth century tended to see it as a way to reduce social tensions arising from the employment relationship; others saw it as a type of incentive pay.

One of the difficulties with studying profit sharing is that the term has historically been used loosely. For example, Henry Ford's famous $5-a-day plan was essentially a wage premium for workers who had been with the firm for at least 6 months and who met company standards of thrift and morality. The Ford premium was unrelated to profits; yet it was termed "profit sharing" at the time (Emmet 1917, pp. 94-122).

This tradition of vague and misleading nomenclature continues up to the present time. For example, a 1986 union-management contract in the shipbuilding industry included what the parties described as "profit sharing" bonuses. Yet the bonuses were guaranteed regardless of profitability (Bureau of National Affairs, Inc. 1986b). More generally, employers have been prone to designate various forms of tax-deferred savings arrangements as profit sharing, even if no formula links the employer contribution to company profits.

The Early Twentieth Century

Profit sharing was considered a sufficiently important phenomenon early in this century to be the subject of a BLS survey conducted in 1916. According to the survey's introduction, profit sharing arrangements were seen by advocates at the time as "the permanent solution to the so-called labor problem" and a way of "fostering the development of a larger spirit of harmony" (Emmet 1917, p. 5). Religious views influenced the establishment of some plans (U.S. Bureau of Labor Statistics 1920).

In the background of this interest in profit sharing was a general concern about labor unrest and about the growth of unionization during the World War I period. Union leaders during this period had uniformly negative views about profit sharing, which they perceived as primarily an anti-union tool of management (National Civic Federation 1920, pp. 368-381). Proponents of profit sharing argued—in part to counter such attitudes—that proper profit sharing plans should always include payment of the going wage, so that the share bonus would be clearly perceived by the workers as something extra, a kind of gravy on top of the expected level of pay (Burritt et al. 1918, pp. 8, 83-84). It might be noted that this gravy approach—which is still often advocated—would tend to defeat the Weitzman effect, which depends in part on a lowering of the base wage.

While proponents of profit sharing had strong views concerning the socially beneficial effects of their idea, public policy in the early twentieth century did not favor its implementation. The BLS study noted that profit sharing bonuses were viewed legally as "mere gratuities" given by the employer to workers, and were, therefore, not deductible from corporate income taxes as a business expense (Emmet 1917, p. 6). Given this disadvantageous treatment, it is hardly surprising that profit sharing was not extensively used in 1916.

BLS found only 60 plans to study; some of which—as in the case of the Ford program—were not really profit sharing at all. The earliest plan included in the 1916 report dated from 1886, but over three-fourths of the plans listed were no more than a decade old. This finding suggests, therefore, that a minority of employers during this early period felt a need to experiment with their personnel practices. Those employers were open to consideration of financial participation by employees in their companies. Although hard data are not available, there is some indication of a growing interest in profit sharing by employers during the 1920s, although clear differentiation between profit sharing and worker stock ownership was not always made (Bloomfield 1923, p. 58).

There is a potential linkage between financial participation by workers and other forms of participation. Although most company unions and employee representation plans were established in the early New Deal period, some were created initially with government encouragement during the World War I era (Guzda 1984). Government policy aimed at ensuring a climate of friendly labor-management relations, and representation systems were seen as a progressive employment policy. In some cases, these plans had profit sharing elements attached (Mitchell 1985c). However, government interest in profit sharing was not triggered again until the late 1930s, another period of labor tensions and union growth.

The Great Depression Era: Labor and Management Attitudes

Not surprisingly, the Great Depression placed severe strains on profit sharing plans, many of which found themselves without profits to share. Some of the older plans may have provided a financial cushion for laid-off workers (U.S. Bureau of Labor Statistics 1932). But a National Industrial Conference Board study published in 1934 found that out of 134 surveyed plans, 48 were "suspended" and 6 had been discontinued. In one case, a plan had been terminated after a newly organized union struck to end the program's bonus system and substitute a fixed hourly wage. And even where plans were not discontinued, some firms took steps to limit employee eligibility for participation (Jeuck 1949, p. 158).

Responding to the BLS 1916 survey, employers gave profit sharing only a mixed review with regard to its ability to stimulate workforce efficiency.

However, during that era of high employee turnover, profit sharing plans—which often required that the employee remain on the payroll for a year before receiving a bonus—were credited with holding down turnover. Excessive quits were not a general problem during the Great Depression, and the Conference Board's 1934 report did not focus on reduced turnover as a positive effect of profit sharing. However, the report did find that employers of the period viewed profit sharing as having had only "indifferent success" in stimulating efficiency or improving morale (National Industrial Conference Board 1934, pp. 26-27).

As the economy began to recover in the 1930s, some revival of employer interest in profit sharing was also evidenced. For example, Westinghouse resumed a suspended plan in 1936 (National Industrial Conference Board 1937). At the same time, certain economists began to argue that there were macroeconomic benefits to be had from profit sharing, foreshadowing Weitzman's recent proposal. Political leaders again began to look to profit sharing as a way of dealing with labor-management tensions.

Union officials in the late 1930s, however, generally were not enthusiastic about such ideas. At Congressional hearings held in 1938, William Green, president of the American Federation of Labor (AFL), testified that while "labor is not opposed to principles involved in profit sharing" it was "opposed to the way in which it has developed and operated" (U.S. Senate 1939, pp. 104-109). He specifically cited the use of profit sharing as part of corporate strategies to form employee representation plans (company unions) which would substitute for independent unions. He also expressed concern about the manipulation of profit figures: "Labor cannot be asked to accept blindly management's decision on what constitutes profits. All of the facts must be available."

According to Green, profit sharing must be based on a "partnership" between labor and management with management acknowledging that, just as shareholders had invested financial capital, so workers had invested human capital ("experience and work ability"). His testimony represented an idealistic statement of what the collective bargaining relationship, in his view, should be. Were such a state of affairs to be brought about, benefits such as profit sharing would naturally follow. Absent that idyllic state, profit sharing was suspect and should not, Green argued, be the recipient of tax advantages.

John L. Lewis, president of the Congress of Industrial Organizations (CIO), made similar points, but in stronger language (U.S. Senate 1939, pp. 189-199). He argued that conventional collective bargaining could be used to share profits without a formal plan. A company that wanted to share profits "will have no difficulty at all under collective-bargaining practices in making the necessary adjustments of the wage structure..." But his testimony seemed to contradict this assertion, since the essence of profit sharing is its variable nature. Lewis argued that such variability rendered profit sharing "a delusionary snare" since workers needed stable incomes.

In some respects, management may have been more put off by the "moderate" remarks of the AFL's Green than by Lewis' more strident tone. The chairman of General Motors, Alfred P. Sloan, Jr., noted with concern Green's argument that financial participation through profit sharing was necessarily associated with worker and union participation in management. Such managerial participation, according to Sloan, "would be very objectionable and ... quite dangerous..." (U.S. Senate 1939, p. 475).

The union viewpoint expressed to Congress was not just a product of the 1930s. As noted above, it had in fact been the prevailing AFL view since the nineteenth century, in contrast to those of the more utopian Knights of Labor (Kruger and Bearup 1986). After the 1930s, the "management rights" movement—foreshadowed by Sloan's remarks—and management resistance to union restrictions on long-standing prerogatives, dampened the participative elements that might have gone along with widespread profit sharing (Jacoby 1985b). Some unions—notably the Auto Workers—did make profit sharing proposals to employers in the post-World War II period. But such proposals served to frighten the management community; unions who talked of profit sharing seemed to be threatening the returns to capital investment (Thompson 1949, pp. 38-42). In the 1950s, continued proposals by Auto Workers' president Walter Reuther that profits be shared between worker, consumer, and stockholder produced angry responses from business representatives (Chamber of Commerce 1958). Not surprisingly, given this history, when the Auto Workers finally negotiated a profit sharing plan with American Motors in the early 1960s, it received substantial attention as a possible new wave of collective bargaining (Jehring, Howell, and Tripp 1962).

The American Motors experiment with profit sharing of the early 1960s really foreshadowed the profit sharing negotiated in autos and elsewhere as part of the concession bargaining of the 1980s. It provided an element of flexible pay to a marginal firm. In any case, until the 1980s, profit sharing remained a negligible element of compensation in the union sector. For example, a 1978 survey of major union contracts found profit sharing was referenced in less than 2 percent of the contracts studied and that it covered less than 1 percent of the workers in the sample (U.S. Bureau of Labor Statistics 1980, p. 42).

Economists and Profit Sharing in the 1930s

A key debate among American economists in the 1930s concerned the role of wage rate determination in causing, exacerbating, or curing the Depression. Two competing theories initially existed. Orthodox economic analysis suggested that unemployment was a sign of oversupply in the labor market. As in the case of any market, so this view went, the price (or in this case, the wage) should be reduced to alleviate excess supply. An opposing view, held by many New Deal officials and some prominent economists, was that *raising* wages was the appropriate Depression remedy. According to this argument, higher wages would mean higher consumption and more demand.

By the late 1930s, Keynesian views, which downplayed manipulating wages as a way of reducing unemployment, added to the confusing stew of economic ideas in the United States (Mitchell 1986b). Still, it appears that a majority of economists believed that economic conditions of the period were being worsened by wage rigidity (Slichter 1934, pp. 139-142). This view, in turn, suggested that profit sharing bonuses—which would tend to fluctuate with business cycle conditions—might add a kind of *ersatz* flexibility to the wage setting system (King 1941, pp. 324-330b). That is, profit sharing was proposed as a route to improved macroeconomic performance.

Political Leaders and Public Policy in the 1930s and After

As already noted, the prevailing thrust of New Deal policy was that income stability was desirable, that minimum "decent" incomes should be provided, and that to the extent that wages were considered as a tool of economic policy, they should be pushed up. This latter objective was initially to be accomplished through NIRA codes; when that route became unavailable, the objective was pursued by encouraging unions and collective bargaining (Mitchell 1986a).

However, the 1930s were marked by industrial unrest as new unions formed, old ones expanded, and employers resisted union encroachment and demands. The old idea was revived that profit sharing might be a means of reconciling labor and capital. In addition, given the limited scope of pension plans then prevailing, and given the search by some in Congress for private alternatives to expanding Social Security, use of profit sharing programs as retirement vehicles seemed attractive.

As a result, a Senate subcommittee recommended favorable tax treatment for retirement-related profit sharing in 1939 (U.S. Senate 1939). The recommendation led to tax code changes which, in broad terms, are still applicable. Employers were permitted to deduct contributions to profit sharing plans (within limits) as business expenses from profits in calculating corporate income tax liability. Payments into profit sharing trust funds were not taxable to the employee until they were actually received (e.g., as benefits received after retirement).

Union Wage Concessions and Profit Sharing in the 1980s

During the 1980s, union attitudes toward profit sharing shifted in a more favorable direction, although under conditions of duress. Official representatives of organized labor still questioned whether pay variability under profit sharing was desirable from the viewpoint of the individual worker or the economy. But at the same time there was recognition that profit sharing could be useful in some circumstances to recoup wages lost in concession bargaining (Oswald 1986; Zalusky 1987). These views are not surprising because in a number of prominent bargaining situations, profit sharing plans were introduced as a quid pro quo for wage and benefit concessions on the part of the union. Mitchell estimated that the number of union workers covered by profit sharing plans negotiated as part of wage concessions stood at 500,000-600,000 as of mid-1985 (Mitchell 1985a, p. 594). The bulk of these workers were at General Motors and Ford, pursuant to concession agreements made in 1982.

If concessions are defined as first-year wage freezes or cuts, the concession movement can be dated as beginning in 1981. However, it was not until 1982 that a substantial proportion of negotiated outcomes fell into the concession classification. In that year, 6 percent of concession contracts contained profit sharing. The proportion varied in subsequent years, but averaged 5 percent during the entire 1981-1987 period.[17] Apart from the automobile cases, profit sharing has figured prominently in a number of concession bargains in the steel and lumber industries.

Perhaps more significant has been the spread of profit sharing in nonconcession agreements. A number of such contracts were negotiated in the telephone communications industry in 1986. Moreover, in the automobile industry, profit sharing was retained in negotiations which produced wage and benefit increases after 1982. Both union and management seemed to see profit sharing as a component of the income security arrangements which were negotiated for senior workers in the 1982 contracts (and which were extended in subsequent negotiations). Profit sharing represented a substitution of labor cost flexibility for employment flexibility.

In the automobile industry, profit sharing developed in relation to job and income security innovations. It is also possible that, over time, a profit sharing element could arise from the lump sum bonus plans which became a major feature of U.S. collective bargaining in the mid-1980s. Under these programs, workers receive a fixed bonus—often either a flat amount or an amount proportionate to earnings—rather than a wage rate increase. During 1987, for example, about one-fourth of the new union settlements included lump sums (Bureau of National Affairs 1988, p. B3).

If lump sums become standard practice in union contracts, they might take on a variable element related to profitability along the lines of the Japanese bonus system. At this point, however, no such development has occurred. Even conventional profit sharing's hold in the union sector remains tenuous. It is doubtful that the proportion of private sector union workers under *major* contracts (agreements covering 1,000 or more workers) with profit sharing exceeds one-tenth. For all private contracts (major and minor), the proportion would be significantly lower.

Tax and Regulatory Incentives

When Congress permitted employers to deduct profit sharing contributions as business expenses originally, it was simply removing the earlier disadvantage placed on profit sharing by the tax code. The favorable treatment of profit sharing in the tax code comes not from the employer deduction, but from the exemption of *deferred* contributions from the current tax liabilities of employees. Put another way, profit sharing plans that pay current cash bonuses receive no net stimulus from the tax code; tax advantages accrue only to deferred plans.

It is again important to point out that profit sharing plans that do provide for deferred benefits—while they obtain a net tax subsidy—are receiving no more favorable tax treatment than are other deferred retirement programs. Qualified pension plans, for example, also are permitted deductibility of employer payments to the associated trust fund. There is no tax liability to the employee accruing from current employer pension contributions. Moreover, because the issue of whether the employer or employee makes the contribution to a savings arrangement is a legal distinction—not an economic one—plans such as 401(k)s and Individual Retirement Accounts (IRAs) essentially receive the same benefits as deferred profit sharing. Under such plans, the employee places pre-tax income in a fund designated primarily for retirement.

Thus, the tax subsidy by itself, while favoring employment-related savings plans, does not favor deferred profit sharing among the various alternatives. However, there are some regulatory aspects of alternative savings plans that may tilt employers toward profit sharing. Requirements that the plan maintain a balanced investment portfolio, for example, do not apply to profit sharing trust funds, which may invest their assets in the stock of the employer. Moreover, the rules concerning employer contributions give the firm more flexibility with regard to the timing and magnitude of such payments.

Gain Sharing

As in the case of profit sharing, it is impossible to determine when gain sharing was invented. One study attributes the concept to the ancient Romans (Ross and Hauck 1984, p. 9). Histories of modern gain sharing in the United States typically begin with the first Scanlon Plan in the 1930s (Lesieur 1958). The Scanlon Plan was named after a Steelworkers union official who developed an innovative plan in the 1930s to rescue a failing employer. Scanlon's system involved both a financial sharing arrangement and encouragement of worker participation in raising productivity and cutting costs. As noted above, the idea of a group bonus related to productivity and/or labor cost or time savings certainly could be found in American industry by the late nineteenth century, although without the participative element.

Despite a few exceptions, before the 1930s employers generally felt that rewards for productivity or savings should be at the individual—rather than at the group—level. Those firms that did have group bonuses argued that their plans induced an esprit de corps or that peer pressure was put on slackers to improve performance (National Industrial Conference Board 1930, pp. 116-118). But prevailing opinion had it that such systems might inadvertently reward slackers, whose shirking could be hidden by overall group effort. Thus, group bonuses were to be used only in situations when individual effort could not be discerned (i.e., in cases of true team production). They were basically simple incentive systems in situations where the incentive could not be aimed at the individual for technical reasons.

As will be seen from the section on plan usage (below), it is not at all clear that this viewpoint has substantially changed. Sometimes the term "gain sharing" is used loosely to cover programs such as profit sharing, or any bonuses awarded on a group basis, or virtually any management system that emphasizes and links teamwork, cooperation, and rewards (Ross and Ross 1984; Profit Sharing Research Foundation 1984). But if gain sharing plans are defined narrowly, that is, as Scanlon, Rucker, Improshare, or similar arrangements, their incidence in the workforce is extremely rare. Thus, the history of gain sharing in the United States is one of much discussion, but little implementation.

Perhaps the most widely publicized gain sharing program was the Kaiser Steel Long Range Sharing Program established in 1963. The program was an outgrowth of a major strike in the steel industry in 1959 and the general automation scare of the early 1960s. During this period, there was concern that workers would resist productivity improvements if job loss resulted. Hence, the Long Range Sharing Program was surrounded by provisions regarding job security in cases of potential technological displacement. It provided bonuses linked to productivity-based cost savings (estimated by complex formulas), and was compared with the Scanlon Plan in contemporary accounts (U.S. Bureau of Labor Statistics 1963).

Despite the initial hoopla at the time of its creation, the Kaiser program slowly faded from public consciousness; economic pressures eventually killed it. Its job security arrangements could not have handled the demand declines experienced by the steel industry in the 1980s, and could not have protected workers from them. Perhaps the greatest lesson from the Kaiser experience relates not to the plan itself, but to a failing of academics and journalists.

Gain sharing (and other innovative programs) are widely discussed when they are implemented. Often, the resulting literature has been disproportionately written by advocates. Successes have invited continued attention; failures seem to disappear without analysis. Calls for follow-up studies (e.g., Schuster 1984, pp. 223-224) are well taken, but seldom heeded. Part of the problem is the small number of examples to study.

Employee Stock Ownership Plans

The notion that workers should own part or all of the enterprises which employ them is quite old. We have already cited the interest of nineteenth century authors in the concept, as well as their doubts about its viability. Various utopian and cooperative schemes from that period to the present have been based on the concept that worker ownership is inherently to be desired (Mitchell and Thompson 1986). However, with the important exception of small family owned and operated businesses and farms, such arrangements have always been extremely rare in the United States.

Modern corporations have been known to encourage and/or subsidize purchase of their stock by ordinary employees since at least the 1920s (National Industrial Conference Board 1928). Although not phrased in this way by practitioner/proponents, there is an assumption, noted earlier, that owner-principals and worker-agents will share a common interest by virtue of stock ownership. Literary proponents of worker stock ownership are more likely to link worker participation in management than are the companies (certainly those of the 1920s) who foster share ownership schemes.

Of course, employees of publicly traded firms can always buy shares in them as individuals, regardless of whether they are encouraged to do so. However, during the 1970s, public policy—expressed in the tax code—began to tilt toward ESOPs as the preferred arrangement of employee ownership.

Arguments for ESOPs have been made at two levels. First, there is a broad social question about the distribution of wealth. Louis Kelso, who is often viewed as the father of the modern ESOP, stressed this aspect in co-authored books written in the 1950s and 1960s (Kelso and Adler 1958; Kelso and Hetter 1968). However, once the tax code became more favorable to implementation of ESOPs, a second idea—one designed to appeal to managers—began to be stressed. Arguments were made that ESOPs would stimulate productivity, cooperation, and, ultimately, profitability.

It is doubtful that Congress would have provided the tax subsidies to ESOPs without the intervention of Senator Russell B. Long, chair of the Committee on Finance until his retirement at the end of the 1986 session. Kelso's notion of spreading wealth appealed to Long, whose father—the legendary Huey Long—led a "share the wealth" movement in the 1930s. However, it is noteworthy that the heavy tax subsidy to PAYSOP plans,[18] an offshoot of ESOPs, was not extended by the tax code modifications of 1986 (see below). Although the tax subsidies to basic ESOPs were continued, their long-term future without a well-placed Congressional patron is uncertain.

Tax History

The first general tax law change applied to ESOPs was enacted in 1974. ESOPs became recognized as qualified benefit plans. This recognition meant that employer contributions to ESOPs were tax-deductible business expenses to the firm, but were not currently taxable to employees. It was often argued that the 1974 law made leveraged ESOPs especially attractive to firms in need of financing. Firms could borrow through the ESOP, issue stock to the ESOP's trust fund in the amount of the loan, and then deduct payment of principal as well as interest. The deductibility of principal—not permitted under conventional financing—was touted by advocates of ESOPs as a major tax break (U.S. Senate, Committee on Finance 1980, pp. 18-23).

However, it is unclear that a real tax break was involved, *if the employer's contribution of stock was appropriately valued.* The repayment of loan principal was supposed to be matched by an equivalent contribution of stock to the ESOP. Thus, the borrowing firm should have incurred a real business expense, equal in value to the principal. A neutral tax code ought to have recognized business expenses for employee compensation of all types, whether wages, benefits, contributions of stock, or Thanksgiving turkeys. Because the 1974 tax code change did no more than that (Federal Reserve Bank of Atlanta 1983, p. 26), it at best removed discrimination *against* ESOPs.

Nevertheless, there was a jump in basic leveraged and leverageable ESOP formation immediately after the 1974 tax changes. A report by the U.S. General Accounting Office (GAO) has linked this activity to the new law (U.S. General Accounting Office 1986a, p. 10). If there was no net tax subsidy, why should such a jump have occurred? Still another GAO report suggested the answer.

For closely held companies, a problem arises concerning the valuation of stock issued to the ESOP. Put bluntly, the tax code creates a temptation to overvalue the contributed stock. Overvalued stock contributions can, of course, create a net tax subsidy where none was intended by Congress to exist. Such overvaluation has been a problem according to GAO. In addition, the GAO report found that voting rights of the shares were often retained by the employer, thus permitting continued control of the firm in the hands of the original owners (U.S. General Accounting Office 1980).

Although the initial tax changes may not have amounted to a true tax subsidy, after 1974 a series of more favorable tax treatments of ESOPs and related plans were enacted. Each new tax bill seemed to contain an ESOP-subsidizing provision. For example, when Congress adopted investment tax credits to stimulate the economy in the 1970s, additional credits were given to firms that created tax-credit ESOPs (then known as TRASOPs) (Marsh and McAllister 1981). Of course, only firms that were undertaking eligible investment projects could benefit from a TRASOP. Thus, a search was begun for a more general form of tax-credit ESOP. Congress' search ended in 1983 with the creation of the PAYSOP to supersede previous tax-credit ESOPs.

Under a PAYSOP, the employer received a tax *credit* for stock contributions (rather than just a deduction), effectively making the U.S. Treasury the contributor. PAYSOP contributions were not linked to investment projects;

any private employer could make them. The tax credit effect was amplified by the exemption of the employee from current taxation on the contribution. Thus, the effective tax subsidy exceeded 100 percent (U.S. Office of Management and Budget 1986, pp. 629-630). Not surprisingly, when Congress looked for tax loopholes to close in 1986, the PAYSOP tax subsidy was permitted to expire.

The use of basic leveraged ESOPs as a financial tool received a substantial boost from the tax code in 1984. Banks and other institutions lending to a firm through an ESOP were permitted to deduct one-half of their interest income on such loans from taxation. As a result, lower interest rates are currently available to ESOP-related borrowers than to conventional borrowers.

Employee Buyouts and Concessions

About one-third the firms reporting to the ESOP Association's 1987 survey were more than 50 percent owned by their ESOPs (ESOP Association 1988). This proportion is undoubtedly substantially exaggerated—relative to all ESOPs—by the fact of membership in the association. An earlier GAO study, for example, found that only about one-third of ESOPs (excluding tax-credit ESOPs) had as much as 25 percent ownership in their sponsoring firms (U.S. General Accounting Office 1986a, p. 39). Thus, most ESOPs do not involve either worker control or control on behalf of workers. However, because of the economic dislocations of the 1980s, instances of employee buyouts of firms through ESOPs have received substantial attention in the United States (Wintner 1983).

When ESOPs are used to save a plant or a company from a planned shutdown, the restructured enterprise is obviously starting from an economic disadvantage. Because it was failing under conventional ownership, the risk of failure under an ESOP must also be high. Indeed, some firms, such as Hyatt Clark (a former General Motors parts plant) and Rath Packing were not saved by ESOP takeovers and went bankrupt.

In contrast to most other instances of ESOP failure, the Rath case has been extensively documented (Hammer and Stern 1986). It appears, based on that case, that in the face of severe economic distress, the motivation for continued union cooperation can be weakened, and a noble experiment can easily turn to ruin. The Rath purchase by the workers involved a company on the verge of failure which negotiated both an ESOP buyout and a system of worker representation on the company board in the late 1970s. Eventually, a former union president became the firm's CEO. Despite the cooperative trappings, however, the road to bankruptcy involved strikes, hiring of replacement workers (by the former union president!), and a struggle for control of the company by union representatives on the board. Rath closed about five years after the buyout occurred.

ESOPs and Wage Concessions

Even in apparently successful cases of ESOP/worker takeovers, such as Weirton Steel, wage and benefit reductions were a major element of the rescue package (Greenhouse 1985). A variety of worker involvement and participation devices are part of the personnel program of the new company. Weirton was characterized in 1987 as "the best-known success story of employee ownership" (Bureau of National Affairs 1987, p. 73).

Many factors in the Weirton case were favorable to a successful buyout. The Weirton purchase involved an independent union representing workers at a former plant of National Steel; as such, the union did not have to consider the effect of keeping the company afloat on other firms in the industry. A great deal of community support was also available. From National Steel's viewpoint, a plant closure would have been expensive because of pension obligations; thus, National Steel had a strong incentive to facilitate the ESOP takeover. The financial package for the buyout left Weirton in debt to National Steel with obligations coming due in the 1990s. Whether Weirton remains a success story will depend importantly on how it deals with those obligations.

Apart from the few cases such as Weirton that involve 100 percent worker ownership, ESOPs involving minority ownership have been included in several union wage concession negotiations in the 1980s. Such ESOPs have been used in the deregulated trucking and airline industries (Rosen 1985). Some resistance by union dissidents to ESOP/concession deals has been reported (Bureau of National Affairs, Inc. 1985). But generally, unions in the 1980s took a pragmatic view of ESOPs in the context of the economic problems they faced (Olson 1982). Management pressure for wage concessions was not welcomed by unions, but worker receipt of some ownership in the firm through an ESOP lessened the blow.

Employer Buyouts

ESOPs have also been used by corporate management in the 1980s to fend off unfriendly mergers and takeovers by other firms and investors. The tax subsidy available to borrowing through ESOPs can make them a useful tool to the incumbent management in a leveraged purchase of the firm. With sufficient stock in the hands of the ESOP, the unwanted raider is effectively rebuffed. However, apart from external borrowing, there have been instances in which pension fund assets have been diverted into ESOPs to accomplish leveraged buyouts (*Business Week* 1984, 1986). Such uses of ESOPs have made proponents of these plans uncomfortable; buyouts may spread the use of ESOPs but also raise questions in the public and Congressional mind about the desirability of the ESOP tax subsidy (Rosen and Caudell-Feagan 1984).

DATA ON CURRENT USAGE OF FLEXIBLE PAY PLANS

Historical examination of flexible pay plans (above) has indicated that no systematic effort has been made by researchers to trace the various types of plans or their use in different employment settings. Differences in plan definitions and in survey samples made it difficult to compare or summarize the information that was available. This problem is still present for studies of contemporary plan usage. A recent investigation by the authors concerning the incidence of alternative pay plans turned up only one survey providing detail on the number and characteristics of employers and employees involved in several types of flexible pay plans. This survey was recently completed by the American Productivity Center (O'Dell 1986; O'Dell and McAdams 1987), and covers member firms of the American Compensation Association.

As an illustration of what current sources of information are available, Table 2 briefly summarizes information from the American Productivity Center survey and four other major surveys covering flexible pay plans. Undoubtedly, there are other specialized surveys taken by trade associations, compensation consultants, and so forth for their own use or the use of their clients. But based on the limited *published* data, the following conclusions about pay plan usage can be reached.

Simple incentive plans are still used with some frequency, especially in the manufacturing sector. In 1984, some 17 percent of manufacturing, as opposed to 8 percent of nonmanufacturing firms reported using incentive plans (Bureau of National Affairs, Inc. 1984). Among manufacturing firms, such plans are still most common in situations where output can be easily measured (e.g., textile, apparel, basic steel). Where production workers in these firms are unionized, roughly 29 percent of their contracts included wage incentive provisions, according to a 1986 survey.[19] Nevertheless, simple incentive plans have declined in popularity over the long run and in recent years. The BLS (Carlson 1982) reports that the proportion of manufacturing production workers covered by such plans dropped from 30 percent in 1947 to 18 percent in 1980. Hourly rates are by far the more common pay method.

Gain sharing plans (as narrowly defined in a preceding section) appear to be so rarely used that they might be regarded as curiosities (Hewitt Associates 1986; Bureau of National Affairs, Inc. 1984; U.S. General Accounting Office 1986). GAO estimates that there are between 500-1,000 plans currently installed. The American Productivity Center survey (O'Dell and McAdams 1987)—using a definition of gain sharing that includes some unit level profit sharing—still reports that only about 13 percent of their sample reported using these plans.[20] There are no comparable data on the use of gain sharing plans by type of employer or on coverage for different types of employees, although the GAO report indicates that the plans are more likely to be found in manufacturing than elsewhere.

Table 2.   Flexible Compensation Plans: Major Data Sources

---

1. Bureau of National Affairs, Inc., *Basic Patterns in Union Contracts* (1986a). Survey of 400 union contracts in mid-1980s. Reports that about 29 percent of the contracts have simple incentives, concentrated in manufacturing.

2. Bureau of National Affairs, Inc., *Productivity Improvement Programs* (1984). Survey of 195 employers. 19 percent had profit sharing, 18 percent had employee stock ownership (no distinction between ordinary ESOPs and tax-credit ESOPs), 1 percent had Scanlon, 1 percent had Improshare, 40 percent had performance bonuses (merit), 10 percent have piecework plans.

3. U.S. General Accounting Office, *Employee Stock Ownership Plans* (1986a and 1986b). Special survey of 4,200 ESOPs and tax-credit ESOPs based on Internal Revenue Service reports. Plans covered 7 million workers as of 1983. 90 percent of these workers were under tax-credit ESOPs.

4. U.S. Bureau of Labor Statistics, *Employee Benefits in Medium and Large Firms, 1986* (1987). Survey of 1,308 establishments in a sample representing 24.1 million workers. In 1986, 22 percent of workers covered by the survey had profit sharing, 2 percent had ESOPs, and 28 percent had tax-credit ESOPs.

5. O'Dell and McAdams, *People, Peformance and Pay* (1987). Special survey of 1,598 firms in 1986. 32 percent had profit sharing, 13 percent had gain sharing (including certain types of profit sharing), 14 percent had small group incentives.

Note: Complete references appear in reference section.

Profit sharing plans cover no more than one-fifth of private sector employees (U.S. Bureau of Labor Statistics 1987). Most of these plans are deferred. Hewitt Associates (1986) estimate that only 4 percent of the private sector firms in their survey offered cash-based profit sharing plans. Overall, these statistics indicate that profit sharing coverage is not at a level high enough to meet the Weitzman proposal.

Finally, data on ESOPs can be misleading. The U.S. GAO (1986a, p. 19) estimated that as many as 90 percent of the workers covered by these plans in 1983 were under tax-credit ESOPs, not ordinary ESOPs. BLS data suggest a still-higher proportion of ESOP-covered workers were under tax-credit ESOPs at medium- and large-sized firms in 1986 (U.S. Bureau of Labor Statistics 1987, p. 81). With the 1986 end to tax subsidy for tax-credit ESOPs, it is difficult to predict whether the use of other ESOPs will grow. However, some survey data to be presented below suggest that firms that had tax-credit ESOPs were more likely to have ordinary ESOPs as well. Thus, discontinuing the former could conceivably reduce the frequency of the latter.

The limitations of these data on plan use certainly underscore the need for consistent definitions of plans and systematic tracking of the adoption and discontinuance of different types of plans. Also of interest would be information on the characteristics of employers using particular plans and the types of employees covered. Detailed information on plan effectiveness and cost is also needed (as the next section makes clear). The development of such data bases, especially over time, is beyond the resources of any individual researcher. Yet, without them it will be difficult, if not impossible, to undertake research regarding public policy on flexible pay.

DATA ON ATTITUDES TOWARD FLEXIBLE PAY PLANS AND THEIR EFFECTS

Research literature tracing the actual effects of different types of flexible pay plans on workforce measures such as productivity, cooperation, commitment or loyalty, and labor costs is dominated by qualitative case studies. There is little research which traces the effectiveness of a single plan across several firms using common workforce measures and virtually none which compares the effectiveness of two or more plans.[21] The reason for this lack of systematic evaluation is not difficult to find. BNA (1984) reports that less than 6 percent of the firms using different types of flexible pay plans attempt any sort of objective evaluation of plan effectiveness. Hence, researchers who question managers must of necessity rely on respondent impressions.

Table 3 presents selected resources that summarize the research on the effectiveness of the different types of flexible pay plans. Although limited by the data, four conclusions can be reached. First, there are no recent data on the effectiveness of simple incentive plans. Earlier lab and field studies (Campbell and Pritchard 1976) indicate that the plans do increase productivity in work settings where output can be easily measured. However, the decline in the use of these plans since 1960 indicates disenchantment with their ability to increase worker productivity without undesirable side effects (such as poor labor-management relations, administrative overloads, and negative work norms). These side effects have long been well documented (Roethlisberger and Dickson 1939; Whyte 1955; Yukl, Latham, and Pursell 1976).

Second, both U.S. GAO (1981) and Hewitt Associates (1985) report case studies in which the implementation of gain sharing plans resulted in cost savings averaging 16 percent (ranging from 8-77 percent). Plans that have been in effect more than five years yielded higher cost savings. GAO also reported that 80 percent of the firms interviewed felt that gain sharing had improved labor-management relations, one-half felt that grievances had been reduced, and one-third felt that turnover and absenteeism had been reduced. White's (1979) review of Scanlon plans indicated that "success" (whether or not the plan had been retained and attitudes toward the plan) was highly correlated with employees' participation in decision making and the length of time the plan had been in effect.

Table 3. Flexible Compensation Plans: Selected Evaluation Studies

1. Lawler, *Motivation in Work Organizations* (1973). Summarizes many field studies on individual and group incentives in chapter 6.

2. Campbell and Pritchard, "Motivation Theory in Industrial and Organizational Psychology" (1976). Summary of lab and field studies of simple incentive plans.

3. White, "The Scanlon Plan: Causes and Correlates of Success" (1979). Summary of 40 studies (case and empirical) of Scanlon Plan implementations.

4. Bullock and Lawler, "Gainsharing: A Few Questions, and Fewer Answers" (1984). Review of 33 case studies of gain sharing plans. Proposes factors influencing successful gain sharing outcomes.

5. Schuster, *Union-Management Cooperation: Structure, Process and Impact* (1984). Chapter 4 analyzes qualitative data from many case studies of gain sharing plans.

6. Profit Sharing Council of America, *Profit Sharing: Philosophy, Practices and Benefits to Society* (1984). Summarizes the results of both case and empirical studies on profit sharing.

7. U.S. General Accounting Office, *Employee Stock Ownership Plans* (1986a, 1986b, 1987). Summarizes evidence on the effectiveness of ESOPs in meeting Congressional objectives: productivity, corporate financing, and distribution of corporate wealth. ESOPs found generally to be ineffective in raising productivity or profitability. Some evidence found that a combination of worker participation and an ESOP raises productivity.

8. Marsh and McAllister, "ESOPs Tables: A Survey of Companies with Employee Stock Ownership Plans" (1981). Survey of 165 firms using ESOPs; covers both attitudes and some productivity measures.

9. Whyte, Hammer, Meek, Nelson, and Stern, *Worker Participation and Ownership* (1983). Summary of evidence from case and empirical studies on firms using ESOPs as a vehicle for worker ownership (particularly the chapter by Hammer and Stern).

Note: Complete references appear in reference section.

Bullock and Lawler (1984), in a review of 33 case studies of gain sharing, propose a number of plan design and implementation factors as well as organization conditions that could influence gain sharing success in organizations. Design factors include the formal mechanisms developed for encouraging employee participation in work decisions, the types of performance measures used, the frequency of plan payout, and so forth. Implementation factors include employee attitudes toward the plan, whether consultants are used in establishing the program, and its performance focus (productivity, better labor-management relations, and so forth). Conditions that might influence gain sharing success include organization size and technology, unionization, and management style. However, Bullock and Lawler conclude that the evidence did not allow them to draw any conclusions about which plans are most effective in meeting different types of performance objectives, nor about how organization conditions would interact with design and implementation factors.

Third, like simple incentive and gain-sharing plans, the effectiveness of profit sharing is rarely evaluated. Some firms seem to favor profit sharing plans because their dependence on bottom line statistics that are routinely collected makes administration relatively simple (Hewitt Associates 1985). BNA (1984) reports that profit sharing plans are believed to increase employee commitment or loyalty by the majority of firms who have adopted them.

Profit sharing plans have been more commonplace in executive pay than in pay for other employee groups (Hewitt Associates 1986). Payouts under profit sharing often account for at least part of the executive's short-term incentive or annual bonus. Studies of executive pay and firm performance have only recently begun to investigate the relationship between individual elements of the executive pay package (base salary, short-term incentives, long-term incentives, and other benefits) and firm performance. The empirical work relating bonuses and firm performance has been inconclusive with some researchers reporting a significant positive relationship (Coughlan and Schmidt 1985; Murphy 1985) and others reporting a weak or no relationship (Redling 1981; Kerr and Bettis 1987).

Advocates of profit sharing believe that well-designed plans can, at a minimum, positively influence employee loyalty and commitment to the firm. Such influence could be the result of employee perceptions of increased employment stability, if such, in fact, occurs. There is at least some evidence that such greater stability occurs (Kruse 1987). Or the influence might result from the increased convergence of interests of principals and agents. Loyalty and commitment need not translate into higher productivity, but instead might increase retention and decrease grievances and absenteeism.[22]

Fourth, and finally, the literature on ESOPs is prodigious. Proponents of worker ownership have turned out a number of case and field studies of the effects of ESOP adoption on workers. However, most of these studies focus on changes in worker attitudes toward the firm and on workplace democracy, not on measures of productivity or labor costs.

All these studies indicate that management-supported employee authority in work-related decision making, and opportunities to receive information and provide input about decisions critical to organization success (product decisions, marketing, major investments, etc.) help sustain employee enthusiasm for ESOP arrangements (Rosen 1985). And the higher the portion of worker-owned equity in the firm, the more likely that ESOPs will be associated with worker loyalty (Whyte et al. 1983). However, the tendency of the ESOP literature to be written by ESOP proponents strongly suggests a need for independent corroboration. The fact that the basic ESOPs are rare, despite the very strong tax incentives they have enjoyed, could indicate that management is dubious about what ESOPs can accomplish. Survey evidence collected by the authors (reported below) supports this proposition.

The tax preference afforded ESOPs has led to studies examining the extent to which the objectives presumably set by Congress have been met. Undoubtedly, the most comprehensive of these is that conducted by the U.S. GAO (1986a, 1986b, 1987). Three major goals Congress intended for ESOPs, according to GAO, are: (1) to increase employee productivity, (2) to finance corporate programs, and (3) to broaden the ownership of corporate stock. In its study, the GAO found that productivity and profitability were not higher for firms with ESOPs, although there was weak evidence that an ESOP combined with the worker participation program could raise productivity. The GAO also found no clear-cut evidence that the use of ESOPs in funding corporate programs has been important. Nor did GAO find that the distribution of corporate stock ownership was significantly more widely dispersed in the mid-1980s due to ESOPs (basic and tax credit) than it was in the mid-1970s.

This summary of previous research, like that on plan use, confirms the need for systematic research in the United States on the impact of alternative plans on different performance objectives, on plan design and implementation factors that influence effectiveness, and on the relationship between organization conditions and plan results. Conspicuous in its absence is any study of the tradeoffs between different types of flexible pay plans in terms of either objective or attitudinal measures. However, the survey described in the next section does address this issue. Obviously, it is an important question to resolve if recommendations about tax preference for one plan over another are to be made.

A SURVEY OF MANAGEMENT ATTITUDES

To supplement the previous literature on attitudes toward flexible pay systems of U.S. managers, the authors conducted their own survey during 1986. An important goal of this survey was to develop information on the issue of substitution between different types of flexible pay plans, both as perceived by management, and as actually practiced. Does having one type of plan preclude having another? More pointedly, because the tax code favors ESOPs, does it have the indirect effect of reducing the use of the other plans? In addition, we looked at the issue of perceived effectiveness of the various plans in achieving management objectives.

Because we were seeking knowledgable respondents—particularly those who may have had experience with one or more types of flexible pay—we used three mailing lists for the survey likely to be biased toward such managers. These were (1) the management mailing lists of the U.C.L.A. Institute of

Industrial Relations,[23] (2) management and business members of the Industrial Relations Research Association reported in the IRRA's membership directory, and (3) managers in larger firms reporting the presence of ESOP-type plans to the Internal Revenue Service (IRS) on form 5500.[24] In the case of the third group, where names of the managers in charge of the plans were not supplied by the IRS, the American Compensation Association directory was used to identify the top compensation executive in the firms listed in IRS records.

Attempts were made to remove consultants, as opposed to practicing managers, from the survey. Only managers from private, profit-making firms were included. Ultimately, a sample of 545 respondents who met the survey criteria was gathered.[25]

Respondents who did not reply to the first request for information were sent a follow-up (reminder) questionnaire a few weeks later. Analysis of responses from those who answered the follow-up questionnaire (i.e., the reluctant respondents) can be used as a source of information about nonrespondents. The analysis suggests that nonrespondents to the survey were more likely to be from smaller, nonunion firms than respondents. They were less likely to have flexible pay plans at their firms or to have had long experience in the personnel/industrial relations field.

In short, the respondents, both because of the authors' selection of mailing lists and the response bias, turned out as expected to be heavily weighted toward managers knowledgeable about flexible pay plans. Over one-half reported that their firm had profit sharing, one-fourth reported having an ESOP, 39 percent reported a tax-credit ESOP, 6 percent reported gain sharing, and 23 percent reported having simple incentives. Eighty-two percent were employed by firms having at least one of these plans in operation (see Appendix).

Respondents were asked various questions about their firm and background. The survey then requested scaled attitudinal responses (strongly agree, generally agree, no opinion, generally disagree, strongly disagree) concerning profit sharing, ESOPs, tax-credit ESOPs, gain sharing, and simple incentives (piece rates and commissions). Some questions also requested respondents to indicate which plan they thought was top ranked on the basis of some attribute. In all cases, respondents were asked to base their reply on the application of the plans to *nonexempt* employees.[26]

Management Attitudes Concerning Plan Effects and Operations

Table 4 summarizes highlights of the responses. Generally, simple incentives were seen as best for raising productivity. Profit sharing was more likely to be viewed as a device to increase employee loyalty, and, in its tax deferred version, as a retirement vehicle. In addition, profit sharing was seen as a good method of linking labor costs to the firm's economic condition.

Table 4. Attitudes of Management Respondents Toward Selected Plans
(In percent)

		Profit Sharing	ESOP	Tax-Credit ESOP	Gain Sharing	Simple Incentives
Plan best for:						
raising productivity		28(30)	5(5)	-(-)	26(59)*	42(55)*
increasing loyalty		48(49)	17(22)	2(2)	18(41)*	15(20)*
retirement income	(TD)	81(88)*	12(24)*	7(9)	n.a.	n.a.
linking labor costs to firm's economic condition		53(56)*	n.a.	n.a.	28(57)*	19(23)*
Agrees that plan:						
raises productivity	(CB)	43(45)	18(24)*	10(10)	38(80)*	n.a.
	(TD)	32(32)				
increases loyalty	(CB)	51(51)	32(39)*	20(22)*	19(51)*	n.a.
	(TD)	50(52)				
needs more tax incentives	(TD)	29(25)*	25(29)*	24(30)*	n.a.	n.a.
creates demands for participation in management	(CB)	44(39)*	26(25)*	17(15)*	34(69)*	n.a.
	(TD)	39(33)*				
links labor costs to firm's economic conditions		63(64)	n.a.	n.a.	42(74)*	n.a.
Plan easiest to:						
administer		39(50)*	7(14)*	13(29)*	3(15)*	38(50)*
explain		32(39)*	8(18)*	7(17)*	4(18)*	49(62)*
Disagree that plan is:						
difficult to administer	(CB)	50(57)*	35(53)*	35(59)*	16(43)*	n.a.
	(TD)	43(54)*				
difficult to explain	(CB)	54(61)*	37(52)*	34(54)*	22(40)*	n.a.
	(TD)	47(54)*				

Notes: Figures in parentheses refer to respondents whose firm had plan listed in column. CB refers to cash bonus plans with regard to profit sharing; TD refers to tax-deferred profit sharing plans.

* Chi-squared test on a contingency table indicated that pattern of responses by those whose firms had the plan was significantly different from that of other respondents at the 5 percent level.

Given the history of flexible pay described earlier, these attitudes are entirely expected. Such views can be found as part of the conventional wisdom of the trade in personnel texts dating back to the 1920s (Tead 1929, especially pp. 263-264). The fact that the views are conventional suggests that the survey respondents—although not a representative sample of all U.S. human resource managements—nevertheless are not so startlingly different in their attitudes that the opinions expressed should be distrusted.

As a rule, those respondents whose companies actually had a plan were *more* likely to see such programs in a positive light, and were *less* likely to view them as difficult to explain to workers or to administer. Only a minority of respondents thought that the three types of plans which received favored tax treatment needed still further incentives. However, *what emerges most sharply from Table 4 is a sense of diversity of opinion and widespread skepticism on the part of knowledgeable respondents about the touted effects of the various plans.*

For example, barely one-half thought that profit sharing increased employee loyalty and an even smaller percentage thought it had a positive productivity impact. Generally, ESOPs (and especially tax-credit ESOPs) were seen as ineffective as either loyalty or productivity enhancers. They were also seen as rather difficult to administer and explain. The small number of respondents with gain sharing were very enthusiastic about the effect of such plans on productivity. But the vast majority of those responding had no direct knowledge of gain sharing, at least based on the compensation practices of their current employers.

The Key Question of Substitutability

A surprising and important result of the survey was that the various plans are typically neither regarded as substitutes, nor treated as substitutes. Table 5 shows that only a relatively small minority viewed having one plan as precluding implementation of one of the others. The only exceptions were the few respondents who had gain sharing. Four out of 10 of these individuals viewed gain sharing as a close substitute for simple incentives and for cash-bonus profit sharing.

Actual implementation of flexible pay plans is reported in Table 6. Roughly one-half of the respondents indicated that their firms had profit sharing, regardless of what other plans they had. Those with tax-credit ESOPs were somewhat more likely to have basic ESOPs, probably because knowledge of one form of ESOP was helpful in implementing the other. Despite the attitudes they expressed, those with gain sharing reported roughly the same incidence of profit sharing as the other respondents and a *higher* incidence of simple incentives.

Table 5. Management Attitudes Toward Substitutability of Selected Plans
(In Percent)

Firm doesn't need → if it has:	Profit Sharing	ESOP	Tax-Credit ESOP	Gain Sharing
ESOP	CB 14(18)[14] TD 15(18)[13]	—		
Tax-credit ESOP	CB 13(9)[12] TD 12(10)[10]	22(22)[28]	—	
Gain sharing	CB 27(41)[21] TD 23(26)[15]	13(6)[14]	9(9)[9]	—
Simple incentives	CB 17(16)[13] TD 13(13)[9]	4(3)[4]	5(4)[3]	23(22)[40]

Notes: Figures in parentheses ( ) refer to respondents whose firm had the plan listed on the same row. Figures in brackets [ ] refer to respondents whose firm had the plan listed in the same column. CB refers to profit sharing plans with cash bonuses; TD refers to tax-deferred profit sharing plans.

Table 6. Incidence of Plans Reported by Management Respondents
(In percent)

	Have Profit Sharing	Have ESOP	Have Tax-Credit ESOP	Have Gain Sharing	Have Simple Incentives
All Respondents	53	25	39	6	23
Respondents in firms with:					
profit sharing	—	27	37	6	25
ESOP	56	—	50*	4	27
tax-credit ESOP	50	32*	—	11*	24
gain sharing	49	17	66*	—	40*
simple incentives	59	30	41	11*	—

Note: * Chi-squared test applied to a contingency table indicates that respondents with plan in row had a different response pattern from other respondents.

The evidence concerning substitution possibilities across flexible pay plans has implications for public policy. Tax treatment of ESOPs is especially favorable compared with other plans. While the wisdom of Congress in providing this favored treatment can be questioned, the promotion of ESOPs by itself does not appear to be directly retarding the use of other forms of flexible pay. Of course, if the tax expenditures for ESOPs were dropped and the monies saved used to promote other flexible pay plans, the usage of the latter might well increase.

Table 7. Management Attitudes Toward Unionization and
Demands for Employee Participation
(Percent Agreeing that Implementation of Plan Leads to
Demands for Employee Participation in Management)

	Unionization Rate for Nonexempt Employees in Respondent's Firm (in percent)		
Type of Plan	*Zero*	*.1-49.9 percent*	*50 percent or greater*
Profit sharing			
Cash bonus	39	46	55
Tax deferred	33	40	50
ESOP	22	26	36
Tax-credit ESOP	16	16	20
Gain sharing	25	43	45

Participatory Implications

According to Table 5, managers who actually worked for companies which had profit sharing or the two forms of ESOPs were somewhat less likely to believe that these plans created worker demands for participation in management than were other respondents. But we know that, on other dimensions, managers in firms with plans tended to think more highly of those plans than those in firms without them. Thus, it may be that some managers saw participatory demands as a potentially *negative* aspect of flexible pay systems; those with the plans may have been anxious to emphasize that this negatively perceived effect was actually unlikely to occur.

The few individuals with gain sharing experience in the sample are given an exception to this response pattern. They were much more likely to think of gain sharing as inducing demands for participation than other respondents. In at least the Scanlon variety of gain sharing, employee participation is overtly encouraged. Thus, firms adopting these plans are likely to have a positive attitude toward worker participation, or they would not have installed their pay systems in the first place.

Generally, however, it was the presence or absence of a union which seemed to condition managerial responses with regard to worker participation. Table 7 shows that respondents from nonunion firms were less likely to believe that flexible pay systems caused worker demands for participation in management than those from unionized firms. The higher the unionization rate in the firm, the more likely the respondent was to think that participatory demands would be induced by a flexible pay system. This finding may simply reflect the fact that, even if participatory demands were created, nonunion workers would not automatically have a channel of expression. However, in terms of actual practice, the degree of unionization within our sample did not have a statistically significant impact on the likelihood that the firm had some type of flexible pay system.

CONCLUSIONS ON FLEXIBLE PAY
IN THE AMERICAN CONTEXT

Although certain forms of flexible pay plans may have macroeconomic (Weitzman-type) benefits, the persons making the decisions on whether or not to install such compensation arrangements respond to perceived *micro*-level benefits. The chief method of public policy which has been used to influence this choice has been tax incentives. For example, tax inducements created tax-credit ESOPs; these plans were entirely an artifact of the tax code.

Basic ESOPs have also been the recipient of generous Congressional favors. However, even with the tax subsidy, surprisingly few workers are covered by basic ESOPs, according to the BLS data discussed earlier. This finding suggests that, despite the literature by proponents extolling the influence of ESOPs on firm efficiency and profitability, most managers do not anticipate that ESOPs would produce such benefits for their companies. Managers, in short, are reluctant to put in place plans which they do not believe will actually advance enterprise goals, even in the face of tax incentives. Where managers are skeptical, tax incentives must be extremely attractive—as with the tax-credit ESOPs—to induce a managerial response. Tax-credit ESOPs were installed only because the government essentially paid for them.

Redirecting Tax Subsidies

Inducements for tax-credit ESOPs have now been ended, leaving only those for basic ESOPs. Yet ESOPs do not have the macro features (along the lines specified by Weitzman) which would justify a social subsidy. There is a strong indication, based on GAO research, that ESOPs are prone to abuse, particularly if found in small, closely held companies. When a firm's stock does not have an objective external market value, there is an incentive for tax reasons to overstate the value of the shares put in trust.

As already noted, even if the various forms of flexible pay are not viewed as substitutes by managers, the scarcity of tax dollars makes them substitutes in terms of tax-favored treatment. In particular, the tax subsidy going to ESOPs might be better directed toward profit sharing—both cash and deferred. Any such subsidy, however, must be targeted only toward genuine profit sharing (i.e., to plans in which the bonus is determined by formula, not by managerial discretion). Otherwise, abuse of the subsidy is probable.

Our review and survey provide several reasons for a tax subsidy of profit sharing. First, there is some micro-level support for Weitzman's proposals, at least with regard to employment stabilization (Kruse 1987). Our survey found that managers believe profit sharing does link labor costs to the firm's economic fortunes. Second, case studies indicate that profit sharing—coupled with other human resource practices—can have a positive impact on productivity and employee commitment to the firm. Our survey suggests that the adoption of profit sharing will not prevent firms from also experimenting with simple incentives and gain sharing plans which might further enhance the effectiveness of human resource utilization.

Finally, profit sharing now enjoys a climate of receptivity, thanks in part to the wage concession movement of the 1980s, which softened (and, in some cases, reversed) union opposition. In addition, economic pressures on employers have produced a greater willingness on their part to experiment with alternative pay systems. The political climate is also improving. During the 1980s, a number of liberal-to-moderate Democrats expressed interest in, and even made proposals for, a tax subsidy for profit sharing.

It would be unfortunate, however, if profit sharing came to be viewed as a liberal/left idea in the United States. The fact that a conservative government in Britain has also found merit in the Weitzman proposal should be proof enough that the proposal can encompass a broad political spectrum. Much depends on packaging. On the left, profit sharing can be viewed (positively) as ersatz socialism or, alternatively (and negatively), as a devious right-wing plot to undermine unions and disguise class conflict. On the right it can be viewed (positively) as teaching workers the benefits of free enterprise, or, alternatively (and negatively), as a sly leftist device to weaken owner and management control of private companies. Thus, along with tax incentives, there must be an educational campaign to allay fears and enliven hopes if a shift toward a share economy is to be successfully encouraged.

Participation and Union-Management Relations

The presence or absence of a profit sharing or gain sharing plan does not inherently create a climate of greater worker participation in management. However, our survey suggests—and common sense indicates—that where unions exist, such plans could have important industrial relations impacts. It has become commonplace to point to the tacit "understanding" reached in the 1940s and 1950s that unions would not play a managerial role. But if the compensation system now tilts toward arrangements which encourage worker participation, the traditional union role as a nonmanagerial demander and griever could be importantly altered.

Compensation systems that are geared to company or group performance are inherently more difficult for workers to verify than simple hourly wages or piece rates. At the very least, therefore, unions could play an "auditing" role where such pay systems exist. To do so, however, union officials would need access to internal firm information. Thus, information sharing demands by unions are likely to be linked to the establishment of flexible pay arrangements.

As our survey suggests, information sharing may in turn give way to demands for sharing in the managerial role itself. It is important to stress, however, that in the U.S. context, with only 14 percent of private wage and salary earners represented by unions (as of 1987), union-management issues are not the critical factor they once were in labor market policy. Were a share economy to develop, most workers affected would be nonunion.

Research Implications

Our review of the literature and our own survey results leave many questions about flexible pay systems unanswered. We have presented some evidence, for example, concerning the degree to which the various plans are substitutes for one another, an important public policy issue. However, our sampling methodology is open to question, and confirming studies, both involving attitudes and actual practice, are needed. In any case, our finding that the various plans are generally not viewed as close substitutes begs the question of optimality. What mix of plans is optimal, given a set of managerial objectives?

We have also noted the limited research that combines actual firm performance measures with information on particular compensation practices. Data sets are potentially available to make this linkage. The GAO study on ESOPs took such an approach, for example. But studies are needed on the other forms of flexible pay as well.

Pay systems are not implemented in a vacuum. Sometimes, flexible pay plans are accompanied by innovative human resource techniques. The GAO report on ESOPs, as a case in point, found weak evidence that ESOPs *combined* with worker participation programs have a positive productivity effect. Data sets providing information on internal personnel practices along with pay system incidence will help in sorting out the various influences on firm performance, and provide clues to the optimal circumstances for implementing flexible pay.

Once the presence of particular plans is linked to firm performance, there will be a need for more data and analysis of the particular formulas used in flexible pay systems. Even simple incentives come in many varieties, as do the others. Profit sharing plans, for example, may share on a first-dollar basis, or may share only the increment above some specified amount of profits. Most studies have not been able to take account of these differences.

Also lacking is information on administrative costs. Are simple incentives, for example, cost-effective substitutes for time-based systems with close supervision? Or do the administrative problems long associated with incentives, (e.g., the need for appropriate standard setting), entail large costs? Our survey provides some information on what managers *think* about the relative costs of administering the various plans. But do firms generally make systematic estimates of such costs? Even the answer to that simple question is unknown at present.

Finally, there are research issues raised by the newer macro views of flexible pay. The Weitzman proposal regarding profit sharing highlights the gap between the macro and micro approaches. These alternative perspectives create a need for dialogue between economists, policymakers, and those who have traditionally implemented or studied flexible pay systems.

In fact, detailed micro information may be needed to evaluate the macro implications. For example, the Weitzman plan assumes that firms using profit sharing will pay a lower base wage than they would in the absence of sharing. Yet compensation specialists often suggest that share plans should be add-ons to the going rate of pay, so that workers will perceive they are earning something extra. The micro issue of whether expected share bonuses substitute for guaranteed pay, thus, is critical for informed macro discussions.

Bringing Together Diverse Viewpoints

The fact that flexible pay systems potentially have various types of impacts has attracted considerable interest in compensation innovations during the 1980s. However, the discussions that have ensued—while nominally about the same topic—have been hindered by diverse alternative perspectives. Macroeconomists, psychologists and behavioral scientists, compensation specialists, and industrial relations practitioners have largely exchanged views in separate forums.

Congress, despite its interest in compensation from a tax subsidy and revenue viewpoint, does not appear to have a coherent policy regarding flexible pay. It has considered such arrangements largely from a perspective of retirement income and wealth redistribution. Macroeconomic aspects—although they began to be discussed in the 1980s—have not been a significant element in actual Congressional policy.

The Reagan administration, after the installation of Labor Secretary Brock, adopted a policy of loosely favoring labor-management cooperation and seems interested in employee participation arrangements.[27] However, this interest has not been clearly linked to fostering pay systems that might reinforce cooperation and participation. Nor has it been extended to applications in nonunion workplaces. As in the case of Congress, the macro side has not been an important element in administration policy.

Because of the economic difficulties felt by many sectors in the 1980s, there is now a greater willingness to consider "new" ideas in compensation, industrial relations, and human resource management than existed a decade ago. However, the diversity of interests and viewpoints, left in isolation, is unlikely to produce a consensus regarding how employees should be paid. Unless the disparate views are brought together, the current lack of clear direction in American public policy and private practice will continue. That outcome would be a loss for the U.S. economy.

APPENDIX

Summary of Respondent Characteristics

Category	Proportion in Category (in percent)	
Responded to initial questionnaire	53	
Responded to follow-up (reminder) questionnaire	47	
Firm produces goods (mining, manufacturing, agriculture)	63	(59)
Firm produces services	37	(41)
Firm has less than 1,000 employees	49	(59)
Firm has at least 1,000 employees	51	(41)
Unionization rate for nonexempt employees:		
0 percent	56	(65)
.1-49.9 percent	18	(13)
50-100 percent	26	(22)
Firm's stock is publicly traded	62	(56)
Firm's stock is not traded	38	(44)
Respondent has less than 10 years' experience	34	(40)
Respondent has at least 10 years' experience	66	(60)
Firm has a profit sharing, ESOP, tax-credit ESOP,		
gain sharing, or simple incentive plan	82	(78)
Firm has no plans	18	(22)
Firm has profit sharing of which:	53	
cash bonus only	27	
tax deferred only	47	
mixed (cash bonus and tax deferred)	26	
Firm has ESOP of which:	25	
leveraged	33	
nonleveraged	61	
Firm has tax-credit ESOP	39	
Firm has gain sharing	6	
Firm has simple incentive plan	23	

Note: Figures in parentheses refer to respondents who answered reminder (follow-up) questionnaire. Where percentages sum to less than 100, missing responses have been omitted. Where percentages sum to more than 100, firms had more than one type of plan. A total of 545 responses are included in the sample.

ACKNOWLEDGMENTS

The authors would like to thank Mark Kuga and Maury Pearl who provided research assistance for this project. Mark E. Thompson, Joseph M. Weiler, W. Craig Riddell, Craig C. Pinder, and two anonymous reviewers provided helpful comments on an earlier version of this essay.

NOTES

1. The original version of this paper was presented to the Pacific Rim Comparative Labour Policy Conference held in Vancouver, British Columbia, Canada in June 1987.

2. Keynes interpreted wage rigidity in terms of collective action and "bargaining" by workers and referred explicitly to unions at key points in his exposition (see, for example, Keynes 1936, pp. 13-15, 264-267).

3. Wage structure within firms may be rigid, due to such institutional practices as job evaluation. To the extent that firms use similar job evaluation systems, a force for interfirm rigidity may be present in the United States. We are not arguing that there are no forces operating which tend to rigidify American wage structure; only that these are weaker than may be found in other countries and that they are not part of a public policy.

4. Initial reports suggest that the complexity of the tax rules adopted have inhibited an employer response. See "Few Major British Employers Favor Profit-Related Plans," *Daily Labor Report* (January 20, 1988), p. A3.

5. Some readers may prefer the term "individual incentives" for these plans. Because piece rates are sometimes applied to small work teams (and thus are not based on the individual), we use the alternative expression "simple incentives."

6. Although our primary focus is on nonsupervisory workers, it should be noted that plans containing aspects of simple incentives are sometimes used in management and executive ranks. Typically, these plans tie a portion of a bonus to quantitative performance targets believed to be within the individual's control (e.g., winning contracts, cutting costs). Bonuses are distributed annually, reflecting a longer time span of discretion associated with managerial occupations (Jacques 1961). However, to the extent that such bonuses are tied to profit-related measures, they can be classified as profit sharing plans (defined below).

7. See the following sections titled "Economic Impact and Tax Treatment of Flexible Pay Plans" and "Employee Stock Ownership Plans."

8. See the section "Employee Stock Ownership Plans."

9. The exception here would be the executive or top management group. For these employees, profit measures are more directly tied to individual or group performance, although there are still many uncontrollable factors affecting profits.

10. Since the proportion of profits shared will typically be well below 100 percent, the dilution effect is further enhanced.

11. There are exceptions when profit sharing is applied at the executive level. Executive pay linked to profits is often viewed as an application of agency theory. The interests of the executive (agent) and the owners (principals) are more tightly linked if their payoffs are tied together. If executives can be assumed to have an important influence on profits, then the outcome might be similar to simple incentives for nonsupervisory workers.

12. See the section titled "Data on Current Usage of Flexible Pay Plans" below.

13. 401(k) plans permit employees to lower their pay and place the resulting "saving" into a tax-deferred trust. Employers may provide matching payments.

14.   Data on the proportion of production workers in total manufacturing employment appear monthly in *Employment and Earnings.*

15.   The low merit system usage rate for unionized workers does not mean that the bulk of such employees were under simple incentive systems. Rather, most were time-rated workers with wage progression systems related to seniority.

16.   Some employers use merit ratings to distribute bonuses to employees who have reached the top of their salary grades, have performed well, but are not being promoted. These bonuses do not become part of base salary; thus, employers do not have to expand their salary structure ranges. O'Dell and McAdams (1987, p. 8) report that 30 percent of surveyed employers used lump sum bonuses. But these included bonuses not tied to specific performance measures, and other types of pay practices. Presumably, merit-related bonuses would have been found in a lower percentage of employers.

17.   These estimates are based on data compiled by Mitchell from listings appearing biweekly in the *Daily Labor Report.* For published data through mid-1986, see Mitchell (1987, p. 315).

18.   See below. Earlier discussion of PAYSOPs appeared in the section titled "Flexible Pay Plan Types."

19.   The Bureau of National Affairs survey of union contracts indicates that 33 percent had wage incentive provisions, but 11 percent of these involved prohibitions or limits on the right of management to install wage incentives. Thus, it can be assumed that 29 percent (e.g., 89 percent of 33 percent) had actual incentives in place for some workers (Bureau of National Affairs 1986a, pp. 122-123, 125).

20.   The American Productivity Center survey was not based on a random sample. It can be assumed that firms with pay plans of the type surveyed were more likely to respond to the questionnaire.

21.   The authors found only one study which compared the effectiveness of two different plans across firms, and this was in a Japanese setting (Barney 1984).

22.   See Freund and Epstein (1984) and Florkowski (1987) for summaries of case studies and surveys supporting these propositions.

23.   The authors wish to thank Rosalind Schwartz of the Center for Management Research and Education, Institute of Industrial Relations, for her assistance in obtaining this list.

24.   Form 5500 is a report required of employers with a variety of deferred compensation plans. Surprisingly, the form is not a confidential document. The Internal Revenue Service will make computer files, based on these forms, available at reasonable cost. Names drawn from this list were obviously biased toward experience with ESOPs. The Management Center mailing lists of the U.C.L.A. Institute of Industrial Relations are biased towards larger firms and "sophisticated" firms concerned with human resource issues. Management members of the IRRA also tend to come from larger employers and—by virtue of their membership in a quasi-academic organization—might be more likely to respond to a questionnaire.

25.   Because it was not always possible to exclude nonprofit entities based on employer name, a question was included on the survey asking employers who were either nonprofit or government entities to return the form unanswered. A total of 6,948 were mailed of which 512 were rejected (primarily by the Postal Service) (e.g., "no such person at this address"). There is reason to suspect that a substantially larger number did not reach their destination, however. In particular, the management mailing list of the Institute of Industrial Relations includes many names of individuals who are no longer at the firms recorded. Because the list is used for advertising rather than survey work, it is assumed that a brochure mailed to such a person will be passed on to an appropriate person or department. But such a substitute person would probably not fill out a questionnaire addressed to someone else. In addition, many such incorrectly addressed surveys may simply have been discarded rather than rejected. Apart from the mailing problem, the low response rate was undoubtedly due in part to the length of the questionnaire (50 questions including one open-ended comment section). However, as will be discussed below, it is evident that those who chose to

respond were not a random sample; they tended to be individuals in firms where flexible pay plans existed. Having a plan in effect acted as a motivator in eliciting a response.

26. "Nonexempt" employees are workers who are not exempted from the overtime provisions of the federal Fair Labor Standards Act. Exempt employees are basically executives, administrators, and professionals. Hence, nonexempt workers are basically nonprofessional, nonsupervisory employees.

27. The Labor Department has issued reports designed to give prominence to cases of innovative labor-management cooperation and has engaged in legal research to find potential legislative barriers to cooperative arrangements.

REFERENCES

Administrative Management Society. 1984. *1984 AMS Guide to Management Compensation.* Willow Grove, PA: AMS.

Alchian. A. and H. Demsetz. 1982. Production, Information Costs, and Economic Organization. *American Economic Review* 62(December): 777-795.

Barney, J.B. 1984. *Employee Stock Ownership, Profit Sharing Bonuses, and a Firm's Cost of Capital: Business Finance Through Compensation Policy.* Working paper, Graduate School of Management, University of California, Los Angeles.

Bloomfield, D. ed. 1923. *Financial Incentives for Employees and Executives,* vol. II. New York: H.W. Wilson Co.

Bullock, R.J. and E.E. Lawler. 1984. Gainsharing: A Few Questions, and Fewer Answers. *Human Resource Management* 23(Spring): 23-40.

Bureau of National Affairs, Inc. 1981. *Wage & Salary Administration,* Personnel Policies Forum No. 131. Washington, DC: BNA.

_____. 1984. *Productivity Improvement Programs,* Personnel Policies Forum No. 138. Washington, DC: BNA.

_____. 1985. Dissident Teamsters Discuss Strategy to Combat Concessions Disguised as Stock Ownership Plans. *Daily Labor Report* (October 9), pp. A2-A5.

_____. 1986a. *Basic Patterns in Union Contracts,* 11th ed. Washington, DC: BNA.

_____. 1986b. No Strike Called Despite Pay Cuts for Todd Shipyard Workers. *Daily Labor Report,* December 2, p. A3.

_____. 1987. *Employee Ownership Plans: How 8,000 Companies and 8,000,000 Employees Invest in Their Futures.* Washington, DC: BNA.

_____. 1988. Median First-Year Pay Increase Holds at 2.4 Percent for 1987. *Daily Labor Report,* January 15, pp. B3-B7.

Burritt, A.W. et al. 1918. *Profit Sharing: Its Principles and Practice.* New York: Harper & Brothers.

Business Week. October 15, 1984. The Tax Magic That's Making Employee Stock Plans Multiply, pp. 158-159.

_____. April 15, 1986. ESOPs: Revolution or Ripoff?, pp. 94-108.

Campbell, J.P., M.D. Dunnette, E.E. Lawler III, and K.E. Weick, Jr. 1970. *Managerial Behavior, Performance and Effectiveness.* New York: McGraw-Hill.

Campbell, J.P. and R.D. Pritchard. 1976. Motivation Theory in Industrial and Organizational Psychology. In *Handbook of Industrial and Organizational Psychology,* edited by M.D. Dunnette. Chicago: Rand McNally.

Carlson, N.W. 1982. Time Rates Tighten Their Grip on Manufacturing Industries. *Monthly Labor Review* 105(May):15-22.

Chamber of Commerce of the United States. 1958. *Reuther's Profit-Sharing Demand.* Washington, DC: Chamber of Commerce.

Cooper, L.W. 1934. Profit Sharing. Pp. 487-492 in *Encyclopedia of the Social Sciences,* edited by R.A. Seligman and A. Johnson. New York: Macmillan.

Coughlan, A.T. and R.M. Schmidt. 1985. Executive Compensation, Management Turnover, and Firm Performance. *Journal of Accounting and Economics* 7(April):43-66.

Cox, J.H. 1971. Time and Incentive Pay Practices in Urban Areas. *Monthly Labor Review* 94(December):53-56.

Denison, E.F. 1979. *Accounting for Slower Economic Growth: The United States in the 1970s.* Washington, DC: Brookings Institution.

Dyer, L., D.R. Schwab, and R. Theriault. 1976. Managerial Perceptions Regarding Salary Increase Criteria. *Personnel Psychology* 29(Spring):233-242.

Ehrenberg, R.G. and G.T. Milkovich. 1987. Compensation and Firm Performance. Pp. 87-122 in *Human Resources and the Performance of the Firm,* edited by M.M. Kleiner, R.N. Block, M. Roomkin, and S.W. Salsburg. Madison, WI: Industrial Relations Research Association.

Emmet, B. 1917. *Profit Sharing in the United States,* U.S. Bureau of Labor Statistics Bulletin 208. Washington, DC: U.S. Government Printing Office.

ESOP Association. 1988. *ESOP Survey 1987.* Washington, DC: ESOP Association.

Federal Reserve Bank of Atlanta. 1983. Employee Stock Ownership Plans: Economic Boon for the Southeast. *Economic Review* 68(October):20-33.

Fein, M. 1981. *Improshare: An Alternative to Traditional Managing.* Norcross, GA: American Institute of Industrial Engineers.

Florkowski, G.W. 1987. The Organizational Impact of Profit Sharing. *Academy of Management Review* 12(October):622-636.

Freedman, S.J. and J.R. Montanari. 1980. An Integrative Model of Managerial Reward and Allocation. *Academy of Management Journal* 5(July):381-390.

Freeman, R.B. and M.L. Weitzman. 1987. Bonuses and Employment in Japan. *Journal of the Japanese and International Economies* 1:168-194.

Freund, W.C. and E. Epstein. 1984. *People and Productivity: The New York Stock Exchange Guide to Financial Incentives and the Quality of Work Life.* Homewood, IL: Dow Jones-Irwin.

Galbraith, J.R. 1977. *Organization Design.* Reading, MA: Addison-Wesley.

Gellerman, S.W. 1963. *Motivation and Productivity.* New York: American Management Assoc.

Gilman, N.P. 1891. *Profit Sharing Between Employer and Employee: A Study in the Evolution of the Wage System.* Boston: Houghton, Mifflin.

Greenhouse, S. 1985. Employees Make a Go of Weirton. *New York Times,* January 6, Section III, p. 4.

Guzda, H.P. 1984. Industrial Democracy: Made in the U.S.A. *Monthly Labor Review* 107(May):26-33.

Haire, M., E.E. Ghiselli, and M.E. Gorden. 1967. A Psychological Study of Pay. *Journal of Applied Psychology Monograph* 51(4).

Hammer, T.H. and R.N. Stern. 1986. A Yo-Yo Model of Cooperation Union Participation in Management at the Rath Packing Company. *Industrial and Labor Relations Review* 39(April):337-349.

Hashimoto, M. 1979. Bonus Payments, On-the-Job Training and Lifetime Employment in Japan. *Journal of Political Economy* 77(October):1086-1104.

Hewitt Associates. 1985. *An Overview of Productivity-Based Incentive Systems.* Newport Beach, CA: Hewitt Associates.

————. 1986. *1986 Profit Sharing Survey (1985 Experience).* In cooperation with the Profit Sharing Council of America. Lincolnshire, IL: Hewitt Associates.

Hoxie, R.F. 1916. *Scientific Management and Labor.* New York: D. Appleton & Co.

Jacoby, S.M. 1985a. *Employing Bureaucracy: Managers, Unions, and the Transformation of Work in American Industry, 1900-1945.* New York: Columbia University Press.

_____. 1985b. Environmental Pressure and Union-Management Cooperation: Historical Evidence from the United States, 1920-1965. In *The Future Directions of Employee Relations,* edited by E.G. Flamholtz and F. Hinman. Los Angeles: UCLA Institute of Industrial Relations.

Jacques, E. 1961. *Equitable Payment.* New York: Wiley.

Jehring, J.J., W.J. Howell, Jr., and L.R. Tripp. 1962. *A New Approach to Collective Bargaining?: Progress Sharing at American Motors.* Madison, WI: Center for Productivity Motivation, University of Wisconsin.

Jeuck, J.E. 1949. *A Case Study in the Evolution of Personnel Management: Sears, Roebuck and Company.* Doctoral dissertation, University of Chicago.

Kahneman, D., J.L. Knetsch, and R. Thaler. 1986. Fairness as a Constraint on Profit Sharing: Entitlements in the Market. *American Economic Review* 76(September):728-741.

Kelso, L.O. and M. Adler. 1958. *The Capitalist Manifesto.* New York: Random House.

Kelso, L.O. and P. Hetter. 1968. *How to Turn Eighty Million Workers into Capitalists on Borrowed Money.* New York: Random House.

Keynes, J.M. 1936. *The General Theory of Employment, Interest, and Money.* New York: Harcourt, Brace & World.

Kerr, J. and R.A. Bettis. 1987. Boards of Directors, Top Management Compensation and Shareholder Returns. *Academy of Management Journal* 30(December):645-664.

Kerr, S. 1975. On the Folly of Rewarding A, While Hoping for B. *Academy of Management Journal* 18(December):769-783.

_____. 1982. *Some Characteristics and Consequences of Organizational Reward Systems.* Working paper, University of Southern California.

King, W.I. 1941. *The Causes of Economic Fluctuations.* New York: The Ronald Press Co.

Kopelman, R.E. and L. Reinharth. 1982. Research Results: The Effect of Merit-Pay Practices on White Collar Performance. *Compensation Review* 14:30-40.

Kruger, D.H. and R.S. Bearup. 1986. *Collective Bargaining and Profit-Sharing.* Working paper, Michigan State University.

Kruse, D.L. 1987. *Profit-Sharing and Employment Variability: Microeconomic Evidence.* Unpublished paper, Harvard University, Department of Economics.

Laud, R.L. 1984. Performance Appraisal Practices in the Fortune 1300. In *Strategic Human Resource Management,* edited by C. Fombrun, N. Tichy, and M.A. Devanna. New York: Wiley & Sons.

Lawler, E.E. III. 1971. *Pay and Organizational Effectiveness: A Psychological Approach.* New York: McGraw-Hill.

_____. 1973. *Motivation in Work Organizations.* Belmont, CA: Wadsworth.

_____. 1981. *Pay and Organization Development.* Reading, MA: Addison-Wesley.

_____. 1984. The Strategic Design of Reward Systems. In *Strategic Human Resource Management,* edited by C. Fombrun, N.M. Tichy, and M.A. Devanna. New York: Wiley & Sons.

Lesieur, F.G. ed. 1958. *The Scanlon Plan: A Frontier in Labor-Management Cooperation.* Cambridge, MA: MIT Technology Press.

Lewis, L.E. 1960. The Extent of Incentive Pay in Manufacturing, May 1958. *Monthly Labor Review* 83(May):460-463.

Locke, E.A. 1982. The Ideas of Frederick W. Taylor: An Evaluation. *Academy of Management Review* 7(January):14-24.

Loomis, C.J. 1982. The Madness of Executive Compensation. *Fortune* 106(June):45-52.

March, J.G. and H.A. Simon. 1958. *Organizations.* New York: McGraw-Hill.

Marsh, T.R. and D.E. McAllister. 1981. ESOPs Tables: A Survey of Companies with Employee Stock Ownership Plans. *Journal of Corporation Law* 6(Spring):551-619.

Marx, K. 1906. *Capital: A Critique of Political Economy.* New York: Modern Library.

Mathewson, S.B. (1931) 1969. *Restriction of Output Among Unorganized Workers.* Carbondale, IL: Southern Illinois University Press.

McCabe, D.A. 1912. *The Standard Rate in American Trade Unions.* Baltimore: Johns Hopkins Press.

McKersie, R.B., C.F. Miller, Jr., and W.E. Quarterman. 1964. Some Indicators of Incentive Plan Prevalence. *Monthly Labor Review* 87(March):271-276.

Metzger, B.L. 1975. *Profit Sharing in 38 Large Companies,* vol. 1. Evanston, IL: Profit Sharing Research Foundation.

———. 1978. *Profit Sharing in 38 Large Companies,* vol. 2. Evanston, IL: Profit Sharing Research Foundation.

Mitchell, D.J.B. 1985a. Shifting Norms in Wage Determination. *Brookings Papers on Economic Activity* 2:575-599.

———. 1985b. Wage Flexibility: Then and Now. *Industrial Relations* 24(Spring):266-279.

———. 1985c. Wage Flexibility in the United States: Lessons from the Past. *American Economic Review* 75(May):36-40.

———. 1986a. Inflation, Unemployment, and the Wagner Act: A Critical Reappraisal. *Stanford Law Review* 38(April):1065-1095.

———. 1986b. Wages and Keynes: Lessons from the Past. *Eastern Economic Journal* 12(June-September):199-208.

———. 1987. Wage Trends and Wage Concessions: Implications for Medium-Term Economic Expansion. Pp. 266-335 in *Research Seminar in Quantitative Economics, The Economic Outlook for 1987.* Ann Arbor, MI: RSQE, Department of Economics, University of Michigan.

Mitchell, W. and J.K. Thompson. 1986. Book Review: Through the Employee Ownership Maze. *California Management Review* 28(Summer):115-128.

Murphy, K.J. 1985. Corporate Performance and Managerial Remuneration. *Journal of Accounting and Economics* 7(April):11-42.

National Civic Federation. 1920. *Profit Sharing by American Employers.* New York: National Civic Federation.

National Industrial Conference Board. 1928. *Employee Stock Purchase Plans in the United States.* New York: NICB.

———. 1930. *Systems of Wage Payment.* New York: NICB.

———. 1934. *Profit Sharing.* New York: NICB.

———. 1937. *Profit-Sharing and Other Supplementary-Compensation Plans Covering Wage Earners.* Studies in Personnel no. 2. New York: NICB.

New York Times. March 28, 1985a. Best Idea Since Keynes (editorial), Section 1, p. 30.

———. April 25, 1985b. How to Cut Unemployment, Without Magic (editorial), Section I, p. 20.

O'Dell, C.S. 1981. *Gainsharing, Involvement, Incentives, and Productivity.* New York: American Management Association.

———. 1986. *Major Findings from People, Performance and Pay Survey.* Houston, TX: American Productivity Center.

O'Dell, C.S. and J. McAdams. 1987. *People, Performance and Pay: A Full Report on the American Productivity/American Compensation Association National Survey of Non-Traditional Reward and Human Resource Practices.* Houston: American Productivity Center.

Olson, D.G. 1982. Union Experiences with Worker Ownership: Legal and Practical Issues Raised by ESOPs, TRASOPs, Stock Purchases and Co-operatives. *Wisconsin Law Review* 5:729-823.

Opinion Research Corporation. 1949. *Productivity from the Worker's Standpoint.* Princeton, NJ: ORC.

Oswald, R.A. 1986. Comment. *Industrial and Labor Relations Review* 39(January):287-290.

Pearce, J. 1986. *More Symbol Than Substance: Actual Pay Allocations Under Merit and Nonmerit Pay Plans.* Working paper, Graduate School of Management, University of California, Irvine.

Pearce, J., W.B. Stevenson, and J.L. Perry. 1985. Managerial Compensation Based on Organizational Performance: A Time Series Analysis of the Effects of Merit Pay. *Academy of Management Journal* 28(June):261-278.

Pencavel, J.H. 1977. Work Effort, On-the-Job Screening, and Alternative Methods of Remuneration. Pp. 225-258 in *Research in Labor Economics,* vol. 1, edited by R.G. Ehrenberg. Greenwich, CT: JAI Press.

Pinder, C.C. 1984. *Work Motivation Theory, Issues, and Applications.* Glenview, IL: Scott, Foresman and Co.

Profit Sharing Council of America. 1984. *Profit Sharing: Philosophy, Practices and Benefits to Society.* Evanston, IL: Profit Sharing Council.

Profit Sharing Research Foundation. 1984. *Participative Gainsharing.* Evanston, IL: Profit Sharing Research Foundation.

————. 1985. *Cumulative Growth in Number of Qualified Deferred Profit Sharing Plans and Pensions in the United States 1939 through 1984.* Mimeo. Evanston, IL: Profit Sharing Research Foundation.

Rabin, B. 1986. *Executive Pay and Firm Performance.* Working paper, New York State School of Industrial and Labor Relations, Cornell University.

Redling, E.T. 1981. Myth versus Reality: The Relationship Between Top Executive Pay and Corporate Performance. *Compensation Review* 13:16-24.

Roethlisberger, F.J. and W.J. Dickson. 1939. *Management and the Worker: An Account of a Research Program Conducted by the Western Electric Company, Hawthorne Works, Chicago.* Cambridge, MA: Harvard University Press.

Rosen, C. 1985. Worker Ownership and Labor-Management Cooperation. In *Selections for the Second National Labor-Management Conference,* U.S. Bureau of Labor-Management Relations and Cooperative Programs, Department of Labor. Washington, DC: U.S. Government Printing Office.

Rosen, C. and M. Caudell-Feagan. 1984. Using ESOP's to Thwart Hostile Takeovers—Beware! *Pension World* 20(February):18-20.

Ross, T.L. and W.C. Hauck. 1984. Gainsharing in the United States. *Industrial Management* 26(March-April):9-14.

Ross, T.L. and R.A. Ross. 1984. Productivity Gainsharing: Resolving Some of the Measurement Issues. *National Productivity Review* 3(Autumn):382-394.

Schuster, M.H. 1984. *Union-Management Cooperation: Structure, Process and Impact.* Kalamazoo, MI: W.E. Upjohn Institute for Employment Research.

Scott, W.D. and M.H.S. Hayes. 1921. *Science and Common Sense in Working with Men.* New York: Ronald Press.

Shepard, J.L. 1938. *Human Nature at Work.* New York: Harper & Brothers.

Shister, J. 1943. The Theory of Union Wage Rigidity. *Quarterly Journal of Economics* 57(August):522-542.

Simon, H.A. 1957. *Models of Man: Social and Rational.* New York: Wiley.

Slichter, S.H. 1934. *Towards Stability: The Problem of Economic Balance.* New York: Holt and Co.

Smith, A. 1937. *An Inquiry into the Nature and Causes of the Wealth of Nations.* New York: Modern Library.

Taylor, F.W. 1914. A Price Rate System: Being a Step Toward Partial Solution of the Labor
    Problem. Pp. 636-665 in *Scientific Management: A Collection of the More Significant
    Articles Describing the Taylor System of Management,* edited by C.B. Thompson.
    Cambridge, MA: Harvard University Press.
Taylor Society. 1929. *Scientific Management in American Industry.* New York: Harper & Brothers.
Tead, O. 1929. *Human Nature and Management: The Applications of Psychology to Executive
    Leadership.* New York: McGraw-Hill.
Thompson, K.M. 1949. *Profit Sharing: Democratic Capitalism in American Industry.* New York:
    Harper & Brothers.
Toedt, T.A. et al. 1962. *Managing Manpower in the Industrial Environment.* Dubuque, IA: W.C.
    Brown.
U.S. Bureau of International Labor Affairs. March 1985. *United States-Japan Comparative Study
    of Economic Adjustment.* Washington, DC: U.S. Bureau of International Affairs.
U.S. Bureau of Labor Statistics. 1920. Application of the Golden Rule in Business. *Monthly Labor
    Review* 11(December):1222-1223.
————. 1932. Results of Profit-Sharing Plan of Sears, Roebuck & Co. During the Depression.
    Monthly Labor Review 34(May):1066-1067.
————. 1963. The Labor Month in Review. *Monthly Labor Review* 86(January):III-IV.
————. 1980. *Characteristics of Major Collective Bargaining Agreements, January 1, 1978,*
    Bulletin 2065. Washington, DC: U.S. Government Printing Office.
————. 1987. *Employee Benefits in Medium and Large Firms, 1986,* Bulletin 2281. Washington,
    DC: U.S. Government Printing Office.
U.S. Commissioner of Labor. 1886. *The First Annual Report of the Commissioner of Labor.*
    Washington, DC: U.S. Government Printing Office.
————. 1904. *Regulation and Restriction of Output,* eleventh special report of the Commissioner
    of Labor. Washington, DC: U.S. Government Printing Office.
U.S. General Accounting Office. 1980. *Employee Stock Ownership Plans: Who Benefits Most
    in Closely Held Companies?,* HRD-80-88. Washington, DC: U.S. Government Printing
    Office.
————. 1981. *Productivity Sharing Programs: Can They Contribute to Productivity
    Improvement?,* AFMD-81-22. Washington, DC: U.S. Government Printing Office.
————. 1985. *Initial Results of a Survey on Employee Stock Ownership Plans and Information
    on Related Economic Trends,* GAO/PEMD-85-11. Washington, DC: U.S. Government
    Printing Office.
————. 1986a. *Employee Stock Ownership Plans: Benefits and Costs of ESOP Tax Incentives
    for Broadening Stock Ownership,* GAO/PEMD-87-8. Washington, DC: U.S. Government
    Printing Office.
————. 1986b. *Employee Stock Ownership Plans: Interim Report on a Survey and Related
    Economic Trends,* GAO/PEMB-86-4BR. Washington, DC: U.S. Government Printing
    Office.
————. 1987. *Employee Stock Ownership Plans: Little Evidence of Effects on Corporate
    Performance,* PEMD-88-1. Washington, DC: U.S. Government Printing Office.
U.S. Office of Management and Budget. 1986. *Special Analyses: Budget of the United States
    Government, Fiscal Year 1987.* Washington, DC: U.S. Government Printing Office.
U.S. Senate, Committee on Finance. 1939. *Survey of Experiences in Profit Sharing and
    Possibilities of Incentive Taxation,* hearings 75th Congress, third session. Washington, DC:
    U.S. Government Printing Office.
————. 1980. *Employee Stock Ownership Plans: An Employer Handbook,* 96th Congress,
    second session. Washington, DC: U.S. Government Printing Office.
Van Dusen, K. 1945. *Union Policy and Incentive Wage Methods.* New York: Columbia University
    Press.

Vanek, J. 1970. *The General Theory of Labor-Managed Market Economies.* Ithaca, NY: Cornell University Press.

Walker, F.A. 1876. *The Wages Question: A Treatise on Wages and the Wages Class.* New York: Holt & Co.

Weisskopf, T.E., S. Bowles, and D.M. Gordon. 1983. Hearts and Minds: A Social Model of U.S. Productivity Growth. *Brookings Papers on Economic Activity* 2:381-441.

Weitzman, M.L. 1983. Some Macroeconomic Implications of Alternative Compensation Systems. *Economic Journal* 93(December):763-783.

————. 1984. *The Share Economy: Conquering Stagflation.* Cambridge, MA: Harvard University Press.

————. 1985. The Simple Macroeconomics of Profit Sharing. *American Economic Review* 75(December):937-953.

White, J.K. 1979. The Scanlon Plan: Causes and Correlates of Success. *Academy of Management Journal* 22(June):292-312.

Whyte, W.F. ed. 1955. *Money and Motivation: An Analysis of Incentives in Industry.* New York: Harper.

Whyte, W.F., T.H. Hammer, C.B. Meek, R. Nelson, and R.N. Stern. 1983. *Worker Participation and Ownership.* Ithaca, NY: ILR Press, New York State School of Industrial and Labor Relations, Cornell University.

William M. Mercer, Inc. 1980. *Employer Attitudes Toward Compensation and Employee Productivity.* New York: William M. Mercer, Inc.

————. 1983. *Employer Attitudes Toward Compensation Change and Corporate Values.* New York: William M. Mercer, Inc.

Wintner, L. 1983. *Employee Buyouts: An Alternative to Plant Closings,* Research Bulletin no. 140. New York: Conference Board.

Wolf, W.B. 1957. *Wage Incentives as a Managerial Tool.* New York: Columbia University Press.

Wyatt Company. 1988. *The 1987 Performance Management Survey.* Chicago: Wyatt.

Yukl, G.A., G.O. Latham, and E.D. Pursell. 1976. The Effectiveness of Performance Incentives Under Continuous and Variable Ratio Schedules of Reinforcement. *Personnel Psychology* 29(June):221-231.

Zalusky, J.L. 1987. Labor's Collective Bargaining Experience with Gainsharing and Profit-Sharing. In *Proceedings of the Thirty-Ninth Annual Meeting,* December 28-30, 1986, edited by B.D. Dennis. Madison, WI: Industrial Relations Research Association.

EQUAL PAY FOR WORK
OF EQUAL VALUE:
CANADA'S EXPERIENCE

Morley Gunderson and Roberta Edgecombe Robb

In the United States, after a flurry of activity in the comparable worth area in the 1970s, comparable worth legislation has largely been "on hold," being implemented in a few states and confined to the public sector (Cook 1985, p. 43; Ehrenberg and Smith 1987). In contrast, in Canada such initiatives have been expanding steadily since the 1970s.

As illustrated in Table 1, nine of the twelve Canadian jurisdictions have implemented comparable worth (also termed *equal pay for work of equal value* or *pay equity*).[1] While most of this legislation is either restricted to the public sector, or in fact applied mainly to the public sector, the situation in Ontario (Canada's most populous province) is particularly noticeable since it will be applied to the private sector. Furthermore, Ontario will not rely on a complaints-based system but rather will follow what is termed a "proactive," system-wide regulatory approach, requiring employers to utilize job evaluation procedures and to implement pay equity whether or not there is prima facie evidence of discrimination.

Advances in Industrial and Labor Relations, volume 5, pages 151-168.
Copyright © 1991 by JAI Press Inc.
All rights of reproduction in any form reserved.
ISBN: 0-89232-940-8

Table 1. Existence of Comparable Worth in Various Canadian Jurisdictions, 1990

Jurisdiction	Year	Private Sector	Enforcement
Comparable Worth			
Quebec	1977	Yes[a]	Complaints-based
Federal	1978	Yes[a]	Complaints-based
Manitoba required[b]	1985	No	Proactive, plans
Yukon	1987	No	Complaints-based
Ontario required[b]	1987[c]	Yes	Proactive and complaints
Newfoundland	1988	No	Part of collective bargaining
Prince Edward Island	1988	No	Proactive and complaints
Nova Scotia	1988	No	Proactive
New Brunswick	1989	No	Proactive
Conventional Equal Pay[d]			
British Columbia	1953	Yes	Complaints-based
Alberta	1957	Yes	Complaints-based
Saskatchewan	1952	Yes	Complaints-based

Notes: [a] Almost all cases have been in the public sector.
[b] Employers are required to initiate gender-neutral job evaluation and to adjust wages in female-dominated jobs to ensure equal pay for work of equal value.
[c] The legislation was passed in 1987 to commence on January 1, 1988. Wage adjustments are to commence no later than January 1, 1990 in the public sector and no later than January 1, 1991 in the private sector, beginning first with larger employers.
[d] All jurisdictions implementing or proposing comparable worth previously followed the conventional approach of requiring equal pay for *equal work* before moving to the comparable worth approach requiring equal pay for work of equal value.
More detailed analysis is given in Weiner and Gunderson (1990).

152

Before outlining the main features of the legislation, this paper provides a brief discussion of the male-female earnings gap in Canada and its implications for comparable worth. This is important because equal value legislation in Canada evolved in large part because of a perceived failure of existing policy initiatives to reduce the persistent earnings gap, especially that portion which arose because of differences in the occupational distribution between men and women.

EARNINGS GAP AND IMPETUS FOR COMPARABLE WORTH

There is considerable controversy in Canada, as elsewhere, on the extent to which the male-female earnings gap reflects discrimination, especially discrimination by employers in the labor market. The standard empirical procedure[2] used in most studies is to estimate separate human capital earnings equations for males and females and to decompose the earnings gap into two component parts: one attributed to differences in endowments of wage determining characteristics, and a residual component attributed to differences in pay for the same endowments of wage determining characteristics. The latter component is often taken as a measure of discrimination, although critics have termed it a measure of our ignorance in that it reflected factors that were not adequately controlled for in the regression procedure.

In particular, most data sets that were used in the conventional decomposition studies did not include important variables like actual work experience and the continuity of that experience, hours or work, absenteeism or preferences for certain occupations[3] that are compatible with differential household responsibilities especially the interruption of careers associated with childbearing and childraising. While many of these factors may themselves reflect discrimination prior to entry into the labor market, or an unequal division of household tasks or sex stereotyping in educational institutions, they need not be the result of employer discrimination in the labor market.

While there remains considerable controversy over the importance of employer discrimination in the labor market, there are a number of generalizations that tend to emerge from the empirical studies and that have implications for policy responses like comparable worth.[4]

1. Differences in the occupational distribution between males and females are a more important contributor to the earnings gap (see, for example, Treiman and Hartman 1981, p. 33), than are wage differentials within the same narrowly defined occupation within the same establishment, the latter being extremely small. This highlights the potential importance of comparable worth (since comparison can be made across establishments) and the limited scope of conventional equal pay laws.

2. There is some evidence, based mainly on U.S. studies, that the earnings gap (see Blau and Beller 1988 and references cited therein) and occupational segregation (see Beller 1985 and references cited therein) are being reduced over time, especially after controlling for compositional changes in the male and female workforce. However, the changes are small and the remaining gap and differences in the occupational distribution are substantial. Whether or not all of the remaining differences reflect discrimination, these unequal outcomes for men and women are regarded by many (although not all) as socially unacceptable.

3. The limited empirical evidence for Canada suggests that conventional equal pay policies requiring equal pay for *equal work* (as opposed to work of *equal value*) have not narrowed the male-female earnings gap (Gunderson 1975, 1985b).

These empirical generalizations have provided the impetus for many of the comparable worth initiatives, at least in Canada.[5] That is, comparable worth has been rationalized in large part because of the perceived failures of conventional equal pay policies to deal with the persistent earnings gap, especially that portion attributed to differences in the occupational distribution between men and women. While equal employment opportunity and affirmative action initiatives may help younger, mobile females and new entrants into the labor market, comparable worth may be necessary to help older women who are likely to remain in their existing job.

OPPOSITION TO COMPARABLE WORTH

Opposition to comparable worth has been based on a variety of considerations.[6] First, there is the potential for efficiency losses resulting from the fact that the legislation requires wages to be determined by an administrative procedure (job evaluation) as opposed to the market. This is akin to the search for a "just price," to be established independent of what people are willing to accept to do a job, and what others are willing to pay to have the job done.

Second, there is concern over the administrative costs of the job evaluation procedures—procedures that were originally used to establish the ordinal ranking of a job, not the cardinal value to attach to a job. Third, as with any wage fixing legislation, comparable worth may reduce the employment opportunities of the same groups it is designed to help.

Lastly, comparable worth may only be dealing with the symptom and not the cause of the problem. If the problem arises because of constraints originating from outside of the labor market, then policies should be directed at that source, not at employers in the labor market. If occupational segregation is the problem, then equal employment opportunity may be the answer. In fact, by reducing the wage gap between male-dominated and female-dominated jobs, comparable worth may reduce the incentive for women to leave the low wage, female-dominated jobs.

PUBLIC POLICY ANALYTICAL FRAMEWORK

Whatever the merits of these arguments, the debate in Canada has shifted from the pros and cons of comparable worth[7] to issues pertaining to how it should best be implemented. Specifically, whether or not discrimination actually exists in the labor market, and whether or not comparable worth is the appropriate policy response, no longer seems to be the major issue in Canada. Rather, the debate has moved to the level of how to design and implement comparable worth so as to maximize its benefits while minimizing its adverse consequences. Issues in this debate may be of broader relevance to jurisdictions contemplating policy changes in this area.

For this reason, this paper focuses on the main design features of comparable worth: (1) coverage, (2) a complaints-based versus a system-wide proactive model, (3) the definition of establishment and comparisons across establishments, (4) the definition of gender dominance, (5) allowable differences in compensation, (6) job evaluation and estimating pay lines, (7) wage adjustments, and (8) phasing.

Each of these design features is examined through a public-policy analytical framework that emphasizes their efficiency and equity implications. Efficiency is broadly construed to refer to administrative efficiency (minimizing real resource costs and bureaucratic intervention) as well as allocative efficiency (minimizing interference with the efficient allocation of resources). The concept of equity is also broadly construed to include both horizontal equity and vertical equity. Horizontal equity (the equal treatment of equals) refers to the ability of a policy to help all those in the target group and to remedy their unequal treatment as much as possible. Vertical equity (the unequal treatment of unequals) refers to the ability of a policy to remedy the situation of the target group without having the benefits spill over into the hands of the nontarget group.

In the case of comparable worth, the target group is persons in female-dominated jobs that are undervalued where value is determined by a job evaluation procedure. A design feature would facilitate the attainment of vertical and horizontal equity if it closed the earnings gap between male- and female-dominated jobs of the same value for all persons in the female-dominated job, without having the benefits spill over into the hands of those not in the female-dominated job. Obviously, spillover benefits to those who are *near* the cutoff of female dominance (i.e., in mixed occupations) are not as undesirable as spillover benefits to those in "over-valued" male-dominated jobs.

In the comparable worth area, it is important to remember that the concept of equity refers to the redress for persons (both males and females) in undervalued female-dominated jobs, wherever they are in the distribution of income. It is not designed per se to improve the wages of low wage women, although that broader distributional issue obviously is of potential relevance.

The remainder of the paper assesses the equity and efficiency implications of the main design features of comparable worth, as they have been discussed in the Canadian context. Rather than deal with all of the various dimensions of the equity and efficiency criteria, the focus is on those that are most relevant to each design feature.

DESIGN FEATURES: ONTARIO AND FEDERAL SECTORS

The design features analyzed are from the Ontario and the federal jurisdictions.[8] These two jurisdictions were selected because the federal jursidiction has the most experience with applying the legislation, and Ontario has the most comprehensive system, with a proactive approach being applied to the private as well as the public sector.

Coverage

The Ontario legislation completely exempts firms with fewer than 10 employees, and does not require formal job evaluation in firms of 10-99 employees. This was done in recognition of the fact that, in small establishments, formal job evaluations are not common[9] (and hence would have to be introduced); and, when they are used, they are more costly (because the fixed cost component is amortized over fewer employees).[10] In essence, uniform coverage to small business would likely have implied a disproportionate burden on small establishments given the difficulty and greater cost of job evaluation.

The differential treatment of small establishments may also have resulted from the political pressure of that constituency. They have considerable force, in part because small business is often regarded as the engine of economic growth and job creation. There is concern that excessive regulation of small business may reduce efficiency, growth, and job creation.

The coverage of the private sector in Ontario was a major step because elsewhere comparable worth is largely a public sector phenomenon. Why this innovative step was first taken in Ontario is by no means obvious. It did occur under an accord between the Liberals and the left-of-center New Democratic Party, and hence, it may have reflected a dominance of equity versus efficiency considerations—the latter being associated with business interests in the private sector. It also occurred at a time when the Ontario economy was incredibly prosperous and, hence, there may have been a perception that it could absorb the adjustment consequences, and any efficiency costs, with a minimum of disruption.

In the federal jurisdiction, coverage is complete. Approximately 10 percent of the Canadian workforce is under federal jurisdiction, mainly in the federal civil service, crown corporations and agencies, and in private corporations mainly in transportation, communications, and banking. While all firms are covered regardless of size, 93 percent of the employees in the federal sector work for employers of 100 or more employees. Hence, the exemption of small business is not a major issue. As well, although coverage is extended to the private sector, it is a heavily regulated private sector and virtually all cases so far have been in the public sector.

Complaints-Based Versus System-Wide, Proactive Model

Undoubtedly, the most important design feature of comparable worth is whether it will be administered on a complaints basis or on a more proactive basis that will require employers to have an acceptable comparable worth policy in place, irrespective of a complaint. The complaints-based model is currently used in the federal sector, although they are proposing to move to the proactive model.

Under the current system, the legislation has to be activated by a complaint, usually from an employee (or group of employees) or a bargaining agent. Some of these complaints may be subsequently dismissed because comparisons are not being made between predominantly male and female jobs, or the jobs are not in the same establishment, or they are exempt because the pay difference is based upon one of the "reasonable factors" recognized by the Human Rights Commission. If the complaint goes forward, then appropriate steps are taken to institute a job evaluation procedure that is free of gender bias. Once the results are obtained, the commission may act as a conciliator to foster a voluntary settlement. If that does not occur, a tribunal is appointed to give a binding decision which can only be challenged in a federal court.

From an employee's point of view, the complaints-based system is costly both because of the time-consuming and elaborate procedure that is involved, and also because of the possibility of employer reprisals. Furthermore, the individual complainant bears the burden of these costs, while other similarly situated groups may "free-ride" on the benefits if they too receive an adjustment. This violates the principle of horizontal equity and it may lead to a less than socially optimal number of complaints because complainants bear the full cost, while others may receive some of the adjustment benefits. For these reasons, few equal value complaints have been lodged in the federal sector,[11] and when they are, it is usually by a union.

The complaints-based system can also lead to horizontal inequities among otherwise similarly situated firms, only some of which are subject to a complaint.

If the adjustment is large enough, they could be placed at a competitive disadvantage relative to firms that have not had to adjust their wages.

Because of these perceived problems, Ontario adopted a system-wide, proactive, regulatory approach. This requires all employers (with 100 or more employees) to utilize a bona fide job evaluation plan, to develop and post a pay equity plan, and ultimately to achieve pay equity by eliminating any wage differential between male- and female-dominated jobs of the same value as determined by the job evaluation plan. It is the combination of this proactive approach *and* the application to the private sector that makes the Ontario legislation virtually unique.

While the proactive approach solves some of the problems of the horizontal inequities and the "free-rider" problem of the complaints-based system, it creates the potential for conflicts with efficiency. It involves the substantial administrative cost of a job evaluation procedure that is required whether or not there is a complaint or prima facie evidence of discrimination. Given the system-wide application, especially to the private sector, it also involves the potential to interfere with efficiency, at least as dictated by market forces of supply and demand.

Definitions of Establishment and Comparisons Across Establishments

Under the federal act, an establishment is defined in functional terms whereby employees of the same company covered by a common set of personnel and compensation policies (notwithstanding any collective agreement or geographical location), are considered to be one establishment. This, in all likelihoood, minimizes interference with the efficient allocation of labor because a common personnel policy can reflect labor market realities. This is especially the case when wage differentials based on regional pay structures are allowed, as is the case in the federal jurisdiction.

In Ontario, an establishment is defined as a corporate entity within a specific geographical area (county, territorial district, or regional municipality). The employer can (with the consent of the union, if any) expand the definition of establishment to include more than one geographic division, but the employer cannot subdivide a geographic division; that is, all work places in a given geographic division must be included as part of the establishment.

The corporate definition, as used in Ontario, raises the possibility that an employer could establish separate geographic branches for its male- and female-dominated jobs. The federal functional definition precludes this possibility, but at the cost of having to establish whether a common personnel and compensation policy prevails, or whether the differential reflects legitimate regional pay structures.

In both Ontario and the federal jurisdictions, wage comparisons are to be made *within* the same establishment, as is the case with virtually all comparable worth legislation.[12] This is done in recognition of the fact that job evaluation comparisons within an establishment have numerous problems; those problems would be compounded if comparisons were made across different establishments (and hence possibly across different regions and industries as well). It should be emphasized, however, that these are practical problems. If—and this is an important if—the principles of comparable worth are correct, there is nothing conceptually inappropriate about extending them to comparisons across establishments. Of course, if the application of comparable worth creates administrative costs and interferes with the efficient allocation of resources, then any extension of the legislation compounds such inefficiencies. The extent to which such inefficiencies are compounded depends on the extent to which such inter-establishment differentials were necessary to induce the efficient allocation of labor, and such legitimate wage differentials could not be exempted.

Restricting comparisons to within the same establishment creates horizontal inequities in that large numbers in predominantly female establishments (e.g., day care, textiles) have no avenue for redress because of the absence of male-dominated comparison groups. This is especially the case given the empirical evidence that the economy-wide effect of comparable worth is severely limited by its inability to make comparisons across establishments (Johnson and Solon 1986). It may also create inequities across employers, some of whom may have no predominantly male occupations for internal comparison. Those employers that practiced the most occupational segregation by having all-female workforces would, in fact, be exempt.

Gender Dominance

In both Ontario and the federal sector, earnings comparisons must take place between male- and female-dominated groups. Under the federal act, gender dominance depends on the size of the occupational group: 70 percent of one sex for groups with less than 100 employees, 60 percent for groups of 100-500 employees, and 55 percent for groups of more than 500 employees. In Ontario, a predominantly female group of jobs generally means a group of jobs that has 60 percent or more of the positions filled by women, and a predominantly male job has 70 percent or more of the positions in the group occupied by men. There is also the provision, however, that a male- or female-dominated job class is one that the Pay Equity Commission, or the employer with the agreement of the bargaining agent (if any) designates as such.[13]

A broader definition of female dominance (e.g., 60 percent as opposed to 70 percent female) obviously expands the number of people who are potentially eligible for a wage adjustment. However, this expansion of the target population means that more males will receive the adjustment, and the adjustment will be going to people who are in more mixed occupations and whose wage is thereby more likely to be determined by the male wages in those mixed occupations. If there is binding budgetary constraint on the magnitude of the wage adjustment (e.g., maximum 1 percent of payroll cost), then these spillover benefits mean that persons in the more female-dominated groups receive less.

Whatever definition of female dominance that is adopted, there will always be a margin of people who feel inequitably treated because they just miss being included in the group that is eligible for wage adjustments. Expanding the definition, say from 70 to 60 percent, simply displaces that margin, albeit perhaps to a group that is less subject to the effects of occupational segregation.

A broader definition of *male* dominance expands the likelihood that a male-dominated comparison group is available for comparison purposes. It will likely involve smaller wage adjustments, however, because wages in the more mixed occupations are likely to be lowered by the larger number of females.

Allowable Differences in Compensation

In both Ontario and federal jurisdictions, wage differences between male- and female-dominated jobs are allowed if they can be shown to be the result of the following: a seniority system that does not discriminate on the basis of gender, a merit compensation plan, a temporary training position, red-circling (downgrading of a position resulting in wages that are temporarily fixed or wage increases that are temporarily curtailed), or a skills shortage. The federal legislation also allows differences based on a rehabilitation assignment, demotion pay procedures, and regional pay structures. Ontario's list further excludes "casual" positions (where the work is performed on a nonregular basis for less than one-third of the normal work period that applies for similar full-time work). Also, in Ontario, once pay equity is achieved in an establishment, subsequent wage differences based on different bargaining strengths (union premiums) will be allowed.

Such allowable differences clearly reduce the extent to which comparable worth interferes with market forces of efficiency. Of course, this very process opens the door for loopholes and for bureaucratic judgment calls as to what is a legitimate exemption. It is in this area of exemptions where many of the compromises between efficiency and equity will be carried out.

Job Evaluation and Estimating Pay Lines

In both the federal sector and Ontario, the value of work is based on the job components or "compensable factors" of skill, effort, and responsibility. In the federal sector, the Human Rights Commission will accept assessments based on the employer's own job evaluation scheme as long as the plan is deemed (by the commission) to be free from gender bias. The commission will provide its own job evaluation in cases where employers may not have existing plans. In Ontario, Bill 154 specifies that the job evaluation plans are to be determined by the employers (in the case of nonunionized employees) and negotiated jointly by employers and unions in the case of unionized employees. If employer/union agreement on a plan cannot be reached, or if nonunionized employees challenge the employer's plan, then the Pay Equity Commission will resolve the issue.

In Ontario, there must be a separate plan for *each* bargaining unit within the establishment, and one for the nonunionized employees (if any). In unionized situations, male job class comparisons for female-dominated job classes are first sought within the bargaining unit. If no male-dominated job comparison exists within the bargaining unit, the search for comparison extends throughout the establishment. For a nonunionized female job class, comparisons should first be sought in the nonunionized sector. If none is available, then comparison can be extended elsewhere in the firm.

Once the process of job evaluation has been completed, the process of making the actual comparable worth wage assessments often involves the estimation of separate pay lines for predominantly male and female jobs in the organization. The precise method for estimating the pay lines has not been specified in the federal act. The Ontario legislation requires comparisons of female-dominated jobs with male-dominated jobs of the same value (or the next lowest value, if jobs of the same value are not available). The role of pay lines is unspecified.

The conventional procedure for estimating pay lines is to regress pay on job evaluation point scores, separately for male- and female-dominated jobs. The job evaluation point score is obtained by simply summing the separate point scores assigned to the various factors pertaining to the skill, effort, responsibility, and working conditions of the job. Summing the separate scores in this fashion implicitly assumes that points for each factor merit equal weight; that is, a point assigned for skill equals a point assigned for effort, and so forth. This seems reasonable only if the ranges and the assignment of the points were designed very carefully to ensure such an equality of weights.

An alternative would be to enter the separate scores for each compensable factor as separate regressors in a multivariate regression equation. The separate regression coefficients for each compensable factor, based on the predominantly male jobs, would give the shadow price or weight that the market or the process of collective bargaining attaches to a point score for each compensable factor. These weights could then be applied to the average point scores in each of the female-dominated jobs to get an estimate of the hypothetical wage that they would be paid if female-dominated jobs were compensated according to the pay structure of the male-dominated jobs.

This is termed a "policy capturing" approach in that it simply extends the pay structure that is generated in the male-dominated jobs into the female ones (see Treiman and Hartman 1981, p. 72; Aaron and Lougy 1986, p. 28; and

Wilborn 1986, p. 64). That pay structure may reflect the forces of competition, collective bargaining, or nepotism; however, it will not reflect the direct effect of discrimination against females. It is analogous to the conventional procedure of estimating separate pay lines based on the aggregate of the component scores, except that it does not restrict the weight (regression coefficient) associated with each component to be the same. Market forces or collective bargaining are allowed to give rise to different weights for the compensable factors, and then those "nondiscriminatory" weights are simply applied to the predominantly female jobs.

In fact, the equality of the weights could be tested for by a conventional hypothesis test on the simultaneous equality of the regression coefficients from each of the compensable factors. Although their analysis was not designed with that purpose in mind, Ehrenberg and Smith (1987) did estimate separate coefficients for each compensable factor in such a regression. They found no significant differences across coefficients. Whether their results are generalizable, however, is an empirical unknown.

One other important issue which arises in the estimation of pay lines is the question of functional form. Conventionally, a linear relationship with an intercept is assumed. However, in some cases, piece-wise regression is used with separate linear relationships estimated over different ranges of the data, largely because the scatter plot of the observations indicates this to be the case. Also, in some cases, unusual outliers are discarded on the grounds that they are not representative.

Obviously, other functional forms are possible, such as a quadratic or a polynomial relationship between pay and point scores. However, neither economic theory nor basic principles of job evaluation suggest an appropriate functional form. The linear relationship would be appropriate, according to economic theory, if the job evaluation points were equal substitutes for each other (and hence merited the same shadow price) at all levels of the points. For example, if the one-hundredth point were equal to the one-hundred-and-fiftieth point (where that value would be given by the estimated regression coefficient) then the linear relationship would be appropriate.

Even if the linear relationship is deemed appropriate, there remains the further question of whether the same linear relationship should be imposed upon the male and female pay lines. This would be the equivalent of a single regression with a dummy variable shift parameter distinguishing the predominantly male and female jobs. That is, the pay lines would have the same slope; they would simply have different intercepts. This assumes that the level of discrimination is independent of the level of the job, where the latter is represented by job evaluation point scores.

This seems an unduly restrictive assumption. It seems more reasonable to let the data "speak for itself" indicating whether unequal pay for work of equal value differs by the level of the job (i.e., to allow different slopes for the predominantly male and female jobs). Extending the logic of allowing the data to speak for itself, however, would also suggest a very flexible functional form between pay and points. This, however, could give rise to very substantially different adjustments for groups that had only slightly different point scores. This, in turn, can create problems of internal equity even within the predominantly female jobs; *differential* redress can create as many problems as no redress.

Once the pay lines are estimated, there is also the issue of whether interpolation of the pay line should be allowed within the range of the point scores in the data. Interpolation would allow comparisons of the pay in a predominantly female job with the pay that would be *expected* in a predominantly male job of that same job evaluation point score; the expected male wage would be estimated by interpolation of the male pay line. This would allow comparisons where female-dominated jobs did not have a male-dominated job for comparison purposes at the same point score. (For this reason, the phrase *comparable* worth is sometimes used to denote situations where equal worth is not required before a comparison can be made; rather, the worth only has to be comparable as established, for example, by interpolation.)

If interpolation is not allowed, then some criterion has to be established for making comparisons with female-dominated jobs that do not have a predominantly male comparison group at the same job evaluation point score. Comparable male-dominated jobs could be the one at the closest point score, or the next lowest point score (the latter being the criteria adopted in Ontario).

More controversial than the issue of interpolation is whether extrapolation or projection of the male pay line should be allowed outside of the range of the point scores of the predominantly male jobs. This can occur especially because there may not be any male jobs to compare with the predominantly female jobs at the low end of the job evaluation point score. Extrapolating the male pay line into that range provides an estimate of the hypothetical male wage that would prevail if the male job did have that point score.

Extrapolation involves the same basic principle as interpolation except that the accuracy of the estimate of the hypothetical male wage is reduced by the fact that extrapolations are being made outside of the range of the data. Formally, the confidence interval increases as estimates are made away from the mean of the data; hence, the confidence that one can place on the expected male wage is reduced under extrapolation.

Allowing interpolation or extrapolation of the male pay line is tantamount to recognition of the principle of proportionate-pay-for-work-of-proportionate-value. Without that principle, if a female-dominated job were found to have 80 percent of the value of a male-dominated job (as determined by job evaluation scores) but only 60 percent of its pay, there would be no grounds for redress. Comparisons could only be made with jobs of equal or substantially similar value (e.g., within 5 percent of each other). Interpolation within the range of the data, or extrapolation outside of that range, would allow such comparison and on the same basis as other comparable worth comparisons are made (i.e., on the basis of estimating pay lines).

Wage Adjustments

Once the separate pay lines have been estimated, there is then the issue of the appropriate adjustment procedure for raising the wages of the undervalued female-dominated jobs.[14] In Ontario, pay equity is regarded as being achieved when the rate for the female job class is at least as great as the rate in the male job class if the work performed is of equal or comparable value. If there is no male job class of comparable value, then one uses the male rate of the job with the next highest value. If more than one male comparison group is available, then the lowest male rate is used if jobs are of the same value, and the highest male rate is used if the male job is of lower value because there are no male jobs of the same value. This might be thought of as a point-to-point procedure.

In the federal sector, a point-to-line procedure is used whereby the wages in each of the undervalued female jobs is raised to the male pay line. This removes both the systematic underevaluation in female pay (i.e., the difference between the male and female lines) as well as the random variation in female pay (i.e., the variation about the female pay line). This implies a larger adjustment for those female jobs that are below the female pay line, and a smaller adjustment for those that are above the female pay line. After the adjustment, all female jobs are on the male pay line. However, there will still be random variation in the male-dominated jobs about their pay line.[15]

An alternative procedure to that used in either Ontario or the federal sector would be to leave the random variation about both pay lines and to simply raise the female pay line to the male pay line. If the pay lines were to have the same slope, then this would imply an equal absolute adjustment for each female-dominated job. If the slopes differed, then the magnitude of the adjustment would depend upon how the gap varied by the level of the job evaluation score. In general, the average magnitude of the adjustment in this line-to-line procedure would be the same as in the point-to-point procedure because the female pay line "averages out" the random deviations about this line (i.e., a property of regression analysis is that the sum of the absolute deviations about the line equals zero). However, the adjustment to particular jobs will obviously be different when both random and systematic variation in wages are being removed.

The rationale for the line-to-line procedure is that it removes only the systematic underevaluation of female-dominated jobs. The random variation (i.e., deviation about the pay lines) reflects random variation in pay that prevails for both male- and female-dominated jobs. Because its existence does not reflect gender discrimination and because it will remain in the male-dominated jobs, there is a rationale for not removing it in the female-dominated jobs, at least through pay equity procedures. Following a line-to-line adjustment procedure also means that the adjustments will be more equal, and this may be more acceptable for purposes of internal equity within the female-dominated jobs. However, the line-to-line adjustment procedure means that those female-dominated jobs that previously were "overpaid" (i.e., above the female pay line) relative to other female-dominated jobs will remain overpaid after the award, and vice-versa for the "underpaid" female-dominated jobs that were below the female pay line. Clearly, trade-offs are involved.

Phasing

Both the federal and the Ontario legislation allow for a phase-in of wage increases. In the federal sector, the precise phase-in time is not specified in the act. The commission appears to operate on a case-by-case basis. In Ontario, the phase-in period is outlined directly in the act and is dependent on firm size. Firms in the broader public and private sector will have from 2-6 years (effective January 1, 1988) before wage adjustments will have to be started, and adjustment costs (in any given year) will be limited to 1 percent of the previous year's payroll. The exception to this latter constraint is in the public sector, where *all* wage adjustments must be completed within 5 years of the start of the adjustments.

Phasing clearly represents a pragmatic compromise to facilitate the adjustment process. It provides firms with time to adopt their existing job evaluation scheme or to implement a new one. Allowing a longer phasing period for smaller firms seems equitable because it partly offsets the fact that the adjustment process is otherwise likely to be more costly for them given that they tend not to use job evaluation procedures. For all firms, it may reduce any disemployment effects. This is important because otherwise disemployment effects imply horizontal inequities—substantial wage increases for those who receive the adjustment, but perhaps unemployment for those who bear the brunt of any adverse employment effect.

CONCLUDING OBSERVATIONS

Comparable worth is, and will likely remain, a controversial policy initiative. The debate in Canada has shifted away from the pros and cons of comparable worth and toward how to design and implement the legislation effectively. These issues should be of broader relevance to other jurisdictions contemplating changes in these areas, especially given some of the features of Canadian implementation. These features include a proactive system-wide application, the extension to the private sector, implementation through collective bargaining, and the use of a complaints-based procedure.

As with so many issues of policy design, the implementation and design features of comparable worth represent a judicious balance of the trade-offs between various equity and efficiency considerations. As well, issues of pure political expediency are likely to be involved.

Unfortunately, there is very little literature, academic or otherwise, on these issues of design and implementation. This likely reflects the fact that it requires information from a variety of areas—job evaluation procedures and compensation, statistical procedures, collective bargaining, legal issues, and economics. As well, the newness of the procedure means that we do not have a legacy of experience from which to draw. This paper is an attempt to fill some of that void by outlining some of the Canadian experience, focusing on the equity and efficiency implications of the most important design features. As that experience unfolds, further dialogue becomes even more important.

NOTES

1.   Throughout the paper, the terms comparable worth (the phraseology used in the United States), equal pay for work of equal value (the term conventionally used in Canada and internationally), and pay equity (the term used recently in Ontario with respect to its initiatives) are used interchangeably, although some parties attach different meanings to the terms. Specifically, comparable worth is sometimes used to denote the principle that the jobs do not have to be precisely *equal* before comparisons have to be made; they only have to be comparable, where comparable may be defined, for example, as within five points of each other on a job evaluation point ranking. In a more technical sense, comparable worth is also sometimes used to denote the possibility that estimated pay lines in job evaluation procedures can be used to establish the worth of jobs, through interpolation or projection, even if there is no male-dominated job at that particular point score. However, in general, the terms are used interchangeably, and that practice is followed in this paper unless otherwise stated.

2.   See, for example, Canadian studies by Robb (1978), Gunderson (1979), Shapiro and Stelcner (1981), and Miller (1987), all variants of the procedure outlined in Oaxaca (1973). For a discussion of the earnings gap based on U.S. data and some of the controversy surrounding the estimation of the gap, see the U.S. Commission on Civil Rights (1984), Treiman and Hartman (1981), Wilborn (1986), and Gunderson (1989).

3.   Recent work with data sets that contain information on these otherwise conventionally "omitted variables" tends to find them to be important determinants of the occupational structure and earnings. See, for example, Filer (1986) and references cited therein.

4.   See, for example, Gunderson (1989) as well as other survey studies cited therein.

5.   For a more detailed discussion of these points, see Robb (1987). Alternatively, one referee indicated "there are additional explanations for the emergence of comparable worth. An example is the public choice approach, namely that a large and powerful interest group seeks higher wages independent of any negative ramifications on aggregate productivity and growth." Our personal assessment is that this is not a fruitful approach for explaining the existence of comparable worth and that even if such a hypothesis could be tested, it would not be verified.

On the question of who gains and who loses by comparable worth, Smith (1988) indicates that, because of differential coverage, higher wage females are likely to gain at the possible expense of lower wage females (even though in the cases where it is applied, the gains may go to lower wage women). This latter proposition of the gains going to lower wage women in the case where it is applied is confirmed in Orazem and Matilla (1988), who find that in the implementation of comparable worth for state employees in Iowa, the greatest gains went to low wage workers, women in general and union workers. The majority of workers gained because of the infusion of public funds. This infusion is unlikely to be sustained, however, suggesting that males may eventually experience real wage cuts as a result of comparable worth.

6.   For a detailed discussion of these points in the Canadian context, see Gunderson (1985a) and Robb (1987).

7.   For a detailed discussion of the more basic issue of the pros and cons of comparable worth, see Aaron and Lougy (1986), Gunderson (1989), Hartman (1985, especially the articles by Bergman and Killingsworth), Robb (1987), U.S. Commission on Civil Rights (1984), and Wilborn (1986).

8.   The federal legislation is described in the *Canada Gazette* (1986) and the Ontario legislation in Ontario (1987). Many of the design features are described in Ontario (1985, 1986).

9.   Robb (1987, p. 453) cites evidence from Labour Canada indicating that some form of job evaluation plan is used in 67 percent of large firms (1,000-4,999 employees), 70 percent of medium-size firms (200-999 employees), and 50 percent of smaller firms (50-199 employees). Of these, 71, 52, and 42 percent, respectively, are plans that would be suitable for equal value comparisons. Thus, the proportion of firms with job evaluation plans suitable for equal value comparisons are 48 percent for large firms, 36 percent for medium-size firms, and 21 percent for smaller firms.

10.   Robb (1987, p. 453) cites Canadian evidence indicating that the administrative cost of setting up a job evaluation procedure is in the neighborhood of $200-300 per employee for large firms and $300-400 per employee for small firms.

11.   Between 1978 and 1987, 77 complaints were made in the federal sector. Of these, 32 were dismissed, 21 were settled, 6 were before a tribunal, 12 were under investigation, and 6 were withdrawn. It is estimated that only some 6,000 workers (in a sector that has 903,000 workers of which one-third are women) have been affected by the equal value policy.

12.   The Ontario Pay Equity Commission is currently considering the feasibility of making wage comparisons across establishments.

13.   The Ontario legislation allows for what is called "historical incumbency," which refers to the historical pattern of employment for a particular job class within an employer's establishment. For example, if a job class in question is one that has traditionally been filled by men, but has recently been filled by women, it may still be considered a male job class. Similarly, a gender-neutral job class may currently exist which historically had been considered a female job class.

14.   In both the federal and the Ontario legislation, differences in wages between the male- and female-dominated jobs must be eliminated by raising the wages in the female-dominated jobs, not by lowering wages in male-dominated jobs.

15.   With this type of adjustment, there is the concern that under the Canadian Charter of Rights, males (whose wages are now under the pay line) will apply to have their wages compared to the (now higher) earnings in some female- or other male-dominated jobs.

REFERENCES

Aaron, H. and C. Lougy. 1986. *The Comparable Worth Controversy*. Washington, DC: Brookings Institution.

Beller, A. 1985. Changes in the Sex Composition of U.S. Occupations, 1960-1981. *Journal of Human Resources* 20(2):235-250.

Blau, F. and A. Beller. 1988. Trends in Earnings Differentials by Gender, 1971-1981. *Industrial and Labor Relations Review* 41(4):513-529.

Canada Gazette. 1986. The Canadian Human Rights Act Employers Guide, II:120:25.

Cook, A. 1985. *Comparable Worth: A Case Book of Experiences in States and Localities.* Manoa, HI: Industrial Relations Center, University of Hawaii.

Ehrenberg, R. and R. Smith. 1987. Comparable Worth in the Public Sector. Pp. 243-288 in *Public Sector Compensation,* edited by D. Wise. Chicago: University of Chicago Press.

Filer, R. 1986. The Role of Personality and Tastes in Determining Occupational Structure. *Industrial and Labor Relations Review* 39(3):412-424.

Gunderson, M. 1975. Male-Female Wage Differentials and the Impact of Equal Pay Legislation. *Review of Economics and Statistics* 57(4):462-469.

———. 1979. Decomposition of Male-Female Earnings Differentials: Canada, 1970. *Canadian Journal of Economics* 12(3):479-485.

———. 1985a. Discrimination, Equal Pay, and Equal Opportunities in the Labour Market. Pp. 219-265 in *Work and Pay: The Canadian Labour Market,* edited by W.C. Riddell. Toronto, Canada: Royal Commission on the Economic Union and Development Prospects for Canada, University of Toronto Press.

———. 1985b. Spline Function Estimates of the Impact of Equal Pay Legislation: The Ontario Experience. *Relations Industrielles/Industrial Relations* 4(4):775-791.

———. 1989. Male-Female Wage Differentials and Policy Responses. *Journal of Economic Literature* 27(1):46-72.

Hartman, H. ed. 1985. *Comparable Worth: New Directions for Research.* Washington, DC: National Academy Press.

Johnson, G. and G. Solon. 1986. Estimates of the Direct Effects of Comparable Worth Policy. *American Economic Review* 76(3):1117-1125.

Miller, P. 1987. Gender Differences in Observed and Offered Wages in Canada, 1980. *Canadian Journal of Economics* 20(2):225-244.

Oaxaca, R. 1973. Male-Female Wage Differentials in Urban Labour Markets. *International Economics Review* 14(3):693-709.

Ontario. 1985. *Green Paper on Pay Equity.* Toronto, Canada: Attorney General's Office.

———. 1986. *The Report of the Consultation Panel on Pay Equity.* Toronto, Canada: Attorney General's Office.

———. 1987. *Pay Equity Act, 1987,* Bill 154. Toronto, Canada: Queen's Printer for Ontario.

Orazem, P. and J.P. Mattila. 1988. *The Political Economy of Comparable Worth: The Iowa Case 1983-1987.* Ames, IA: Department of Economics, Iowa State University. Mimeo.

Robb, R.E. 1978. Earnings Differentials Between Males and Females in Ontario, 1971. *Canadian Journal of Economics* 11(2):350-357.

———. 1987. Equal Pay for Work of Equal Value: Issues and Policies. *Canadian Public Policy* 13(4):445-461.

Shapiro, D.M. and M. Stelcner. 1981. Male-Female Earnings Differentials and the Role of Language in Canada, Ontario and Quebec, 1970. *Canadian Journal of Economics* 14(2):341-348.

Smith, R. 1988. Comparable Worth: Limited Coverage and the Exacerbation of Inequality. *Industrial and Labor Relations Review* 41(2):227-239.

Treiman, D. and H. Hartman, eds. 1981. *Women, Work and Wages: Equal Pay for Jobs of Equal Value.* Washington, DC: National Academy Press.

U.S. Commission on Civil Rights. 1984. *Comparable Worth: Issue for the 80's.* Washington, DC: A Consultation of the U.S. Commission on Civil Rights.

Weiner, N. and M. Gunderson. 1990. *Pay Equity: Issues, Options and Experiences.* Toronto: Butterworths.

Wilborn, S. 1986. *A Comparable Worth Primer.* Lexington: Heath.

CONTINENTAL DIVIDE:

THE DIRECTION AND FATE OF

NORTH AMERICAN UNIONS

Gary N. Chaison and Joseph B. Rose

The merger of the American Federation of Labor (AFL) and Congress of Industrial Organizations (CIO) in 1955 led many "to expect a fresh impetus to organize the increasing numbers of unorganized workers" (Chamberlain, Cullen, and Lewin 1980, p. 116). A similar expectation was created in Canada the following year when the Trades and Labour Congress (TLC) and the Canadian Congress of Labour (CCL) merged to form the Canadian Labour Congress (CLC).[1] By 1980, there was clear evidence that the Canadian labor movement had consistently outperformed its American counterpart in terms of union growth, union density (the proportion of nonagricultural employment organized by unions), and the certification of new bargaining units. The divergent trends were not the result of market factors, but differences in the legal framework and the incidence and intensity of employer opposition to union organizing in the two countries. It also was recognized that union-related variables (e.g., militancy and the desire and ability to organize) might be important determinants of union performance (Rose and Chaison 1985).

Advances in Industrial and Labor Relations, volume 5, pages 169-205.
Copyright © 1991 by JAI Press Inc.
All rights of reproduction in any form reserved.
ISBN: 0-89232-940-8

The purpose of this paper is to update our earlier research and to expand the scope of that study. First, we present evidence of the extent of the divergent trends in the United States and Canada. In addition to considering aggregate trends in union membership and union density, cross-sectional data are presented on union membership by sex, education, employment status (part-time and full-time employees), occupation, and industry. Additional data were gathered on union organizing in both countries. In a second section we review studies and analyze data to determine the roles of five explanatory factors: market shifts, public policy, employer resistance, union organizing efforts, and public opinion. Conclusions are then reached about the relative importance of these factors and their interaction.

Recent prescriptions for labor law reform (e.g., Weiler 1983, 1985; Dickens 1988) have cited differences in Canadian and U.S. certification procedures (viewing the former positively and the latter negatively), and have related these to trends in union growth in the two countries. In our study we go beyond these limited comparisons and examine the relative contributions of four explanatory factors in addition to public policy. There have also been some studies which take the approach of first presenting a "body" or malady in the form of declining union membership, density or organizing ability, and then evaluate "suspects" or likely causes (e.g., Freeman 1985, 1987; Goldfield 1987). Our analysis follows a similar pattern but from a comparative perspective which we believe will result in a more revealing investigation. As we noted in our earlier article (Rose and Chaison 1985, p. 109):

> ... a better perspective on the state of American unions requires the simultaneous examination of a labor movement that is significantly different yet that shares enough common elements for meaningful comparison. The Canadian labor movement is the obvious, though often overlooked, choice for making such a comparison.

DIVERGENT TRENDS

Union Membership

Table 1 presents comparative union membership data for the period 1956 to 1986 and reveals that North America's labor movements are moving in opposite directions. In the United States, unions have experienced stagnation and decline. Union membership increased steadily between 1956 and 1975, peaked in the late 1970s, and declined in the 1980s. According to the Troy and Sheflin series, the net membership increase was 1,910,000 members (11.6 percent) from 1956 to 1984; the BLS series (with Gifford's updated figures) reports an increase of 2,273,000 members (13 percent) between 1956 and 1982. The CPS survey shows that unions have lost 742,000 members (4.2 percent) from 1983 to 1986. As well, union density has fallen from more than 30 percent in 1956 to below 18 percent in 1986.

Table 1a. Union Membership[a] and Union Density[b]
in the United States and Canada

	United States					
	Troy and Sheflin		CPS		BLS	
Year	Membership	Density (%)	Membership	Density (%)	Membership	Density (%)
1956	16,396	31.4			17,490	33.4
1960	15,516	28.6			17,049	31.4
1965	16,949	30.1			17,299	28.4
1970	20,990	29.6			21,248	30.0
1975	22,207	28.9			22,361	28.9
1976	22,153	27.9			22,662	28.3
1977	21,632	26.2			22,456	27.2
1978	21,757	25.1			22,757	26.2
1979	22,025	24.5			22,579	25.1
1980	20,968	23.2			22,366	24.7
1981	20,647	22.6			—	—
1982	19,571	21.9			19,763	22.1
1983	18,634	20.7	17,717	20.4		
1984	18,306	19.4	17,340	19.1		
1985			16,996	18.0		
1986			16,975	17.5		

Notes: [a] Union membership expressed in thousands.

[b] Union membership as a percent of nonagricultural employment.

The Troy and Sheflin series is a continuation of an earlier series developed for the National Bureau of Economic Research. The data are derived primarily from union financial records and represent annual averages of full-time dues-paying union members.

The CPS series is derived from a survey of 60,000 households conducted by the Census Bureau for the Bureau of Labor Statistics. It covers employed wage and salary workers but excludes union members who are retired, self-employed, unemployed, or laid-off. Data were not collected for 1982, and the earlier series is not comparable with the post-1982 series because of differences in data collection and presentation.

The BLS series was derived from a mail survey to union officers conducted biannually by the Bureau of Labor Statistics until it was discontinued in 1980. The data were periodically published in the BLS *Directory of National Unions and Employee Associations.* Gifford (1982) updated the series with his own survey in 1982.

Sources: Troy and Sheflin series: Troy and Sheflin (1985, p. 3.10) for years 1960, 1970, 1975-1984; Bain and Price (1980, p. 89) for years 1956 and 1965.

CPS series: United States Bureau of the Census (1987, p. 409) for years 1983-1985; *Daily Labor Report* (February 23, 1987, p. B8) for year 1986.

BLS series: Gifford (1982, p. 1) for years 1975-1980, 1982; Bain and Price (1980, p. 89) for years 1956, 1960, 1965, and 1970.

In contrast, Canadian unions have experienced robust membership growth. The Labour Canada data reveal that between 1956 and 1986 union membership rose from 1,352,000 to 3,730,000 members (176 percent) and union density increased to 37.7 percent from 33.3 percent. A broadly similar pattern in union growth is reflected in the series collected under the reporting requirements of

Table 1b.   Union Membership[a] and Union Density[b]
in the United States and Canada

	Canada			
	Labour Canada		CALURA	
Year	Membership	Density (%)	Membership	Density (%)
1956	1,352	33.3		
1960	1,459	32.3		
1965	1,589	29.7	1,761	30.0
1970	2,173	33.6	2,268	33.1
1975	2,884	36.9	2,736	32.2
1976	3,042	37.3	2,779	32.2
1977	3,149	38.2	2,822	32.6
1978	3,278	39.0	2,908	31.9
1979	—	—	3,036	29.9
1980	3,397	37.6	3,093	31.8
1981	3,487	37.4	3,160	32.5
1982	3,617	39.0	3,054	33.3
1983	3,563	40.0	3,391	35.7
1984	3,651	39.6	3,439	35.1
1985	3,666	39.0		
1986	3,730	37.7		

Notes: [a] Union members expressed in thousands.

[b] Union membership as a percent of nonagricultural employment.

The membership figures in the Labour Canada series are provided by union officers. Data for all years up to and including 1949 are as of December 31. In 1950 the reference date was moved ahead one day to January 1, 1951. The data for subsequent years are as of January 1. Data were not collected in 1979.

The figures in the CALURA series are provided by union officers in accordance with the requirements of the Corporations and Labour Unions Returns Act. CALURA membership figures are lower than those reported by Labour Canada because CALURA only includes organizations formed for the purpose of regulating employer-employee relations. Consequently, most teachers' organizations and, in the past, nurses' associations have been excluded. Membership figures are for December 31 of each year and union density is calculated on December figures for paid workers.

Sources: Labour Canada series: Eaton (1975, pp. 648-649) for years 1956, 1960, 1965, and 1970; Labour Canada (1986, p. 18) for years 1975-1986.

CALURA series: Statistics Canada (1962-1984).

the Corporations and Labour Unions Returns Act (CALURA). Although Canada also experienced a severe recession in the 1980s, Canadian unions continued to outperform their American counterparts. Since 1980, union membership rose by 333,000 members (or 10 percent) and union density remained relatively stable (i.e., in the 37-40 percent range). While union density in 1956 stood at about one-third of the workforce in both countries, in Canada the proportion is now more than double that of the United States.

Part of the difference in the membership figures reflects the virtually complete unionization of the public sector in Canada (Rose 1984). One reason

Table 2. Changes in the Membership of Selected International Unions
(1980-1983)

Union	Change in Membership		Canadian as a percent of total membership	
	United States	Canada	1980	1983
Teamsters	-298,700 (-15.6%)	+1,000 (+1.1%)	4.8	5.8
Automobile Workers	-331,400 (-24.4%)	-81,000 (-6.2%)	9.6	11.9
Steelworkers	-272,500 (-28.2%)	-1,500 (-.8%)	20.5	28.4
Electrical (IBEW)	-70,700 (-7.5%)	+2,300 (+3.3%)	7.3	8.2
Machinists	-214,700 (-28.5%)	+1,300 (+2.1%)	8.4	11.9
Carpenters	-37,500 (-5.2%)	0 (0%)	12.4	13.1
Food and Commercial Workers	+92,800 (+9.5%)	+6,200 (+4.8%)	11.7	11.2

Source: Troy and Sheflin (1985).

union penetration in the Canadian public sector is substantially higher than
in the United States is the existence of a more supportive public policy in
Canada (Feuille and Anderson 1980). At the same time, important gains have
also been made in the private sector. An examination of Canadian membership
in American-based international unions (a proxy for private sector unionism)
reveals an increase from 947,498 to 1,458,863 members (54 percent) between
1956 and 1986.[2] It is noteworthy that aggregate union growth by international
unions in Canada outpaced union growth in the United States by a wide margin
in this period. Since 1980, international union membership in Canada has fallen
by 112,000 members or by 7 percent. Nevertheless, these losses were
substantially smaller than those experienced by American unions generally.
Indeed, the Canadian sections of many large international unions continued
to grow as a percentage of total membership in parent organizations between
1980 and 1983 (Table 2). A notable exception is the United Food and
Commercial Workers, which grew more slowly in Canada than in the United
States.

Cross-sectional union membership data reveal further differences between
the United States and Canada. Union density figures by sex, part-time/full-
time employment status, age, education, occupation, and industry are broadly

Table 3. United States and Canadian Union Membership Profile (1985)[a]

Category	Union Members as a Percent in Each Category	
	United States	*Canada*
Men	22.1	41.5
Women	13.2	31.9
Age		
16-24 years[b]	7.3	18.6
25-34 years	16.7	39.7
35-44 years	22.7	46.1
45-54 years	25.1	44.4
55-64 years	24.8	44.7
65 years and over	8.7	14.1
Full-time Workers	20.4	40.9
Part-time Workers	7.3	18.8
Education		
Elementary (grade 8 and below)	19.7	45.7
Some High School	17.8	34.1
High School Graduate	19.7	30.2[c]
Some College	15.2	41.6[d]
College Graduate		
4 years	12.1	
5 years	20.8	42.6[e]
6+ years	19.1	
Occupation		
Managerial and Professional Specialty	15.2	40.9
Technical, Sales, and Administrative Support	10.8	24.1
Service Occupations	14.4	28.5
Precision Production, Craft, and Repair	28.5	57.2
Operators, Fabricators, and Laborers	31.8	46.9
Farming, Forestry, and Fishing	5.5	28.4
Industry		
Agriculture, Wage and Salary	2.1	N/A
Mining	17.3	32.8
Construction	22.3	38.9
Manufacturing	24.8	45.0
Transportation and Public Utilities	37.0	60.0
Wholesale and Retail Trade	7.2	12.5
Finance, Insurance, and Real Estate	2.9	9.2
Services	6.6	38.1
Government Workers	35.8	66.6

Notes: [a] Canadian figures are for December 1984.

[b] Canadian figures are for age 15-24 years.

[c] Some post-secondary education.

[d] Post-secondary graduate.

[e] University degree (level unspecified).

Sources: United States: *Monthly Labor Review* (1986, p. 45).

Canada: Statistics Canada (1984); Kumar, Coates, and Arrowsmith (1986).

consistent with the aggregate data.[3] For most categories, union density in Canada is about twice the level reported in the United States (Table 3). This is even the case for the purportedly "harder to organize" workers and sectors (e.g., women, younger workers, better educated workers, part-time workers, and white-collar occupations). In the service industry, union density is more than five times greater in Canada. These data suggest that the Canadian unions generally have less difficulty organizing new recruits and/or have concentrated more intensely their organizing drives in the emerging sectors of the economy.

New Union Organizing

As reported in our earlier study, the sagging fortunes of U.S. unions are reflected in their performance in new organizing. Not only has there been a long-run decline in union victories in National Labor Relations Board (NLRB) certification elections (from 65.3 percent to 46.0 percent between 1955 and 1978), but the size of the election districts fell from 122 to 57 workers in the same period (Seeber and Cooke 1983). As well, there was a major decline in the proportion of cases that were consent elections, a large increase in the incidence of unfair labor practice charges, and a record backlog of unfair labor practice charges. These factors have contributed to delays in deciding representational issues and, thereby, reduced the probability of union success.

More recent data indicate virtually no improvement in the election performance of U.S. unions. The victory rate for certification elections increased to 47.9 percent in 1980, fell to 43.7 percent in 1982, and then reached 46.5 percent in 1985. The fact remains that U.S. unions have not won a majority of NLRB elections since 1974. In 1983 there were 28,995 unfair labor practice complaints issued against employers, a decline of 7.3 percent from the 1980 figure. One-half of these were for illegal discrimination or discharge of employees. In the same year, the NLRB ordered reimbursements of over $32 million to employees who were discharged or discriminated against and obtained 6,029 orders of reinstatement (U.S. National Labor Relations Board 1986).

Labor board data (1971-1985) from the federal jurisdiction and Ontario and British Columbia indicate that Canadian unions are more successful than American unions in new organizing.[4] Of the more than 30,000 certification applications disposed of between 1971 and 1985, nearly 70 percent of the applications were granted. Although there is no discernable trend in overall certification outcomes, the percentage of certification applications granted to British Columbia unions declined steadily in recent years (from 77 percent in 1982 to 56 percent in 1985). Nevertheless, this still represents a higher success rate than U.S. unions are experiencing.

In Canada, union membership cards rather than elections remain the primary method for determining union representation. It is estimated that only about 15-20 percent of certification applications resulted in elections. But even when elections were held, unions were victorious 55 percent of the time.[5] The election results are even more impressive in British Columbia, where the *Labour Code Amendment Act, 1984* required representation votes in virtually all applications for certification.[6] The British Columbia Labour Relations Board (BCLRB) has adopted streamlined procedures designed to ensure votes are conducted 10 calendar days after the application for certification (British Columbia Labour Relations Board 1984). Of the 349 elections conducted in 1984 and 1985, unions achieved 270 victories (a success rate of 77.4 percent).

The success of Canadian unions occurred despite concerns over unfair labor practices. As we previously reported, between 1974 and 1980 there was a threefold increase in the number of unfair labor practices (from 386 to 1,210) and such complaints rose from 6-15 percent of the total case load (Rose and Chaison 1985). The upward trend has moderated in recent years. For example, there were 1,331 complaints in 1984 (up only 10 percent since 1980) and these complaints comprised 16.2 percent of the total case load. While the incidence of alleged misconduct continues to grow in Canada, it is quite modest when compared to the situation in the United States.

EXPLANATORY FACTORS

Market Shifts

A common explanation for the decline in union membership rates in the United States is the changing structure of product and labor markets. It is frequently claimed that those industrial sectors with the highest unionization rates, notably manufacturing and construction, are experiencing the lowest growth, while the service sector is rapidly expanding and remains relatively unorganized (*Daily Labor Report* June 13, 1986; Troy 1986; AFL-CIO Committee on the Evolution of Work 1985). Moreover, there has been an increase in the number of better educated, white-collar, younger, and female workers in the labor force. These groups are said to have a lower propensity to join unions or to vote for unions in certification elections (e.g., Greenhouse 1985; Edwards and Podgursky 1986). It is often claimed that union growth has been reversed as employment expansion takes place in those industrial sectors and among those workers where there are no strong traditions of collective bargaining. As Troy (1986, p. 89) summarized the situation:

...the crisis of American trade unionism now and for the foreseeable future [is that] unions are slipping sharply in declining industries, the historic mainstays of union organization, and have failed to take hold in the growth portions of the labor market.

While these arguments seem quite logical, the importance of market shifts is not supported by recent empirical evidence. Freeman (1985) found little relationship between the decline in union success in NLRB representation elections and the changing proportions of workers in categories of age, education, sex, occupation, and industry. Farber (1985) concluded that structural changes (i.e., the shift toward the South, white-collar and female workers, and away from manufacturing) accounted for only about 40 percent (3.9 of the 9.4 percentage points) of the decline in union density between 1956 and 1978. Farber (1987) found that only about one-fifth of the decline in unionization from 1977 to 1984 was the result of changes in labor force structure. Doyle (1985) found that less than one-quarter of the decline in the collective bargaining agreement coverage of production workers from 1961 to 1984 could be accounted for by employment shifts between industries.

An analysis by Meltz (1985) showed that shifts in employment from the manufacturing to the service sector cannot explain the higher density rate in Canada. Structural shifts are even less useful in explaining the divergence between union density in the United States and Canada. Indeed, Meltz (1985) estimated that, if the employment distribution had been the same in both countries in 1980, the union density rate in Canada would have been about 10 percent higher than it was. This was confirmed by our own calculations. Using the CALURA union membership data, we found that the density rate in Canada would have been 11.4 percent higher than it was in 1984.

Lipset (1986a) examined the ratio of service/industrial sector employment for Canada, the United States, and selected OECD countries and found that in all of the countries the service sector had become considerably larger than the industrial sector. However, the analysis could not uncover any consistent pattern in the degree and direction of union density in the eleven selected countries. In four countries, including Canada, density increased, while it decreased in three and remained stable in the remainder. There was no apparent relationship between the rankings in the service/manufacturing ratio and union density. It appears that shifts in labor and product markets play only a very limited role in explaining changes in certification election outcomes and union density in the United States and cannot account for the differences in union density in the United States and Canada.

Public Policy

It has become a fairly common practice to link the differences in the degrees of unionization in the United States and Canada to the underlying philosophies and procedures of their respective labor legislation. We did this in our earlier review of the state of the unions in the two countries (Rose and Chaison 1985) and the public policy differences have been emphasized in the works of Weiler (1983, 1985), Meltz (1985), and Gunderson and Meltz (1986). The apparent links between union membership and public policy in the United States and Canada have been used to justify labor law reform in the United States. For example, the AFL-CIO's Committee on the Evolution of Work (1985, p. 15) claimed that:

> The Canadian experience is instructive. Canada has roughly the same type of economy, many similar employers and has undergone the same [demographic and industrial] changes that we previously have described with respect to the United States. But, in Canada, unlike the United States, the government has not defaulted in its obligation to protect the right of self organization; rather, Canada's law carefully safeguards that right.

While there are clear differences in the legislation in the two countries, the impact of public policy on union growth is not as simple and direct as implied by the AFL-CIO. The principal area for comparison has been the procedures for safeguarding employee choice in the selection of bargaining agents. Canadian public policy is directed at encouraging employee choice without protracted employer campaigns (Weiler 1983, 1985; Rose and Chaison 1985). Union representation is determined by signed membership cards rather than elections in most jurisdictions and, in those where elections are required, there are expedited procedures (e.g., Craig 1986, pp. 129-134). In the United States, we find a strong reliance on elections and this results in prolonged campaigns, opportunities for employer unfair labor practices, and employer challenges of unit composition and employee ballots. As a result, the election procedure is often contentious, protracted, and necessitates frequent appeals to the NLRB. Faced with the deluge of cases, the NLRB annual case backlog has more than doubled from 535 in 1980 to 1,196 in 1985 (Levitan, Carlson, and Shapiro 1986, p. 137).

There is a wealth of data pointing to widespread employer violations of the National Labor Relations Act. Between 1980 and 1983, charges of employer discrimination against union supporters (violations of section 8(a)(3) of the National Labor Relations Act) have averaged 17,036 cases per year. This is almost double the 1970 figure. The number of reinstatement cases during the same period averaged 2,456 per year, or nearly triple the level in 1970 (Cooke 1985b, p. 426). Compensation for illegally discharged employees also increased dramatically. From 1980 to 1983, the NLRB awarded an annual average of $32.6 million in back pay to employees who were illegally discriminated against or discharged because of their union activity. The annual average for the preceding 4-year period was $14.7 million (U.S. National Labor Relations Board 1986). Back pay reached a record high of $62.2 million in 1985 before declining to $27.8 million in 1986 (*AFL-CIO News* March 21, 1987).

Both employer discrimination and election delays have been shown to have a significant negative impact on the probability of union election victories (Seeber and Cooke 1983; Weiler 1983; Cooke 1985b; Hunt and White 1985).

As a result, unions are no longer able to use certification elections as the principal means for the replenishment of union members. Weiler (1985, pp. E6-E7) observed:

> The stark reality is that private sector unions are now able, through the NLRB procedures, to replace only one quarter of the members which they lose through the normal attrition process in an economy within which existing plants are constantly being closed or moved, and replaced by new business enterprises.

After calculating the net gains in union membership resulting from the election process, Freeman (1987, p. 17) concluded: "...it is apparent that the legally established mode of organizing labor in the private sector in the U.S. has run dry for unions."

American labor legislation has been harshly criticized by labor leaders for its failure to protect and promote employee free choice, and for lacking corrective power. For example, Lane Kirkland, AFL-CIO president, recently stated that the NLRB

> has become an instrument not just of employers generally, but of those employers who have most aggressively engaged in practices contrary to the spirit of the law to deny working people the right to self-organization, self-representation (Galenson 1986, p. 69).

Kirkland suggested that unions might be better off if all government regulation of industrial relations was eliminated and labor and management returned to "the law of the jungle" (Weiler 1985, p. E1; Galenson 1986, p. 99). The AFL-CIO Executive Council has suggested that affiliates might have to radically alter organizing strategies and, when possible, pursue alternatives to the NLRB procedures (AFL-CIO 1985). Some unions have indicated that they would rather bypass the NLRB by filing cases with state agencies with concurrent jurisdictions, as well as by pressuring employers into granting recognition through corporate campaigns and consumer boycotts (Samoff 1987). For example, John Sweeney, president of the Service Employees, explained why his union was successful in organizing in 1986:

> We got recognition and contracts through a combination of economic and community pressure techniques, and it certainly proved less costly and time consuming than the traditional process (*AFL-CIO News* March 14, 1987).

While there seems to be a consensus among union officers and industrial relations scholars about the need for labor law reform in the United States,[7] we should recognize that reform alone may only have a limited impact on the extent of unionization. For example, Kochan, Katz, and McKersie (1986, p. 252) believe:

...if rules governing union representation elections were to be reformed—for example, to eliminate delays, stiffen penalties for illegal conduct, and eliminate the problems experienced in achieving initial contracts—unions will increase their organizing success rates with low wage workers in service industries and occupations and in small bargaining units. These changes will not, however, make any significant differences in the unionization rate of large firms or in the quality of the union-management relationship in existing bargaining units. Thus union membership will continue to decline...

Analyses of membership data have reached similar conclusions. Dickens and Leonard (1985) found that if unions in the United States had been able to win the representation rights for the same proportion of workers as they did in 1950-1954, union density still would have fallen from 1960 to 1980 by almost as much as it did. Even if unions had won every election they were involved in since 1950, density would have fallen. These results are certainly not encouraging for those who assign the exclusive blame for union membership decline on the policies and procedures of the NLRB and who believe that changes modeled after the Canadian procedures would quickly reverse the trend. On the other hand, they can argue that U.S. labor legislation, by failing to protect employees from the coercive anti-union tactics of employers, has encouraged increased employer resistance to union organizing in particular and the process of collective bargaining in general. In the next section, we examine the forms and intensity of employer resistance in the United States and Canada.

Employer Resistance

There can be little doubt that employer resistance to union organizing efforts has reached its highest level in the United States since the 1920s:

Not since the twenties has it been as socially and politically acceptable for American management to embrace publicly a "union free" approach. Many companies now make union avoidance or union containment a very high priority (Kochan, McKersie, and Capelli 1984, p. 18).

What remains unclear is the relative contribution of the various forms of employer resistance to the recent decline in union membership and to the difference in union density in the United States and Canada.

Most studies of employer resistance have been confined to the conduct surrounding representation election campaigns and the negotiation of the first agreement. As we already noted, concerns have been expressed about the growing number of employer unfair labor practices, the frequent recourse to procedural delays to thwart employee free choice (Weiler 1983, 1985; Seeber and Cooke 1983; Lawler and West 1985; Goldfield 1987; Dickens 1988),[8] and the increasing inability of unions to achieve first contracts following certification (Cooke 1985a,c; Weiler 1984).[9] Employer opposition is said to occur in about 95 percent of organizing campaigns (AFL-CIO Committee on the Evolution of Work 1985) and has been shown to be an underlying factor behind the decline in union success rates in certification elections (e.g., Freeman 1985, 1987; Stephan and Kaufman 1987; Dickens 1988). Behind this employer resistance is the "expanding and lucrative occupation of consultants who provide legal advice on how to keep the unions out" (Galenson 1986, p. 68). It has been estimated that as many as 75 percent of employers in the United States use such consultants at an annual cost of about one hundred million dollars (AFL-CIO Committee on the Evolution of Work 1985; Raskin 1986b). As Barkin (1986, p. 10) described the situation:

> Representation elections have become veritable miniature class wars. Employer opposition to unions has converted the election primarily into a contest on worker censure of outsiders and a vote of support for management, departing from its purpose of determining bargaining agents for a specific workplace.

The impact of employer resistance in election campaigns is highlighted when we consider the relatively high rate of unionization in the public sector in the United States. Elected or appointed public employers offer little or no resistance to union organizing efforts because they are much less concerned than private sector employers about being competitive and because they do not want to appear to oppose collective bargaining (de Bernardo 1986; Freeman 1986, 1987). As Freeman (1987, p. 27) observed:

> In the public sector...there has been no outburst of anti-union activity by management. Charges of unfair labor practices concern interpretation of state bargaining laws—whether a particular topic is subject to collective bargaining or is a management prerogative—not to the existence of unionism per se. Public sector managers rarely hire union preventing firms to discourage organization by their workers.

Recent studies conducted as part of the Industrial Relations in Transition project at MIT have suggested that union avoidance strategies, rather than employer resistance during election campaigns, may be the major force behind the decline in union membership in the United States. Briefly stated, there has been a major transformation of the labor-management relationship:

> ...the emergence of a large non-union sector in the United States since 1960 was a function of a changing environment, deep seated managerial values opposed to unions, and increased opportunities and incentives to avoid unions resulting from competitive and cost conditions. Management responded by shifting power from its staff experts most deeply committed to working within the union-management relationship. Line and staff managers who were willing and able to introduce innovative new systems of human resource management gained power and were successful in helping to develop and stabilize a new non-union system (Kochan, Katz, and McKersie 1986, p. 79).

The emerging nonunion model placed the greatest emphasis on individual employee concerns and participation, and provided employees with greater discretion through the design of broader jobs. Nonunion and partially unionized employers targeted expansion, new investment, and workplace innovations at "greenfield sites," locations where there are lesser possibilities of unionization, and introduced their new human resource management approach to present and new nonunion plants. In effect, the union avoidance strategies, developed at the highest levels of corporate decision making, enabled employers "to control the pre-conditions of the employment relationship so as to prevent unions from establishing a basis for holding representation elections" (Kochan, Katz, and McKersie 1986, p. 232). Employee choice through elections became a moot issue; "...wherever plants were designed and run on the new human resource management model they were essentially immune from unionization..." (Kochan, Katz, and McKersie 1986, p. 64). Certification elections were never even held in the vast majority of the new employment relationships created in the past two decades.[10]

Employer resistance during election campaigns and the broader union avoidance strategies are both manifestations of the dramatic increase in employer animosity toward unions in the United States and the strong desire to operate on a nonunion or partially unionized basis. There has developed an explosively expanding confrontation sector in the industrial relations system (Kerr 1986) marked by continued concession bargaining, plant relocation, and employer offensives aimed at the simplification of work rules, the reduction in job classifications, and greater flexibility in outsourcing. It is widely believed, particularly among labor leaders, that the confrontation was intensified as employers were emboldened by the Reagan Administration's discharge of the striking air traffic controllers in 1981; "the handling of the air traffic controllers provided a signal to, and model for, anti-union employers" (AFL-CIO Committee on the Evolution of Work 1985, p. 11; Molotsky 1987). We now see a greater tendency for U.S. employers to replace strikers. This has been most evident in the widely publicized disputes at Greyhound, Hormel, Phelps-Dodge, and in the airline industry (Raskin 1987). It was recently estimated that about 40 percent of employers continue operations during strikes (*New York Times* April 5, 1987).

Although there is no supporting data, a consensus seems to have developed that employer resistance to unions in Canada is not as extensive or intense as in the United States. Canadian employers, both private and public, are said to be more receptive to unions (Craig 1986). Huxley, Kettler, and Struthers (1986, p. 116) believe that:

Canada is conditioned by public economic policies to manage the labor market in the interests of economic growth. Compared to the U.S., however, this management has proceeded more frequently through negotiations at the highest level or through ad hoc

> interventions that regulate or supersede collective bargaining...rather than a weakening of the competitive position of organized labor within the adversarial system.
>
> Employers in America are more apt in general to pursue the goal of "union-free organizations," especially in new and growing sectors, and unions accept limitations imposed by employer resistance. Canadian employers and unions are more willing to accept one another and commit themselves more directly and [bindingly] to political parties.

Adams' (1981) theoretical framework may help to explain the divergence in employer behavior. He argues that employer attitudes in North America are fundamentally the same (i.e., employers place a high value on the right to manage the enterprise and perceive unions as a threat to managerial control). Employer behavior toward unions will not only be shaped by this value orientation, but also by labor philosophy and strategy and government action. In Canada, the labor movement has experienced large membership gains, become increasingly nationalistic, and supported the policies of the social democratic New Democratic Party. A strong labor movement and broad support in Canada for government intervention in the marketplace have profoundly influenced the industrial relations system. Although Canada does not have a highly developed tripartite system by western European standards, in contrast to the United States there has been a movement toward tripartite consensus-building on socioeconomic issues. Adams (1985) asserts that economic upheaval has pushed the Canadian and U.S. systems in different directions. In Canada, there has been "more cooperation by labor, management and government in search of consensus and the expansion of workers' participation by right," whereas in the United States, many employers "have abandoned their commitment to unions and collective bargaining" and "rather than being embraced as a social partner, organized labor finds itself to be the object of the most forceful assault on its integrity in more than a half-century" (Adams 1985, p. 115).

What appears to be a broader acceptance of unions may also be conditioned by the lack of opportunities to avoid them. Considering that certification is normally based on membership card majorities, there may be less recourse to the use of union avoidance consultants or the dismissal of union supporters. As Weiler (1983) observed, the number of discriminatory discharge complaints per certification campaign is substantially lower in Canada than in the United States.[11] Additionally, there are no equivalents of greenfield sites in Canada (Meltz 1985) and "lacking a non-union hinterland to which they could easily relocate, Canadian employers did not...embrace the 'non-union' alternative to collective bargaining as vigorously as their U.S. counterparts" (Adams 1985, p. 125).

In summary, while many Canadian employers may face the same competitive and cost pressures as their U.S. counterparts, there is a general belief that they are less likely to resolve their difficulties through union confrontation and union avoidance strategies. Unfortunately, there are no empirical measures of this difference in employer approaches and, consequently, it is difficult to determine how much of the difference in union density in the two countries is attributable to employer resistance.

Union Organizing Efforts

There is a substantial body of empirical and anecdotal evidence suggesting that unions in the United States have a diminished motivation and ability to organize. Unions have been repeatedly blamed for devoting too few resources to organizing (e.g., Craft and Extejt 1983; Voos 1983; Weiler 1985) and Freeman (1985) estimated that the reduced union organizing effort in terms of real expenditures per member is responsible for about one-third of the decline in union success rates in certification elections. These failings have figured prominently in union self-appraisals such as the AFL-CIO's *The Changing Situation of Workers and Their Unions* (1985), the Communications Workers' *Committee on the Future Report* (Communications Workers of America 1983) and the United Steelworkers' *Forging a Future* (United Steelworkers of America 1984). There have been numerous suggestions for broadened jurisdictions, improved training for organizers, and better coordination of organizing campaigns and selection of organizing targets. Unions have been urged to devote greater effort to internal organizing (i.e., recruiting the nonunion employees in their bargaining units) and to strengthening the ties with past members who lost or left their jobs. AFL-CIO affiliates also have started to experiment with alternative forms of representation, including associate memberships for unemployed members or union supporters in units where there were election defeats (AFL-CIO Committee on the Evolution of Work 1985; Reynolds 1986; *CWA News* March, 1987). There have also been attempts to make union membership more appealing by expanding the array of services that are provided; the AFL-CIO has initiated legal service, life insurance, and investment service plans, as well as low interest credit cards for affiliates' members (Kirkland 1987; McDonald 1987).

The reduced motivation and ability to organize can be blamed on the destabilizing influence of the severe membership declines during the past recession as well as the unions' intense concerns with the issues of job security and concession bargaining. There is little possibility that unions faced with a threatening environment and reduced resources can substantially increase or even maintain past levels of organizing activity. For some unions, a case may be made that the costs of organizing are outweighed by the monetary benefits to the membership because of the increased bargaining power and collective agreement coverage in their industries (Voos 1983). But decisions to fund and implement organizing programs are often made on the local union level and within a political as well as economic framework. Officers and members would have to be convinced of a favorable cost/benefit equation before there is sufficient political pressure to allocate funds to recruit new members. This might be very difficult in the presence of scarce financial resources, rising concerns about immediate threats to the members' job security, increasing employer resistance to organizing, the low chances of success, and the small number of members gained through certification elections.

Levitan, Carlson, and Shapiro (1986, p. 147) observed:

> With union membership falling, it is increasingly difficult for union leaders to justify ...[organizing] expenditures to a membership preoccupied with stagnating, if not declining, real wages and lack of security. If union leaders are to maintain their own job security, they need to respond to the pressing needs of present members, instead of crafting a future oriented strategy.

In addition, the precipitous membership declines in the past decade may have depleted many unions' treasuries and resulted in cutbacks in the budgets of organizing departments and layoffs among organizing staffs (Rose and Chaison 1985). Membership levels and dues income may have fallen too low for unions to fully exploit the growth potential of their jurisdictions (Weiler 1985; Voos 1987).

The decline in union organizing in the United States is likely to result in some major changes in the structures and relationships within the labor movement. First, large unions with declining memberships (e.g., the Steelworkers) may find that the most efficient way to maintain economies of scale in their operations is by absorbing smaller unions, in effect recruiting members that are already organized. Second, these absorptions, as well as the increased recruitment among workers in the service industries, may make organizing jurisdictions largely irrelevant and could create conglomerate and general unions (Chaison 1986). Finally, the AFL-CIO may become considerably more active and influential in coordinating and financing affiliate organizing and arranging affiliate mergers (Chaison 1986; Raskin 1986a). Two steps in this direction were taken in 1986 when the Federation implemented the *Procedure for Determining Organizing Responsibilities,* which resolves nonraid organizing disputes of affiliates (*Daily Labor Report* February 20, 1986), and adopted guidelines for affiliate mergers (AFL-CIO Committee on the Evolution of Work 1985).

The extent to which organizing activity has fallen off in the United States is indicated by NLRB certification election data (see Table 4). The number of single union elections petitioned for by unions fell by 56 percent from 1976 to 1985, with major declines in 1978, 1981, and 1982. The last four years of the series could be characterized as a period of severely depressed union organizing.

Table 4. NLRB Certification Elections[a]
(Total Cases and Cases in the Service Sector, White-Collar Units and Professional and Technical Units: 1976-1985)

Year	Total Cases	Service Sector[b]		White-Collar[c]		Professional and Technical[d]	
		Cases	Percent of total	Cases	Percent of total	Cases	Percent of total
1976	7,475	1,322	17.7	746	10.0	396	5.3
1977	7,744	1,325	17.1	753	9.7	355	4.6
1978	6,622	1,077	16.3	567	8.6	291	4.4
1979	6,496	1,111	17.1	610	9.4	293	4.5
1980	6,443	1,305	20.3	599	9.3	410	6.4
1981	5,786	1,224	21.2	504	8.7	254	4.4
1982	3,275	795	24.3	195	6.0	196	6.0
1983	3,067	717	23.4	141	4.6	182	5.9
1984	3,325	806	24.2	155	4.7	139	4.2
1985	3,314	743	22.4	125	3.8	110	3.3

Notes: [a] Single union certification elections petitioned for by unions.
   [b] Service sector consists of SIC 70-89.
   [c] White-collar units are those categorized by the NLRB as code "W"—"Office, Clerical, and Other White-Collar."
   [d] Professional and technical units are those categorized by the NLRB as code "P"—"Professional and/or Technical."

Source: Computer tape provided by the Data Systems Branch of the National Labor Relations Board.

In contrast to the situation in the United States, there is evidence that Canadian unions have rebounded from the 1981-1982 recession. A survey of labor boards in Canada's eleven jurisdictions found the number of certifications granted fell from 3,378 in 1980 to 2,509 in 1983 (a 26 percent decrease) before rebounding in 1984 and 1985 (2,707 and 2,907 certifications, respectively). Of particular significance is the fact that unions acquired new bargaining rights for nearly 100,000 employees in 1985 compared to 67,000 in 1984. The increase in organizing activity and the recruitment of new members is evident in all regions except western Canada (which has not experienced an economic recovery) (Wood and Kumar 1984; Kumar, Coates, and Arrowsmith 1986).

In order to compare organizing activity in both countries, we developed a general index of union organizing effort. It consists of determining the number of employees that unions attempt to organize through certification procedures and dividing this figure by the total union membership in the previous year.[12] Table 5 shows the number of employees that unions attempted to organize (in absolute terms and as a percentage of union members) for 1976 to 1985 in the United States and Ontario. Figures are presented for Ontario because it publishes the most comprehensive certification data.[13] Although there are some fluctuations in both the Ontario and the U.S. series, organizing effort is considerably higher in Ontario. Unions in Ontario attempted to increase membership by 3.0-4.6 percent through new organizing, whereas U.S. unions attempted to increase membership by .9-2.3 percent through new organizing. Moreover, the differential in organizing effort increased. In the early years of the series, the ratio of Ontario to U.S. percentages was around 1.5 to 1; in the later years of the series, it increased to 3 to 1 or greater.

In addition to the levels of organizing activity and the overall organizing effort, there is the question of labor's willingness to organize in the emerging frontiers of employer growth (e.g., the service industry and white-collar workers). These so-called "harder to organize" sectors are essential to the long-run survival of the labor movement. As the union density data in Table 3 suggest, Canadian unions have been more actively recruiting new members in these sectors of the economy than their American counterparts. In 1971, 15.7 percent of the certifications granted in British Columbia and Ontario were in the service industries; in 1985, service industries accounted for 36.4 percent of all certifications. Approximately 40 percent of the newly certified employees were employed in the service sector. As well, certification success was greater in the service sectors of both provinces than in any other major industry grouping. Evidence of white-collar organizing comes from Ontario, where, since 1980, 24 percent of the bargaining units certified consisted of white-collar workers. This is an increase from 19 percent between 1974 and 1979.

Compared to their Canadian counterparts, American unions are considerably less active in organizing where unions traditionally have been weak. Table 4 shows the decline in election activity in the service sector in the

Table 5.   Union Organizing Efforts in the United States and Ontario
(1976-1985)

	Employees Attempted in Union Organizing			
	Ontario		United States	
Year[a]	Number of Employees	Percent of Total Union Membership	Number of Employees	Percent of Total Union Membership
1976	34,218	3.4	477,811	2.2
1977	38,271	3.8	519,581	2.3
1978	35,809	3.4	457,850	2.1
1979	44,094	4.1	494,512	2.3
1980	45,070	4.0	463,573	2.1
1981	50,638	4.6	377,214	1.8
1982	33,778	3.0	213,986	1.0
1983	33,339	3.0	181,257	.9
1984	46,431	3.8	206,503	1.1
1985	47,060	3.8	231,014	1.3

Note: [a] U.S. data for the calendar year. Ontario data are for the fiscal year April 1 to March 31.

Source: Computer tape provided by the Data Systems Branch of the National Labor Relations Board and tabulations derived from annual reports of the Ontario Ministry of Labour and the Ontario Labour Relations Board.

United States from 1976 to 1985. Service sector cases increased as a proportion of total cases, but this was largely the result of the overall decline in union election activity; over the ten years the actual number of cases in the service sector fell by 44 percent.

White-collar cases fell precipitously in terms of both the number of elections and the proportion of total cases. The number of cases involving white-collar units declined by 83 percent over the 10-year period, and in 1985 such cases comprised only 3.8 percent of the certification elections petitioned for by unions.

Professional and technical employees are also considered to be very difficult to organize but critical to future union growth. Table 4 shows fluctuating but small proportions of NLRB certification elections among professional and technical employees. The number of elections among these employees fell in the last four years of the series at an even faster rate than the overall decline in election activity. Over the 10-year period the number of cases in professional and technical units fell by 72 percent.

While it may be too strong a statement to characterize union organizing in Canada as booming (e.g., Slotnick 1986) the data point to a clearly higher level of activity than in the United States. This may be partly the result of the survival needs of the many small Canadian national unions which must grow to retain or achieve economies of scale in operations, as well as the desire of the Canadian sections of internationals to increase their stature and influence in, or independence from their parent unions (Rose and Chaison 1985). There is also a strong possibility that we are witnessing the impact of the differences in public policy and employer resistance in the two countries. In the United States, union avoidance strategies may have severely restricted the number of potential organizing targets while employer tactics during organizing campaigns may have reduced both the number of elections and the chances of union success. In Canada, because the potential for employer resistance is lower and certification normally takes place without elections, unions may have been encouraged to devote greater resources and energy to organizing.

Public Opinion and National Values

In a recent study, Lipset argued that the loss of public support for unions is more important than socioeconomic and legal structures in explaining the 30-year decline in union density in the United States (Lipset 1986a). Statistical analysis of opinion polling data revealed first that "as public approval of unions declines, so too do union density and the certification win rate of unions" (Lipset 1986a, p. 440) and second that public approval measures provided close predictions of union density in any given year. He concludes:

> studies that seek to explain the decline of labor organizations by reference to the factors which differentiate union members from non-members, or environments that are more or less conducive to union strength, clearly cannot solve the conundrum of why American workers are so much less organized than their compeers elsewhere (Lipset 1986a, pp. 441-442).

In a comparison of the United States and Canada, Lipset submits that, to a major extent, "the effects of structural changes on the strength of the labor movements are mediated by diverse national values" (Lipset 1986a, p. 442).

Lipset's analysis is problematic for two reasons. First, it ignores Canadian polling data. Although the Canadian data are not as comprehensive as data gathered in the United States, they are, nevertheless, instructive (see Table 6). For many years the Gallup poll has asked respondents whether they think labor unions are good or bad for Canada. In the period 1950-1958, between 12 and 20 percent responded "bad" and between 60 and 69 percent "good" (the remainder gave qualified responses or expressed no opinion). For the period 1976-1984, between 30 and 41 percent of the respondents answered "bad" and between 42 and 52 percent answered "good" (Labour Canada 1983). In the intervening years, three polls (asking a slightly different question) recorded a modest increase in public disapproval of unions (Johnston 1986). Although these data preclude us from unambiguously concluding that there has been a sharp decline in the public acceptance of Canadian unions, it appears most probable that public support for unions declined in both countries. Moreover,

Table 6. Public Approval of Labor Unions in the United States and Canada

| | Percent of Respondents Approving and Disapproving | | | |
| | U.S. Surveys[a] | | Canadian Surveys[b] | |
Year	Approve	Disapprove	Approve	Disapprove
1936	72	20	—	—
1937	72	20	—	—
1939	68	24	—	—
1940	64	22	—	—
1941	61	30	—	—
1947	64	25	—	—
1949	62	22	—	—
1950	—	—	62	14
1952	—	—	60	15
1953	75	18	—	—
1956	—	—	69	12
1957: (1)	76	14	—	—
(2)	64	18	—	—
1958	—	—	62	20
1959	68	19	—	—
1961: (1)	70	18	66	23
(2)	63	22	—	—
1962	64	24	—	—
1963	67	23	—	—
1965: (1)	71	19	—	—
(2)	70	19	—	—
1967	66	23	—	—
1970	—	—	54	30
1973	59	26	—	—
1975	—	—	57	26
1976	—	—	42	36
1978	59	31	46	41
1979	55	33	50	35
1980	—	—	54	30
1981	55	35	—	—
1982	—	—	48	42
1984	—	—	51	35
1985	58	27	—	—

Notes: [a] The U.S. Gallup polls asked: "In general, do you approve or disapprove of labor unions?" Two polls were conducted in 1957, 1961, and 1965.
[b] The Canadian Gallup poll asked: (1961-1975)—"In general, do you approve or disapprove of labor unions?"; (1950-1958, 1976-1985)—"Generally speaking, do you think that labor unions have been a good thing or a bad thing for Canada?"

public disapproval of unions in Canada and the United States was roughly comparable in the early 1980s. Thus, whereas union density fell as U.S. public opinion became increasingly negative, in Canada unions were not adversely affected by public disapproval of labor unions.

Other polls suggest that the standing of Canadian unions is weak, perhaps even weaker than in the United States. During the 1980s, Decima reported that only about 9 percent of the public expressed a "great deal" of confidence in Canadian union leaders (see Table 7). Almost 90 percent of the respondents expressed "hardly any" or "only some" confidence in union leaders. According to Riddell (1986, p. 12):

> Canadians consistently expressed less confidence in the leaders of labour unions than those of any other institution when asked to rate their confidence in the leaders of twenty institutions (including banks, schools, provincial governments, oil companies, federal government, multinational corporations, newspapers and the tobacco industry).

Although public confidence in American unions and their leaders is low, their standing appears to be marginally higher than their Canadian counterparts. Six national surveys conducted by the National Opinion Research Corporation between 1975 and 1985 asked respondents to assess the level of trust and confidence they had in fourteen institutions. U.S. unions were among the least esteemed institutions, consistently ranking thirteenth (Lipset 1986b). Respondents expressing complete trust in unions fell from 22 percent in 1975 to 15 percent in 1985. Public confidence in union leaders is even lower. Thirty surveys conducted by Harris and the National Opinion Research Center between 1966 and 1985 found a smaller percentage expressing "a great deal of confidence" in trade union leaders than the heads of other institutions. As shown in Table 7, the percentage expressing a great deal of confidence in U.S. trade union leaders has steadily declined, but remains higher than the Canadian average and is almost double the Canadian figure in 1985.

Another measure of public attitudes toward organized labor is the perception of union power (see Table 8). Decima polls asked respondents to choose between the statements "unions in Canada have become too powerful" and "unions are necessary in Canada to protect workers from exploitation" (Johnston 1985). The average for five polls conducted from 1981 to 1986 reveals 53 percent of the respondents chose "too powerful" and 40 percent chose "necessary" (the remainder expressed "no opinion"). A similar poll was conducted by Gallup from 1968 to 1984. The average for five polls shows that 65 percent of respondents felt unions were too powerful or strong. In the United States, eight National Opinion Research Corporation polls conducted between 1971 and 1985 asked respondents whether unions were "too powerful," "not powerful enough," or "power about right" (Lipset 1986b). The dominant response in each survey was "too powerful" (ranging from 42 percent in 1974 to 55 percent in 1971). Considering that in Canada union density and strike activity are higher than in the United States and concessionary bargaining has not been as prevalent (Adams, 1985), it is not surprising that a larger percentage of Canadians perceive unions as too powerful.

Table 7.   Confidence in Labor Union Leaders in the United States and Canada

| | | Percent of Respondents Expressing a Great Deal of Confidence in Labor Union Leaders | | |
| | | United States[b] | | Canada[c] |
Year[a]		Harris Survey	NORC Survey	Decima Survey
1966		22	—	—
1967		20	—	—
1971		14	—	—
1972		15	—	—
1973:	(1)	20	16	—
	(2)	16	—	—
1974:	(1)	17	18	—
	(2)	18	—	—
1975:	(1)	14	10	—
	(2)	18	—	—
1976		—	12	—
1977:	(1)	14	15	—
	(2)	15	—	—
1978		15	11	—
1979		10	—	—
1980:	(1)	14	15	13
	(2)	—	—	8
	(3)	—	—	11
	(4)	—	—	10
1981:	(1)	12	—	11
	(2)	—	—	9
	(3)	—	—	10
	(4)	—	—	11
1982:	(1)	8	12	10
	(2)	—	—	10
	(3)	—	—	10
	(4)	—	—	7
1983:	(1)	10	8	10
	(2)	—	—	8
1984:	(1)	12	9	8
	(2)	—	—	9
1985:	(1)	13	—	6
	(2)	—	—	7
1986:	(1)	—	—	9
	(2)	—	—	10
1987:	(1)	—	—	10
	(2)	—	—	9
Average		15	13	9

Notes: [a] The U.S. polls were conducted annually with the exception of the Harris surveys in 1973 to 1977. The month of the Harris surveys varied from year to year. NORC surveys were conducted in March of each year. Decima polls were conducted on a quarterly basis from 1980 to 1982 and semi-annually since 1983.

[b] The Harris and NORC surveys asked the following question: "As far as the people running (organized labor or other institutions) are concerned, would you say you have a great deal of confidence, only some confidence, or hardly any confidence at all in them?"

[c] The Decima survey asked the following question: "Now I'm going to name some institutions in this country and I'd like you to consider the people who run these institutions. How about the people who run labor unions? Would you say you have a great deal of confidence in them, only some confidence in them, or hardly any confidence in them?"

Table 8. Attitudes Toward the Power of Unions
in the United States and Canada

| | Percent of Respondents Who Feel Unions are Too Powerful | | |
| | *United States* | *Canada* | |
Year	*NORC*[a]	*Decima*[b]	*Gallup*[c]
1968	—	—	62
1971	55	—	—
1972	46	—	—
1974	42	—	—
1975	50	—	—
1976	52	—	—
1977	51	—	—
1979	—	—	68
1980	—	—	65
1981	—	52	—
1982	48	61	67
1984	—	53	62
1985	46	50	—
1986	—	50	—
Average	49	53	65

Notes: [a] The question asked was: "Please tell me which one statement best describes the way you feel about labor unions in this country: (1) Labor unions today are not strong enough. I would like to see them grow in power. (2) Labor unions today have grown too powerful. I would like to see their power reduced. (3) The power that labor unions have today is about right. I would like to see it stay the way it is."

[b] The question asked was: "Some people say that unions in Canada have become too powerful. Others say unions are necessary in Canada to protect workers from exploitation. Which of these points of view best reflects your own?"

[c] The question asked prior to 1979 was: "Do you think labor unions are getting too strong in Canada, or not?" The question asked in 1979 and in subsequent years was: "Do you think that labor unions are becoming too powerful, or not powerful enough, or are about right?"

There are, of course, many inherent problems associated with interpreting public opinion polls. While it is beyond the scope of this paper to provide a comprehensive assessment of these and other polling data, we believe that this brief comparison of polls is revealing. The evidence suggests that in both Canada and the United States, approval of unions has fallen, unions and their leaders are held in low esteem, and unions are perceived as too powerful.

A second concern with Lipset's analysis involves the linkage between public acceptance of unions and union density. In the United States, these measures declined in tandem over thirty years. Notwithstanding the impreciseness of public opinion measures in Canada, it seems very probable that union density grew in Canada as public acceptance of unions declined (or alternatively, as unions remained generally unpopular).

GARY N. CHAISON and JOSEPH B. ROSE

As one of the most astute observers of North American culture, Lipset correctly identifies important differences in national values (e.g., an electorally viable social democratic party and public enterprise culture in Canada and the free market and competitive individualism of the United States). Given that there probably has been a long-run decline in the public acceptance of unions in both countries, can national values intervene to produce such vast differences in the propensity of workers to join unions, management's pursuit of union-avoidance strategies, and the legal protection afforded by collective bargaining legislation? While some support exists for Lipset's thesis, we remain skeptical about its explanatory power.[14]

Despite a large body of scholarly research pointing to management resistance as a major contributor to union decline in the United States (e.g., Freeman 1985), Lipset is only willing to concede that "the greater use of legal methods to intimidate or otherwise undermine support of labor organizations cannot be dismissed..." (Lipset 1986a, p. 437). More recently he wrote: "There is at best only ambiguous evidence that American employers successfully use intimidating tactics to campaign against unions in representation elections" (Lipset 1986c, p. 26). This appears at variance with studies revealing that American workers are at far greater risk of discharge for legally protected union organizing activities than their Canadian counterparts (Weiler 1983). (Indeed, one examination of state-level Gallup polls for 1978 to 1981 even concluded that "there exists a strong negative association between the public's approval of labor and management's apparent willingness to break the country's labor law" [Medoff 1984, p. D22].) Moreover, as we noted earlier, American corporate values and strategies increasingly are emphasizing union avoidance. For example, a recent study found that U.S. firms that placed a high priority on union avoidance were able to substantially reduce union representation and the probability of unionization at new facilities (Kochan, McKersie, and Chalykoff 1986).

While we agree that Canadian and American employers generally face similar pressures to cut costs (Lipset 1986a) and are more antagonistic toward unions than their European counterparts (Adams 1981), American employers are more likely to stress union avoidance. In the context of new organizing, American firms have discovered that the benefits of union avoidance outweigh the costs of noncompliance with the law. One study of Section 8(a)(3) violations of the National Labor Relations Act concluded that the Act did not act as a deterrent "to management violations and may be considered a relatively low cost of doing business" (Kleiner 1984, p. 241). Greer and Martin (1978) have even been able to develop a calculative decision model which shows that, under some circumstances, employers can achieve economic gains by committing unfair labor practices and forestalling the unionization of their enterprises.

Union growth will also depend on the ability of unions to influence workers' propensity to join. The decision of individual workers to join unions may be shaped by many factors including organized labor's public image. However, "the relationship between workers' *general* beliefs or *image* of the American labor movement and their actual willingness to support unionization on their job is rather weak" (Kochan 1980, p. 146). Far more important are pragmatic considerations such as workers' job conditions and the perceived instrumentality of unions in altering conditions. In a recent review of survey and polling data, Kochan, Katz, and McKersie (1986) report that the preference for unionizing is greatest among workers who are dissatisfied with their pay, job security, on-the-job recognition, and promotional opportunities, and perceive unions as instrumental in improving job conditions. They also point out that one-third of the nonunion workforce in the United States sees "unionization as a vehicle for improving specific job conditions and would prefer to have a union represent them, if given the opportunity" (Kochan, Katz, and McKersie 1986, p. 217). To the extent that American employers seek to reduce the need for unions and actively oppose organizing drives, the propensity to unionize can be affected. Wheeler (1985) has observed that, while there may be innate human predispositions which ready individuals for aggressive action (e.g., union organizing), such behavior may be impeded by fears of employer retaliation.

Although systematic comparative analyses of employer strategy in Canada and the United States do not exist, we believe that the greater hostility of American employers has had a chilling effect on union joining. Moreover, given the greater prevalence of concession bargaining in the United States than in Canada in recent years, the perceived instrumentality of unions may be lower among American workers. Farber (1987) examined data from 1977 and 1984 surveys and uncovered a significant decline in the perceived instrumentality of unions among nonunion workers in the United States. Along with increases in job satisfaction, this change in perceived instrumentality resulted in a decrease (from 38.6 percent to 32.4 percent) in the demand for union representation. It has also been observed:

> Paradoxical as it may seem, collective bargaining is not losing ground in the United States because unions are less attractive, but unions are less attractive because collective bargaining is losing ground (Huxley, Kettler, and Struthers 1986, pp. 128-129).

Turning to the more "liberal" collective bargaining laws in Canada, there can be no doubt that the existence of social democratic governments (or strong social democratic opposition parties) has contributed to labor law reforms.[15] At the same time, not all provinces have electorally viable social democratic parties or institutional frameworks that can be described as "union user friendly." While national values may impart a "social democratic tinge" to all political parties in Canada this begs the point. To begin with, Canadian labor policy has, until recently, followed innovations in the United States (e.g., the

Wagner Act and extending bargaining rights to federal civil servants). Although Canada adopted a "liberal" approach to public sector collective bargaining, this has not precluded federal and provincial governments from adopting draconian measures to regulate unions (e.g., suspending collective bargaining rights for up to two years, including the right to strike). Indeed, these measures enjoyed broad public support (Swimmer 1985).

There also is growing evidence that unions are on the defensive in western Canada, where several provinces have embraced privatization and decentralization programs similar to those of the Thatcher government in the United Kingdom. The situation is probably most acute in British Columbia, where, in 1987, the government introduced a controversial bill to overhaul the province's labor code. The changes, which were aimed at curtailing or undermining union power, prompted the British Columbia Federation of Labour to boycott the law and the new Industrial Relations Council which oversees the law (Cruickshank 1987). It is noteworthy that, notwithstanding the government's fervor for promoting free enterprise and restraining union power, labor policy in British Columbia retains the broad features and basic rights of the Wagner Act model.

Curiously, with all the emphasis put on differences in national values, the fact remains that Canada imported the Wagner Act bargaining model (and some aspects of the Taft-Hartley Act). In the United States, it has been argued that inconsistencies exist between the Wagner and Taft-Hartley Acts, with the earlier law providing strong encouragement for collective bargaining and the latter law elevating free choice and individual rights to a level equal to that of the right to collective bargaining. As described by Gross (1985, pp. 13-14):

> ...the concept of government as a *neutral* guarantor of some equal or reasonably balanced rights of labor and management and as a *neutral* guarantor of employee free choice between individual or collective action is clearly inconsistent with the Wagner Act's concept of a government *partial* to the practice of collective bargaining; yet the Taft-Hartley Act contains both conceptions of government. Interweaving assumptions of employee free choice (the right to refrain) and equality of rights between labor and management, for example, lead to conclusions that are unfavorable to the encouragement of collective bargaining...

Such "tensions" are not unknown in Canada. For example, it was not until the early 1970s that the neutral preamble of the federal labor code was replaced by a positive commitment to collective bargaining (Task Force 1968). Ironically, it is the Canadians who have endeavored to maintain a balance of power between employers and employees by ensuring that employees' rights to self-organization are protected.

In summary, what Lipset appears to be suggesting is that the Wagner Act principles are incompatible with contemporary American values. We would simply observe that, not only do there appear to be conflicting statutory purposes in the United States, but it is questionable whether public opinion unambiguously reflects national values. As noted above, polling data are subject to numerous problems of interpretation. To this we would add that polls often reveal different images of unions. For example, whereas "most of the American public has a poor image of unions in general, an equally strong majority agrees that the functions unions traditionally have performed for their members and for the larger society continue to be relevant and needed today" (Kochan, Katz, and McKersie 1986, p. 216). Our analysis suggests that it is far from certain how public attitudes toward unions will affect the behavior of the actors in the industrial relations system.

CONCLUSIONS

In an earlier paper (Rose and Chaison 1985), we indicated the extent of the differences in union growth in Canada and the United States up to 1980 and described some possible causes for the diverging trends. In this paper, we examined data up to 1986 and further developed our analysis of possible determinants. As we realized in our earlier attempt, it is far easier to document the growth patterns than it is to isolate and measure determinants.

There is clear evidence of a 2 to 1 (or even greater) ratio of Canadian/U.S. union density when measured for various occupational, industrial, and membership characteristics. We also found that Canadian unions are more actively organizing, carry out more campaigns among the more difficult to organize types of bargaining units, and have enjoyed considerably higher success rates in attaining certification even during the difficult years of the past recession.

Our analysis suggests that the trends in union growth may largely result from the complex interplay between employer resistance, public policy, and union organizing efforts. The primary factor appears to be the differences in the public policy in the two countries, with the United States requiring protracted election contests in which employers may fully utilize their union-avoidance strategies, while the Canadian jurisdictions rely on card counts or expedited elections to determine the employees' choice quickly and with the least opportunity for employer coercion or intimidation. These differences in the certification process have important and direct roles in shaping the intensity of both union organizing efforts and employer resistance.

Operating within a public policy framework that they perceive to be generally effective, the Canadian unions are actively pursuing organizing targets, while their American counterparts seem discouraged in their ability to use certification elections to replenish lost membership and make inroads in companies that are practicing the new human resource management. American unions have become wary of the election process and have increasingly resorted to alternative avenues for growth. Among the emerging methods to recruit new members are associate memberships, internal organizing, the absorption of small unions, the affiliation of local independent unions, and the use of corporate campaigns and consumer boycotts to gain employer recognition.

It has long been observed that the certification election procedures in the United States provide employers with an opportunity for action, an arena for the demonstration of legal and illegal resistance to union organizing. We are particularly concerned, along with others (e.g., Weiler 1983, 1985; Freeman 1987; Dickens 1988), that this certification process not only provides an opportunity but also an incentive to resist unionization through intimidation and coercion of employees and procedural delays.

While we have argued that there is a greater acceptance of unions by Canadian employers, we have also suggested that this acceptance has been conditioned by the movement toward tripartite consensus-building and by fewer opportunities to avoid unions. We could speculate about the level and consequence of employer resistance if the Canadian jurisdictions suddenly adopted the U.S. approach to certification. Faced with such increased opportunity to defeat organizing campaigns, some Canadian employers might show a greater resistance than they would otherwise, and Canadian unions might reduce their organizing efforts if protracted campaigns became too costly and produced lower success rates. Such a legislative reversal, however, would be highly unlikely because it would be alien to the broader employer acceptance of unions in Canada and the general orientation of Canadian legislation to provide choice with minimum opportunity for conflict. It is even more interesting (and realistic) to speculate about the consequences if the United States were to adopt a variant of the Canadian certification procedures. This seems to be the objective of many of the efforts that are encompassed under the term "labor law reform." Employer resistance during union organizing campaigns would probably be reduced, but might resurface during initial negotiations. Additional safeguards, such as first contract arbitration or restrictions on the use of permanent strike replacements, might be needed to strengthen the ability of unions to achieve first collective agreements. Faced with the possibility of faster, less expensive, and more successful campaigns, unions might accelerate their organizing efforts and we could see a spurt in union growth. Would such growth continue and would it be sufficient to offset normal attrition in union membership? Would the differential in union density in the United States and Canada narrow? The answer to these questions would depend on whether enough unions had the financial resources and staff to launch campaigns among large units and major unorganized employers, the number of potential organizing targets available, and the ability of unions to significantly improve certification success rates.

If there are no changes in the underlying causes, the differences in union growth in Canada and the United States will continue and could lead to two significant trends. First, many Canadian sections of internationals may be growing and placing a high priority on devoting resources and staff for organizing, while their parent unions in the United States may be adopting primarily defensive postures with the major concern for job security for the present membership rather than membership expansion. The appearance of having different priorities and chances for expansion may fuel the arguments for the greater autonomy of Canadian sections. Furthermore, some international unions which are beset with financial difficulties because of declining membership may no longer feel that they can support Canadian sections and might agree to an amicable severance. In summary, the significant difference in the state of the unions in Canada and the United States may accelerate the trend toward autonomy for Canadian sections of international unions.[16]

Second, we can expect a renewed interest on the part of American labor leaders (and academics) in the Canadian industrial relations system. The two labor movements seem to be moving farther apart, with the Canadian showing an ability and desire to expand and having the vibrancy and optimism that is associated with such growth, while the American appears discouraged and preoccupied in an intense search for solutions. The attempts to reverse the membership declines in the United States have created a new openness to alternative industrial relations systems, particularly public policy approaches, and this will lead to continuing and closer examinations of the situation in Canada.

ACKNOWLEDGMENTS

An earlier version of this paper was presented at the Annual Meetings of the Canadian Industrial Relations Association at McMaster University, Hamilton, Ontario (June 6, 1987). The authors thank Margo Schwab for research assistance and H. Jacek and two anonymous reviewers for their comments on an earlier draft of this paper.

NOTES

1. The T.L.C. largely consisted of U.S.-based craft unions affiliated with the A.F.L., and the C.C.L. largely consisted of U.S.-based industrial unions affiliated with the C.I.O.

2. Canadian membership in the U.S.-based unions may underestimate private sector union membership in Canada, particularly in recent years, because of the increasing nationalization of the Canadian labor movement through the creation of Canadian unions and the succession of Canadian sections of international unions in the private sector. For example, see Thompson and Blum (1983).

3. There may be minor discrepancies in the occupational groupings "processors, production, craft, and repair" and "operators, fabricators, and laborers" between the two countries. These differences do not distract from the overall findings.

4. Sources include: British Columbia Department of Labour (1970-1973), British Columbia Labour Relations Board (1974-1985), Canada Department of Labour (1970-1973), Canada Labour

Relations Board (1973/1974-1984/1985), Ontario Ministry of Labour (1970/1971-1980/1981), and Ontario Labour Relations Board (1981/1982-1985/1986). Union membership in these jurisdictions is approximately 50 percent of the Canadian total.

5.   Election results were only available for British Columbia and Ontario.

6.   The exception is the construction industry.

7.   While the American labor movement has recently regained its influence in Congress, there are indications that its legislative agenda will not focus on labor law reform. The major emphasis will be on proposals that help both union and nonunion workers (e.g., plant closure notification, job hazard notification, minimum wage increases, minimum health insurance, and provisions for parental leave) (Hughey 1987).

8.   Contrary to these studies, Cooper (1984) found that election delay did not reduce union election success. A critique of Cooper's methodology is found in the appendix to Dickens (1988).

9.   In the United States the union success rate in obtaining first contracts after certification has declined from 86 percent in 1960 to 78 percent in 1970 and 63 percent in 1980. This is largely attributed to increased employer resistance as evidenced in the greater employer tendency to commit unfair labor practices during the organizing compaign and initial bargaining sessions (Weiler 1984, pp. 354-355). Although Canadian data are sketchy, in British Columbia unions consistently negotiated first collective agreements (within 18 months of certification) in 75-85 percent of the newly certified bargaining units (1974-1985). There has been a modest drop in the percentage of first agreements achieved in the past two years, but nothing comparable to the trend in the United States. However, direct comparisons are difficult because in British Columbia the labor relations board can impose first contracts and construction unions often conclude agreements prior to certification (British Columbia Labour Relations Board 1986).

10.   Kochan, Katz, and McKersie (1986, p. 64) "found that firms that implemented the average amount of these innovations [in work organization, design and practices] (compared to those not using any of the innovations) reduced the probability that a new plant will be organized by approximately 17 percentage points."

11.   Complaints per certification campaign were 25 times higher in the United States than in British Columbia and 6 times higher than in Ontario (Weiler 1983).

12.   While not perfectly compatible, there are some important similarities in the coverage of the U.S. and Ontario certification data. The U.S. figures are based on membership gains through NLRB elections and provide a conservative estimate because they exclude employees covered by federal and state public sector legislation as well as the Railway Labor Act. The Ontario figures include some public employees (e.g., municipal workers) but exclude public employees covered by provincial and federal public sector labor legislation. The Ontario data also exclude the industries in the federal jurisdiction (e.g., airlines, shipping, and railroads).

13.   In Ontario, the number of employees attempted was estimated by multiplying the average size of the bargaining units certified by the number of units certified and adding the average size of bargaining units not certified (applications withdrawn, dismissed, or elections lost) multiplied by the number of unsuccessful certification applications. The average size of the bargaining units not certified was based on average unit size in union election defeats (the only available data on unit size).

14.   Another reason for skepticism is that within the United States it is possible to contrast union membership trends between the private and public sector (Freeman 1987; Burton and Thomason 1988).

15.   As well, Canada has gone further with government substitution for union services. Statutory procedures, including binding arbitration, exist for protecting nonunion employees against unjust dismissal and for resolving disputes involving occupational health and safety, mass layoffs, and redundancies (Adams 1985).

16.   For example, in January 1987 the delegates to the convention of the International Woodworkers of America voted to split the union into Canadian and U.S. units. It was reported:

The number one reason for breaking up the international, most leaders agreed, was the unwillingness to fund an international office, due largely to a drop in membership during the 1980s. It cost twice as much today on a per capita basis to maintain the international structure compared with the late 1970s when membership was well over 100,000... Membership in the international has declined more steeply in the U.S. than in Canada (*Daily Labor Report* January 28, 1987).

REFERENCES

Adams, R.J. 1981. A Theory of Employer Attitudes and Behavior Toward Trade Unions in Western Europe and North America. Pp. 277-293 in *Management Under Differing Value Systems,* edited by G. Dlugos and K. Weiermair. Berlin: Walter de Gruyter.

———. 1985. Industrial Relations and the Economic Crisis: Canada Moves Toward Europe, Pp. 115-149 in *Industrial Relations in a Decade of Change,* edited by H. Juris, M. Thompson and W. Daniels. Madison, WI: Industrial Relations Research Association.

AFL-CIO. 1985. *Proceedings of the Sixteenth Constitutional Convention of the AFL-CIO, Vol. II, Report of the Executive Council.* Washington, DC: AFL-CIO.

AFL-CIO Committee on the Evolution of Work. 1985. *The Changing Situation of Workers and Their Unions.* Washington, DC: AFL-CIO.

AFL-CIO News. March 14, 1987. SEIU Chalks Up Major Gains on Organizing Front, p. 8.

———. March 21, 1987. Labor Board's Caseload Increases, p. 3.

Bain, G.S. and R.J. Price. 1980. *Profiles of Union Growth.* Oxford: Blackwell.

Barkin, S. 1986. The Current Unilateralist Counterattack on Unionism and Collective Bargaining. *Relations Industrielles* 41:3-16.

British Columbia Department of Labour. 1970-1973. *Annual Reports.* Victoria: British Columbia Department of Labour.

British Columbia Labour Relations Board. 1974-1986. *Annual Reports.* Victoria: British Columbia Labour Relations Board.

Burton, J.B., Jr. and T. Thomason. 1988. The Extent of Collective Bargaining in the Public Sector. Pp. 1-51 in *Public Sector Bargaining,* 2nd ed., edited by B. Aaron, J.M. Najita and J.L. Stern. Washington, DC: Bureau of National Affairs.

Canada Department of Labour. 1970-1973. *Annual Reports.* Ottawa: Canada Department of Labour.

Canada Labour Relations Board. 1973/1974-1984/1985. *Annual Reports.* Ottawa: Canada Labour Relations Board.

Chaison, G.N. 1986. *When Unions Merge.* Lexington, MA: Lexington Books.

Chamberlain, N., D. Cullen, and D. Lewin. 1980. *The Labor Sector,* 3rd ed. New York: McGraw-Hill.

Communications Workers of America. 1983. *Committee on the Future Report.* Washington, DC: CWA.

CWA News. March 1987. 80 Laid-off MCI Workers Sign as CWA "Associates," p. 4.

Cooke, W.N. 1985a. The Failure to Negotiate First Contracts: Determinants and Policy Implications. *Industrial and Labor Relations Review* 38(2):163-178.

———. 1985b. The Rising Toll of Discrimination Against Union Activists. *Industrial Relations* 24(3):421-442.

———. 1985c. *Union Organizing and Public Policy: Failure to Secure First Contracts.* Kalamazoo, MI: W.E. Upjohn Institute for Employment Research.

Cooper, L. 1984. Authorization Cards and Union Representation Outcome: An Empirical Assessment of the Assumption Underlying the Supreme Court's *Gissel* Decision. *Northwestern University Law Review* 79(March):87-141.

202   GARY N. CHAISON and JOSEPH B. ROSE

Craft, J.A. and M. Extejt. 1983. New Strategies in Union Organizing. *Journal of Labor Research* 4(Winter):19-32.

Craig, A. 1986. *The System of Industrial Relations in Canada,* 2nd ed. Scarborough, Ontario: Prentice-Hall.

Cruickshank, J. 1987. The Battle for B.C. *Globe and Mail,* June 27, pp. D1, D3.

Daily Labor Report. February 20, 1986. Statements Adopted by AFL-CIO Executive Council at Winter Meeting, pp. E1-E4.

————. June 13, 1986. Congressional Research Service Report on Implications for Economic Policy and Labor Legislation of Decline in Union Membership, pp. D1-D16.

————. January 28, 1987. IWA Splits into U.S., Canadian Units at 34th Annual Convention, pp. A1-A3.

————. February 23, 1987. Union Membership Decline Eases Somewhat in 1986 as Proportion Reaches 17.5 Percent, pp. B6-B8.

de Bernardo, M. 1986. Public Sector Sees Organizing Labor Boom. *Wall Street Journal,* December 18, p. 26.

Dickens, W.T. 1988. *Does the NLRA Still Protect Workers' Right to Organize?: Testimony of Professor William T. Dickens Before the Labor Subcommittee of the Senate Committee on Labor and Human Resources, January 29, 1988.* Unpublished manuscript, University of California, Berkeley.

Dickens, W.T. and J.S. Leonard. 1985. Accounting for the Decline in Union Membership, 1950-1980. *Industrial and Labor Relations Review* 3(April):223-334.

Doyle, P.M. 1985. Area Wage Surveys Shed Light on Declines in Unionization. *Monthly Labor Review* 108(September):13-20.

Eaton, J.K. 1975. The Growth of the Canadian Labour Movement. *Labour Gazette* 75(September):643-650.

Edwards, R. and M. Podgursky. 1986. The Unraveling Accord: American Unions in Crisis. Pp. 14-60 in *Unions in Crisis and Beyond: Perspectives from Six Countries,* edited by R. Glover, P. Garonna, and F. Todtling. Dover, MA: Auburn House.

Farber, H.S. 1985. The Extent of Unionization in the United States. Pp. 15-44 in *Challenges and Choices Facing American Labor,* edited by T.A. Kochan. Cambridge, MA: MIT Press.

————. 1987. The Recent Decline in Unionization in the United States. *Science* 238(November):915-920.

Feuille, P. and J.C. Anderson. 1980. Public Sector Bargaining: Policy and Practice. *Industrial Relations* 19(Fall):309-324.

Freeman, R.B. 1985. Why Are Unions Faring Poorly in NLRB Representation Elections? Pp. 45-64 in *Challenges and Choices Facing American Unions,* edited by T.A. Kochan. Cambridge, MA: MIT Press.

————. 1986. Unionism Comes to the Public Sector. *Journal of Economic Literature* 24(March):41-86.

————. 1987. *Contraction and Expansion: The Divergence of Private Sector and Public Sector Unionism in the U.S.* Working paper no. 2399, National Bureau of Economic Research, Cambridge, MA.

Galenson, W. 1986. The Historical Role of American Trade Unionism. Pp. 39-74 in *Unions in Transition,* edited by S.M. Lipset. San Francisco: Institute for Contemporary Studies.

Gifford, C. ed. 1982. *Directory of U.S. Labor Organizations, 1982-1983.* Washington, DC: Bureau of National Affairs.

————. 1984. *Directory of U.S. Labor Organizations, 1984-1985.* Washington, DC: Bureau of National Affairs.

Goldfield, M. 1987. *The Decline of Organized Labor in the United States.* Chicago: University of Chicago Press.

Greenhouse, S. 1985. Reshaping Labor to Woo the Young. *New York Times,* September 1, pp. F1, F6.

Greer, C.R. and S.A. Martin. 1978. Calculative Strategy Decisions During Union Organizing Campaigns. *Sloan Management Review* 19(Winter):61-74.

Gross, J.A. 1985. Conflicting Statutory Purposes: Another Look at Fifty Years of NLRB Law Making. *Industrial and Labor Relations Review* 39(October):7-18.

Gunderson, M. and N.M. Meltz. 1986. Canadian Unions Achieve Strong Gains in Membership. *Monthly Labor Review* 109(April):48-49.

Hughey, A. 1987. Congress Takes Up Labor's Cause. *New York Times,* August 23, Section 3, pp. 1, 28.

Hunt, J.C. and R.A. White. 1985. The Effects of Management Practices on Union Election Returns. *Journal of Labor Research* 6(Fall):389-403.

Huxley, C., D. Kettler, and J. Struthers. 1986. Is Canada's Experience "Especially Instructive"? Pp. 113-132 in *Unions in Transition,* edited by S.M. Lipset. San Francisco: Institute for Contemporary Studies.

Johnston, R. 1986. *Public Opinion and Public Policy in Canada.* Toronto: University of Toronto Press.

Kerr, C. 1986. Introduction: A New Industrial Relations? A Four (or Perhaps Six) Sector Approach to An Answer. Pp. xi-xvi in *Teamwork: Joint-Labor Management Programs in America,* edited by J.M. Rosow. New York: Pergamon Press.

Kirkland, L. 1987. Goal of New Benefit Programs: Extend Unionism from Workplace to Marketplace. *AFL-CIO News,* February, 24, Supplement p. 1.

Kleiner, M.W. 1984. Unionism and Employer Discrimination: Analysis of 8(a)(3) Violations. *Industrial Relations* 23(Spring):234-243.

Kochan, T.A. 1980. *Collective Bargaining and Industrial Relations.* Homewood, IL: Irwin.

Kochan, T.A., H. Katz, and R.B. McKersie. 1986. *The Transformation of American Industrial Relations.* New York: Basic.

Kochan, T.A., R.B. McKersie, and P. Capelli. 1984. Strategic Choice and Industrial Relations Theory. *Industrial Relations* 23(Winter):16-39.

Kochan, T.A., R.B. McKersie, and J. Chalykoff. 1986. The Effects of Corporate Strategy and Workplace Innovations on Union Representation. *Industrial and Labor Relations Review* 39(July):487-501.

Kumar, P., M.L. Coates, and D. Arrowsmith. 1986. *The Current Industrial Relations Scene in Canada, 1986.* Kingston, Ontario: Industrial Relations Centre, Queen's University.

Labour Canada. 1983. Labour and Labour Issues in the 1980s. Presentation on the MacDonald Royal Commission on the Economic Union and Development Prospects for Canada, Ottawa.

————. 1986. *Labour Organizations in Canada, 1986.* Ottawa: Labour Canada.

Lawler, J.J. and R. West. 1985. Impact of Union Avoidance Strategies on Representation Elections. *Industrial Relations* 24(Fall):406-420.

Levitan, S., P.E. Carlson, and I. Shapiro. 1986. *Protecting American Workers.* Washington, DC: BNA Books.

Lipset, S.M. 1986a. North American Labor Movements: A Comparative Perspective. Pp. 421-452 in *Unions in Transition,* edited by S.M. Lipset. San Francisco: Institute for Contemporary Studies.

————. 1986b. Labor Unions in the Public Mind. Pp. 287-321 in *Unions in Transition,* edited by S.M. Lipset. San Francisco: Institute for Contemporary Studies.

————. 1986c. Why Do Canada's Unions Prosper? *Wall Street Journal,* December 18, p. 26.

McDonald, C.J. 1987. The AFL-CIO's Blueprint for the Future—A Progress Report. *Proceedings of the Thirty-Ninth Annual Meeting of the Industrial Relations Research Association,* pp. 276-282. Madison, WI: Industrial Relations Research Association.

Medoff, J.L. 1984. Study for AFL-CIO on Public's Image of Unions. *Daily Labor Report,*
    December 24, pp. D1-D23.
Meltz, N. 1985. Labor Movements in Canada and the United States. Pp. 315-334 in *Challenges*
    and Choices Facing American Labor, edited by T.A. Kochan. Cambridge, MA: MIT Press.
Molotsky, I. 1987. Air Controllers Vote New Union Over Issues that Led to '81 Strike. *New York*
    Times, June 12, pp. 1, B8.
Monthly Labor Review. May 1986. Union Membership of Employed Wage and Salary Workers,
    1985, vol. 109, pp. 44-46.
New York Times. April 5, 1987. Prospects: On Strike, In Business, p. 1F.
Ontario Labour Relations Board. 1981/1982-1985/1986. *Annual Reports.* Toronto: Ontario
    Labour Relations Board.
Ontario Ministry of Labour. 1970/1971-1980/1981. *Annual Reports.* Toronto: Ontario Ministry
    of Labour.
Raskin, A.H. 1986a. Big Labor Tries to End its Nightmare. *New York Times,* May 4, pp. 1F,
    8F.
––––––. 1986b. Labor: A Movement in Search of a Mission. Pp. 3-38 in *Unions in Transition,*
    edited by S.M. Lipset. San Francisco: Institute for Contemporary Studies.
––––––. 1987. Even Football Players Find Labor's Glory Has Faded. *New York Times,* October
    25, p. E4.
Reynolds, J. 1986. Steelworkers Press Organizing and Coordinated Bargaining. *Monthly Labor*
    Review 109(November):48-49.
Riddell, W.C. 1986. Canadian Labour Relations: An Overview. Pp. 1-93 in *Canadian Labour*
    Relations, edited by W.C. Riddell. Toronto: University of Toronto Press.
Rose, J.B. 1984. Growth Patterns of Public Sector Unions. Pp. 83-119 in *Conflict or Compromise:*
    The Future of Public Sector Industrial Relations, edited by M. Thompson and G. Swimmer.
    Montreal: The Institute for Research on Public Policy.
Rose, J.B. and G.N. Chaison. 1985. The State of the Unions: United States and Canada. *Journal*
    of Labor Research 6(Winter):97-111.
Samoff, B.L. 1987. What Lies Ahead for the NLRB. *Labor Law Journal* 38(June):259-270.
Seeber, R.L. and W.N. Cooke. 1983. The Decline in Union Success in NLRB Representation
    Elections. *Industrial Relations* 22(Winter):34-44.
Slotnick, L. 1986. Labor Intensive Drives Net Unions New Recruits. *Globe and Mail,* September
    1, pp. A1-A2.
Statistics Canada. 1962-1984. *The Corporations and Labor Unions Returns Act Annual Report.*
    Ottawa: Statistics Canada.
––––––. 1984b. *Survey of Union Membership, 1984.* Unpublished manuscript, Statistics Canada,
    Ottawa.
Stephan, P.E. and B.E. Kaufman. 1987. Factors Leading to the Decline in the Union Win Rates:
    1973-1981. *Proceedings of the Thirty-Ninth Annual Meeting of the Industrial Relations*
    Research Association, pp. 296-305. Madison, WI: Industrial Relations Research
    Association.
Swimmer, G. 1985. Dispute Resolutions in the Ontario Public Sector: What's So Wrong About
    the Right to Strike? Pp. 154-178 in *Public Sector Compensation,* edited by D. Conklin.
    Toronto: Ontario Economic Council.
Task Force on Labour Relations. 1968. *Canadian Industrial Relations.* Ottawa: Queen's Printer.
Thompson, M. and A. Blum. 1983. International Unionism in Canada: The Move to Local
    Control. *Industrial Relations* 22(Winter):71-86.
Troy, L. 1986. The Rise and Fall of American Trade Unions: The Labor Movement from FDR
    to RR. Pp. 75-109 in *Unions in Transition,* edited by S.M. Lipset. San Francisco: Institute
    for Contemporary Studies.

Troy, L. and N. Sheflin. 1985. *Union Sourcebook: Membership, Structure, Finance, Directory.* West Orange, NJ: Industrial Relations Data and Information Services.

United States Bureau of the Census. 1987. *Statistical Abstract of the United States, 1987.* Washington, DC: U.S. Government Printing Office.

United States National Labor Relations Board. 1986. *Forty-Eighth Annual Report of the National Labor Relations Board, 1983.* Washington, DC: U.S. Government Printing Office.

United Steelworkers of America. 1984. *Forging a Future: Report of the Convention Committee on the Future Directions of the Union.* Pittsburgh: USWA.

Voos, P. 1983. Union Organizing: Costs and Benefits. *Industrial and Labor Relations Review* 36(July):571-591.

_____. 1987. Union Organizing Expenditures: Determinants and Their Implications for Union Growth. *Journal of Labor Research* 8(Winter):18-30.

Weiler, P. 1983. Promises to Keep: Securing Workers' Rights to Self-Organization Under the NLRA. *Harvard Law Review* 96(June):1769-1827.

_____. 1984. Striking a New Balance: Freedom of Contract and the Prospects for Union Representation. *Harvard Law Review* 98:351-420.

_____. 1985. Reflections on the NLRA at 50. *Daily Labor Report,* June 11, pp. E1-E11.

Wheeler, H.N. 1985. *Industrial Conflict: An Integrative Theory.* Columbia: University of South Carolina Press.

Wood, W.D. and P. Kumar, 1984. *The Current Industrial Relations Scene in Canada, 1984.* Kingston: The Industrial Relations Centre, Queens University.

MEASURING THE PERCEPTIONS OF THE EFFECTIVENESS OF A WORKPLACE COMPLAINT PROCEDURE

Karen E. Boroff

There are several significant benefits that can accrue to firms, employees, and, where applicable, worker representatives as a result of establishing particular systems for handling workplace conflict. Employers, unionists, and employees want to resolve workplace conflict and reduce worker discontent. Complaint procedures permit conflict to be addressed without disrupting workplace operations. Furthermore, complaint systems can be a source of information to those who manage or represent employees. By analyzing the issues presented in the complaints that surface as well as by tracking the managers "against" whom complaints are registered, companies and, where applicable, union representatives, can identify potential weaknesses in an organization's policies (both human resources and operational policies), practices, and management team (Chamberlain, Cullen, and Lewin 1980). Also, complaint systems can improve a firm's responsiveness to public law. Charges of race or sex discrimination, for example, that surface in internal complaints may be able to be rectified without having to resort to state or federal agencies (Berenbeim

Advances in Industrial and Labor Relations, volume 5, pages 207-233.
Copyright © 1991 by JAI Press Inc.
All rights of reproduction in any form reserved.
ISBN: 0-89232-940-8

1980; Chamberlain and Kuhn 1986; Kochan and Katz 1988; Lewin 1983; Slichter, Healy, and Livernash 1960).

In addition, in unionized firms unionists can, through the filing of grievances, minimize fair representation suits charged by dissatisfied union members. Because the grievance machinery is considered to be an extension of collective bargaining (Kuhn 1961), the grievance process allows the company and the union to resolve ambiguities or omissions in the collective bargaining agreement during the term of the agreement. Freeman and Medoff (1984) conclude that, by providing "voice" to employees, the grievance process can reduce turnover for a firm. This voice, in turn, is claimed to have positive productivity implications for the firm. Despite the purported productivity gains associated with union voice, in the nonunion setting the existence of a complaint system may diminish the need for a union in the eyes of the unorganized. Thus, a firm may hope to maintain a union-free environment via a complaint system (Foulkes 1980; Ichniowski and Lewin 1987).

These many benefits notwithstanding, there is little agreement on how one measures the effectiveness of grievance and complaint systems (g/c systems). It is the purpose of this paper to put forth and empirically test conceptual models on the effectiveness of g/c systems. This will be accomplished by examining the perceptions that complainants, potential complainants, and respondents to complaints have regarding a g/c system. In so doing, this paper will set forth a framework from which future work on g/c system effectiveness can be researched.

THE EXISTING RESEARCH

The existing literature on grievance and complaint systems effectiveness is diverse and can be divided into three broad categories, each of which provides insights, directly or indirectly, on g/c system effectiveness. The first category focuses on studies on grievance usage. These studies implicitly assume that, because grievance usage can be differentiated by the personal characteristics of system users, this implies that workers perceive g/c system effectiveness differently. As a result, these studies suggest variables for which the researcher must control when attempting to model g/c system effectiveness. The second category of research concentrates on the benefits of g/c systems. This literature suggests dimensions that may well contribute to the effectiveness of a g/c system. The third category attempts to assess directly the effectiveness of g/c systems. This body of research offers still another set of factors that may be related to g/c system effectiveness. These three major areas of research are briefly summarized.

The research on grievance usage generally compares the demographics of those who file grievances or complaints with those who do not (Ash 1970; Lewin

1987; Lewin and Peterson 1987a) or focuses on grievance rates (Lewin 1984). These authors report a positive relationship between usage and education. Furthermore, males and veterans seem to use the g/c system more than females and nonveterans. One also finds that usage is negatively associated with age, although the relationship between minority status and usage is reported to be both positive and negative. Finally, one sees that grievance rates (generally measured as grievances per 100 employees) varies by industry.

The literature on the benefits of g/c procedures reveals that complainants, unions (where applicable), and employers can each benefit from both the establishment and the use of g/c systems. As an example, Berenbeim (1980), Chamberlain, Cullen, and Lewin (1980), Foulkes (1980), Freeman and Medoff (1984), and Kochan and Katz (1988) collectively suggest that employers and union leaders can obtain information about the efficacy of company policies as well as the collective bargaining agreement by studying issues that surface in the g/c system. In addition, g/c systems can help pinpoint weak or poor supervisors. Third, g/c systems can help employers and unions abide by equal employment legislation; when apparent violations do occur, g/c systems can provide a less costly avenue of redress than civil litigation. Fourth, g/c systems may help a firm reduce the possibility of unionization. Complainants, too, can benefit from g/c systems. They can air their concerns with dignity and without fear of reprisal. Furthermore, complainants are provided with an alternative and peaceful means to correct what they perceive to be industrial injustices.

The third research stream focuses directly on the question "what makes a g/c process effective," primarily from the perspective of the complainant. One can conclude from these studies that perceptions of a fair hearing, timeliness of resolution, ease of use, feedback about the g/c process, and protection from recrimination are important elements in evaluating appeal systems. Furthermore, adversarial fact-finding, the use of external decisionmakers if the complaint cannot be resolved, and perceived equity of the settlement are additional dimensions to consider in analyzing the effectiveness of g/c systems (Aram and Salipante 1981; Chamberlain and Kuhn 1986; Knight 1985; Kuhn 1961; Lewin 1983; Sheppard 1983; Slichter, Healy, and Livernash 1960; Thibaut and Walker 1978). From this research, one sees that there are both objective and subjective measures of g/c system effectiveness.

While these various works have enriched our understanding of g/c systems, there are, nevertheless, several gaps in our body of knowledge on measuring the effectiveness of g/c processes. First, the studies on grievance usage really do not answer the question "what makes a grievance or complaint process effective?" Instead, such studies attempt to model the probability of filing a complaint. This difference in focus is not trivial. One of the factors that *may* influence the probability of using a complaint system is the perceived effectiveness of a complaint process.[1] If so, effectiveness can be conceived as an independent variable in a model predicting usage. The research question posed here, however, is "what factors influence the perceived effectiveness of a g/c process?" The dependent variable is *not* usage but perceived effectiveness. Furthermore, studies on the characteristics of grievance filers need to be treated cautiously even in developing probability of usage models. These studies compare those who file complaints with those who do not. The more appropriate level of analysis on usage would be to study *all* employees who have experienced or who perceive themselves to have experienced unfair treatment. Then, one would study patterns of usage within this group. With this latter focus, the results on, say, sex or race differences between users and nonusers that have been previously observed may really be insignificant when one studies only complaint system users and nonusers when *both* groups perceived themselves to have experienced unfair treatment.

Another gap is that the existing empirical work generally has not studied perceived effectiveness from the needs and viewpoints of *all* the individuals who are participants in the g/c process (for exceptions, see Briggs 1982; Jennings 1974a,b; and Lewin 1987). These various participants include, obviously, the complainant but also include the line managers who respond to complaints, the personnel staff manager, the union steward, and other union officers. It is conceivable that these players evaluate effectiveness differently. For example, we know that one of the dimensions with which a complainant may measure the perceived effectiveness of a g/c process is in terms of the speed of resolution of the complaint (Lewin 1984). But it is easy to imagine that the same may not be said for the line manager against whom a complaint is filed or the personnel staff manager or union official who oversees the administration of the g/c system.

In a related manner, because the focus of the existing literature on g/c systems has generally been on the complainant, we have not fully considered how "winning a grievance" relates to the perceived effectiveness of g/c systems. At first blush, one would expect that "winning" (i.e., having the complaint decided in the complainant's favor) would be essential to one's perceptions of effectiveness. The literature on procedural and distributive justice is insightful, yet equivocal, in this respect.[2] For example, both Tyler and Caine (1981) and Thibaut and Walker (1978) assert that perceived effectiveness is composed of both *process* and *outcome* fairness, and that these two dimensions can be distinguished from each other. Further, Thibaut and Walker (1978) state that higher *process* fairness ratings should improve overall effectiveness ratings of justice systems, regardless of the outcomes obtained by the complainant. Leventhal, Karuza, and Fry (1980), on the other hand, suggest that outcomes obtained and not procedures used will be the more important factor in evaluating processes that attempt to distribute scarce resources. Note these studies do not rule out outcomes as a correlate of perceived effectiveness— just that the weight given to winning one's complaint varies in estimating perceived effectiveness.

However, in the industrial relations and sociology literatures, there is research to suggest that winning may play an insignificant role in evaluating g/c system effectiveness for certain participants in the g/c system. For example, Sayles and Strauss (1953) suggest that "winning" the grievance may not necessarily be the objective for some unionists. These scholars assert that union officials may support a grievance because they are more interested in communicating a message to management, a message that may be totally unrelated to the issue at hand in the grievance. For these unionists, then, winning the specific complaint may play a minor role in evaluating perceived effectiveness of the grievance system. A similar argument can be made regarding winning a grievance for managers who respond to complaints or personnel staff managers. As expressed by Kanter (1977), managers are socialized to conform for the good of the corporation (as opposed for the good of the individual). As a result, managers may be less influenced by the results of specific grievances because their focus is on the "larger" welfare that a g/c system brings to the workplace. This may be especially evident when a company unilaterally establishes a complaint system. Regardless, though, of how the g/c system is established, winning the grievance may differentially affect the perceived effectiveness of g/c systems, depending on whether one is the "owner" of the specific grievance (i.e., the complainant) or one is the "owner" of the g/c process (i.e., the union leader or manager). Existing research does not address this issue.

Another gap in our body of knowledge on the effectiveness of g/c processes is that there exists no empirical test that attempts to integrate the various determinants of perceived effectiveness into one index. For example, Knight (1986) examines the impact that feedback about grievances and the grievance process has on a measure of grievance process effectiveness, namely, resolution of grievances. Yet, he does not incorporate or control for other factors that may influence effectiveness, such as the outcomes or consequences of the complaint itself. In a similar vein, Lewin (1984) examines perceived effectiveness as it correlates to such elements as grievance rates and speed of settlement. These elements are not analyzed in a multivariate and, hence, more comprehensive manner. As a result, it becomes difficult to conclude which are the more salient components of perceived complaint system effectiveness.

This study narrows these research gaps in two important respects. First, I empirically investigate, in a multivariate analysis, the relationship between perceived effectiveness and the various elements of g/c systems which are purported to enhance g/c system effectiveness. Second, I analyze perceived effectiveness from the perspectives of both the complainants and those respondent to complaints.

THE RESEARCH QUESTIONS AND THE MODELS

The previous literature review suggests several research questions. These research questions focus, in part, on the different participants in the g/c system. In order to facilitate the discussion of these research questions and the various players in the complaint system, the following diagram is provided.

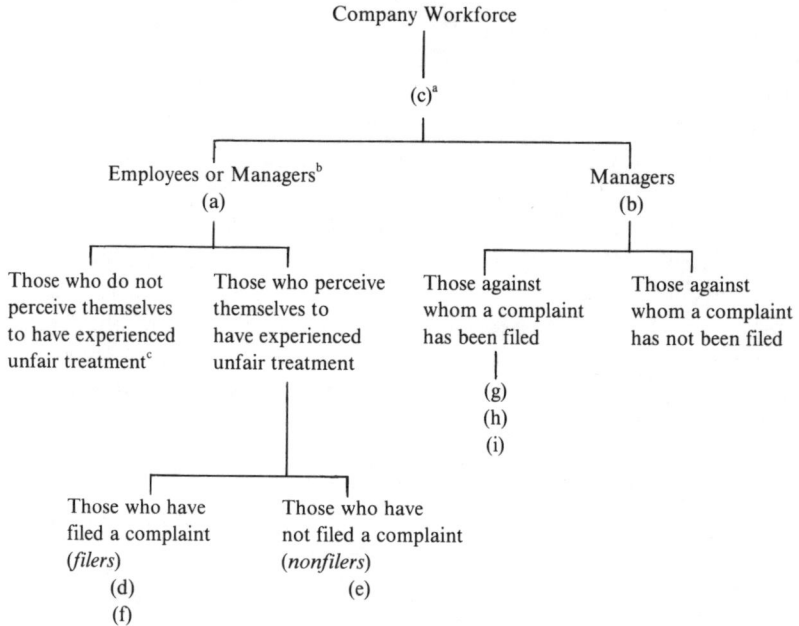

Company Workforce

$(c)^a$

Employees or Managers[b]
(a)

Managers
(b)

Those who do not perceive themselves to have experienced unfair treatment[c]

Those who perceive themselves to have experienced unfair treatment

Those against whom a complaint has been filed

(g)
(h)
(i)

Those against whom a complaint has not been filed

Those who have filed a complaint (*filers*)
(d)
(f)

Those who have not filed a complaint (*nonfilers*)
(e)

Notes: [a] The letters in parentheses refer to regression equations that will be developed for the specific groups. These regression equations will be subsequently discussed.

[b] The term "manager," as subsequently used in this paper, refers to all supervisor and managerial employees, including senior company officials. The term "employee" refers to all nonsupervisory employees.

[c] One may argue that an individual may not necessarily have to experience unfair treatment in order to file a complaint, but this issue is beyond the scope of this paper.

First, the aggregate determinants of g/c system effectiveness, as measured by the perceptions of employee-complainants (or potential employee-complainants) will be investigated. This overcomes the already identified research deficiency which has examined effectiveness on a one-by-one independent variable basis. Second, I will investigate whether or not managers, in their role of complainants or potential complainants, perceive g/c system effectiveness differently from employees to see whether perceived effectiveness does vary based upon the players' orientations. In other words, employees and managers may weigh the same correlates of effectiveness differently and this will be researched by comparing perceived effectiveness from the viewpoints of these two groups.[3]

The third research question will examine perceived effectiveness from the perspective of employee filers and nonfilers.[4] By focusing solely on those who have experienced unfair treatment, the findings obtained here will not be confounded by those who have never perceived a need to file a complaint. (Recall that the failure to control for those who have never felt a need even to consider filing complaints was a shortcoming of the "characteristics of grievance system user" stream of research discussed earlier). In addition, this third research question will explore the importance that "winning" one's grievance (i.e., whether or not the complaint is decided in the complainant's favor) has in determining perceived complaint system effectiveness among filers. Thus, the weights given to an element of distributive justice, namely the content of the decision, and to elements of procedural justice as components in an overall measure of perceived effectiveness will be better understood.

In order to investigate these first three research questions, the following model (Model I) is put forth. Model I studies perceived effectiveness from the viewpoint of the complaint system user or potential user.[5] In Table 1, the conceptual and the empirical research which supports the inclusion of the independent variables in the model is provided.

PERCEIVED EFFECTIVENESS MODEL I

$$\text{PERCEIVED EFFECTIVENESS}_1 = B_0 + B_1\text{ADVRSARY} + B_2\text{IMPRTIAL}$$
$$+ B_3\text{SPEED} + B_4\text{SOURCE}$$
$$+ B_5\text{FEEDBACK} + B_6\text{EASY}$$
$$+ B_7\text{REPRISAL} + B_8\text{LVLSREV}$$
$$+ B_9\text{OTHRTINK} + B_{10}\text{OUTCOME}$$

where: PERCEIVED EFFECTIVENESS$_1$ is an overall measure of the perceptions of individuals about the g/c system, from the perspective of complaint system users or potential users.

ADVRSARY is the degree to which individuals believe an adversarial fact-gathering/fact-presentation feature is absent in the g/c system.

IMPRTIAL is the degree to which individuals feel the g/c system is impartial.

SPEED is the degree to which individuals feel that their complaints are quickly resolved via the g/c system.

SOURCE is the degree to which the grievance is resolved as close as possible to the source of the complaint.

FEEDBACK is the degree to which individuals feel that they are informed about the g/c process.

EASY is the degree to which individuals feel that the g/c system is easy to use.

REPRISAL is the degree to which individuals believe g/c system users experience reprisal for filing complaints.

LVLSREV is the degree to which individuals feel that multiple levels of review of their complaints is important to g/c system effectiveness.

OTHRTINK is the degree to which individuals feel that coworkers think badly about g/c system users.

OUTCOME is the degree to which the grievance or complaint is decided in the complainant's favor.

In addition, because there is evidence to suggest that use may be an indicator of perceived effectiveness, the model controls for the following personal characteristics of the complainants: sex (Lewin 1987; Lewin and Peterson 1987a), education (Lewin and Peterson 1987a), race (Ash 1970; Lewin and Peterson 1987a), and age (Ash 1970; Lewin and Peterson 1987a). According to the research streams developed by the respective authors listed in Table 1, the coefficients B_2, B_3, B_4, B_5, B_6, B_8, and B_{10} are hypothesized to be positive; B_1, B_7, and B_9 are hypothesized to be negative.

Drawing upon the review of the literature, one recognizes that there is another research question, one that focuses on the perceived effectiveness of the g/c process from the perspectives of managers who have responded to complaints (herein called "manager-respondents"). Kochan and Katz (1988) state that one measure of grievance process effectiveness may be the degree to which it assists a firm in complying with employment regulation. Chamberlain, Cullen, and Lewin (1980) note that grievance processes can provide managers information about problems and concerns in the workplace. Foulkes (1980) suggests that g/c systems can help a firm thwart union organizing attempts. These factors may not necessarily be relevant in the model of perceived effectiveness for complainants but may, nonetheless, combine to measure perceived effectiveness from a different vantage point—that of the manager-respondent. As a result, one needs to investigate whether or not there exists a second set of factors that correlate with g/c effectiveness. Furthermore, as a subset of this fourth research question, there is a need to investigate the degree to which perceived effectiveness for manager-respondents is influenced by whether or not the complaint is resolved in the complainant's favor. In order to address this fourth research question, a second model (Model II) has been developed.

Model II studies perceived g/c process effectiveness from the perspective of manager-respondents. In Table 2, the conceptual and the empirical research which supports the inclusion of the independent variables in the model is provided.

Table 1. Perceived Effectiveness Model I:
Research References for the Independent Variables

Independent Variable	Research Source(s)
Absence of Adversarial Fact-finding	Chamberlain and Kuhn (1986), Sheppard (1983)
Impartiality of g/c System	Aram and Salipante (1981), Briggs (1982), Chamberlain and Kuhn (1986)
Speed of Resolution	Aram and Salipante (1981), Chamberlain and Kuhn (1986), Kochan and Katz (1988), Kuhn (1961), Lewin (1983, 1984*)
Resolution as Close to the Source of the Complaint as Possible	Lewin (1983), Slichter, Healy, and Livernash (1960)
Feedback about the Process	Knight* (1986)
Ease of Use	Aram and Salipante (1981)
Perceptions of Reprisal for Filing a Complaint	Aram and Salipante (1981)
Multiple Levels of Review	Chamberlain and Kuhn (1986)
Concern over what Others Think about g/c System Users	While there is no direct citation for this variable, we do know that reference groups can exert an influence on one's behavior and attitudes. This has been addressed generally by Homans (1950) and specifically in the industrial relations context by Ross (1948) and Lipset, Trow, and Coleman (1956). For example, Ross (1948) asserts that one's reference group (or, in his words, "orbits of coercive comparison") can influence one's satisfaction with a collective bargaining agreement. Thus, it is reasonable to hypothesize that if one's reference group has negative perceptions about complainants, such may dampen one's perceptions about a given g/c system.
Outcome in Favor of the Complainant	Lewin (1983, 1984*)

Note: * This research empirically investigates the asserted relationship between the independent variable and perceived effectiveness.

PERCEIVED EFFECTIVENESS MODEL II

$$\text{PERCEIVED EFFECTIVENESS}_2 = B_0 + B_1\text{LOSSFLEX} + B_2\text{DUEPROC}$$
$$+ B_3\text{EFFECT} + B_4\text{OTHROUTCM}$$
$$+ B_5\text{TRNG} + B_6\text{INFOSOURCE}$$
$$+ B_7\text{PUBLICPOLICY}$$
$$+ B_8\text{UNIONAVOID}$$
$$+ B_9\text{OUTCOME}$$

where: PERCEIVED EFFECTIVENESS$_2$ is an overall measure of the perceptions of individuals about the g/c system, from the perspective of manager-respondents.

LOSSFLEX is the degree to which manager-respondents feel that they lose managerial flexibility in supervising their subordinates as a result of the g/c system.

DUEPROC is the degree to which manager-respondents feel that the g/c system affords their subordinates fairer treatment at work.

EFFECT is the degree to which manager-respondents feel that the g/c system has a positive effect on the complainant's productivity and morale.

OTHROUTCM is the degree to which manager-respondents feel that the g/c system has a positive effect on the output of their subordinate team.

TRNG is the degree to which manager-respondents are satisfied with the amount of training they receive on the g/c system.

INFOSOURCE is the degree to which manager-respondents feel that the g/c system provides them information about poor company policies/practices and weak managers.

PUBLICPOLICY is the degree to which manager-respondents feel that the g/c system helps them comply with employment regulation.

UNIONAVOID is the degree to which manager-respondents believe that the presence of the g/c system helps the company avoid unions.

OUTCOME is the degree to which the grievance or complaint is decided in the complainant's favor.

The control variables are, again, sex, education, race, and age. Based upon the conclusions drawn by the scholars listed in Table 2, the coefficients B_2, B_3, B_4, B_5, B_6, B_7, and B_8 are hypothesized to be positive; B_1 is hypothesized to be negative. The coefficient B_9 is indeterminate and might even be insignificant.

Table 2. Perceived Effectiveness Model II:
Research References for the Independent Variables

Independent Variable	Research Source(s)
Loss in Flexibility of Managerial Prerogatives	Lewin (1983), Loewenberg (1984)
Due Process for Subordinates	Aram and Salipante (1981), Betton (1986), Yenney (1977)
Positive Performance and Morale Effects for Complainant	Lewin (1983)
Positive Outcomes for the Workgroup of the Complainant	Lewin (1983)
Training on the g/c Process	Knight* (1986)
The g/c Process Provides Information on Policies/Managers	Chamberlain, Cullen, and Lewin (1980), Lewin (1983)
The g/c Process Assists Company in Abiding with Employment Regulation	Kochan and Katz (1988)
The g/c Process is a Good Union Avoidance Strategy	Foulkes (1980), Ichniowski and Lewin (1987)
Outcome in Favor of the Complainant	Lewin* (1984), Sayles and Strauss (1953), Kanter (1977)

Note: * This research empirically investigates the asserted relationship between the independent variable and perceived effectiveness.

METHODOLOGY

Background

In order to test the models, the complaint system of a nonunion firm is studied. The study of the effectiveness of a nonunion complaint system, unlike a union complaint system, is not confounded by internal union administration considerations that may influence system effectiveness in the unionized firm.[6] Because the research in this paper represents the first attempt to build models of perceived effectiveness, it is appropriate to attempt to remove potential internal union political dimensions that may influence effectiveness, as evaluated from the individual user's perspective (see, for instance, Knight 1987a,b). In subsequent research on effectiveness, the question of whether a g/c system is perceived to be effective because it satisfies other objectives of complainants can be studied.

The company under study employs several thousand workers. Approximately 85 percent of these individuals, because they are nonsupervisory employees, are protected under the National Labor Relations Act, should they decide to join a union. However, the company is strongly committed to operating with a nonunion workforce and clearly identifies this as a company objective in its various publications to its workers.

As part of this strategy to remain union-free, the company has established a complaint system, herein called the Company Complaint Procedure (CCP), for all its workers, both managers and employees alike. The complaint system contains several steps, each of which provides complainants an opportunity to air their grievances either to peers or company officials, or both. The decisions made by high level company officials in the last step of the process are final and binding on the affected parties.

The Data Set

The data used in this research were drawn, with permission, from the results of a survey developed and administered to employees and managers at this company by Dr. Alan F. Westin, Professor of Public Law and Government, Department of Political Science, Columbia University, to be used in a book on fair procedure systems that Professor Westin is writing. In 1987, this questionnaire was distributed to three random samples of the company's workforce. The first and second samples consisted of 950 employees and 900 managers, respectively, who may or may not have registered or responded to complaints via the CCP. The third group consisted of a random sample of 600 CCP users (both employees and managers) who were not part of the first two samples. The survey instrument was identical for employees and managers with regard to CCP use and personal characteristics. However, the manager's questionnaire also included questions on whether or not the manager had ever participated in the CCP as a respondent to another employee's or manager's complaint. Furthermore, there were questions on the degree to which the managers felt that the CCP assisted the company in meeting its various objectives.

Of the 2450 surveys distributed, 1107 were returned, representing a response rate of 45.2 percent, and 1062 were fully usable.[7] Of these surveys, 579 were completed by employees and 483 by managers. In the case of the usable surveys, it was possible to determine the respondents' perceptions about the CCP, regardless of CCP use. Furthermore, I was able to determine who perceived themselves to have experienced unfair treatment.[8] It was also possible to determine who filed a complaint and its final disposition. Because there were only 9 CCP filers in the manager sample (this, in itself, is an interesting finding), it was not possible to study differences in the CCP effectiveness rating between employee and manager CCP *filers*. However, the difference in perceived effectiveness of the CCP between the two groups, regardless of CCP use, was analyzed.[9]

The Variables

Perceived effectiveness of the CCP was operationalized by the following question: "Overall, on a scale of 1 to 10, with 10 being 'excellent,' 5 being 'average,' and 1 being 'poor,' how would you rate the CCP?" The independent variables for Models I and II are operationalized in the Appendix.

RESULTS AND DISCUSSION

The Aggregate Correlates of Perceived g/c System Effectiveness

Using ordinary least squares multiple regression, Model I is estimated. The results are provided in Table 3. Note that equation (a) estimates perceived effectiveness for the employee population and that equation (b) is the estimate for managers. Because of the nature of the survey instrument, there are no independent variables in the regression equation which measure the importance of the speed of resolution of the CCP, its ease of use, and resolution as close to the source of the complaint as possible.[10] With this understated model, we see that equation (a) accounts for 46 percent of the variance in the CCP perceived effectiveness rating, which is the median of variance explained in the seven Model I perceived effectiveness equations. The signs on the significant coefficients are uniformly in the hypothesized direction.[11]

Comparing Perceived Effectiveness Between Employees and Managers

One observes from Table 3 that the independent variables used to measure the effectiveness of the CCP of employees and managers account for different "percent explained" in the two groups. In order to determine whether or not equations (a) and (b) are structurally different, a Chow test is performed on the regression results and the results are provided in Table 4. In Panel A of Table 4, one sees that the two equations are structurally different, and in Panel B one sees the variables that account for this difference. First, employees assess the CCP to be less effective because of its lack of an adversarial fact-gathering system. This variable is insignificant in the managers' equation.[12] Clearly, one would expect managers to feel that unions or outside representatives would not be necessary to make the CCP effective—the CCP was established in order to avoid such third parties.

The two groups also differ in the extent to which impartiality is important in perceived CCP effectiveness. The employee group clearly links the CCP's impartiality to its overall perceived effectiveness. Although the mean of IMPRTIAL (not shown here) is higher for managers, it is nonetheless an insignificant variable in their equation. Interestingly, both groups see this

Table 3. Correlates of Perceived Effectiveness: Model I

Dependent Variable: CCP Rating

Independent Variables		Equation				
	(a) Employees	(b) Managers	(c) Combined Population	(d) Employee Filers	(e) Employee Nonfilers	(f) Employee Filers/Outcome
ADVRSARY	-.18*** (-3.87)	.04 (.94)	-.10*** (-3.37)	-.19*** (-3.03)	-.05 (-.56)	-.20*** (-3.28)
IMPRTIAL	.27*** (6.24)	.04 (.80)	.17*** (5.75)	.28*** (4.46)	.29*** (3.06)	.25*** (4.14)
FEEDBACK	.15*** (3.69)	.15*** (3.41)	.18*** (5.73)	.14*** (2.30)	.17*** (2.10)	.12*** (2.14)
REPRISAL	-.17*** (-3.74)	-.13*** (-2.85)	-.18*** (-5.71)	-.10 (-1.45)	-.36*** (-4.30)	-.07 (-1.15)
LVLSREV	.24*** (5.67)	.34*** (7.16)	.32*** (9.91)	.28*** (4.52)	.19*** (2.16)	.23*** (3.78)
OTHRTINK	.01 (.15)	-.17*** (-3.76)	-.07*** (-2.42)	.04 (.61)	-.01 (-.07)	.03 (.48)
SEX	.06 (1.55)	-.00 (-.06)	.04 (1.27)	.01 (.24)	.14* (1.88)	-.01 (-.13)

EDUCATN	.03	.04	.04	.01	.04	.05
	(.89)	(1.02)	(1.52)	(.24)	(.51)	(.97)
MINORITY	-.00	.03	.01	-.05	.10	-.02
	(-.05)	(.70)	(.47)	(-.95)	(1.35)	(-.41)
AGE	-.00	-.01	.01	.02	-.10	.03
	(-.04)	(-.16)	(.21)	(.29)	(-1.27)	(.60)
OUTCOME						.27***
						(4.67)
CCP Mean	6.58	7.65	7.13	6.21	6.19	6.26
N	397	410	807	196	96	191
R^2	.46	.28	.39	.45	.55	.50
F-test	32.68***	15.39***	50.14***	14.80***	10.45***	15.94***

Notes: Standardized coefficients are reported; t-statistics are in parentheses.

* Significant at the .10 level
** Significant at the .05 level
*** Significant at the .01 level

Table 4.

**Panel A: Measuring the Structural Difference in the Regression Equations of
Employees v. Managers for Model I**

	N	Error Sum of Squares
Employees	397	1461.35
Managers	410	1331.38
Combined Equation	807	2928.89

F-test$_{(11,785)}$ = 3.47***

**Panel B: Measuring the Difference in the Independent Variables in the Regression of
Employees v. Managers for Model I**

Independent Variable	t-Statistic
ADVRSARY	-2.77***
IMPRTIAL	3.77***
FEEDBACK	-.25
REPRISAL	-.75
LVLSREV	2.69***
OTHRTINK	2.65***
SEX	1.07
EDUCATN	.01
MINORITY	.56
AGE	.11

Notes: * Significant at the .10 level
            ** Significant at the .05 level
            *** Significant at the .01 level

information about the CCP (FEEDBACK) and fear of reprisal (REPRISAL) as important correlates of effectiveness. However, while both groups see multiple levels of review (LVLSREV) as significant, the perceived effectiveness of the CCP is apparently more sensitive to LVLSREV for managers than for employees. Last, employees differ significantly from managers on the issue of what others think (OTHRTINK) about CCP users. For employees, OTHRTINK is not a significant variable; for managers, though, one observes a negative relationship between perceived CCP effectiveness and OTHRTINK. It is of interest to see that REPRISAL is distinct from the concern about what others think about CCP users. So, at least with regard to perceived CCP effectiveness, the manager reference group influences managers' perceptions of CCP effectiveness; I am unable to measure the same effect in the employee equation.

These series of equations, then, not only provide support for the perceived effectiveness model for employees; they also indicate that the same independent variables combine differently to explain perceived effectiveness for complainants or potential complainants between the employee and the manager populations. As a result, combining perceptions of employee-complainants with those of manager-complainants may mask certain relationships between perceived effectiveness and a given independent variable. For example, the variable OTHRTINK is significant in equation (c) for the combined population, but, as noted earlier, is not significant in equation (a), the employee equation.

Comparing Perceived Effectiveness of Employee Filers and Nonfilers

The next research question focuses again on Model I. However, the unit of analysis here is the group of employees who perceive themselves to have experienced unfair treatment. In equation (d), I study those who actually filed a CCP (filers) while in equation (e) I study those who did not file a complaint (nonfilers). The results of these regressions are also given in Table 3. From these series of regressions several observations can be drawn. First, fear of reprisal (REPRISAL) is insignificant in the employee filers' perceptions of effectiveness. For nonfilers, however, REPRISAL is not only a significant variable but it is also the independent variable to which perceived effectiveness is most responsive. Second, one sees that, even though nonfilers are concerned about REPRISAL, the absence of adversarial fact-finding (ADVRSARY) is insignificant in their perceived CCP effectiveness rating. Third, women nonfilers rate the CCP as more effective than men. Note that the other personal characteristics are insignificant in both equations (d) and (e). Considering previous empirical research on characteristics of g/c users which linked g/c usage to g/c effectiveness, one now sees some evidence that begins to question the appropriateness of that relationship. The fact that no differences have been found along dimensions such as age and minority status may be due to the fact that, as mentioned earlier, previous studies on the characteristics of grievance filers (Ash 1970; Lewin 1987) did not analyze usage across only that population that perceived themselves to have experienced unfair treatment.

In equation (f) I focus on employee filers. This equation is identical to equation (d) except for one variable. The variable that measures the degree to which the complaint is resolved in the complainant's favor (OUTCOME) is added. From equation (f) one sees that OUTCOME is significant and perceived effectiveness is most sensitive to this variable. This demonstrates that perceived effectiveness is responsive to winning one's complaint. So, the reader sees that filers appear to be able to sort out elements of procedural due process and what Folger and Greenberg (1985) would consider to be an element of distributive justice—the content of the outcome. Because of the significance of OUTCOME, coupled with the desire for a more adversarial CCP, the possibility that employment-related conflict resolution can represent a primarily integrative game and not a zero-sum game may need to be examined further. For example, Winkelgren (1974) suggests that the "fixed pie" perception in conflict resolution is a false assumption that hinders finding creative or "win-win" solutions to problems. However, here at least, one party to the complaint process, the filer, seems to link his/her perceptions of the effectiveness of a problem-solving mechanism with specific results achieved from that mechanism. To ignore this focus may well lull managers into overlooking the fact that no matter how well one attempts to understand the other side's perspective, there are real and persistent areas of conflict in the workplace. In this sense, the term "dispute resolution" as applied to complaint systems may, in part, be a misnomer. Certainly, for the complainant who "loses" his/her complaint, the dispute may not have really been resolved; at the very least, the perceived effectiveness of the process has been diminished for the complainant, regardless of how well he/she feels that the process itself was fair.

Perceived Effectiveness of g/c Systems for Manager-Respondents

The fourth research question examines the extent to which the original model of effectiveness, Model I, is appropriate in estimating the CCP effectiveness rating for managers against whom a CCP has been filed. As has already been shown in Tables 3 and 4, manager and employee *complainants* (or potential complainants) weigh the components of perceived effectiveness differently. How do manager-respondents measure perceived effectiveness? The results of this regression are provided below in equation (g) (standardized coefficients are reported and *t*-statistics are provided in parentheses).

$$\begin{aligned}
\text{PERCEIVED EFFECTIVENESS}_1 = \\
.08(\text{ADVRSARY}) + .04(\text{IMPRTIAL}) \\
(1.27) \qquad\qquad (.70) \\
+ .17(\text{FEEDBACK}) - .08(\text{REPRISAL}) \\
(2.67) \qquad\qquad (-1.17) \\
+ .34(\text{LVLSREV}) - .20(\text{OTHRTINK}) \\
(5.16) \qquad\qquad (-3.19) \qquad\qquad\qquad (g) \\
- .05(\text{SEX}) + .02(\text{EDUCATN}) \\
(-.76) \qquad\qquad (.34) \\
+ .02(\text{MINORITY}) - .08(\text{AGE}) \\
(.40) \qquad\qquad (-1.38)
\end{aligned}$$

The CCP mean is 7.47 and the sample size is 217. The R^2 and the F-test are .30 and 8.65, respectively. However, one needs to examine perceived effectiveness of manager-respondents under the framework of Model II. The results of this phase of the research are provided on Table 5.

Table 5. The Determinants of Perceived Effectiveness for Managers Against
Whom a CCP Was Filed: Model II

Dependent Variable: CCP Rating

	Equation	
		(i)
	(h)	*Manager*
	Manager	*CCP Respondents/*
Independent Variables	*CCP Respondents*	*Outcome*
LOSSFLEX	-.30***	-.29***
	(-4.29)	(-3.98)
DUEPROC	.12*	.13*
	(1.84)	(1.91)
EFFECT	.09	.08
	(1.31)	(1.11)
OTHROUTCM	.18***	.17***
	(2.71)	(2.52)
TRNG	-.02	-.02
	(-.34)	(-.35)
INFOSOURCE	.17**	.15**
	(2.32)	(2.06)
PUBLICPOLICY	-.07	-.06
	(-.99)	(-.90)
UNIONAVOID	.14**	.14*
	(2.00)	(1.91)
SEX	.00	.00
	(.03)	(.05)
EDUCATN	.07	.07
	(1.13)	(1.05)
MINORITY	.06	.05
	(.96)	(.72)
AGE	-.08	-.08
	(-1.27)	(-1.30)
OUTCOME		-.09
		(-1.33)
CCP Mean	7.48	7.46
N	200	193
R^2	.33	.33
F-test	7.66***	6.81***

Notes: Standardized coefficients are reported; *t*-statistics are in parentheses.
  * Significant at the .10 level
  ** Significant at the .05 level
  *** Significant at the .01 level

Equation (h) on Table 5 is Model II without the variable OUTCOME; OUTCOME is included in equation (i). One notes that the F-statistic for both equations (g) and (h) (Model I and II, respectively) are significant, indicating that in each model the independent variables as a group are significant. This supports the possibility that perceived effectiveness needs to be measured by considering the interests and objectives of all the individuals who may operate under the context of g/c systems. Second, the signs of all the statistically significant coefficients in equation (h) are in the hypothesized direction. Third, while managers do feel that the loss in their flexibility to manage employees detracts from the effectiveness of the CCP (LOSSFLEX is the largest coefficient), they also feel that the effectiveness of the CCP is enhanced because the workgroup's productivity is improved (OTHROUTCM). These managers believe that providing information to the company (INFOSOURCE) is positively associated with perceived CCP effectiveness.

Furthermore, the effectiveness of the CCP is significantly influenced by the managers' beliefs that the CCP helps the company avoid unions (UNIONAVOID). One could assert that managers appear willing to forego some managerial flexibility in the form of the CCP in order to avoid perhaps greater losses in flexibility that might come about with unionization. One also finds from equation (i) that the variable OUTCOME is not significant in the manager-respondents' model on perceived effectiveness. In addition, there is no support for the notion that this complaint system is perceived as effective because it assists the firm in abiding by employment opportunity regulations. In all, it appears that managers seem to be able to assess perceived effectiveness of the CCP from two perspectives—a perspective where the CCP hopes to ensure users (including themselves) a chance to air complaints, and a second perspective, one of respondents to complaints, whereby the CCP helps the company meet other specific organizational objectives.

CONCLUSIONS

It is hoped that this research can advance our understanding of grievance/ complaint system effectiveness in several important respects. First, this research demonstrates that g/c system effectiveness, as measured by the perceptions of individuals, needs to be studied from the roles one assumes as a participant in the g/c system. Employee and manager complainants (or potential complainants) assess perceived effectiveness differently; manager-respondents have still another roster of dimensions, as shown in Model II, with which to measure perceived effectiveness. Therefore, the method researchers use to *measure* effectiveness (i.e., scoring, perception ratings, etc.) notwithstanding, the researcher will have to specify from whose perspective effectiveness is studied.

Second, for the employee population, an adversarial fact-finding feature enhances perceived g/c effectiveness. In light of the debate on the relative effectiveness of collective voice over individual voice, this is an interesting and potentially important finding. For example, Freeman and Medoff (1984) have suggested that collective voice is more effective than individual voice. This is because many of the goods at work are "public goods" and representation of these issues to management is more appropriate at the group level. Moreover, these authors state that collective voice minimizes the threat of reprisal to individual complainants. Assuming for a moment that collective voice is more effective than individual voice, this research suggests still another reason why collective voice may be more effective than individual voice. Collective voice contains adversarial fact-gathering and fact-presentation features, the absence of which has been shown here to be negatively related to perceived effectiveness.

Third, this research suggests that future research on g/c system effectiveness must control for whether or not individuals experienced (or perceive themselves to have experienced) unfair treatment. Otherwise, one's results on effectiveness may be distorted by an improper aggregation of individuals' perceptions. Furthermore, the findings reported here suggest that more work is needed on the issue of how distributive justice and procedural justice correlate with g/c system effectiveness. Only one aspect of distributive justice, that which focuses on the complaint's specific outcome, was investigated here. However, it would be worthwhile to investigate whether the weight given to procedural and distributive justice does vary in evaluating g/c system effectiveness, depending on the role one assumes in the system. If, in fact, distributive justice is of greater importance for some players in the g/c system, the next research question is to understand *why* this is observed. Clearly, practitioners in the field of conflict resolution (i.e., union officials, labor relations managers, ombudsmen, mediators, and arbitrators) would certainly be interested in understanding whether or not such predispositions to outcomes and consequences can be changed or at least de-emphasized.

Finally, this research has also introduced the possibility that one's reference group may influence perceptions of g/c system effectiveness. For reasons that cannot be answered with the data set at hand, perceived complaint system effectiveness is negatively associated with the concern managers have about what their reference group believes about CCP users. If such a finding is replicated in other settings, then practitioners will want to consider how this orientation can be changed. After all, if one objective of g/c systems is to resolve the workplace disputes of aggrieved employees without their resorting to tribunals outside the company, than an impediment to meeting that objective may well be reference groups within the company.

Obviously, the work here has some limitations. As noted, not all of the independent variables in Model I could be included because of deficiencies in the survey instrument. Furthermore, this study is limited to one company, so a concern may be raised over the generalizability of the results. Specifically, it may be argued that this company may not be representative of all companies because it is a relatively young company, or because its complaint system is, perhaps, more sophisticated than most nonunion complaint systems. Having said this, though, by focusing initially on one company, this research has been able to control for inter-company differences. Certainly, it is easy to conceive of those situations where differences such as management philosophy toward employees could alter g/c system effectiveness ratings. Nevertheless, it is hoped that this research will provide a point of departure for future studies on g/c system effectiveness and, perhaps, more generally on dispute resolution.

APPENDIX: OPERATIONALIZING THE INDEPENDENT VARIABLES

Model I

ADVRSARY.   The relevant questions on the survey ask the respondents whether they feel that union representation or an attorney for employees would assist them in presenting their complaints; it ranges from a low of 1 to a high of 4.

IMPRTIAL.   The relevant questions on the survey ask the respondents to assess the need for an outside arbitrator to hear final appeals, to assess how fair they feel their superiors are in listening to their concerns, and to assess the perceived impartiality of the Board of Review as well as the review of CCPs by the CEO; it ranges from a low of 1 to a high of 14.

FEEDBACK.   The relevant questions on the survey ask the respondents to give their assessment about their present knowledge of the CCP, the amount of information they receive about the CCP, and how specific complaints are resolved via the CCP; it ranges from a low of 1 to a high of 9.

REPRIsAL.   The relevant question on the survey asks the respondents to give their perceptions on whether they believe some kind of reprisal is taken against CCP users; it ranges from a low of 1 to a high of 4.

LVLSREV.   The relevant questions on the survey ask the respondents to assess four different levels of appeals review in the CCP; it ranges from a low of 1 to a high of 16.

OTHRTINK.   The relevant questions on the survey ask the respondents to assess how others would think about them were they to file a CCP; it ranges from a low of 1 to a high of 8.

SEX is the sex of the respondents and is coded 1 for females and 0 for males.

EDUCATN is the number of years of formal education that the respondents received.

MINORITY identifies the race of the respondents and is coded 1 for all nonwhite respondents and 0 for white respondents.

AGE is the age of the respondents and is measured in number of years.

OUTCOME represents the degree to which the CCP is decided in the complainant's favor; it ranges from a low of 1 (the CCP is denied) to a high of 3 (the CCP is upheld)—the middle value of 2 represents a compromise in the CCP decision.

Model II

LOSSFLEX.   The relevant questions on the survey ask the respondents to assess whether or not it is harder to be effective operating with the CCP, whether the CCP undercuts management authority, and whether managers have opted not to take disciplinary action against employees because of the CCP; it ranges from a low of 1 to a high of 12.

DUEPROC.   The revelant questions on the survey ask the respondents to assess whether or not the CCP makes managers act more fairly and more carefully in applying company policies; it ranges from a low of 1 to a high of 8.

EFFECT.   The relevant question on the survey asks the respondents to assess whether the CCP has had a positive effect on the complainant's productivity and morale; it ranges from a low of 1 to a high of 3.

OTHROUTCM.   The relevant questions on the survey ask the respondents to assess the degree to which they feel that the CCP has had a positive effect on the output of their subordinate team; it ranges from a low of 1 to a high of 9.

TRNG.   The relevant questions on the survey ask the respondents to assess the three types of training/information programs they participate in on the CCP; it ranges from a low of 1 to a high of 12.

INFOSOURCE.   The relevant questions on the survey ask the respondents to assess whether the CCP helps them to identify weak company policies and poor managers, as well as to provide a method to improve communication within the company; it ranges from a low of 1 to a high of 9.

PUBLICPOLICY.   The relevant questions on the survey ask the respondents to assess how the CCP helps them to comply with EEO requirements, and to settle civil suits without resort to outside litigation; it ranges from a low of 1 to a high of 9.

UNIONAVOID.   The relevant question on the survey asks the respondents to assess whether they believe that the presence of the CCP helps the company avoid unions; it ranges from a low of 1 to a high of 3.

AGE, SEX, EDUCATN, MINORITY, and OUTCOME are as they have been previously operationalized in Model I.

ACKNOWLEDGMENTS

This research was made possible by a joint grant from the National Institute for Dispute Resolution (#88-004) and the Industrial Relations Research Center, Columbia Business School (Columbia University). The author acknowledges the insights provided by John T. Delaney, David Lewin, Donna Sockell, and two anonymous reviewers. In addition, she is appreciative of Drew Claxton's programming assistance.

NOTES

1.   Kuhn (1961) notes that use of the grievance process in unionized firms may also be indicative of fractional bargaining. In this case, use does not necessarily reflect effectiveness but is instead an element in a bargaining strategy.

2.   Procedural justice focuses on *how* decisions are made; distributive justice is concerned with the *content/outcome* and the *consequences* of decisions (Folger and Greenberg 1985).

3.   As will be subsequently discussed in greater detail, the g/c system under study here is in a nonunion firm. Both employees *and* managers are permitted to file complaints with their superiors. As a result, while not all employees and managers may actually use the g/c system, they may still, nevertheless, have perceptions about the process's effectiveness.

4.   Recall that I have defined, from the above chart, "filers" as those individuals who perceive themselves to have experienced unfair treatment *and* have filed a complaint; "nonfilers" are those individuals who perceive themselves to have experienced unfair treatment but have *not* filed a complaint.

5.   Recall that g/c system users or potential users may either be managers or employees in this study.

6.   As noted by Sayles and Strauss (1953), certain *individual* grievance system users in the unionized firm may well file grievances in order to make a statement to a political opponent within the union membership. Because of this, the effectiveness of the system from this individual's perspective may include variables not relevant in a model of effectiveness of another individual who seeks to reverse a company decision, say, on sick pay. This is not to say that employees in a nonunion firm do not file complaints for reasons unrelated to the issue of the grievance or complaint. However, such behavior has not, as yet, been documented. Second, employees in nonunion firms do not represent their peers in any legally binding manner, as union representatives do. As such, the potential need to platform grievances or complaints for the nonunion employee is not as pressing vis-à-vis the union representative.

7.   The reasons why 45 surveys were not usable are two-fold: some of the surveys for managers were incorrectly sent to employees and the remaining surveys were not completed.

8.   Respondents were specifically asked whether or not, within the past year, they (had) *personally* experienced unfair treatment by higher management.

9.   It should be pointed out that the company was extremely concerned with maintaining confidentiality among all respondents and especially CCP users. As a result, it was decided *not* to establish a mechanism which would track the returned questionnaires to determine which ones were completed by individuals from either the "950," the "900," or the "600" sample.

10.   As noted earlier, Dr. Westin has shared this data set with the Industrial Relations Research Center. Because Dr. Westin's research interests had a different focus as he constructed the survey instrument, measures for these independent variables were not anticipated.

11.   As can be seen in the Appendix, the scales of the independent variables differ in range. This is because the respective variables are created by combining responses to the relevant questions. As recommended by an anonymous referee, regressions were rerun (not shown here) adjusting for the different independent variables' scales. There were no differences in the sign, the significance, the F-test or the R^2 of these scale-adjusted regression runs. As also noted by the same referee, the relatively large sample size here can allow small values to achieve statistical significance. Even so, of primary concern here is to test hypotheses regarding different independent variables. As such, the results here, I feel, are not just statistically significant but also important. Finally, although not reported here, correlations were run among the independent variables; multicolinearity is not an issue with this (and subsequent) regression equations.

12.   Recall that ADVRSARY, as defined in Table 3, measures the absence of adversarial fact-gathering in the CCP, as indicated by the respondents' desire for union representation or outside counsel for CCP users.

REFERENCES

Aram, J.D. and P.F. Salipante, Jr. 1981. An Evaluation of Organizational Due Process in the Resolution of Employee/Employer Conflict. *Academy of Management Review* 6(2):197-204.

Ash, P. 1970. The Parties to the Grievance. *Personnel Psychology* 23(Spring):13-37.

Berenbeim, R. 1980. *Nonunion Complaint Systems: A Corporate Appraisal,* Report No. 770. New York: Conference Board.

Betton, J. 1986. The Three Faces of Unionism: Managerial Opposition to Labor Unions, An Empirical and Theoretical Analysis. *Labor Law Journal* 37(August):555-559.

Briggs, S. 1982. The Steward, the Supervisor, and the Grievance Process. *Proceedings of the Thirty-Fourth Annual Meeting,* pp. 313-319. Madison, WI: Industrial Relations Research Association.

Chamberlain, N.W., D.E. Cullen, and D. Lewin. 1980. *The Labor Sector,* 3rd ed. New York: McGraw-Hill.

Chamberlain, N.W. and J.W. Kuhn. 1986. *Collective Bargaining,* 3rd ed. New York: McGraw-Hill.

Folger, R. and J. Greenberg. 1985. Procedural Justice: An Interpretive Analysis of Personnel Systems. Pp. 141-183 in *Research in Personnel and Human Resources Management,* vol. 3, edited by K. Rowland and G. Ferris. Greenwich, CT: JAI Press.

Foulkes, F.K. 1980. *Personnel Policies in Large Nonunion Companies.* Englewood Cliffs, NJ: Prentice-Hall.

Freeman, R.B. and J.L. Medoff. 1977. The Two Faces of Unionism. *The Public Interest* (48):69-93.

————. 1984. *What Do Unions Do?* New York: Basic.

Gordon, M.E. and S.J. Miller. 1984. Grievances: A Review of Research and Practice. *Personnel Psychology* 37(1):117-146.

Ichniowski, C. and D. Lewin. 1987. Grievance Procedures and Firm Performance. Pp. 159-193 in *Human Resources and the Performance of the Firm,* edited by M.M. Kleiner, R.N. Block, M. Roomkin, and S.W. Salsburg. Madison, WI: Industrial Relations Research Association.

Jennings, K. 1974a. Foremen's Views of Their Involvement with Other Management Officials in the Grievance Process. *Labor Law Journal* 25(May):305-316.

———. 1974b. Foremen's View of Their Involvement with the Union Steward in the Grievance Process. *Labor Law Journal* 25(September):540-549.

Kanter, R.M. 1977. *Men and Women of the Corporation.* New York: Basic.

Knight, T.R. 1985. Toward a Contingency Theory of the Grievance/Arbitration Systems. Pp. 269-318 in *Advances in Industrial and Labor Relations,* vol. 2, edited by D.B. Lipsky. Greenwich, CT: JAI Press.

———. 1986. Feedback and Grievance Resolution. *Industrial and Labor Relations Review* 39(4):585-598.

———. 1987a. The Role of the Duty of Fair Representation in Union Grievance Decisions. *Relations Industrielles/Industrial Relations* 42(4):716-736.

———. 1987b. Tactical Use of the Duty of Fair Representation: An Empirical Analysis. *Industrial and Labor Relations Review* 40(2):180-194.

Kochan, T.A. and H.C. Katz. 1988. *Collective Bargaining and Industrial Relations,* 2nd ed. Homewood, IL: Irwin.

Kuhn, J.W. 1961. *Bargaining in Grievance Settlement.* New York: Columbia University Press.

Leventhal, G.S., J. Karuza, Jr., and W.R. Fry. 1980. Beyond Fairness: A Theory of Allocation Preferences. In *Justice and Social Psychology,* edited by G. Mikula. Bern, Switzerland: Huber.

Lewin, D. 1983. Theoretical Perspectives on the Modern Grievance Procedure. Pp. 127-147 in Suppl. 2: *New Approaches to Labor Unions, Research in Labor Economics,* edited by J.D. Reid, Jr. Greenwich, CT: JAI Press.

———. 1984. Empirical Measures of Grievance Procedure Effectiveness. *Proceedings of the Thirty-Fourth Annual Spring Meeting,* pp. 491-495. Madison, WI: Industrial Relations Research Association.

———. 1987. Dispute Resolution in the Nonunion Firm: A Theoretical and Empirical Analysis. *Journal of Conflict Resolution* 31(3):465-502.

Lewin, D. and R.B. Peterson. 1987a. *Behavioral Outcomes of Grievance Activity.* Working paper, Columbia University.

———. 1987b. *The Modern Grievance Procedure in the United States.* Westport, CT: Greenwood Press.

Lipset, S.M., M.A. Trow, and J.S. Coleman. 1956. *Union Democracy.* Glencoe, IL: Free Press.

Loewenberg, J.J. 1984. Structure of Grievance Procedures. *Labor Law Journal* 35(January):44-51.

Peterson, R.B. and D. Lewin. 1982. A Model for Research and Analysis of the Grievance Process. *Proceedings of the Thirty-Fourth Annual Meeting,* pp. 303-312. Madison, WI: Industrial Relations Research Association.

Ross, A.M. 1948. *Trade Union Wage Policy.* Berkeley, CA: University of California Press.

Sayles, L.R. and G. Strauss. 1953. *The Local Union: Its Place in the Industrial Plant.* New York: Harper and Brothers.

Sheppard, B.H. 1983. Managers as Inquisitors: Some Lessons From the Law. Pp. 193-213 in *Negotiating in Organizations,* edited by M.H. Bazerman and R.J. Lewicki. Beverly Hills, CA: Sage.

Slichter, S., J. Healy, and E.R. Livernash. 1960. *The Impact of Collective Bargaining on Management.* Washington, DC: Brookings Institution.

Thibaut, J. and L. Walker. 1978. A Theory of Procedure. *California Law Review* 66(3):541-566.

Tyler, T.R. and A. Caine. 1981. The Influence of Outcomes and Procedures on Satisfaction with Formal Leaders. *Journal of Personality and Social Psychology* 41(1):642-655.

Winkelgren, W.A. 1974. *How to Solve Problems.* San Francisco, CA: Freeman.

Yenney, S.L. 1977. In Defense of the Grievance Procedure in a Nonunion Setting. *Employee Relations Law Journal* 2(4):434-443.

THE ANALYSIS OF NONWAGE
BARGAINING OUTCOMES:
EVIDENCE FROM THE
CANADIAN PRIVATE SECTOR

Richard P. Chaykowski

INTRODUCTION

While there has been extensive analysis of collective agreement wage outcomes, in general there is a dearth of studies of bargaining outcomes which include nonwage clauses as a part of the analysis. This research follows the growing body of industrial relations literature that examines collective bargaining outcomes at the level at which negotiations occur by examining the determinants of nonwage outcomes in the Canadian private sector at the firm level.[1] One of the primary questions of this research is: Why observe a particular range of nonwage outcomes in one bargaining relationship yet observe a quite different set of outcomes in another? This study, therefore, constitutes an analysis of the determinants of union demand for various disaggregated categories of nonwage clauses.

Advances in Industrial and Labor Relations, volume 5, pages 235-289.
Copyright © 1991 by JAI Press Inc.
All rights of reproduction in any form reserved.
ISBN: 0-89232-940-8

The analysis of the underlying determinants of collective bargaining outcomes will contribute to our understanding of variations in bargaining outcomes across the economy and, consequently, will contribute to the evaluation and formulation of alternative public policies.[2] In the broader context, Kochan and Block (1977, p. 432) point out that the development of public policy in the realm of the employment relationship makes the analysis of all aspects of collective bargaining particularly relevant:

> This expansion of government into areas that previously had been left to collective bargaining suggests that it may be time to examine the conditions under which the bargaining process can most effectively respond to the needs of workers and the conditions under which it may need to be supplemented by public policy or other strategies.

By analyzing the nature of union demand for clauses across collective bargaining agreements, this study will examine how underlying economic factors, the characteristics of the union and firm, and bargaining power determine observed outcomes in a particular collective agreement.

Studies of the determinants of collective bargaining outcomes in the public sector began with the pioneering work of both Kochan and Wheeler (1975) and Gerhart (1976) who examined the environmental factors (particularly legal, economic, and political factors), as well as characteristics of both the management and the union, as determinants of variations in the outcomes observed across collective agreements.[3] The methodology used by Kochan and Wheeler (1975) basically involves two steps: first, they score each clause in a contract "according to the degree to which they [the outcomes] approached the attainment of union bargaining goals" (p. 49). These individual scores are then aggregated into a total score (index) that measures the "favorableness" of a collective agreement to union interests, thereby analyzing bargaining effectiveness. Similarly, as one aspect of a public sector analysis, Perry and Levine (1976) constructed an index of contractual change by calculating the difference in the respective scores of contract items between successive collective agreements.

In an attempt to expand this line of research for Canada, Anderson (1979a) analyzed longitudinal data from the Canadian federal government sector for the years 1968 through 1975.[4] In a similar analysis of Canadian municipal public sector collective bargaining outcomes, Anderson (1979b) separately examines wage and nonwage outcomes, essentially following the previous work of Kochan and Wheeler (1975), Gerhart (1976), and Perry and Levine (1976).

In the first study of private sector bargaining outcomes, Kochan and Block (1977) follow Kochan and Wheeler (1975) and Gerhart (1976) in constructing indexes of collective agreement outcomes.[5] In particular, they develop one index reflecting the overall outcome of the contract and also five sub-indexes reflecting each of wage supplement, fringe benefit, working conditions, job security, and equity in administration outcomes, respectively.[6] Finally, Fiorito and Hendricks (1987) examined the question of whether or not union characteristics, including union democracy, union membership levels, the militancy of union ideology, and the degree of national (centralized) control over decision making have an impact on wage and nonwage collective bargaining outcomes.[7] Following Kochan and Block (1977), Fiorito and Hendricks (1987) (in addition to the analysis of wage and nonwage contract indexes) analyze six individual subgroups of nonwage contract outcomes including equity, job security, work rule, pay supplement, and fringe outcomes. Each outcome group is measured using a contract index constructed in a manner similar to previous studies.

This study generally follows the private sector United States studies of Feuille, Hendricks, and Kahn (1981) and Fiorito and Hendricks (1987) by focusing on both pecuniary and nonpecuniary (nonwage) outcomes. However, this empirical analysis is based on Canadian private sector collective agreement data from both manufacturing and nonmanufacturing over the period from 1975 to 1984. Specifically, the empirical analysis of bargaining outcomes makes use of a unique data set of collective agreements that cover approximately one million workers in over 2,000 bargaining units. The dependent variables used in the regression analysis are the observed outcomes or clauses of the negotiated contracts. The empirical investigation extends previous United States research of the determinants of bargaining outcomes by separately analyzing the determinants of each of the following outcomes in the Canadian private sector: an overall nonwage collective bargaining agreement outcome, a total (nonwage) pecuniary outcome, a total (nonwage) nonpecuniary outcome, and each of 12 subcategories of nonwage contract outcomes.[8] Furthermore, the analysis extends past research by also examining the determinants of tradeoffs between aggregate outcomes. Finally, the study includes an extensive discussion of various methodological issues inherent in this line of industrial relations research.

The second section presents a discussion of the reduced form equations used in the empirical analysis of bargaining outcomes and contains a detailed discussion of the types and sources of data used and descriptive summary statistics of the contracts. The third section describes the results of the analysis of both aggregated and disaggregated bargaining outcomes. The fourth section discusses various methodological issues related to the analysis of bargaining outcomes. The paper concludes with a summary of major results as well as methodological directions for future research that examines the determinants of collective bargaining outcomes.

THE ANALYSIS OF CANADIAN
COLLECTIVE BARGAINING AGREEMENT OUTCOMES

Collective Bargaining Outcomes

This analysis follows Kochan and Wheeler (1975), Gerhart (1976), and Anderson (1979) in using the concept of the total *net* union power that a union uses to obtain desired outcomes. The net power that the union has at its discretion to obtain the jth contract outcome is assumed to be a function of a vector of characteristics of the union (W). Also, we expect certain union characteristics (Y) to directly affect union tastes for alternative bargaining outcomes.

Each quantity of net power that the union must expend to obtain a given outcome is expected to be different, depending upon the resistance of the firm to the clause. The stronger the clause, the greater the expected quantity of net union power that the union must expend ceteris paribus. Consequently, the resistance of the firm to union demands is assumed to be a function of a vector of characteristics of the firm (Z).

If we consider "q" observed contract clauses (c) to be generated by union "demand" for alternative outcomes, then the general form of the jth "demand" equation estimated is given by the following:

$$c^j = c^j[Z,\ W,\ Y,\ \mu^j] \qquad \text{for } j = 1 \ldots q. \qquad (1)$$

Assuming a linear functional form for each equation yields the following general specification of the jth reduced form "demand" equation which is to be estimated (suppressing the jth subscript):

$$c = \beta_0 + \Sigma_i \beta_i Z_i + \Sigma_h \pi_h W_h + \Sigma_n \alpha_n Y_n + \Sigma_f \theta_f M_f + \mu \qquad (2)$$

$$\text{for } i = 1 \ldots I,\ h = 1 \ldots H,\ n = 1 \ldots N, f = 1 \ldots F.$$

Each of these equations represents the measured outcome (associated with the jth clause) as a function of union and firm characteristics and a vector M of environmental control variables, where μ is the stochastic disturbance term.

The dependent variable in each equation is taken to represent a separate bargaining outcome. Following previous analyses of contract outcomes, this study proposes the construction of several nonwage contract outcome indexes (ξ): this approach involves the creation of a series of R sub-indexes over groups of S clauses in the collective agreement. The rth sub-index is of the following form:

$$\xi^r = \Sigma_s K_s^r \cdot CS_s \tag{3}$$

for $s = 1...S$, $r = 1...R$, for $S < q$, $R \ll q$

where: CS_s = the sth contract clause score;

          K_s^r = weight assigned the sth contract clause in the rth sub-index.

Each of these sub-indexes is taken to represent a single (composite) outcome. The maintained assumption about the weight on each clause is that $K_s^r = 1$ for all s, r.[9] Empirical analysis consists of ordinary least squares regression analysis using the rth sub-index (ξ^r) as the dependent variable in the rth bargaining outcome equation. This approach basically involves the estimation of a single "demand" equation for each of the R subcategories of outcomes considered. (At the most disaggregated level of analysis, this study focuses on twelve distinct subcategories of nonwage contract outcomes.)

In general, if the entire collective agreement contains a total of q nonwage contract outcomes, then a *total* nonwage contract index variable is defined as the weighted summation of the q individual contract outcomes, where each contract clause is "scored" (to obtain CS_i) according to the degree to which it is viewed as fulfilling union bargaining goals. The aggregate index for the collective agreement is then typically interpreted as a proxy for union influence or effectiveness (Kochan and Wheeler 1975). Empirical analysis using the notion of an aggregate nonwage index consists of using the aggregate index as the dependent variable in the reduced form bargaining outcome equation: this involves estimating a single "demand" equation for a Total (nonwage) Contract Outcomes index. Similarly, assuming that the Total Nonwage Contract index can be decomposed into "pecuniary" and "nonpecuniary" contract outcomes, further dependent variables include indexes for each of a Total Pecuniary Contract outcome and a Total Nonpecuniary Contract outcome.

All dependent variables used in the empirical analysis are constructed from the observed clauses of approximately 2,148 private sector collective bargaining agreements negotiated during the period from 1975 to 1984.[10] All of the bargaining outcome variables are collective-agreement specific. The unit of observation is the individual collective bargaining agreement by employer.[11] The sample covers approximately 20 manufacturing and 8 nonmanufacturing industries.[12] Table 1 provides the sample frequency of collective agreements by provincial region. As expected from the geographic industrial concentration of Canadian industrial activity, the three provinces with the greatest frequencies of collective agreements are Ontario (41.6% of the sample), Quebec (29.5% of the sample) and British Columbia (11.8% of the sample). Approximately 93 percent of the sample consists of collective agreements negotiated during the period from 1975 to 1980 inclusive. This data is a rich source of information about the nature of collective bargaining agreement outcomes in the Canadian private sector.

Table 1.   Distribution of Collective Agreements by Province[a]

Province	Number of Agreements	Percentage of Agreements
Maritimes[b]	161	7.5
Quebec	634	29.5
Ontario	894	41.6
Prairie[c]	205	9.5
British Columbia	254	11.8

Notes: [a] The sample includes only private sector collective agreements. Both the Yukon and Northwest Territories are excluded from the analysis.

[b] Maritimes include Newfoundland, Prince Edward Island, Nova Scotia, and New Brunswick.

[c] Prairies include Manitoba, Saskatchewan, and Alberta.

Two distinct schemes were used to score each individual outcome for each of approximately 148 possible clauses coded in a collective agreement. The first scheme (designated A), involves coding each possible outcome for each clause in the contract on the basis of how favorable the particular outcome is to the union, using a scale of (−30 to +30).[13] The clause was scored 0 if absent from the contract. Clauses designated as "unfavorable to the union" were scored less than 0 but greater than or equal to −30, where −30 represented the maximum possible "unfavorable to union" outcome. Similarly, clauses which were deemed "favorable to the union" were assigned a score greater than 0 but less than or equal to +30, where +30 represented the maximum possible "favorable to union" outcome. For example, a provision in the collective agreement covering the use of seniority in determining promotions is coded so as to distinguish the use of straight seniority, the use of seniority if other factors are equal, or the use of seniority in conjunction with other factors such as skills, training and ability, in the determination of which employee obtains the job-change. Scheme A provides the method which is the focus of the analysis of collective agreement outcomes. Under scheme B, if a clause is present in the collective agreement it is assigned a code of 1 regardless of the particular outcome associated with each clause, and assigned a code of 0 if the clause is absent. Scheme B is used to explore the robustness of the results to the use of alternative coding schemes (see the section on methodological issues).

Coding scheme A distinguishes not only the presence or absence of a contract clause, but also the degree of (un)favorableness to the union, whereas coding scheme B distinguishes only the presence or absence of a given clause. The bounds (−30 and +30) of the ordinal scale used in scheme A wre chosen arbitrarily, since any ordinal scale which acts as a continuous measure of the degree of "favorableness to the union" will yield the same empirical results. However, the fundamental differences between the −30 to +30 scheme and the 0-1 scheme arises because of the assumption adopted in this analysis that the underlying true "score" variable is typically continuous for most (but not all) individual clauses.[14] Consequently, the use of the 0-1 binary coding scheme

Table 2. Canadian Private Sector Contract Provisions by Major Group[a]

Contract Category	Variable Name	Maximum Possible Number of Clauses
1. Union Security	USEC	4
2. Employee Security	EMPSEC	24
3. Grievance and Arbitration Procedure	GRIEV	5
4. Hours and Days of Work	HOURS	7
5. Vacations and Leaves	VAC	29
6. Allowances and Benefits	ALLOW	19
7. Technological Change Provisions	TECH	8
8. Overtime and Premium Pay	OVERT	15
9. Pay Guarantees	PAYGUAR	7
10. Health, Safety, and Disability Benefits	HEALTH	10
11. Worker-Management Relationship	WMR	5
12. Fringe Benefits	FRINGE	15

Note: [a] Individual clauses included in each major group are provided in the Appendix.

would not be the appropriate measure in those cases in which the true underlying variable is not dichotomous.

For purposes of the analysis of bargaining outcomes, the 148 clauses were organized into the following 12 subcategories (composite outcomes): Union Security; Employee Security; Grievance and Arbitration Procedure; Hours and Days of Work; Overtime and Premium Pay; Pay Guarantees; Vacations and Leaves; Allowances and Benefits; Technological Change; Health, Safety, and Disability Benefits; Worker-Management Relationship; and Fringe Benefits. These categories and the maximum number of clauses included in each are provided in Table 2. The specific clauses assigned to each of the 12 major categories of clauses is provided in the Appendix.[15]

Each scored clause within a given category is summed to form the total category score. For example, the Employee Security category consists of 24 possible clauses. (According to scheme B, the maximum score for this category is 24 and the minimum score is 0.) Using scheme A (favorable to the union on a −30 to +30 scale) the maximum score for the Employee Security category is 720 if all clauses score +30 (maximum possible "favorable to union" score) and the minimum score possible is −720 if all clauses scored −30 (minimum "favorable to union" score). Summary statistics for each of the 12 categories of clauses obtained by using scheme A are provided in Table 3.

The clauses in each of the Union Security, Employee Security, Grievance and Arbitration Procedure, Hours and Days of Work, Technological Change, and Worker-Management Relationship categories are aggregated to form a Total Nonpecuniary Outcomes contract score. Similarly, the clauses in each of the Overtime and Premium Pay, Pay Guarantees, Vacations and Leaves, Allowances and Benefits, Health, Safety, and Disability Benefits, and Fringe

Table 3. Major Collective Bargaining Agreement Categories[a]

Category	Mean Score	Score Standard Deviation	Percent CBA's Score ≤ 0	Percent CBA's Score > 0
1. Union Security	18.8	17.2	22.7	77.3
2. Employee Security	132.0	53.6	2.0	98.0
3. Grievance and Arbitration Procedure	81.1	27.5	0.8	99.2
4. Hours and Days of Work	91.7	24.3	1.7	98.3
5. Overtime and Premium Pay	97.0	47.6	2.7	97.3
6. Pay Guarantees	25.0	19.3	10.8	89.2
7. Vacations and Leaves	215.9	60.9	0.3	99.7
8. Allowances and Benefits	89.7	48.7	2.1	97.9
9. Technological Change	13.7	23.0	63.3	36.7
10. Health, Safety, and Disability Benefits	37.6	31.3	12.3	87.7
11. Worker-Management Relationship	-3.7	18.9	66.9	33.1
12. Fringe Benefits	71.1	51.7	6.9	93.1
Total Pecuniary Outcomes	498.7	146.9		
Total Nonpecuniary Outcomes	371.4	101.7		
Total Contract Score	870.1	224.6		

Note: [a] Based on a sample of 2,148 collective agreements.

242

Benefits categories are aggregated to form a Total Pecuniary Outcomes contract score. All clauses are also aggregated to create a Total Contract Outcomes score. Summary statistics for these three variables also appear in Table 3. The mean Total Contract score in the sample was 870, with a minimum score of 121 and a maximum score of 1,639. The mean Total Pecuniary Outcomes score in the sample was 499 (minimum score of 57 and a maximum score of 985) and the mean Total Nonpecuniary Outcomes score in the sample was 371 (minimum score of 3 and a maximum score of 658), suggesting the relative importance of Pecuniary Outcomes in collective agreements.[16]

Explanatory Variables

The explanatory variables used in the analysis of the outcome equations are derived both from the microdata file of collective bargaining agreements as well as various Canadian government publications. Variables based on this data include characteristics of the individual unions identified in the sample as well as economic and demographic control variables. Complete variable definitions and data sources for each of the variables used in the empirical analysis are presented in Panels A, B, C, and D of Table 4. Summary statistics for each of the explanatory variables are presented in Table 5.

The distribution of collective agreements by size of the bargaining unit is skewed towards smaller bargaining units, with approximately 92 percent of the collective agreements covering employees in bargaining units with fewer than 1,000 employees and approximately 97 percent of the collective agreements covering employees in bargaining units with fewer than 2,000 employees. Over 50 percent of the employers are in the "manufacturing" industrial classification. The second most highly represented industrial classification is the "transportation, communication and other utilities" group with approximately 32 percent of the sample. The least represented industry is "fishing and trapping" with less than 1 percent of the collective agreements in the sample. The "agriculture" and "finance, insurance and real estate" divisions are not represented in the sample.

While approximately 65 percent of the negotiating units are "single-employer and single-plant units, 28 percent are "single-employer and multiplant" units and the remaining 7 percent are "multiemployer or employer association" units. Also, 9 percent of the employers are associated with a single set of negotiations that results in more than one collective agreement (joint bargaining). These general descriptive characteristics indicate a national representative sample of collective agreements which includes contracts across the broad range of industries and bargaining unit sizes.

The following discussion focuses on the independent variables used in the empirical analysis. Five variables are included in the analysis as potential sources of union power. First, the gross domestic product (LGDP) and the

Table 4. Independent Variable Definitions*

Panel A: Economic and Demographic Variable Definitions

1. $LBRIT_p$ — Percent of ethnic British.[a]

2. $PLTU_p$ — Percentage of people 15 years and over with no certificate or diploma, or 15 years and over with high school, trades certificate, or other nonuniversity certificate.[b]

3. $PURBAN_p$ — Percentage total urban population.[c]

4. UR_k — Unemployment rate of experienced persons 15 years and over.[d]

5. $PIMM_k$ — Percentage of the total labor force 15 years and over that immigrated (percentage not Canadian born).[e]

6. $LGDP_{k,t}$ — Logarithm of per capita gross domestic product[f] $[GDP_{k,t}/(\text{Total Population})_p]$

* For all i, j, k, p, t: i = union; j = firm; k = industry; p = province; t = year.

Notes to Panel A:

[a] Source: Statistics Canada, 1981 Census of Canada, Volume 1, *Population: Ethnic Origin,* Catalogue No. 92-911, September 1982, Table 1.
[b] Source: Statistics Canada, 1981 Census of Canada, Volume 1, *Population: School Attendance and Level of Schooling,* Catalogue No. 92-914, January 1984, Table 4.
[c] Source: Statistics Canada, 1981 Census of Canada, Volume 1, *Population: Age, Sex and Marital Status,* Catalogue No. 92-901, September 1982, Table 6.
[d] Source: Statistics Canada, 1981 Census of Canada, Volume 1, *Population: Worked Since January 1, 1980–Industry By Labour Force and Work Activity,* Catalogue No. 92-924, January 1984, Table 1.
[e] Source: Statistics Canada, 1981 Census of Canada, Volume 1, *Population: Labour Force and Industry By Cultural Characteristics,* Catalogue No. 92-922, February 1984, Table 1.
[f] Source: Statistics Canada, *Gross Domestic Product by Industry,* 1984, Catalogue No. 61-213, September 1985, Table 3.

Panel B: Collective Bargaining Variable Definitions[a]

1. $Y(t)_{i,j}$ — Year collective bargaining agreement is effective for t = 75,76,...,84.[b]

2. $JB_{i,j,t}$ — 1 = joint bargaining; 0 = no joint bargaining.[c]

3. $PROV(p)_{j,t}$ — Province variable for each of p = 1,2,3,4,5 where PROV1 = Quebec; PROV2 = Manitoba, Saskatchewan, and Alberta (PRAIRIE); PROV3 = British Columbia; PROV4 = Newfoundland, Prince Edward Island, Nova Scotia, and New Brunswick (MARITIME); and PROV5 = Ontario.[d]

Notes to Panel B:

[a] Source: Labour Canada data file on the Analysis of Collective Bargaining Agreements.
[b] Default year is 1975.
[c] Joint bargaining is defined as a single set of negotiations culminating in more than one collective bargaining agreement.
[d] Ontario is the default category (omitted dummy variable) in the analysis. These regional dummy variables do not correspond to provincial jurisdictions in the cases of PRAIRIE and MARITIME. Also, the Yukon and Northwest Territories are excluded from the analysis.

(continued)

Table 4.   (continued)

Panel C: Firm Variable Definitions[a]

1.	$TU2_{j,t}$	1 = single employer-multiplant negotiating unit.[b]
2.	$TU3_{j,t}$	1 = multiemployer or association of employers.[b]
3.	$IND(h)_{j,t}$	2-digit industry variable for each of $h = 1,2,3,\ldots 7$; where IND1 = Forestry; IND2 = Fishing; IND3 = Mines; IND4 = Transportation (Trans in all tables); IND5 = Trade; IND6 = Services; and IND7 = Manufacturing.[c]

Notes to Panel C:

   [a] Source: Labour Canada data file on the Analysis of Collective Bargaining Agreements.
   [b] Default category is single employer-single plant negotiating unit.
   [c] Default category is Manufacturing.

Panel D: Union Variable Definitions

1.	$LUNITSIZE_{i,t}$	Logarithm of the number of workers covered by the collective bargaining agreement.[a]
2.	$INTL_{i,t}$	1 = affiliated with an international (United States-based) union; 0 = affiliated with a national union.[b,d]
3.	$LOCALS_{i,t}$	Number of union locals in Canada.[b,d]
4.	$LMEMBER_{i,t}$	Logarithm of the number of union members in Canada.[b]
5.	$PFEM_{i,t}$	Percentage of female union members in Canada.[b]
6.	$STRIKES_{i,t}$	Number of strikes and lockouts in existence during the year.[c]
7.	$OCC(Z)_{i,t}$	Occupation variable[e] where $Z = 21,33,\ldots,99$.

Notes to Panel D:

   [a] Source: Labour Canada data file on the Analysis of Collective Bargaining Agreements.
   [b] Source: *Corporations and Labour Unions Returns Act, Part II–Labour Unions,* 1975-1982, Catalogue No. 71-202S, Table 1.
   [c] Source: *Strikes and Lockouts In Canada,* 1975-1984, Labour Canada, Catalogue No. L2-1, Tables 4, 6, and 8; Wood and Kumar (1981-1984).
   [d] "National" unions include those unions affiliated with the Canadian Labour Congress (CLC), the Canadian Federation of Labour (CFL), the Confederation of National Trade Unions (CNTU), the Centrale des syndicats démocratiques (CSD), the Canadian National Federation of Industrial Unions (CNFIU), the Confederation of Canadian Unions (CCU), and various unaffiliated unions. "International" unions include those unions affiliated with the AFL/CIO and various independents.
   [e] $OCC(Z)^e$ = Occupation variable where $Z = 21,33,\ldots,99$ and Z is the 1971 Dictionary of Occupational Classifications 2-digit Major Group Occupational Code.
   OCC21 = Natural Services, Engineering, and Mathematics
   OCC33 = Artistic, Literary, Recreational, and Related
   OCC41 = Clerical and Related
   OCC51 = Sales
   OCC61 = Services
   OCC75 = Forestry and Logging
   OCC77 = Mining and Quarrying (includes some oil and gas)
   OCC81 = Processing (includes minerals, metals, chemicals, petrols, food, wood, textiles)
   OCC83 = Machining and related (includes metals, wood, stone)
   OCC87 = Construction and Trades related
   OCC91 = Transport Equipment Operation
   OCC93 = Material Handling
   OCC95 = Other Crafts and Equipment Operating
   OCC99 = "Other" (includes general labor, inspection, supervisory)
   OCC85 = Product Fabricating, Assembly and Repair (default category)

Table 5. Explanatory Variable Summary Statistics

Variable[a]	Mean	Standard Deviation
OCC21	0.004	0.1
OCC33	0.04	0.2
OCC41	0.04	0.2
OCC51	0.03	0.2
OCC61	0.05	0.2
OCC73	0.003	0.1
OCC75	0.02	0.2
OCC77	0.04	0.2
OCC81	0.23	0.4
OCC83	0.06	0.2
OCC87	0.02	0.1
OCC91	0.19	0.4
OCC93	0.04	0.2
OCC95	0.01	0.1
OCC99	0.05	0.2
OCC85	0.19	0.4
IND1	0.03	0.2
IND2	0.002	0.05
IND3	0.06	0.2
IND4	0.33	0.5
IND5	0.05	0.2
IND6	0.04	0.2
IND7	0.50	0.5
Y75	0.07	0.2
Y76	0.2	0.4
Y77	0.3	0.5
Y78	0.2	0.4
Y79	0.09	0.3
Y80	0.06	0.2
Y81	0.04	0.2
Y82	0.02	0.1
Y83	0.009	0.10
Y84	0.002	0.04
ONTARIO	0.41	0.5
BC	0.12	0.3
PRAIRIE	0.10	0.3
MARITIME	0.08	0.3
QUEBEC	0.30	0.5
LUNITSIZE	5.2	1.6
TU1	0.65	0.5
TU2	0.28	0.5
TU3	0.07	0.3
PIMM	18.6	9.4
PLTU	90.3	0.9
LGDP	11.06	1.09
PURBAN	76.9	7.8
PBRIT	39.5	22.0
UR	6.2	3.5
LOCALS	209.4	304.7
JB	0.09	0.3
LMEMBER	10.5	1.3
STRIKES	75.0	75.3
PFEM	16.1	18.1
INTL	0.75	0.4

Note: [a] Variables are defined in Table 4.

unemployment rate (UR) are economic control variables that reflect general economic conditions in the industry and labor market pressures, respectively (Kochan and Wheeler 1975; Anderson 1979a). We expect a positive coefficient of LGDP and a negative coefficient of UR in each of the six disaggregated pecuniary outcome regressions and no expected sign for either variable in each of the six disaggregated nonpecuniary outcome regressions. In the two aggregate outcome regressions, we expect a positive coefficient of LGDP and a negative coefficient of UR in both the Total Contract and Total Pecuniary outcomes regressions but have no expectations for either variable in the Total Nonpecuniary outcome regression.

Three variables are union characteristics that are expected to affect union power (W), including the size of the bargaining unit (LUNITSIZE), the size of the national union (LMEMBER), and the number of strikes in the industry (STRIKES). Generally, we expect that large bargaining units will be able to impose greater costs of disagreement on management than smaller units, ceteris paribus (Gerhart 1976). This size effect may also be viewed as reflecting increased resources available to the union (Fiorito and Hendricks 1987) or the importance of labor in the production process. Consequently, larger units are expected to have greater bargaining power than smaller sized units (Anderson 1979a; Feuille, Hendricks, and Kahn 1981). Therefore, we expect a positive coefficient for LUNITSIZE in each of the pecuniary and nonpecuniary outcomes regressions (for both aggregated and disaggregated outcomes).

The size of the parent union membership in Canada (LMEMBER) is expected to reflect the aggregate level of resources available to a particular local, so that we expect locals with a large parent union to have more bargaining power than locals belonging to small parent unions, all else equal. We expect a positive coefficient for LMEMBER in all pecuniary and nonpecuniary outcomes regressions (for both aggregated and disaggregated outcomes).

Finally, strike activity has been viewed as either a bargaining process variable (Anderson 1979a) or as a measure of membership "militancy" (Fiorito and Hendricks 1987) when the variable captures bargaining *unit* strike activity. However, while the number of strikes variable (STRIKES) used in this analysis reflects industry strike activity, it more likely approximates the militancy concept. To the extent that high levels of militancy among the membership enhances bargaining power (perhaps through a credible threat effect at the bargaining table), then we expect a positive coefficient for this variable in all pecuniary and nonpecuniary outcome regressions (both aggregated and disaggregated outcomes). However, since this variable is likely to be a poor proxy for militancy and since the effect of union militancy on union bargaining power is likely tenuous, the expectations associated with the signs of the coefficients are also considered tenuous.

The variables in the empirical analysis which are expected to affect the resistance of the firm (Z) include each of the following variables: whether or not the firm is in the manufacturing industrial classification (IND(h)) (for example, due to systematic variations between the manufacturing and nonmanufacturing sectors in the use of continuous operating schedules, or reliance on new technologies); and whether the employer is involved in multiplant (TU2) or multiemployer (TU3) bargaining (these variables may proxy unobserved tastes for outcomes). There are no determinate expected signs associated with the coefficients of these firm characteristics.

One problem inherent in the use of aggregated industrial control variables (such as a manufacturing-nonmanufacturing variable) is that the grouping of industries may obscure important industry-specific variations in work organization, capital intensity, work conditions, or other industrial characteristics that determine the presence or absence of particular classes of clauses across collective agreements. While previous studies have addressed this issue by analyzing bargaining outcomes within a single industry (see, for example, Anderson 1979a,b), in what follows the approach adopted is to estimate the outcome equations including separate controls for each of forestry, fishing, mines, transportation, trade, and services, where the manufacturing sector is the default category.

Finally, consider the union characteristics that directly affect tastes for clauses (Y), hence the demand for clauses. The variables expected to directly affect union utility include whether the union local is affiliated with an international (United States) based union (INTL), the percentage of the union local membership that is female (proxied by the percentage of the parent Canadian union membership that is female, PFEM), the presence or absence of joint bargaining (JB), the number of locals belonging to the parent union (LOCALS), and the occupational classification of the employees (OCC(Z)).

Generally, we expect that locals affiliated with internationals may have different tastes both among alternative outcomes and for the level of a particular outcome, than locals affiliated with nationally (Canadian) based unions. Specifically, we expect that having an international affiliation would have no effect on Union Security outcomes. There are generally no expectations regarding the effect of being internationally affiliated on the level of any of the disaggregated pecuniary outcomes; however, one exception to this could be the Pay Guarantees category. International unions in the United States and Canada are highly represented in the manufacturing industries that were adversely affected by both the recession of the early 1980s and the increased international competition throughout the time period of this analysis. These external economic pressures may induce international unions to be more accommodating to management and, therefore, seek lower wage-related outcomes than nationally based unions (we therefore expect a negative coefficient).[17] Moreover, given the recent interest of United States locals of internationals in allowing the development of management programs designed to improve productivity (such as productivity plans, union-management cooperative ventures, and schemes to enhance management flexibility in the workplace), we may also expect a propensity for similar cooperation with management (at a point in time) by Canadian locals that are affiliated with internationals, in these nonpecuniary areas. Together, this willingness of unions to moderate their bargaining demands may be viewed as coming under the general rubric of "concession bargaining."[18] Consequently, we expect a negative sign of the coefficient of INTL in each of the Employee Security, Grievance and Arbitration Procedure, Technological Change, and Worker-Management Relationship regressions. Finally, we expect an indeterminate sign of the coefficient of INTL in each of the Total Contract, Total Pecuniary Contract and Total Nonpecuniary Contract outcome-demand regressions.

We expect that union locals with a large proportion of female membership will more highly value outcomes which are in particular demand by females than locals with low or virtually no female membership levels, ceteris paribus. There is an uncertain effect of PFEM on each of the pecuniary outcomes except Vacations and Leaves, for which we expect a positive coefficient—reflecting the demand for maternity-related leaves. We also expect higher demand (positive coefficient of PFEM) in both the Employee Security regression (reflecting a demand for management systems which prevent or reduce gender discrimination) and Hours and Days of Work regression (reflecting a demand for flexible work schedules). There are no a priori expectations associated with the coefficient of PFEM in the remaining nonpecuniary outcome regressions. We expect an indeterminate sign of the coefficient of PFEM in the Total Nonpecuniary, Total Contract, and Total Pecuniary outcome-demand regressions.

There are no expectations associated with the sign of the coefficient of either the joint bargaining variable or the number of locals variable in any of the pecuniary or nonpecuniary outcome regressions (aggregated or disaggregated outcomes). Because the presence of joint bargaining may affect union tastes and the number of locals may reflect union structure, both the JB and LOCALS variables are expected to proxy unobserved union preferences, although the direction of the effects are indeterminate a priori.

Another issue related to the analysis of bargaining outcomes concerns the need to control for interoccupational effects on the demand for alternative clauses. For example, Kochan and Wheeler (1975) address this issue by restricting their analysis to a single occupation. Recognizing that occupational variation across unions is an important source of variation in union demands (preferences) for alternative bargaining outcomes, an attempt was made to control for occupational differences by including 15 occupational dummy variables that attempt to measure the presence or absence of the majority occupation in the unionized establishment.[19] Under the assumption that union locals operate democratically, these variables will capture variations in the bargaining outcome demands of the majority occupation across unions. However, these occupational variables are likely to only proxy the true

Table 6. Expected Variable Signs in Private Sector Demand Equations For Bargaining Outcomes

Panel A: Disaggregated Bargaining Outcomes

							Category or Groupings of Clauses[a]					
IV[b]	*NP 01*	*NP 02*	*NP 03*	*NP 04*	*P 05*	*NP 06*	*P 07*	*P 08*	*P 09*	*P 010*	*NP 011*	*P 012*
LGDP	+	?	?	?	+	?	+	+	+	+	?	+
UR	?	?	?	?	−	?	−	−	−	−	?	−
LUNITSIZE	+	+	+	+	+	+	+	+	+	+	+	+
LMEMBER	+	+	+	+	+	+	+	+	+	+	+	+
STRIKES	+	+	+	+	+	+	+	+	+	+	+	+
IND(h)	?	?	?	?	?	?	?	?	?	?	?	?
TU2	?	?	?	?	?	?	?	?	?	?	?	?
TU3	?	?	?	?	?	?	?	?	?	?	?	?
JB	?	?	?	?	?	?	?	?	?	?	?	?
PFEM	?	?	+	?	+	+	?	?	?	?	?	?
INTL	0	−	−	−	?	?	?	?	−	?	−	?
LOCALS	?	?	?	?	?	?	?	?	?	?	?	?
OCC(Z)	?	?	?	?	?	?	?	?	?	?	?	?

(*continued*)

Table 6. (*continued*)

Panel B: Aggregated Bargaining Outcomes

	Category or Groupings of Clauses[a]		
IV^b	TCO	P TPCO	P TNPCO
LGDP	+	+	?
UR	−	−	?
LUNITSIZE	+	+	+
LMEMBER	+	+	+
STRIKES	+	+	+
IND(h)	?	?	?
TU2	?	?	?
TU3	?	?	?
JB	?	?	?
PFEM	?	?	?
INTL	?	?	?
LOCALS	?	?	?
OCC(Z)	?	?	?

Notes: [a] Definition of clause category variables:
01 = Union Security;
02 = Technological Change;
03 = Employee Security;
04 = Grievance and Arbitration Procedure;
05 = Vacations and Leaves;
06 = Hours and Days of Work;
07 = Allowances and Benefits;
08 = Overtime and Premium Pay;
09 = Pay Guarantees;
010 = Health, Safety, and Disability Benefits;
011 = Worker-Management Relationship;
012 = Fringe Benefits;
TCO = Total Contract index;
TPCO = Total Pecuniary index;
TNPCO = Total Nonpecuniary index;
P = Pecuniary;
NP = Nonpecuniary.
[b] Independent variable (*IV*) definitions are provided in Table 4.

underlying occupational structure with error, particularly because the majority occupation is measured with error and these variables do not capture the extent of intra-union-local variation in occupations. Nevertheless, the inclusion of these occupational controls represents an important attempt to control for the variation in bargaining outcome demands across occupational groups. Viewed as a union characteristic that directly affects tastes for alternative outcomes, there are no a priori expectations associated with the signs of the coefficients of these variables. Detailed occupational definitions are provided in Table 4, along with information concerning the default occupational category.

Among the environmental control variables, we expect the year variables to capture several time varying institutional and economic effects during the period of this analysis including: (1) the implementation of the Anti-Inflation Board, the progressively deteriorating performance of the Canadian economy commencing with the 1980 recession and increasing international competition; (2) the attempt to restructure the Canadian manufacturing sector; and (3) commensurate with the two economic trends, the (potential) decline in net union bargaining power and the (potentially) increased willingness of unions to accommodate those firms which experience adverse economic and competitive conditions.

Two specifications of the estimating equations are used. The first specification includes all explanatory variables except the occupational control variables. The results from this specification form the basis of the analysis, and the results for the key variables of interest are provided in Table 7a, 8a, 9a, and 10a. Regression results for the key variables of interest, using the specification of the equation that includes the occupational control variables, are included in Table 7b, 8b, 9b, and 10b.[20] The results for the occupational variables will only be discussed for the aggregate outcome regressions. Finally, a summary of the expected signs for major variables of interest are presented in Panels A and B of Table 6.[21]

EMPIRICAL RESULTS FOR THE
BARGAINING OUTCOMES REGRESSIONS

The following discussion of empirical results for the outcome regressions focuses primarily on the signs of the coefficients of variables representing the firm characteristics that affect its resistance to union demands (Z), the union characteristics affecting power (W), and the union characteristics that directly affect utility (Y). Throughout the discussion, the primary results that are of interest are based on the regressions that use the dependent variable constructed using the "favorable to union" coding scheme. The signs of the coefficients are discussed only in those cases in which the coefficient is statistically significantly different from zero at the .05 level in a two-tailed test.

In what follows, the results are discussed first for each of the Total Contract Outcome, the Total Pecuniary Outcome and the six disaggregated Pecuniary Outcomes, and finally, for the Total Nonpecuniary and six disaggregated Nonpecuniary Outcomes. The empirical analysis concludes with a discussion of results for the outcome-tradeoffs regressions.

The results for the aggregate contract outcomes appear in Table 7a for coding scheme A (favorable to union). The results for the 12 disaggregated outcome regressions, with dependent variables corresponding to each of the Union Security, Technological Change, Employee Security, Grievance and

Table 7a. Collective Bargaining Agreement Outcomes Equations[a]

Dependent Variable/ Explanatory Variable[b]	Pecuniary Outcomes		Nonpecuniary Outcomes		Total Outcomes		Nonpecuniary/ Pecuniary Outcomes	
C	845.36	(1.0)	573.55	(1.2)	1418.92	(1.2)	-0.27	(0.2)
LUNITSIZE	31.18	(9.4)*	15.22	(8.1)*	46.40	(10.2)*	-0.011	(2.2)*
TU2	4.98	(0.6)	-6.072	(1.3)	-1.090	(0.1)	-0.0080	(0.6)
TU3	-50.21	(3.4)*	-31.69	(3.4)*	-81.91	(4.1)*	0.045	(2.0)*
LGDP	2.81	(0.8)	-3.061	(1.5)	-0.26	(0.1)	-0.0062	(1.1)
PURBAN	0.16	(0.1)	-1.31	(1.3)	-1.15	(0.5)	-0.0031	(1.1)
UR	-9.61	(6.1)*	-4.96	(5.6)*	-14.57	(6.7)*	0.0039	(1.6)
LOCALS	-0.023	(1.4)	-0.0075	(0.8)	-0.030	(1.4)	-0.000088	(0.4)
JB	-13.061	(1.1)	9.75	(1.4)	-3.31	(0.2)	0.036	(1.9)
LMEMBER	19.83	(5.3)*	7.0037	(3.3)*	26.83	(5.2)*	-0.0063	(1.1)
STRIKES	-0.41	(3.7)*	-0.15	(2.3)*	-0.55	(3.6)*	0.00017	(1.0)
PFEM	-1.71	(7.4)*	-0.082	(0.6)	-1.79	(5.6)*	0.0029	(8.0)*
INTL	-21.41	(2.4)*	-24.65	(4.8)*	-46.053	(3.7)*	-0.027	(1.9)
FORESTRY	46.66	(1.4)	21.97	(1.1)	68.63	(1.4)	-0.0076	(0.1)
FISHING	-318.62	(3.9)*	-229.51	(5.0)*	-548.13	(4.9)*	-0.14	(1.1)
MINES	-44.40	(2.1)*	-47.58	(3.9)*	-91.98	(3.1)*	-0.010	(0.3)
TRANS	-77.39	(4.6)*	-43.00	(4.5)*	-120.39	(5.2)*	0.012	(0.5)
TRADE	-72.26	(3.5)*	-55.55	(4.7)*	-127.82	(4.4)*	-0.053	(1.6)
SERVICES	-129.61	(5.9)*	-62.66	(5.0)*	-192.26	(6.3)*	0.028	(0.8)
$\bar{R}^2$	0.32		0.23		0.31		0.18	
n	1674		1674		1674		1674	
F	23.7		15.5		23.0		10.2	
Prob > F	0.0001		0.0001		0.0001		0.0001	

Notes: [a] Figures in parentheses are absolute values of t-statistics.
[b] Variables are defined in Table 2 and Table 4. Other explanatory variables included in the analysis but not reported include: PIMM, PLTU, PBRIT, and dummy variables for year |Y(t)| and region |PROV(p)|.
* Coefficient is statistically significantly different from zero at the .05 level in a two-tailed test.

253

Table 7b. Collective Bargaining Agreement Outcomes Equations[a]

Dependent Variable / Explanatory Variable[b]	Pecuniary Outcomes		Nonpecuniary Outcomes		Total Outcomes		Nonpecuniary/ Pecuniary Outcomes	
C	775.59	(0.9)	489.22	(1.0)	1264.81	(1.1)	-0.26	(0.2)
LUNITSIZE	29.58	(8.8)*	14.25	(7.7)*	43.83	(9.6)*	-0.012	(2.2)*
TU2	6.85	(0.9)	-3.29	(0.8)	3.46	(0.3)	-0.0088	(0.5)
TU3	-43.09	(3.0)*	-25.32	(3.2)*	-68.41	(3.4)*	0.049	(2.1)*
LGDP	3.35	(1.1)	-1.96	(1.0)	-2.00	(0.4)	-0.0061	(1.0)
PURBAN	0.093	(0.1)	-1.34	(1.4)	-1.25	(0.5)	-0.0031	(1.1)
UR	-9.20	(5.8)*	-4.36	(5.0)*	-13.56	(6.3)*	0.0043	(1.7)
LOCALS	-0.031	(1.9)	-0.016	(0.8)	-0.047	(2.1)*	-0.0000015	(0.3)
JB	-16.85	(1.4)	8.20	(1.2)	-8.64	(0.5)	0.038	(1.9)
LMEMBER	20.82	(5.3)*	8.78	(4.1)*	29.30	(5.5)*	-0.0053	(0.9)
STRIKES	-0.39	(3.5)*	-0.12	(2.0)*	-0.51	(3.4)*	0.00019	(1.1)
PFEM	-1.85	(7.8)*	-0.18	(1.4)	-2.03	(6.2)*	0.0029	(7.7)*
INTL	-12.00	(1.3)	-15.89	(3.1)*	-27.89	(2.2)*	-0.023	(1.6)
$\bar{R}^2$	0.33		0.28		0.34		0.16	
n	1674		1671		1676		1679	
F	18.2		14.4		19.0		7.5	
Prob > F	0.0001		0.0001		0.0001		0.0001	

Notes: [a] Figures in parentheses are absolute values of t-statistics.
[b] Variables are defined in Table 2 and Table 4. Other explanatory variables included in the analysis but not reported include: PIMM, PLTU, PBRIT, and dummy variables for year [Y(t)], region [PROV(p)], industry [IND(h)], and occupation [OCC(Z)].
* Coefficient is statistically significantly different from zero at the .05 level in a two-tailed test.

254

Arbitration Procedure, Vacations and Leaves, Hours and Days of Work, Allowances and Benefits, Overtime and Premium Pay, Pay Guarantees, Health, Safety and Disability Benefits, Worker-Management Relationship, and Fringe Benefits Outcomes, is presented in Table 9a using the "favorable to union" coding scheme for the construction of the outcome indexes (scheme A). In each of the 12 regressions the computed F-statistic is statistically significant at the 5 percent level of significance.

The Total Contract Outcome Index

In the Total Contract Outcome regression we expected and obtained a negative coefficient for UR. While a positive coefficient for LGDP was expected, no statistically significant result was obtained for this variable. These results indicate that the levels of total contract outcomes decline in times of slack labor market conditions or during an economic downturn—suggesting that under adverse economic conditions either unions have less net bargaining power (these two economic variables are expected to affect power) or firms set higher resistance on pecuniary outcomes, or both.

In the Total Outcome regression we expected a positive coefficient for each of the three union characteristics that affect net union power. Contrary to the expectations for the STRIKES variable, the sign of the coefficient was negative; there is no explanation for this result.[22] The coefficient of both of the union characteristics most likely to reflect bargaining power, LUNITSIZE and LMEMBER, are positive and significant in the Total Contract Outcomes regression, suggesting that union locals with a greater stock of net bargaining power and greater resources can obtain higher levels of outcomes that are favorable to the union, ceteris paribus.

The results for the union characteristics that are expected to directly affect utility are mixed. The joint bargaining variable (no sign expectation) was statistically insignificant and the coefficient of PFEM (no sign expectation) is negative in the Total Outcome regression. There is no explanation for the result that unions with large female memberships are associated with lower total contract outcomes than unions with small female memberships. The expected sign of the coefficient for the INTL variable was indeterminate in the Total Outcome regression. A statistically significant negative coefficient was obtained, this result being consistent with the view that relative to national unions, internationally affiliated unions may have engaged in more concessionary bargaining activity. Finally, the coefficient of the LOCALS variable (no sign expectation) is not statistically significant.

The final vector of explanatory variables developed from the model includes the firm characteristics expected to influence the resistance it sets. There were no expected signs for any of these variables in the aggregate outcome regression. From Table 7a, the coefficients of all industry dummy variables are negative

Table 8a. Collective Bargaining Agreement Outcomes Equations[a]
(Dependent Variable Coding 0-1)

Dependent Variable / Explanatory Variable[b]	Pecuniary Outcomes		Nonpecuniary Outcomes		Total Outcomes		Nonpecuniary/ Pecuniary Outcomes	
C	60.049	(1.3)	34.82	(1.3)	94.89	(1.49)	-0.22	(0.2)
LUNITSIZE	1.57	(9.3)*	0.90	(9.2)*	2.47	(10.3)*	0.00032	(0.09)
TU2	0.45	(1.1)	-0.49	(2.1)*	0.04	(0.07)	-0.019	(2.2)
TU3	-1.95	(2.6)*	-1.92	(4.5)*	-3.87	(3.6)*	-0.028	(1.8)
LGDP	-0.051	(0.3)	-0.22	(2.0)*	-0.27	(1.0)	-0.0058	(1.5)
PURBAN	-0.037	(0.4)	-0.039	(0.7)	-0.076	(0.6)	-0.000048	(0.0)
UR	-0.49	(6.2)*	-0.31	(6.8)*	-0.80	(7.1)*	-0.0015	(0.9)
LOCALS	-0.0013	(1.6)	-0.001	(1.9)*	-0.0022	(1.9)*	1.4×10^{-7}	(0.0)
JB	0.63	(1.0)	0.39	(1.1)	1.02	(1.1)	0.0039	(0.3)
LMEMBER	0.90	(4.7)*	0.46	(4.2)*	1.36	(5.0)*	0.0072	(2.3)*
STRIKES	-0.014	(2.5)*	-0.0074	(2.3)*	-0.021	(2.6)*	0.00017	(1.8)
PFEM	-0.043	(3.6)*	-0.006	(0.8)	-0.049	(2.9)*	0.00023	(1.2)
INTL	-1.24	(2.7)*	-1.26	(4.7)*	-2.50	(3.8)*	-0.031	(4.0)*
FORESTRY	4.10	(2.3)*	1.57	(1.5)	5.65	(2.3)*	-0.057	(1.5)
FISHING	-19.23	(4.7)*	-13.09	(5.5)*	-32.31	(5.5)*	-0.12	(1.4)
MINES	-2.27	(2.0)*	-2.10	(3.3)*	-4.37	(2.8)*	-0.022	(0.9)
TRANS	-4.58	(5.4)*	-2.30	(4.6)*	-6.88	(5.6)*	0.024	(1.3)
TRADE	-3.86	(3.6)*	-2.97	(4.8)*	-6.83	(4.5)*	-0.016	(0.7)
SERVICES	-8.61	(7.7)*	-3.63	(5.6)*	-12.24	(7.6)*	0.063	(2.6)*
$\bar{R}^2$	0.31		0.27		0.33		0.06	
n	1674		1674		1674		1674	
F	22.6		19.1		24.9		4.2	
Prob > F	0.0001		0.0001		0.0001		0.0001	

Notes: [a] Figures in parentheses are absolute values of t-statistics.
[b] Variables are defined in Table 2 and Table 4. Other explanatory variables included in the analysis but not reported include: PIMM, PLTU, PBRIT, and dummy variables for year [$Y(t)$] and region [PROV(p)].
* Coefficient is statistically significantly different from zero at the .05 level in a two-tailed test.

256

Table 8b. Collective Bargaining Agreement Outcomes Equations[a]
(Dependent Variable Coding 0-1)

Dependent Variable / Explanatory Variable[b]	Pecuniary Outcomes		Nonpecuniary Outcomes		Total Outcomes		Nonpecuniary / Pecuniary Outcomes	
C	50.79	(1.1)	27.41	(1.1)	78.20	(1.3)	0.32	(0.3)
LUNITSIZE	1.46	(8.6)*	0.84	(8.8)*	2.30	(9.6)*	0.00004	(0.0)
TU2	0.54	(1.3)	-0.27	(1.2)	0.28	(0.5)	-0.015	(1.7)
TU3	-1.47	(2.0)*	-1.50	(3.6)*	-2.96	(2.9)*	-0.022	(1.4)
LGDP	0.057	(0.3)	-0.15	(1.4)	-0.092	(0.3)	-0.0055	(1.4)
PURBAN	-0.035	(0.4)	-0.044	(0.9)	-0.079	(0.6)	-0.00013	(0.1)
UR	-0.48	(5.9)*	-0.27	(6.1)*	-0.75	(6.6)*	-0.0023	(1.3)
LOCALS	-0.0015	(1.8)	-0.0015	(3.1)*	-0.0030	(2.5)*	-0.000008	(0.5)
JB	0.43	(0.7)	0.28	(0.8)	0.71	(0.8)	0.0039	(0.3)
LMEMBER	0.88	(4.4)*	0.60	(5.4)*	1.48	(5.3)*	0.0049	(1.1)
STRIKES	-0.013	(2.4)*	-0.0062	(2.0)*	-0.019	(2.5)*	0.00009	(0.8)
PFEM	-0.054	(4.5)*	-0.012	(1.8)	-0.066	(3.9)*	0.00055	(2.1)*
INTL	-0.66	(1.4)	-0.72	(2.7)*	-1.38	(2.1)*	-0.0091	(0.9)
$\bar{R}^2$	0.33		0.33		0.37		0.066	
n	1674		1674		1674		1674	
F	18.1		17.9		21.1		3.4	
Prob > F	0.0001		0.0001		0.0001		0.0001	

Notes: [a] Figures in parentheses are absolute values of t-statistics.
[b] Variables are defined in Table 2 and Table 4. Other explanatory variables included in the analysis but not reported include: PIMM, PLTU, PBRIT, and dummy variables for year [$Y(t)$], region [PROV(p)], industry [IND(h)], and occupation [OCC(Z)].
* Coefficient is statistically significantly different from zero at the .05 level in a two-tailed test.

Table 9a.   Level Collective Bargaining Agreement Outcomes Equations[a]

Dependent Variable/ Explanatory Variable[b]	USEC		TECH		EMPSEC	
C	356.50	(3.9)*	-54.64	(0.4)	10.69	(0.0)
LUNITSIZE	-0.44	(1.3)	2.63	(5.5)*	6.46	(5.4)*
TU2	1.46	(0.9)	-0.83	(0.7)	-2.58	(0.9)
TU3	7.50	(1.5)	-5.45	(2.6)*	-26.65	(5.1)*
LGDP	-0.49	(0.4)	-2.57	(4.9)*	-0.12	(0.1)
PURBAN	0.64	(0.2)	0.41	(1.6)	-1.36	(2.1)*
UR	1.17	(0.2)	-1.25	(5.6)*	-2.95	(5.2)*
LOCALS	-0.012	(0.0)	0.0066	(2.9)*	-0.0062	(1.1)
JB	0.96	(1.3)	15.055	(8.4)*	-2.058	(0.5)
LMEMBER	0.76	(0.4)	-0.96	(1.8)	4.85	(3.6)*
STRIKES	0.025	(0.0)	-0.088	(5.5)*	-0.015	(0.4)
PFEM	-0.052	(0.0)	0.028	(0.8)	-0.084	(1.0)
INTL	-1.45	(1.0)	-8.92	(6.8)*	-7.63	(2.3)*
FORESTRY	-12.48	(3.6)*	-6.94	(1.4)	21.64	(1.7)
FISHING	-29.61	(8.4)*	-36.71	(3.2)*	-77.81	(2.7)*
MINES	-0.60	(2.3)*	-19.81	(6.4)*	-19.50	(2.5)*
TRANS	9.51	(1.8)	-13.74	(5.7)*	-18.099	(3.0)*
TRADE	6.71	(2.2)*	-20.13	(6.7)*	-24.20	(3.2)*
SERVICES	-7.036	(2.3)*	-22.059	(7.0)*	-22.059	(2.8)*
$\bar{R}^2$	0.33		0.32		0.16	
n	1674		1674		1674	
F	24.9		24.1		10.6	
Prob > F	0.0001		0.0001		0.0001	

(continued)

(except Forestry, which was not statistically significant). There is no robust explanation for the result that manufacturing firms have consistently greater levels of "favorable to union" outcomes than nonmanufacturing firms (except Forestry). However, it may be the case that relative to nonmanufacturing firms, manufacturing firms tend to have longer established bargaining relationships with their unions and consequently may have developed a more accommodating approach to (or favorable view of) the goals of unions. This could induce manufacturing firms to set lower resistances than nonmanufacturing firms over the range of individual pecuniary and nonpecuniary bargaining outcomes desired by the union. The coefficient of TU2 is not statistically significant but the coefficient of TU3 is negative. That is, relative to a single-plant unit, multiplant units have no effect on the level of outcomes obtained, but the existence of bargaining by an association of employers is associated with lower total contract outcomes. This latter result provides

Table 9a.   (*continued*)

Dependent Variable/ Explanatory Variable[b]	GRIEV		VAC		HOURS	
C	-293.67	(1.9)	345.085	(1.0)	745.88	(4.9)*
LUNITSIZE	3.25	(5.4)*	4.83	(3.6)*	0.87	(1.5)
TU2	-2.46	(1.7)	-1.29	(0.4)	-2.60	(1.9)
TU3	-13.46	(5.1)*	-16.45	(2.8)*	6.081	(2.4)*
LGDP	1.81	(2.7)*	-3.066	(2.1)*	-3.00	(4.7)*
PURBAN	-0.12	(0.4)	0.55	(0.8)	-1.11	(3.6)*
UR	-1.33	(4.7)*	-3.54	(5.6)*	-0.43	(1.6)
LOCALS	-0.0031	(1.1)	-0.0091	(1.4)	-0.0014	(0.5)
JB	-5.71	(2.6)*	2.34	(0.5)	-0.87	(0.4)
LMEMBER	3.19	(4.7)*	5.32	(3.6)*	1.55	(2.4)*
STRIKES	-0.019	(0.9)	-0.23	(5.0)*	-0.024	(1.3)
PFEM	0.063	(1.5)	-0.18	(1.9)	0.077	(1.9)
INTL	-3.85	(2.3)*	-11.76	(3.2)*	2.18	(1.4)
FORESTRY	0.602	(0.1)	18.37	(1.3)	2.22	(0.4)
FISHING	-12.24	(0.8)	-153.40	(4.7)*	-76.41	(5.4)*
MINES	0.62	(0.2)	-39.91	(4.6)*	-4.98	(1.3)
TRANS	-3.66	(1.2)	-39.73	(5.9)*	-10.18	(3.5)*
TRADE	0.79	(0.2)	-33.17	(3.9)*	-6.90	(1.9)
SERVICES	-2.15	(0.5)	-47.65	(5.4)*	-7.053	(1.9)
$\bar{R}^2$	0.22		0.18		0.11	
n	1674		1674		1674	
F	14.7		11.4		6.8	
Prob $>$ F	0.0001		0.0001		0.0001	

(*continued*)

support for the view that employer associations may choose to set higher resistances over the range of bargaining outcomes desired by the union.

An alternative specification of the outcomes regressions includes control variables for occupational classification. Regression results for the specification that includes the occupation control variables are reported in Table 7b for the variables discussed above. With only the exception of the Mining dummy variable, all union and firm variables discussed above that were statistically significant (in the Total Outcomes regression specified without occupation controls) were also significant (and of the same sign) as the corresponding variables in the specification that included occupational controls (refer to Table 7b). Interestingly, relative to "Product Fabricating, Assembly and Repair" (OCC85) occupations, "Construction and Trades" (OCC87) related and "Artistic, Literary and Recreational" (OCC33) related occupation groups are associated with greater contract outcome scores, whereas "Material Handling"

Table 9a. (*continued*)

Dependent Variable/ Explanatory Variable[b]	ALLOW		OVERT		PAYGUAR	
C	130.72	(0.5)	571.15	(2.1)*	-5.65	(0.1)
LUNITSIZE	10.17	(9.2)*	7.90	(7.8)*	1.83	(4.1)*
TU2	-0.44	(0.1)	0.65	(0.3)	0.4	(0.4)
TU3	-13.77	(2.8)*	-7.016	(1.6)	3.17	(1.6)
LGDP	-0.18	(0.1)	3.74	(3.3)*	0.73	(1.5)
PURBAN	0.068	(0.1)	-0.85	(1.6)	-0.074	(0.3)
UR	1.082	(2.1)*	-2.80	(5.9)*	-0.063	(0.3)
LOCALS	-0.016	(2.9)*	0.0099	(2.0)*	-0.0077	(3.5)*
JB	-7.063	(1.7)	-5.18	(1.4)	3.62	(2.1)*
LMEMBER	7.55	(6.1)*	-1.045	(0.9)	0.94	(1.9)
STRIKES	-0.15	(4.2)*	-0.064	(1.8)	-0.035	(2.3)*
PFEM	-0.53	(6.9)*	-0.30	(4.2)*	-0.24	(7.5)*
INTL	0.43	(0.1)	5.40	(1.9)	4.42	(3.6)*
FORESTRY	-18.75	(1.6)	16.48	(1.6)	-4.68	(1.0)
FISHING	-34.59	(1.2)	-67.80	(2.8)*	-19.65	(1.8)
MINES	-5.92	(0.8)	-11.33	(1.7)	-0.46	(0.2)
TRANS	15.33	(2.8)*	-28.84	(5.7)*	0.69	(0.3)
TRADE	-15.28	(2.2)*	-1.70	(0.3)	-8.87	(3.1)*
SERVICES	-17.42	(2.4)*	-46.26	(6.9)*	1.45	(0.5)
$\bar{R}^2$	0.17		0.24		0.13	
n	1674		1674		1674	
F	11.3		16.8		8.6	
Prob $> F$	0.0001		0.0001		0.0001	

(*continued*)

(OCC93) and "Other" (OCC99) (which includes general labor) related occupational groups are both associated with lower contract outcomes. The coefficients of the remaining occupation dummy variables are not statistically significant. (These results are not reported.)

Pecuniary Bargaining Outcomes Regressions

Total Pecuniary Outcomes

In the Total Pecuniary Outcomes regression we expected and obtained a negative coefficient for UR. While a positive coefficient for LGDP was expected, no statistically significant result was obtained for this variable. This result indicates that the level of pecuniary outcomes is lower in times of slack labor market conditions or during an economic downturn, again suggesting

Table 9a. (*continued*)

Dependent Variable/ Explanatory Variable[b]	HEALTH		WMR		FRINGE	
C	-167.11	(0.9)	-191.21	(1.8)	-28.84	(0.1)
LUNITSIZE	1.83	(2.6)*	2.45	(6.0)*	4.62	(4.5)*
TU2	4.77	(2.8)*	0.93	(0.9)	0.85	(0.3)
TU3	-2.055	(0.7)	0.29	(0.2)	-14.092	(3.1)*
LGDP	1.54	(2.0)*	1.32	(2.9)*	-0.031	(0.0)
PURBAN	-0.68	(1.8)	0.21	(1.0)	1.15	(2.1)*
UR	-2.027	(6.2)*	-0.19	(1.0)	-2.25	(4.7)*
LOCALS	-0.0044	(1.3)	0.0090	(4.5)*	0.0040	(0.8)
JB	1.12	(0.4)	2.37	(1.5)	-7.89	(2.1)*
LMEMBER	2.90	(3.7)*	-2.39	(5.2)*	4.17	(3.6)*
STRIKES	0.032	(1.4)	-0.025	(1.9)	0.042	(1.2)
PFEM	-0.090	(1.9)	-0.11	(4.0)*	-0.38	(5.3)*
INTL	-10.69	(5.6)*	-4.98	(4.4)*	-4.20	(3.3)*
FORESTRY	25.79	(3.6)*	16.92	(3.9)*	9.45	(0.9)
FISHING	-26.077	(1.5)	3.26	(0.3)	-17.095	(0.7)
MINES	0.25	(0.1)	-3.31	(1.2)	12.98	(1.9)
TRANS	-10.013	(2.9)*	-6.84	(3.3)*	-14.84	(2.9)*
TRADE	0.18	(0.0)	-11.83	(4.6)*	-13.42	(2.1)*
SERVICES	-2.84	(0.6)	-2.30	(0.8)	-16.89	(2.5)*
$\bar{R}^2$	0.18		0.23		0.37	
n	1674		1674		1674	
F	11.8		15.4		29.5	
Prob $>$ F	0.0001		0.0001		0.0001	

Notes: [a] Figures in parentheses are absolute values of *t*-statistics.

[b] Variables are defined in Table 2 and Table 4. Other explanatory variables included in the analysis but not reported include: PIMM, PLTU, PBRIT, and dummy variables for year [$Y(t)$] and region [PROV(p)].

* Coefficient is statistically significantly different from zero at the .05 level in a two-tailed test.

that under adverse economic conditions either unions have less net bargaining power or firms set higher resistance on pecuniary outcomes, or both.

We expected a positive coefficient for each of the three union characteristics that affect net union power. Contrary to the expectations for the STRIKES variable, the sign of the coefficient was negative and there is no explanation for this result. Both of the union characteristics most likely to reflect bargaining power, LUNITSIZE and LMEMBER, are positive and significant in the Total Pecuniary Outcomes regression, again suggesting that union locals with greater net bargaining power and resources can obtain higher levels of outcomes that are favorable to the union, ceteris paribus.

Table 9b. Level Collective Bargaining Agreement Outcomes Equations[a]

Dependent Variable/ Explanatory Variable[b]	USEC		TECH		EMPSEC	
C	331.70	(3.7)*	-51.8	(0.4)	-83.58	(0.3)
LUNITSIZE	0.24	(0.7)	2.51	(5.2)*	5.97	(5.0)*
TU2	1.43	(1.7)	-0.037	(0.03)	-1.48	(0.5)
TU3	7.04	(4.7)*	-5.23	(2.5)*	-21.64	(4.2)*
LGDP	-0.27	(0.7)	-2.76	(5.2)*	0.82	(0.6)
PURBAN	0.71	(3.9)*	0.38	(1.5)	-1.37	(2.2)*
UR	1.07	(6.5)*	-1.01	(4.5)*	-2.70	(4.8)*
LOCALS	-0.012	(6.7)*	0.0041	(1.7)	-0.0090	(1.5)
JB	1.05	(0.8)	14.67	(8.3)*	-3.05	(0.7)
LMEMBER	0.74	(1.8)	0.057	(0.1)	5.05	(3.7)*
STRIKES	0.025	(2.2)*	-0.080	(5.1)*	-0.0068	(0.18)
PFEM	-0.033	(1.3)	-0.0069	(0.2)	-0.15	(2.7)*
INTL	-1.49	(1.6)	-7.95	(6.0)*	-2.20	(0.68)
$\bar{R}^2$	0.35		0.34		0.21	
n	1674		1674		1674	
F	19.4		18.7		10.3	
Prob > F	0.0001		0.0001		0.0001	

	GRIEV		VAC		HOURS	
C	-333.98	(2.1)*	236.17	(0.7)	818.89	(5.4)*
LUNITSIZE	3.14	(5.2)*	4.65	(3.4)*	0.47	(0.8)
TU2	-1.68	(1.1)	-0.28	(0.1)	-2.44	(1.7)
TU3	-11.43	(4.4)*	-12.24	(2.1)*	6.05	(2.4)*
LGDP	2.23	(3.4)*	-2.37	(1.6)	-3.15	(4.9)*
PURBAN	-0.12	(0.4)	0.55	(0.8)	-1.17	(3.8)*
UR	-1.17	(4.1)*	-3.29	(5.2)*	-0.28	(1.4)
LOCALS	-0.0048	(0.7)	-0.010	(1.5)	-0.0032	(1.1)
JB	-5.86	(1.6)	1.45	(0.3)	-0.80	(0.4)
LMEMBER	3.49	(5.0)*	5.51	(3.5)*	1.56	(2.3)*
STRIKES	-0.015	(0.8)	-0.22	(4.9)*	-0.022	(1.2)
PFEM	0.042	(1.0)	-0.26	(2.7)*	0.076	(1.8)
INTL	-1.48	(0.9)	-6.93	(1.9)	2.68	(1.7)
$\bar{R}^2$	0.25		0.20		0.12	
n	1674		1674		1674	
F	12.5		9.5		5.9	
Prob > F	0.0001		0.0001		0.0001	

(*continued*)

Table 9b. (*continued*)

Dependent Variable/ Explanatory Variable[b]	ALLOW		OVERT		PAYGUAR	
C	-38.29	(0.1)	677.09	(2.5)*	53.26	(0.4)
LUNITSIZE	10.77	(9.8)*	6.96	(6.8)*	1.45	(3.2)*
TU2	0.23	(0.1)	0.93	(0.4)	0.49	(0.4)
TU3	-9.37	(2.0)*	-18.04	(1.8)	2.39	(1.2)
LGDP	1.49	(1.2)	3.33	(2.9)*	0.50	(1.0)
PURBAN	0.19	(0.3)	-0.89	(1.7)	-0.12	(0.5)
UR	0.77	(1.5)	-2.53	(5.4)*	-0.16	(0.8)
LOCALS	-0.010	(1.9)	0.0063	(1.2)	-0.0088	(3.9)*
JB	-7.47	(1.9)	-5.73	(1.5)	3.39	(2.0)*
LMEMBER	0.25	(4.9)*	-0.14	(0.1)	1.06	(2.0)*
STRIKES	-0.16	(4.5)*	-0.054	(1.6)	-0.035	(2.4)*
PFEM	-0.48	(6.2)*	-0.32	(4.3)*	-0.21	(6.5)*
INTL	-4.12	(1.4)	8.55	(2.0)*	3.80	(3.0)*
$\bar{R}^2$	0.23		0.26		0.15	
n	1674		1674		1674	
F	11.3		13.0		7.1	
Prob $> F$	0.0001		0.0001		0.0001	

	HEALTH		WMR		FRINGE	
C	-157.74	(0.9)	-192.06	(1.8)	5.10	(0.02)
LUNITSIZE	1.60	(2.3)*	2.41	(5.7)*	4.15	(4.0)*
TU2	4.84	(2.9)*	0.78	(0.8)	1.13	(0.5)
TU3	-2.29	(0.7)	-0.10	(0.1)	-13.54	(3.0)*
LGDP	1.23	(1.6)	1.17	(2.5)	-0.26	(0.2)
PURBAN	-0.69	(1.9)	0.22	(1.0)	1.05	(1.9)
UR	-1.80	(5.4)*	0.16	(0.8)	-2.14	(4.3)*
LOCALS	-0.0076	(2.2)*	0.008	(3.9)*	0.00023	(0.04)
JB	0.47	(0.2)	2.20	(1.4)	-8.96	(2.3)*
LMEMBER	3.46	(4.2)*	-2.13	(4.4)*	4.37	(3.6)*
STRIKES	0.038	(1.6)	-0.023	(1.7)	0.044	(1.3)
PFEM	-0.15	(2.9)*	-0.11	(3.8)*	-0.44	(5.9)*
INTL	-10.20	(5.3)*	-5.45	(4.8)*	-8.35	(2.9)*
$\bar{R}^2$	0.19		0.24		0.37	
n	1674		1674		1674	
F	9.2		11.77		21.7	
Prob $> F$	0.0001		0.0001		0.0001	

Notes: [a] Figures in parentheses are absolute values of *t*-statistics.

[b] Variables are defined in Table 2 and Table 4. Other explanatory variables included in the analysis but not reported include: PIMM, PLTU, PBRIT, and dummy variables for year [$Y(t)$], region [PROV(p)], industry [IND(h)], and occupation [OCC(Z)].

* Coefficient is statistically significantly different from zero at the .05 level in a two-tailed test.

Table 10a.   Collective Bargaining Agreement Outcomes Equations[a]
(Dependent Variable Coding 0-1)

Dependent Variable/ Explanatory Variable[b]	USEC		TECH		EMPSEC	
C	21.94	(5.4)*	0.97	(0.1)	2.55	(0.1)
LUNITSIZE	-0.025	(1.6)	0.13	(5.1)*	0.47	(7.1)*
TU2	-0.022	(0.6)	-0.0081	(0.1)	-0.26	(1.6)
TU3	0.29	(4.3)*	-0.25	(2.3)*	-1.39	(4.7)*
LGDP	-0.065	(3.8)*	-0.15	(5.4)*	-0.088	(1.2)
PURBAN	0.026	(3.2)*	0.020	(1.5)	-0.062	(1.7)
UR	0.052	(7.2)*	-0.075	(6.2)*	-0.21	(6.5)*
LOCALS	-0.00083	(11.1)*	0.00030	(2.4)*	-0.00054	(1.7)
JB	-0.0052	(0.1)	0.80	(8.4)*	0.017	(0.1)
LMEMBER	0.095	(5.5)*	-0.047	(1.6)	0.25	(3.3)*
STRIKES	0.00038	(0.8)	-0.0043	(5.0)*	-0.0025	(1.1)
PFEM	-0.0016	(1.5)	0.0016	(0.9)	-0.0063	(1.4)
INTL	-0.086	(2.0)*	-0.56	(7.9)*	-0.49	(2.7)*
FORESTRY	-0.82	(5.1)*	-0.35	(1.3)	2.13	(3.1)*
FISHING	-1.94	(5.2)*	-2.17	(3.5)*	-5.95	(3.6)*
MINES	-0.16	(1.7)	-1.16	(6.9)*	-0.89	(2.0)*
TRANS	0.38	(4.9)*	-0.85	(6.6)*	-1.42	(4.2)*
TRADE	0.20	(2.0)*	-1.14	(7.1)*	-1.67	(4.0)*
SERVICES	-0.49	(4.8)*	-1.17	(6.9)*	-1.59	(3.6)*
$\bar{R}^2$	0.40		0.35		0.23	
n	1674		1674		1674	
F	33.7		27.8		15.7	
Prob > F	0.0001		0.0001		0.0001	

(*continued*)

Among the results for the union characteristics that are expected to directly affect utility, the joint bargaining variable (no sign expectation) and the LOCALS variable (no sign expectation) were both statistically insignificant and the coefficient of PFEM is negative (no sign expectation), with no explanation for the result obtained for this latter variable. Finally, the expected sign of the coefficient for the INTL variable was indeterminate in the Pecuniary aggregate-outcome regression: a statistically significant negative coefficient was obtained.

The final vector of explanatory variables developed from the model includes the firm characteristics expected to influence the resistance it sets. There were no expected signs for any of these variables. From Table 7a, the coefficient of TU2 is not statistically significant, and the coefficient of TU3 is negative. The results for TU2 and TU3 again suggest that relative to a single-plant unit,

Table 10a. (*continued*)

Dependent Variable/ Explanatory Variable[b]	GRIEV		VAC		HOURS	
C	-7.73	(1.3)	8.61	(0.46)	24.70	(4.5)*
LUNITSIZE	0.14	(6.4)*	0.31	(4.3)*	0.066	(3.2)*
TU2	-0.11	(2.0)*	0.086	(0.5)	-0.02	(0.4)
TU3	0.58	(5.8)*	-1.34	(4.3)*	0.08	(0.9)
LGDP	0.074	(2.9)*	-0.23	(2.9)*	-0.078	(3.4)*
PURBAN	0.0018	(0.2)	0.0022	(0.1)	-0.035	(3.2)*
UR	-0.049	(4.6)*	-0.24	(7.1)*	-0.017	(1.7)
LOCALS	-0.000019	(0.2)	-0.000029	(0.8)	-0.000021	(0.2)
JB	0.21	(2.4)*	0.079	(0.3)	-0.06	(0.8)
LMEMBER	0.087	(3.4)*	0.24	(3.0)*	0.044	(1.9)*
STRIKES	0.000067	(0.1)	-0.010	(4.4)*	0.0008	(1.2)
PFEM	0.0010	(0.7)	0.0063	(1.3)	0.0018	(1.3)
INTL	-0.12	(2.0)*	-0.63	(3.2)*	-0.037	(0.7)
FORESTRY	0.21	(0.9)	1.099	(1.5)	0.10	(0.4)
FISHING	-0.28	(0.5)	-7.64	(4.4)*	-2.85	(5.7)*
MINES	0.17	(1.1)	-2.87	(6.2)*	-0.24	(1.8)
TRANS	-0.0087	(0.1)	-2.86	(7.9)*	-0.29	(2.7)*
TRADE	-0.16	(1.1)	-0.43	(1.0)	-0.35	(2.7)*
SERVICES	-0.058	(0.4)	-3.24	(6.8)*	-0.33	(2.4)*
$\bar{R}^2$	0.24		0.27		0.08	
n	1674		1674		1674	
F	16.6		18.9		5.1	
Prob > F	0.0001		0.0001		0.0001	

(*continued*)

multiplant units have no effect on the level of outcomes obtained, but the existence of bargaining by an association of employers is associated with lower pecuniary contract outcomes. Again, this latter result provides support for the view that employer associations may choose to set higher resistances over the range of individual pecuniary bargaining outcomes desired by the union. There is no robust explanation for the result that manufacturing firms have consistently greater levels of pecuniary outcomes than nonmanufacturing firms (except Forestry). As noted above, it may be the case that relative to nonmanufacturing firms, manufacturing firms tend to have longer established bargaining relationships with their unions and consequently may have developed a more accommodating approach to (or favorable view of) the goals of unions. These results for the variables that represent firm characteristics are consistent with the results obtained in the Total Outcomes regression.

Table 10a.   (continued)

Dependent Variable/ Explanatory Variable[b]	ALLOW		OVERT		PAYGUAR	
C	-3.29	(0.2)	43.16	(3.4)*	2.20	(0.3)
LUNITSIZE	0.52	(10.1)*	0.37	(7.8)*	0.16	(6.7)*
TU2	-0.040	(0.3)	-0.11	(0.9)	-0.041	(0.7)
TU3	-0.51	(2.2)*	-0.57	(2.7)*	0.085	(0.8)
LGDP	0.058	(1.0)	0.16	(3.0)*	-0.034	(1.3)
PURBAN	0.015	(0.6)	-0.051	(2.0)*	0.011	(0.9)
UR	0.030	(1.2)	-0.12	(5.6)*	0.031	(2.7)*
LOCALS	-0.00085	(3.4)*	0.00032	(1.4)	-0.000053	(0.5)
JB	-0.48	(2.5)*	0.13	(0.8)	0.28	(3.1)*
LMEMBER	0.39	(6.7)*	-0.037	(0.7)	0.020	(0.8)
STRIKES	-0.0047	(2.7)*	-0.0023	(1.5)	0.000031	(0.0)
PFEM	-0.028	(7.9)*	-0.0033	(2.3)*	-0.0022	(1.3)
INTL	-0.096	(0.7)	0.14	(1.1)	0.20	(3.0)*
FORESTRY	0.093	(0.2)	1.31	(2.6)*	0.92	(3.6)*
FISHING	-1.23	(1.0)	-4.91	(4.2)*	-2.35	(4.0)*
MINES	-0.15	(0.4)	0.074	(0.2)	0.12	(0.7)
TRANS	0.67	(2.6)*	-1.49	(6.2)*	-0.39	(3.1)*
TRADE	-0.98	(3.0)*	-1.056	(3.5)*	-1.30	(8.5)*
SERVICES	-1.06	(3.1)*	-1.95	(6.2)*	-1.20	(7.4)*
$\bar{R}^2$	0.18		0.26		0.26	
n	1674		1674		1674	
F	11.8		18.7		18.3	
Prob > F	0.0001		0.0001		0.0001	

(continued)

Again, with only the exception of the Mining and INTL variables, all firm and union variables discussed above that were statistically significant (in the Total Pecuniary Outcomes regression specified without occupation controls) were also significant (and of the same sign) as the corresponding variables in the specification that included occupation controls (refer to Table 7b). Consistent with the above results for the Total Outcomes regression, the model specification that included the occupational control variables yielded results that suggest that relative to "Product Fabricating, Assembly and Repair" (OCC85) occupations, the "Construction and Trades" (OCC87) related and "Artistic, Literary and Recreational" (OCC33) related groups are both associated with greater contract outcome scores but the "Other" (OCC99) group (which includes general labor occupations) is associated with lower contract outcomes.

Table 10a.   (continued)

Dependent Variable/ Explanatory Variable[b]	HEALTH		WMR		FRINGE	
C	5.21	(0.6)	-2.51	(0.6)	4.15	(0.3)
LUNITSIZE	0.054	(1.5)	0.11	(7.8)*	0.16	(3.6)*
TU2	0.20	(2.4)*	-0.068	(1.9)	0.27	(2.4)*
TU3	0.15	(1.0)	-0.069	(1.1)	0.22	(1.1)
LGDP	0.093	(2.4)*	0.091	(5.6)*	-0.094	(1.9)
PURBAN	-0.046	(2.5)*	0.013	(1.6)	0.032	(1.3)
UR	-0.11	(6.6)*	-0.019	(2.7)*	-0.079	(3.7)*
LOCALS	-0.00031	(1.8)	0.00013	(1.8)	-0.00012	(0.6)
JB	0.33	(2.5)*	-0.15	(2.8)*	0.28	(1.7)
LMEMBER	0.13	(3.4)*	0.031	(1.9)	0.081	(1.6)
STRIKES	0.0021	(1.8)	-0.00032	(0.7)	0.0015	(1.0)
PFEM	0.0036	(1.5)	-0.0022	(2.1)*	-0.015	(4.8)*
INTL	-0.67	(7.0)*	-0.047	(1.2)	-0.18	(1.4)
FORESTRY	1.20	(3.3)*	0.49	(3.2)*	-0.52	(1.1)
FISHING	-0.85	(1.0)	0.11	(0.3)	-2.25	(2.0)*
MINES	0.21	(0.9)	0.20	(2.1)*	0.35	(1.2)
TRANS	0.17	(0.9)	-0.12	(1.6)	-0.68	(3.0)*
TRADE	0.78	(3.5)*	-0.17	(1.9)	-0.86	(3.0)*
SERVICES	0.36	(1.5)	-0.10	(1.1)	-1.52	(5.1)*
$\bar{R}^2$	0.14		0.18		0.29	
n	1674		1674		1674	
F	9.1		12.2		21.5	
Prob > F	0.0001		0.0001		0.0001	

Notes: [a] Figures in parentheses are absolute values of t-statistics.

[b] Variables are defined in Table 2 and Table 4. Other explanatory variables included in the analysis but not reported include: PIMM, PLTU, PBRIT, and dummy variables for year [$Y(t)$] and region [PROV(p)].

* Coefficient is statistically significantly different from zero at the .05 level in a two-tailed test.

Disaggregated Pecuniary Outcomes

The results for the two economic control variables that are expected to influence union net bargaining power are quite mixed across the disaggregated categories of pecuniary outcomes. A positive coefficient of LGDP and a negative coefficient of UR was expected in all six pecuniary regressions; the results for LGDP show a negative coefficient in the Vacations and Leaves regression and positive coefficients in the Overtime and Premium Pay and the Health, Safety and Disability Benefits regressions, whereas (except for the Allowances and Benefits regression) the results for UR show negative coefficients, as generally expected. However, the generally statistically

Table 10b.   Collective Bargaining Agreement Outcomes Equations[a]
(Dependent Variable Coding 0-1)

Dependent Variable/ Explanatory Variable[b]	USEC		TECH		EMPSEC	
C	20.24	(5.0)*	1.27	(0.2)	-8.43	(0.5)
LUNITSIZE	-0.010	(0.6)	0.12	(4.8)*	0.43	(6.5)*
TU2	-0.023	(0.6)	0.028	(0.5)	-0.12	(0.8)
TU3	0.29	(4.4)*	-0.26	(2.4)*	-1.052	(3.7)*
LGDP	-0.05	(2.9)*	-0.17	(5.9)*	-0.043	(0.6)
PURBAN	0.029	(3.6)*	0.019	(1.4)	-0.067	(2.0)*
UR	0.047	(6.5)*	-0.063	(5.2)*	-0.18	(5.8)*
LOCALS	-0.00077	(10.1)*	0.00014	(1.1)	-0.00087	(2.7)*
JB	-0.0022	(0.0)	0.78	(8.2)*	-0.061	(0.3)
LMEMBER	0.089	(4.9)*	0.0087	(0.3)	0.32	(4.2)*
STRIKES	0.00034	(0.7)	-0.0038	(4.6)*	-0.0019	(0.9)
PFEM	-0.00063	(0.6)	-0.00025	(0.1)	-0.011	(2.3)*
INTL	-0.075	(1.8)	-0.52	(7.4)*	-0.14	(0.7)
$\bar{R}^2$	0.42		0.37		0.28	
n	1674		1674		1674	
F	26.3		21.4		14.8	
Prob $>$ F	0.0001		0.0001		0.0001	

	GRIEV		VAC		HOURS	
C	-9.15	(1.6)	0.73	(0.0)	25.93	(4.8)*
LUNITSIZE	0.14	(6.1)*	0.29	(4.1)*	0.056	(2.7)*
TU2	0.086	(1.6)	0.15	(0.9)	0.013	(0.3)
TU3	0.51	(5.2)*	-1.12	(3.6)*	0.086	(0.9)
LGDP	0.093	(3.7)*	-0.18	(2.3)*	-0.073	(3.2)*
PURBAN	-0.0016	(0.1)	0.0061	(0.2)	-0.036	(3.3)*
UR	-0.046	(4.3)*	-0.22	(6.5)*	-0.015	(1.5)
LOCALS	-0.000017	(0.1)	-0.00041	(1.2)	-0.00004	(0.4)
JB	0.21	(2.5)*	0.021	(0.1)	-0.068	(0.9)
LMEMBER	0.089	(3.4)*	0.26	(3.2)*	0.050	(2.1)*
STRIKES	-0.00011	(0.1)	-0.010	(4.3)*	0.00070	(1.0)
PFEM	-0.00033	(0.2)	-0.00048	(0.1)	0.0017	(1.2)
INTL	-0.036	(0.6)	-0.36	(1.8)	-0.073	(1.3)
$\bar{R}^2$	0.27		0.29		0.10	
n	1674		1674		1674	
F	13.9		15.3		4.9	
Prob $>$ F	0.0001		0.0001		0.0001	

(*continued*)

Table 10b. (continued)

Dependent Variable/ Explanatory Variable[b]	ALLOW		OVERT		PAYGUAR	
C	-10.50	(0.8)	45.46	(3.6)*	7.84	(1.2)
LUNITSIZE	0.53	(10.5)*	0.33	(6.8)*	0.13	(5.2)*
TU2	-0.039	(0.3)	-0.099	(0.9)	0.052	(0.9)
TU3	-0.29	(1.3)	-0.54	(2.6)*	0.060	(0.6)
LGDP	0.14	(2.5)*	0.14	(2.7)*	-0.042	(1.6)
PURBAN	0.019	(0.7)	-0.053	(2.1)*	0.0064	(0.5)
UR	0.0095	(0.4)	-0.11	(4.9)*	0.022	(1.9)
LOCALS	-0.00058	(2.3)*	0.00021	(0.9)	-0.000043	(0.4)
JB	-0.51	(2.8)*	0.11	(0.6)	0.28	(3.1)*
LMEMBER	0.31	(5.3)*	0.065	(1.2)	0.0066	(0.2)
STRIKES	-0.0051	(3.1)*	-0.0020	(1.2)	-0.000090	(0.1)
PFEM	-0.026	(7.2)*	-0.0095	(2.8)*	-0.00029	(0.2)
INTL	0.086	(0.6)	0.18	(1.4)	0.17	(2.6)*
$\bar{R}^2$	0.24		0.27		0.30	
n	1674		1674		1674	
F	12.3		13.8		15.8	
Prob > F	0.0001		0.0001		0.0001	

	HEALTH		WMR		FRINGE	
C	3.61	(0.4)	-2.45	(0.6)	3.66	(0.3)
LUNITSIZE	0.032	(0.9)	0.10	(7.0)*	0.15	(3.2)*
TU2	0.22	(2.6)*	-0.049	(1.4)	0.26	(2.3)*
TU3	0.18	(1.2)	-0.052	(0.8)	0.23	(1.2)
LGDP	0.082	(2.1)*	0.091	(5.5)*	-0.087	(1.7)
PURBAN	-0.046	(2.5)*	0.013	(1.6)	0.032	(1.3)
UR	-0.091	(5.5)*	-0.016	(2.2)*	-0.085	(3.9)*
LOCALS	-0.00050	(2.8)*	0.000058	(0.8)	0.00019	(0.8)
JB	0.29	(2.2)*	-0.16	(2.9)*	0.25	(1.5)
LMEMBER	0.18	(4.3)*	0.047	(2.7)*	0.058	(1.1)
STRIKES	0.0026	(2.3)*	-0.00022	(0.5)	0.0013	(0.9)
PFEM	-0.0011	(0.4)	-0.0023	(2.2)*	-0.017	(5.2)*
INTL	-0.59	(6.1)*	-0.024	(0.6)	-0.15	(1.2)
$\bar{R}^2$	0.17		0.20		0.30	
n	1674		1674		1674	
F	8.2		9.7		16.0	
Prob > F	0.0001		0.0001		0.0001	

Notes: [a] Figures in parentheses are absolute values of t-statistics.

[b] Variables are defined in Table 2 and Table 4. Other explanatory variables included in the analysis but not reported include: PIMM, PLTU, PBRIT, and dummy variables for year [$Y(t)$], region [PROV(p)], industry [IND(h)], and occupation [OCC(Z)].

* Coefficient is statistically significantly different from zero at the .05 level in a two-tailed test.

insignificant results across pecuniary categories for the coefficient of the LGDP variable suggests that the GDP has no impact on the levels of outcomes obtained by the union—where the coefficient is statistically significant, the signs are mixed across outcome categories. (Consistent with these results, the coefficient of this variable was not statistically significant in the aggregate outcome regressions.) In contrast, the coefficient of UR is typically statistically insignificant or negative (the latter result as expected). Taken together, these results suggest that slack labor markets (hence lower net union bargaining power) lead to lower outcomes over the range of pecuniary categories.

Of the union characteristics that are expected to affect union power, both LUNITSIZE and LMEMBER show the strongest and most consistent results across the pecuniary outcome regressions, whereas the coefficient of the STRIKES variable is seldom statistically significant. The coefficient of the bargaining unit size variable is positive in all six of the pecuniary outcome regressions, providing very strong evidence, consistent with previous studies, that unit size and net bargaining power are positively related. As expected, the greater the membership levels of the parent union in Canada (hence the greater the level of resources available), the greater the level of outcomes for all pecuniary categories except the Overtime and Premium Pay and the Pay Guarantees, in which the coefficients are not statistically significant.

The third vector of variables (including IND(h), TU2, and TU3) are firm characteristics that are expected to determine the resistance it sets for alternative outcomes. None of these variables has sign expectations associated with the variable coefficients for any of the six disaggregated pecuniary categories. Relative to a single-plant unit, the presence of a multiplant unit appears to have no effect on the various pecuniary bargaining outcomes. However, the results for TU3 support the view that relative to a single-plant unit, multiemployer associations tend to place a higher resistance on each of the Vacations and Leaves, Allowances and Benefits, and Fringe Benefits pecuniary outcomes (the coefficient is insignificant in the remaining three pecuniary outcome regressions). While a firm's participation in an association may reflect a preference for lower (favorable to union) outcomes and, therefore, higher resistance (firms holding similar views may be expected to form a coalition), it is likely that the TU3 variable may also capture a bargaining power effect. This latter explanation would imply that employer associations are able to reduce the net bargaining power of unions by forming a coalition. The results for the industry control variables show that with few exceptions, relative to manufacturing, nonmanufacturing industries are typically associated with either lower pecuniary outcomes or no difference.[23] These results are consistent with the view that relative to other industries, manufacturing firms set a *lower* resistance over a range of pecuniary bargaining outcomes.

The final set of variables derived from the model represent the union characteristics that are expected to directly affect tastes for alternative outcomes, including joint bargaining (JB), percentage female (PFEM), international versus national affiliation of the local (INTL), and the number of union locals (LOCALS). There were no expectations associated with the coefficients of the JB variable. The coefficient of JB was statistically significant in only two of the six pecuniary outcome regressions and there is no consistent pattern of results between these two coefficients that were significant. The coefficient of LOCALS, where statistically significant, is either positive or negative with no consistent pattern among the disaggregated pecuniary outcomes. Except in the Pay Guarantees category (expected a negative coefficient), the expected sign of the coefficient for the INTL variable was indeterminate. Except for Pay Guarantees outcomes (positive coefficient), the coefficient of INTL in the remaining five pecuniary equations was either insignificant or negative. A statistically significant negative coefficient is consistent with the view that, relative to national unions, internationally affiliated unions may have engaged in concessionary bargaining activity. The coefficient of PFEM was negative in each of the four pecuniary outcome regressions in which the coefficient was statistically significant. However, while the coefficient of PFEM was expected to be positive in the Vacations and Leaves regression, the coefficient was not statistically significant. The results for the PFEM variable suggest that unionized workforces with a large proportion of females are associated with lower contract indexes for four of the six pecuniary outcomes. These negative coefficients are consistent with the signs of PFEM obtained in the aggregate outcome regressions. One interpretation of these results is that the PFEM variable may capture either unobserved bargaining power effects or gender discrimination effects.

Nonpecuniary Bargaining Outcomes Regressions

Total Nonpecuniary Outcomes

In the Total Nonpecuniary Outcomes regression we had no expectation for the coefficient of either LGDP or UR, but obtained a negative coefficient for UR while the coefficient of LGDP was statistically insignificant. A positive coefficient for each of the three union characteristics that affect net union power was expected. Contrary to the expectations for the STRIKES variable, the sign of the coefficient was negative; there is no explanation for this result. Both of the union characteristics most likely to reflect bargaining power, LUNITSIZE and LMEMBER, are positive and significant in the Total Nonpecuniary Outcomes regression, suggesting that union locals with a greater stock of net bargaining power and greater resources can obtain higher levels of nonpecuniary outcomes that are favorable to the union, ceteris paribus.

The results for the union characteristics that are expected to directly affect utility are mixed. The coefficients of the joint bargaining variable, LOCALS variable and the PFEM variable are all statistically insignificant. The expected sign of the coefficient for the INTL variable was indeterminate. A statistically significant negative coefficient was obtained, consistent with the view that, relative to national unions, internationally affiliated unions may have engaged in more concessionary bargaining activity, particularly in areas involving nonpecuniary outcomes.

Among the firm characteristics expected to influence the resistance it sets there were no expected signs for the coefficients of these variables. The coefficient of TU2 is not statistically significant, and the coefficient of TU3 is again negative. Finally, while there is no robust explanation for the result that manufacturing firms have greater levels of "favorable to union" outcomes than nonmanufacturing firms (except Forestry firms) it appears that manufacturing firms set lower resistances than nonmanufacturing firms over the range of nonpecuniary bargaining outcomes desired by the union.

The regression results for the specification that includes the occupation control variables are reported in Table 7b for the variables discussed above. With the exception of the Mines variable, all variables discussed above were statistically significant and of the same sign in both specifications of the regressions. Among the occupation control variables, relative to "Product Fabricating, Assembly and Repair" (OCC85) related occupations, both "Artistic, Literary and Recreational" (OCC33) and "Construction and Trades" (OCC87) related occupations are associated with greater levels, and both "Material Handling" (OCC93) and "Other" (OCC99) (including general labor) related occupations are associated with lower levels of nonpecuniary bargaining outcomes, respectively. (These occupation variable results are not reported but are available upon request.)

Disaggregated Nonpecuniary Outcomes

The results for the two economic control variables that are expected to influence union net bargaining power are mixed across disaggregated categories of nonpecuniary outcomes. There were no expectations regarding the coefficients of LGDP and UR in all six nonpecuniary regressions. The coefficient of LGDP is negative in the Technological Change and the Hours and Days of Work regressions but positive in the Grievance and Arbitration Procedure regression. The coefficient of UR is negative in each of Technological Change, Employee Security, and Grievance and Arbitration Procedure regressions (no expectations), and statistically insignificant in the remaining regressions. Taken together, these results provide no unambiguous results concerning the relationship between slack labor markets (hence lower net union bargaining power) and union ability to obtain nonpecuniary contract outcomes which provide security to employment levels (for example, through greater Technological Change related outcomes).

Of the union characteristics that are expected to affect union power, both LUNITSIZE and LMEMBER show the most consistent (expected) results across the nonpecuniary outcome regressions.[24] Except in the Union Security and Hours and Days of Work regressions in which the coefficients are not significant, the coefficient of the bargaining unit size variable (reflecting power) is positive in each of the remaining nonpecuniary outcome regressions. As expected, the greater the membership levels of the parent union in Canada (hence the greater the level of resources available), the greater the level of outcomes for most of the nonpecuniary categories (where the coefficient is significant); however, greater parent union size is associated with lower Worker-Management Relationship outcomes. Note that given both size variables are expected to directly determine the available stock of net union power and given the underlying assumption of the model of nonsatiation, then there is no explanation for the negative effect observed for the LMEMBER union characteristic. However, the unexpected result for LMEMBER does suggest that, aside from bargaining power, the parent union size variable may also capture unobserved union tastes that are associated with parent union membership size. Finally, the coefficient of the STRIKES variable is seldom statistically significant.

None of the variables (including IND(h), TU2, and TU3) that is expected to determine the resistance firms set for alternative outcomes has expectations associated with the signs of the coefficients for any of the nonpecuniary outcome categories. The results suggest that manufacturing firms set lower resistances than nonmanufacturing firms on most nonpecuniary outcomes (four of the six nonpecuniary outcome regressions).[25] This pattern of results is consistent with the explanation that relative to most nonmanufacturing firms, manufacturing firms accommodate union demands (membership desires) for favorable technological change provisions (Technological Change), seniority systems (Employee Security), and working conditions related to production scheduling and the organization of the workforce (Hours and Days of Work). One issue raised by these results is why manufacturing firms (appear to) have set lower resistances than nonmanufacturing firms for the broad range of these outcomes; that is, why would manufacturing firms prefer to set lower resistances?

Relative to a single-plant unit, the presence of a multiplant unit again appears to have no effect on the various nonpecuniary bargaining outcomes. The results for TU3 support the view that relative to a single-plant unit, multiemployer associations tend to place a higher resistance on each of the Technological Change, Employee Security, and Grievance and Arbitration Procedure nonpecuniary outcomes (the coefficient is insignificant in two of the remaining three nonpecuniary outcome regressions); only the result for the Hours and Days of Work regression suggests that an employer association ever sets a *lower* resistance.

Among the union characteristics that are expected to directly affect tastes for alternative outcomes [including joint bargaining (JB), percentage female (PFEM), international versus national affiliation of the local (INTL) and the number of union locals (LOCALS)] the coefficient of JB was statistically significant in only two of the six disaggregated nonpecuniary outcome regressions and there is no consistent pattern of results between those two coefficients that were significant; the coefficient of LOCALS is statistically significant in only two of the six nonpecuniary outcomes regressions; and the coefficient of PFEM was statistically significant in only one nonpecuniary outcome regression, Worker-Management Relationship. The only union characteristic with results that are broadly consistent with a priori expectations is local affiliation: union locals affiliated with international unions tend to have lower nonpecuniary outcomes for each of the Technological Change, Employee Security, Grievance and Arbitration Procedure, and Worker-Management Relationship categories. These outcomes represent areas in which we may expect international unions to accommodate firms—particularly during the adverse economic conditions and restructuring of industries (covered by international unions) that characterized much of the time period of this analysis—so that we would expect international unions to experience lower outcomes in these categories. This interpretation is particularly relevant to the results obtained in both the Technological Change and Worker-Management Relationship regressions.

Aggregate Outcome-Tradeoff Results

The results for tradeoffs between the aggregate pecuniary outcome index and aggregate nonpecuniary outcome index are presented in Table 7a. We have several a priori expectations regarding the signs of five of the explanatory variables.

First, we expect adverse economic conditions to have a negative effect on the level of both pecuniary and nonpecuniary outcomes. However, we expect pecuniary outcomes to be more responsive to changes in the firm's financial position than nonpecuniary outcomes, particularly since many pecuniary outcomes represent cost items incurred "up-front." Therefore we expect a positive effect of UR on the nonpecuniary-pecuniary outcomes index, implying a tradeoff in favor of nonpecuniary outcomes.

Second, we expect larger bargaining units to have a positive effect on the level of both pecuniary and nonpecuniary outcomes. However, we expect that the larger the unit, the more complex and comprehensive will be the nonpecuniary outcomes, such as rules (discipline systems) or formalized voice mechanisms (grievance and arbitration procedures). Therefore, we expect a positive effect of LUNITSIZE on the nonpecuniary-pecuniary outcomes index, implying a tradeoff in favor of nonpecuniary outcomes.

Third, we expect union locals with a large female constituency to pursue contract items of particular interest to females, including mechanisms to reduce discrimination in the workplace (Employee Security), maternity and child-care related leaves (Vacations and Leaves), and flexible work schedules (Hours and Days of Work). Therefore, we expect a positive effect of PFEM on the nonpecuniary-pecuniary outcomes index, implying a tradeoff in favor of nonpecuniary outcomes.

Fourth, relative to a single-plant unit, we expect an employer association to have a negative effect on the level of both pecuniary and nonpecuniary outcomes. However, we expect a coalition of employers to be more likely to seek favorable (to the *firm*) pecuniary outcomes, particularly since many pecuniary outcomes represent cost items that could be incurred by all firms in the coalition. Therefore, we expect a positive effect of TU3 on the nonpecuniary-pecuniary outcomes index, implying a tradeoff away from pecuniary outcomes in favor of nonpecuniary outcomes.

As expected, the coefficients of the employer association and percent female variables are positive. However, the coefficient of the unit size variable is negative (not expected). The coefficient of UR is not statistically significant.

METHODOLOGICAL ISSUES

The following discussion presents several important methodological issues inherent in most analyses of bargaining outcomes. While some issues relate to limitations inherent in the current state-of-the-art line of industrial relations research, the resolution of these issues also defines a future research agenda.

First, an important methodological issue in empirical analyses of bargaining outcomes concerns the type of coding scheme to apply to individual contract clauses. The results obtained using the dependent variable constructed with the 0-1 coding scheme are presented in order to investigate whether or not the results are robust using this alternative scheme for constructing (coding) the dependent variable. The question is essentially whether or not a binary (0-1) coding scheme or a continuous (ordinal) coding scheme should be used to code those clauses for which the maintained assumption is that the true underlying variable is continuous. In order to explore this issue, the outcome regressions were estimated separately using both the 0-1 code, for which the true underlying variable was assumed to be discrete, and the (-30 to 0 to $+30$) code, for which the underlying true variable was assumed to be continuous. The regression results obtained using the 0-1 coding scheme (scheme B) for the construction of the outcome indexes are presented in Table 8a for the aggregate contract outcomes and in Table 10a for the disaggregated outcomes.

The empirical results obtained when the 0-1 coding scheme is used to construct each of the Total Contract Outcomes, Total Pecuniary Outcomes and Total Nonpecuniary Outcomes Indexes are very similar to the results obtained using the "favorable to the union" coding scheme for these indexes (see Table 7a and Table 8a for these results). Differences, where they exist, are typically limited to individual coefficients being statistically significant in the regressions with the 0-1 specification of the dependent variables whereas they were insignificant in the regressions in which the "favorable to the union" coding scheme was used.

The regression analysis of disaggregated outcomes (excluding occupational control variables) was replicated using the 0-1 coding scheme for the construction of the outcome indexes. Among the key explanatory variables of interest, including union characteristics (that are expected to affect net union bargaining power), firm characteristics (that determine the resistance set by the firm) and union characteristics that directly affect utility, many of the coefficients are statistically (in)significant in the regressions that use the 0-1 coding scheme. While differences typically occur with respect to whether or not particular coefficients are statistically significant, in general there is no consistent or robust pattern regarding either the sign or statistical significance of the coefficients in the regressions using the first coding scheme compared to the coefficients obtained in the regressions using the second scheme.

The assumption adopted in this analysis was that the true underlying "score" variable for contract outcomes is continuous for most (but not all) clauses, so that any ordinal scale which acts as a continuous measure of the "degree of favorableness" to the union should yield comparable results.[26] The (−30 to +30) coding scheme used in the analysis was intended to measure a variable that captures not only the presence or absence of a given clause, but also the degree of favorableness of the clause to the union. In contrast, the 0-1 coding scheme for each clause imposes a discrete measure on those outcomes which are in fact continuous; that is, the use of a 0-1 coding scheme measures an underlying variable which only captures whether or not a given clause is present or absent in a collective agreement. The resulting contract outcome-index (dependent variable) is therefore distinct from the dependent variable created using the continuous (−30 to +30) coding scheme because the two underlying variables that are measured are different. Consequently, one would not expect, a priori, the coefficients of the explanatory variables that are statistically (in)significant in the regression model with the outcome-index constructed using the continuous coding scheme to necessarily be (in)significant in the regression using what is in fact an alternative dependent variable constructed on the basis of a dichotomous coding scheme. Taken together, the empirical results (see Tables 9a and 10a) suggest that the statistical significance of the coefficient estimates depends on the method of construction of the contract outcome-indexes.[27] This underscores the importance of selecting appropriate coding schemes in order to create outcome-indexes which proxy the intended underlying variable of interest.

Second, presuming that a union will evaluate different clauses differently, another important issue involves the value of the set of weights, (K_i), to attach to the contract clauses (see, for example, Kochan and Wheeler 1975, p. 50). Previous studies have typically circumvented this issue by relying either implicitly or explicitly on "Wilks Theorem" (see Gerhart 1976; Wilks 1938), which implies that as the number of clauses (outcomes) to be weighted becomes sufficiently large, the value of the weights is not of practical concern. That is, previous studies (for example, see Gerhart 1976) suggest that variation of K_i away from one (equal weights) does not produce results that differ from those obtained under the use of the equal (unitary) weighting scheme. Chaykowski (1988b) explores this specific issue and presents preliminary evidence that the weights assigned to individual clauses in the creation of outcome-indexes does matter. Two further related issues include, first, the extent to which the weights assigned to clauses and corresponding to a given union may vary over time and second, the degree to which weights may vary across union locals. While these issues are beyond the scope of this analysis, these aspects of the weighting issue bear further investigation.

In the empirical analysis of bargaining outcomes, the estimation of separate reduced form equations for each of the 12 categories of outcomes relies on the assumption that the dependent variables are not jointly dependent. Corresponding to this formulation of the estimating equations, the union is hypothesized to possess a utility function whose arguments are the observed outcomes in the collective agreement. Essentially, total union utility is assumed to be a function of the 12 general classes of (disaggregated) outcomes. Furthermore, preferences are assumed to be strongly separable among the outcomes partitioned; that is, preferences over individual suboutcomes within each of the 12 groups are assumed to be independent of preferences over outcomes in the other groups. This is a fundamental assumption underlying all analyses of disaggregated bargaining outcome groups in which the outcome equations are estimated separately. However, in a full model of bargaining outcome determination all of the outcomes, and hence the system of equations, would be simultaneously determined.

One important aspect of the characterization of unions as organizations that expend power to obtain desired outcomes is that there exist no "free" outcomes. One implication of this assumption is that the union must expend a nonzero amount of its net bargaining power in order to obtain (resist) each positive (negative) outcome. Stated alternatively, the assumption implies that only distributive issues exist. To the extent that integrative issues are measured as outcomes favorable to the union, then this analysis will bias upwards estimates of the extent of union bargaining power.

The weak results for many of the explanatory variables suggest that many of the variables used in the regression analysis are imperfect measures of the true variables, resulting in the problems of errors in explanatory variables. The difficulty of empirically capturing many of the underlying factors that determine outcomes suggests that further attention should be directed toward the construction of better data sets. For example, the empirical results, taken together, imply a need to more uniquely identify (empirically) further union and firm characteristics that are determinants of union power or the resistance the firm sets. Better measures of variables such as percentage of a union local that is female, and the inclusion of variables that capture firm capital intensity, union financial resources, and the presence of unique constituencies within the local, would likely enhance the explanatory power of the various regressions.

One potentially fruitful area for future research is controlling for unobservable heterogeneity among bargaining units (employers). Unobserved heterogeneity effects (which are likely to be correlated with the other explanatory variables) will result in biased estimates of the coefficients in the regression analysis of outcome-demand equations.[28] If one assumes that the effects of unobservable variables are constant over time, then bargaining unit (employer) fixed effects can be accounted for by first-differencing an outcome-demand equation over successive time periods in order to remove the "fixed effect." Alternatively, assuming that the effects of unobservable variables are random, the outcome-demand equations could be estimated using a random effects model whereby the bargaining unit (employer) specific effects are assumed to be random terms that are viewed as part of the error structure—under the assumption that the unobserved effects are uncorrelated with the other explanatory variables.

CONCLUSIONS

While analyses of collective bargaining outcomes have traditionally focused on union wage (and employment) impacts, recent studies have included both pecuniary and nonpecuniary nonwage contract outcomes. By examining various economic factors, union and firm characteristics, and sources of bargaining power, as underlying determinants of alternative nonwage bargaining outcomes in the Canadian private sector, this study has contributed to the further bridging of these two lines of research. Several important variables expected to determine bargaining outcome levels, including bargaining unit size, the size of the parent union, the affiliation of the union local (national versus international), and the presence of an employer association, each had expected effects on the levels of bargaining outcomes. An important result arising from the analysis of the various outcome indexes (constructed at different levels of aggregation) is that the use of aggregate indexes appears to obscure statistically significant variations in the effects of explanatory variables on levels of alternative disaggregated outcome-categories—these effects are only discernable upon analysis of the disaggregated outcome categories. That is, the results suggest that the effects of the union and firm characteristics vary among alternative outcomes.

Each of the employer association and percent female variables was found to be important factors that determine substitutions between the aggregate pecuniary and nonpecuniary outcomes. However, the effects of many of the explanatory variables in the various individual contract outcomes regressions were statistically significant in only some regressions and the signs of the coefficients varied among the regressions. Together, these results suggest that the effect of union characteristics that determine demand for alternative outcomes varies among categories of clauses and that tradeoffs among categories do exist.

The empirical analysis extends past research methodologies by developing both a comprehensive coding scheme that assesses each outcome (associated with each contract clause) on a "favorable to union" basis as well as a coding scheme that indicates presence or absence of a clause. The analysis of the outcomes regressions was based primarily upon the ordinal coding scheme for the construction of the various contract indexes. However, when these results were replicated using a 0-1 coding scheme, the results obtained are found to differ between the two schemes (in particular, the results for the disaggregated outcomes yield important differences in the effects of the explanatory variables depending upon the method of construction of the outcome indexes), underscoring the importance of the development of appropriate coding schemes in future empirical analyses of contract outcomes.

An area of concern in the study is controlling for bargaining unit and employer specific characteristics that affect tastes for individual outcome levels and demand for alternative configurations of bargaining outcomes (hence tradeoffs), but which cannot be measured. One further area for future empirical research is controlling for unobservable heterogeneity among bargaining units (employers). Second, future empirical analyses of disaggregated bargaining outcomes could be estimated using a simultaneous equations model. Finally, the results of the study also suggest that many of the variables used in the regression analysis are imperfect measures of the true variables, implying that further attention should be directed toward the construction of better data sets.

The introduction to the study began by noting that responsible decision making concerning unions—by political, legal, and economic groups in society—should be based upon the knowledge of the actual effects and consequences of unionism. Furthermore, labor legislation and government programs often arise from a view that the outcomes of collective bargaining are either undesirable or inadequate. Consequently, this study, and continued research in the area of the determination of bargaining outcomes, will contribute to a more thorough and accurate understanding of the outcomes of collective bargaining, thus contributing to the formulation of public policies that better meet the needs of those most affected by government programs.

APPENDIX

The following 12 general categories of collective agreement provisions were constructed for use in the analysis of collective bargaining outcomes. Each category contains specific provisions identified in the sample data set used in the analysis of collective bargaining outcomes. The 12 aggregate categories and the specific clauses to be included in each category were determined a priori. Column 1 contains the percentage of collective agreements in the data sample for which a particular clause was present but scored less than 0 ("unfavorable" to the union). Column 2 presents the percentage of collective agreements in the data sample for which a clause was not present in the contract. Column 3 presents the percentage of collective agreements in the data sample for which a clause was present but scored greater than 0 ("favorable" to the union). For a given clause the total percentage of collective agreements in the sample for which the clause is present is therefore the sum of column 1 and column 3. Finally, the number of outcomes coded for each clause is provided in column 4. Note that the number of outcomes coded, provided in column 4, does not include a "0" code (absence of a clause) but does include an "other" (miscellaneous) outcome. For each clause, if there was no outcome (that is, the clause was absent) the clause was assigned a value of 0. If the clause was present, the outcome was coded on a scale of +1 to +30 if the outcome was deemed "favorable to the union" and coded on a scale of −1 to −30 if the observed outcome was judged "unfavorable to the union."

Composition of Collective Bargaining Agreement Categories[a]

	1 Percent CBA's Score < 0	2 Percent CBA's Score = 0	3 Percent CBA's Score > 0	4 Outcomes Coded
Category 1: Union Security				
Union security—membership	0.2	26.5	74.3	5
Union security—check-off	—	89.2	10.8	5
Jurisdiction of work—each trade	—	95.9	4.1	1
Union security crossing of picket lines, and so forth	—	76.9	23.1	3
Category 2: Employee Security				
Contracting out	15.1	62.5	22.4	6
Length of probationary period after hiring	—	9.7	90.3	9
Special seniority provision for employees with special skills and/or union officials	—	67.1	32.9	3
Seniority on promotion	—	13.8	86.2	3
Seniority on layoff	—	8.0	92.0	3
Retention of seniority during terms of layoff	—	17.4	82.6	8

(continued)

(*Continued*)

	1 Percent CBA's Score < 0	2 Percent CBA's Score = 0	3 Percent CBA's Score > 0	4 Outcomes Coded
Category 2: (cont'd)				
Retention of seniority during illness (omitted)	—	—	—	8
Seniority—bumping	—	46.3	53.7	3
Notice of layoff	—	47.6	54.2	5
Recall procedure	—	12.4	87.6	3
Distribution of work during slack period	—	91.4	8.6	4
Severance pay with SUB	—	63.4	36.6	6
Eligibility for severance pay on layoff	—	77.1	22.9	9
Eligibility for severance pay on resignation	—	98.4	1.6	9
Eligibility for severance pay on retirement	—	9.7	2.5	9
Severance pay—benefits (layoff)	—	75.8	24.2	7
Severance pay—benefits (resignation)	—	98.5	1.5	7
Severance pay—benefits (retirement)	—	97.7	2.3	7
Severance pay—total benefits (on layoff)	—	79.1	20.9	9
Severance pay—total benefits (resignation)	—	98.6	1.4	9
Severance pay—total benefits (retirement)	—	97.6	2.4	9
Posting of job vacancies	—	26.7	73.3	9
Acting pay—qualifying period	—	97.0	3.0	8
Rate on temporary transfer	—	37.2	62.8	4
Category 3: Grievance and Arbitration Procedure				
Employee grievance—initial presentation	—	1.5	98.5	6
Special grievance—disciplinary or dismissal	—	40.4	59.6	4
Compensation for grievance work	0.5	37.2	62.3	5
Compensation of union officials in negotiation of				
agreements	0.2	70.4	29.4	6
Arbitration—number of arbitrators	—	2.0	98.0	6
Category 4: Hours and Days of Work				
Normal work week (days per week)	—	6.9	93.1	14
Daily hours	—	5.6	94.4	23
Maximum hours per run (transportation)	—	95.4	4.6	24
Maximum hours per month (transportation)	—	99.8	0.2	20
Weekly hours	—	6.0	94.0	30
Normal weekly method of operations	—	16.2	83.8	10
Flexible working hours	—	95.9	4.1	5
Category 5: Overtime and Premium Pay				
Overtime compensation after daily hours	5.2	5.6	89.2	11
Overtime compensation after weekly hours	3.9	43.9	52.2	11
Overtime compensation on Saturday or 6th day	4.3	20.7	75.0	11
Overtime compensation on Sunday or 7th day	2.3	15.3	82.4	11
Time off in lieu of overtime pay	—	94.6	5.4	3

(continued)

(*Continued*)

	1 Percent CBA's Score < 0	2 Percent CBA's Score = 0	3 Percent CBA's Score > 0	4 Outcomes Coded
Category 5: (cont'd)				
Right to refuse overtime	6.7	48.4	44.9	8
Equal distribution of overtime among employees	—	45.4	54.6	7
Premium pay for regular scheduled work on Saturday	—	92.3	7.7	12
Premium pay for regular scheduled work on Sunday	—	83.2	16.8	12
Shift premium (second shift)	—	27.1	72.9	30
Shift premium (third shift)	—	30.0	70.0	30
Premium pay (broken or slip shifts)	—	98.2	1.8	30
Premium pay (hazardous, dangerous or dirty work)	—	84.4	25.2	4
Amount of premium pay for hazardous, dangerous or dirty work	—	90.1	9.9	30
Amount of premium rates for work on paid holidays	—	7.4	92.6	11
Category 6: Pay Guarantees				
Guaranteed employment or earnings	—	87.8	12.2	6
Reporting pay guarantee	—	34.9	65.1	9
Call-in (back) pay guarantee	—	21.3	78.7	28
Portal-to-portal	—	94.9	5.1	4
Stand-by pay	—	90.9	9.1	6
Wage incentives	20.5	79.5	0.0	6
Pay guarantee during machinery breakdown or adverse weather conditions	—	78.5	21.5	4
Category 7: Vacations and Leaves				
Number of paid holidays per year	—	1.6	98.4	30
Eligibility for paid holidays (minimum service)	—	48.1	51.9	8
Eligibility for paid holidays (other requirements)	—	24.2	75.8	6
Provision concerning paid holiday falling on Saturday or 6th day (not normally worked)	—	43.1	56.9	5
Provision concerning paid holiday falling on Sunday or 7th day (not normally worked)	—	36.6	63.4	5
Paid vacation—election	—	20.3	79.7	4
Paid vacation (2 weeks)	—	10.7	89.3	12
Paid vacation (3 weeks)	—	4.4	95.6	19
Paid vacation (4 weeks)	—	9.5	90.5	28
Paid vacation (5 weeks)	—	36.0	64.0	30
Paid vacation (6 weeks)	—	76.2	23.8	30
Paid vacation (more than 6 weeks)	—	98.3	1.7	3
Carry-over of vacation	13.4	79.1	7.5	4

(*continued*)

(*Continued*)

	1 Percent CBA's Score < 0	2 Percent CBA's Score = 0	3 Percent CBA's Score > 0	4 Outcomes Coded
Category 7: (cont'd)				
Extended vacation if taken at certain time(s) of year	—	96.9	3.1	4
Extended vacation in designated years of service	—	91.0	9.0	6
Pre-retirement vacation	—	93.3	6.7	7
Special payments	—	83.4	16.6	4
Paid leave—death in immediate family	—	8.2	91.8	7
Paid leave—death other than family	—	60.7	39.3	7
Paid leave—marriage	—	94.2	5.8	7
Paid leave—childbirth (paternal leave)	—	1.0	8.9	7
Paid leave—adoption	—	96.1	3.9	7
Pay for leave—jury duty and/or court witness	—	24.8	75.2	5
Paid leave of absence—education	—	89.8	10.2	5
Sabbatical leave	—	99.9	0.1	3
Leave of absence—union business	1.6	23.5	74.9	6
Women—maternity leave (seniority)	—	77.5	12.5	5
Women—maternity leave (pay)	12.5	85.1	2.4	6
Women—maternity leave: time limitation before and after date of birth	—	68.5	31.5	9
Category 8: Allowances and Benefits				
Travel pay/transportation on call-in (back)	—	96.6	3.4	3
Travel pay/transportation on overtime	—	96.3	3.7	3
Travel pay/transportation—special circumstances	—	89.6	10.4	3
Travel pay on company business	—	65.8	34.2	6
Meal pay (cash or meal) and/or paid meal	—	49.6	50.4	3
Paid wash-up time	—	79.7	20.3	9
Rest period	—	40.7	59.3	9
Moving expenses (not related to technological change)	—	88.6	11.4	5
Clothing and uniforms	—	58.7	41.3	4
Tools	1.0	76.6	22.4	6
Safety equipment	—	43.1	56.9	5
Training or retraining (not related to technological change)	—	56.3	43.7	8
Industrial safety	—	25.3	74.7	3
Rehabilitation programs (alcoholism/drugs)	—	98.3	1.7	1
Legal protection	—	97.7	2.3	2
Environment protection	—	97.8	2.2	5
Longevity pay	—	99.0	1.0	17
Moonlighting	6.3	77.2	16.5	4
Older/handicapped workers	—	70.9	29.1	6

(*continued*)

(Continued)

	1 Percent CBA's Score < 0	2 Percent CBA's Score = 0	3 Percent CBA's Score > 0	4 Outcomes Coded
Category 9: Technological Change				
Advance notice and/or consultation with employee and/or union prior to the introduction of technological changes or new methods	—	73.7	26.3	5
Training or retraining	—	79.6	10.4	4
Relocation allowance	—	98.9	1.1	5
Labor-management committee	—	92.4	7.6	4
Employment security	—	85.0	15.0	5
Notice of layoff	—	92.0	8.0	4
Reopener clause (both wages and/or working conditions)	—	99.4	0.6	3
Technological change—work-sharing techniques	—	99.8	0.2	9
Category 10: Health, Safety and Disability Benefits				
Workers' compensation	—	87.6	12.4	4
Sickness weekly indemnity (period of)	—	21.6	78.4	29
Sickness weekly indemnity (benefit amount)	—	21.2	78.8	30
Paid sick leave (number of days yearly)	—	75.4	24.6	28
Accumulation of unused sick leave	—	81.6	18.4	19
Reimbursement of unused sick leave on termination of employment	1.2	96.3	2.5	7
Reimbursement of unused sick leave on retirement	0.7	96.8	2.5	7
Long-term disability (employer's contribution)	—	81.3	18.7	9
Long-term disability—benefit (amount of)	—	81.6	18.4	30
Administration of health and welfare plan	1.9	95.8	2.3′	4
Category 11: Worker-Management Relationship				
Profit-sharing plans	—	99.3	0.7	1
Productivity plan	1.4	98.6	0.0	3
Labor-management committee	—	54.4	45.6	1
Management rights	84.8	15.2	—	3
Job-enrichment	—	98.3	1.7	7
Category 12: Fringe Benefits				
Basic medicare—employer's contribution	—	44.3	55.7	9
Extended health benefits—employer's contribution	—	17.5	82.5	9
Dental plan—employer's contribution	—	72.6	27.4	9
Life insurance, accidental death and dismemberment—employer's contribution	—	16.9	83.1	9
Life insurance, accidental death and dismemberment—amount of benefit	—	34.9	65.1	15

(continued)

(*Continued*)

	1 Percent CBA's Score < 0	2 Percent CBA's Score = 0	3 Percent CBA's Score > 0	4 Outcomes Coded
Category 12: (cont'd)				
Life insurance—retirees and/or dependents				
(amount of benefit)	—	87.5	12.5	9
Private pension plan—employer's contribution	—	40.9	59.1	9
Private pension plan—benefit (amount of)	—	81.7	18.3	22
Indexation of private pension plans	—	99.9	0.1	5
Early retirement benefit	—	92.8	7.2	5
Death benefits	—	95.7	4.3	14
Death expenses	—	99.8	0.2	13
Administration of pension plans	7.0	87.0	6.0	4
Administration of severance plan	0.2	99.7	0.1	4
Administration of SUB plan	0.5	99.4	0.1	4

Note: [a] The individual clauses listed were those found in the microdata set of Canadian collective bargaining agreements as found in the following source.

Source: Coding Manual for the Analysis of Collective Agreements (1979), Labour Data Branch, Labour Canada.

ACKNOWLEDGMENTS

The author gratefully acknowledges the benefit of the helpful comments and input of John F. Burton, Jr., Ronald Ehrenberg, George Slotsve, and Dane Partridge, on previous versions of this paper. The author also acknowledges the benefit of comments of two anonymous referees. The usual disclaimer applies. This paper was developed from the author's doctoral dissertation. I would also like to thank Labour Canada for making available the necessary data tapes, Brian Lewis for capable research assistance, and Eileen Driscoll for her assistance in facilitating the use of the data.

NOTES

1. Studies of the determinants of pecuniary outcomes in a unionized private sector work environment have traditionally focused on the measurement of wage outcomes and have done so at a level of analysis which is much more aggregated than the level at which negotiations occur. The development of this criticism is presented in Kochan and Wheeler (1975, p. 48).

2. Understanding the determinants of variations in bargaining outcomes is of wider interest than to academics, union leaders, or corporate leaders. Kochan (1980, p. 306) emphasizes the importance of the public perception of bargaining outcomes in the formation of public opinion:

> The importance of understanding why the results of bargaining differ among various industries and occupations cannot be overemphasized. The public's view of collective bargaining is too often influenced by the highly publicized settlements of those unions that enjoy the most powerful bargaining positions. It is a mistake, however, to generalize from these large and highly visible settlements to all bargaining relationships.

Given the significant role of public opinion in the political decision-making process, a thorough public understanding of the effects and outcomes of collective bargaining is an important factor in the long-run formulation of related public policy.

3.   Both of these studies analyze data from the United States local government sector. Also, these studies are restricted to static analyses of bargaining outcomes due to the restriction imposed by cross-section data.

4.   In particular, Anderson (1979a) found that organizational characteristics such as the bargaining unit size, occupational category, percent exclusions, and membership dispersion were most consistent in explaining outcomes. Anderson considered bargaining outcomes both at a point in time as well as across rounds of bargaining. In addition, Anderson focuses on wage and nonwage outcomes as separate dependent variables in the regression analysis. The results of Anderson's study indicate that different variables are important in explaining wage and nonwage outcomes and that different variables are important in determining outcomes across rounds of bargaining (over time).

5.   Kochan and Block (1977) used a data base consisting of collective agreements (covering at least 1,000 workers) from the United States manufacturing private sector for the year 1972 in order to investigate the determinants of wage and nonwage contract outcomes.

6.   Similarly, in a major study of private sector collective bargaining outcomes, Feuille, Hendricks, and Kahn (1981) use a cross-section of 1975 data on United States manufacturing firms to estimate reduced form equations for each of wage and nonwage contract outcomes.

7.   The wage outcome data base consists of collective bargaining agreements from the manufacturing sector covering the time period from 1971 to 1981 and the nonwage contract outcomes data base consists of collective bargaining agreements from both the nonmanufacturing and manufacturing sectors for the year 1975.

8.   The 12 categories of nonwage categories include: employee security; grievance and arbitration procedure; hours and days of work; vacations and leaves; technological change; union security; allowances and benefits; overtime and premium pay; pay guarantees; health, safety, and disability benefits; worker-management relationship; and fringe benefits.

9.   See Chaykowski (1988b) for an analysis that attempts to assess the validity of imposing the constraint that $K_s^r=1$ (for all s, r). The question that arises is which set of weights (K_s^r) to attach to each of the clauses, given the presumption that the union will place a different valuation on different clauses. See the section on methodological issues.

10.   The contract data consists of a vector of individual clauses from collective agreements covering 250 or more employees for agreements negotiated during the period from 1975 to 1981 and individual clauses from collective agreements covering 500 or more employees for agreements negotiated from 1982 to 1984.

11.   The sample of collective agreements used throughout the analysis was the first occurrence of each employer-union collective agreement in the sample period. The result is a sample of "first occurrences" of each collective bargaining relationship (unit).

12.   By design, the data set excludes all contracts negotiated in the "construction" and the "public administration and defense" industries, as well as the "education" and "religious organizations" groups.

13.   The Appendix provides the number of outcomes coded for each clause.

14.   When applying scheme A, the coding allows for assigning a discrete score to those clauses with discrete outcomes. These clauses are listed as having one outcome in column 4 of the Appendix.

15.   Note that no "wages" or "cost-of-living allowance" clauses were included in the analysis; therefore, the analysis is restricted to *nonwage* related collective bargaining outcomes.

16.   Note that there are a total of 11 jurisdictions in Canada: the federal jurisdiction and each of the 10 provincial jurisdictions each have labor legislation covering employees. Of particular relevance to this study are those clauses (outcomes) which are mandated by the various acts or

codes. When mandatory outcomes appear in a contract, the clause is coded as a zero value on the assumption that the parties completely lacked bargaining discretion over the particular clause observed and, therefore, the opportunity to exercise their bargaining power to achieve their (potentially alternative) preferred outcomes for that clause. Examples of areas that may involve mandatory provisions in various Canadian jurisdictions include: dues checkoff, technological change, exclusive representation, resolution of rights disputes, and the minimum term of a collective agreement. For a comprehensive summary of legislative requirements in Canadian jurisdictions, see Wood and Kumar (1984, pp. 139-151).

While treating mandated outcomes as if the clause were not present is the approach adopted in this analysis, it is recognized that alternative coding schemes may be preferred on some other basis. In either case, a potential errors-in-dependent-variables problem is acknowledged. However, under appropriate assumptions regarding the error terms in the regressions, the estimated coefficients will be unbiased.

17. The "international union" variable may also capture both economic environmental effects as well as union-specific characteristics (such as the internal political dynamic of the union organization). However, such unobserved effects are not distinguishable in this empirical analysis.

18. While concession bargaining activity is not confined to international unions, we assume that concession bargaining activities in Canada will be more evident among internationally based unions, under the assumption that manufacturing industries in Canada were the most severely exposed to both the recession and international competition and assuming that international union membership is concentrated in manufacturing. For a discussion of concession bargaining in the United States, see Cullen (1985).

19. The "fishing, hunting, trapping and related" occupational classification was omitted from the regressions since this variable was perfectly correlated with the "fishing" industry control variable.

20. The results for the coefficients of the occupation variables are not reported in Table 7b, 8b, 9b, and Table 10b. However, tables that report all occupation variable results for the full specification of the equations that includes the occupational control variables is available from the author upon request.

21. There are no expected signs associated with the coefficients of the remaining demographic, year, or regional control variables. However, we expect that the regional variables may reflect regional economic and labour market conditions [Feuille, Hendricks, and Kahn (1981)] and the year variables are also expected to reflect general economic conditions or the impact of government programs such as the Federal government's anti-inflation program.

22. The surprising negative result for the coefficient of the STRIKES variable may be the consequence of the fact that the STRIKES variable may be a proxy not only for union militancy, but also for otherwise unobserved and possibly confounding effects. For example, the STRIKES variable may reflect unobserved *employer* bargaining power effects or resistance, in an industry, which may result in *lower* "favorable to union" bargaining outcomes.

23. The only exceptions to these results include Allowances and Benefits (positive coefficient for Transportation), and Health, Safety, and Disability Benefits (positive coefficient for Forestry).

24. The only exception is a negative coefficient for LMEMBER in the Worker-Management Relationship regression.

25. The coefficients of the industry dummy variables are typically either statistically insignificant or, where significant, negative. Two exceptions include a positive (statistically significant) coefficient for Trade in the Union Security regression and for Forestry in the Worker-Management Relationship regression. The coefficient of Forestry is typically insignificant.

26. The analysis used a -30 to $+30$ coding scheme that allowed for the assignment of a discrete score to clauses with a discrete outcome.

27.   Since the outcome-indexes constructed using alternative scoring schemes are different dependent variables one cannot, for example, compare R^2 statistics or perform empirical tests of the extent to which the use of the different scoring schemes may lead to different results.

28.   See Butler and Ehrenberg (1981) for a notable use of a fixed effects model in the industrial relations literature.

REFERENCES

Anderson, J.C. 1979a. Determinants of Bargaining Outcomes in the Federal Government of Canada. *Industrial and Labor Relations Review* 32(2):224-241.

————. 1979b. Bargaining Outcomes: An IR System Approach. *Industrial Relations* 18(2):127-143.

Butler, R. and R.G. Ehrenberg. 1981. Estimating the Narcotic Effect of Public Sector Impasse Procedures. *Industrial and Labor Relations Review* 35(1):3-20.

Chaykowski, R.P. 1988a. *The Determination of Nonwage Collective Bargaining Outcomes: An Application to Canadian Data*. Ph.D. dissertation, NYSSILR, Cornell University, Ithaca, NY.

————. 1988b. *The Empirical Formulation of Nonwage Collective Bargaining Outcomes*. Queen's Papers in Industrial Relations 1988-8, Industrial Relations Centre, Queen's University, Kingston, Ontario.

————. 1988c. *The Determination of Nonwage Collective Bargaining Outcomes in the Canadian Private Sector*. Queen's Papers in Industrial Relations, 1988-7, Industrial Relations Centre, Queen's University, Kingston, Ontario.

Cullen, D. 1985. Recent Trends in Collective Bargaining in the United States. *International Labour Review* 124(3):299-321.

Delaney, J.T. 1986. Impasses and Teacher Contract Outcomes. *Industrial Relations* 25(1):45-55.

Feuille, P., W.E. Hendricks, and L.M. Kahn. 1981. Wage and Nonwage Outcomes in Collective Bargaining: Determinants and Tradeoffs. *Journal of Labor Research* 2(1):39-53.

Fiorito, J. and W.E. Hendricks. 1987. Union Characteristics and Bargaining Outcomes. *Industrial and Labor Relations Review* 40(4):569-584.

Freeman, R.B. 1980. Unionism and the Dispersion of Wages. *Industrial and Labor Relations Review* 34(1):3-23.

————. 1981. The Effect of Unionism on Fringe Benefits. *Industrial and Labor Relations Review* 34(4):489-509.

Freeman, R.B. and J. Medoff. 1979. The Two Faces of Unionism. *The Public Interest* 57(Fall):69-93.

Gerhart, P.F. 1976. Determinants of Bargaining Outcomes in Local Government Labour Negotiations. *Industrial and Labor Relations Review* 29(3):331-351.

Gerhart, P.F. and Krolikowski. 1980. Bargaining Costs and Outcomes in Municipal Labor Relations. *Journal of Collective Negotiations in the Public Sector* 9(3):223-243.

Hendricks, W.E. and L.M. Kahn. 1975. Cost-of-Living Clauses in Union Contracts: Determinants and Effects. *Industrial and Labor Relations Review* 36(3):447-460.

————. 1981. Wage and Nonwage Outcomes in Collective Bargaining: Determinants and Tradeoffs. *Journal of Labor Research* 2(1):39-53.

Hendricks, W., P. Feuille, and C. Szerszen. 1980. Regulation, Deregulation, and Collective Bargaining in the Airline Industry. *Industrial and Labor Relations Review* 34(1):67-81.

Judge, G., R. Hill, W. Griffiths, H. Lutkepohl, and T.C. Lee. 1982. *Introduction to the Theory and Practice of Econometrics*. New York: Wiley and Sons.

Kochan, T.A. 1974. A Theory of Multilateral Collective Bargaining in City Governments. *Industrial and Labor Relations Review* 27(4):525-542.

_____ 1980. *Collective Bargaining and Industrial Relations.* Homewood, IL: Irwin.

Kochan, T.A. and R.N. Block, 1977. An Interindustry Analysis of Bargaining Outcomes, Preliminary Evidence from Two-Digit Industries. *Quarterly Journal of Economics* 91(August):431-452.

Kochan, T.A. and H.N. Wheeler. 1975. Municipal Collective Bargaining: A Model and Analysis of Bargaining Outcomes. *Industrial and Labor Relations Review* 29(1):46-66.

Lewis, H.G. 1963. *Unionism and Relative Wages in the United States.* Chicago: University of Chicago Press.

Perry, J.L. and C.H. Levine. 1976. An Interorganizational Analysis of Power, Conflict, and Settlements in Public Sector Collective Bargaining. *The American Political Science Review* 70(4):1185-1201.

Wilks, S.S. 1938. Weighting Systems for Linear Functions of Correlated Variables When There is no Dependent Variable. *Psychometrika* 3(1):23-40.

Wood, W.D. and P. Kumar, eds. 1981-1984. *The Current Industrial Relations Scene in Canada 1981-1984.* Industrial Relations Centre, Queen's University, Kingston, Ontario.

ORGANIZED CRIME AND UNIONS:

AN EXAMINATION OF THE FREEDOM OF

ASSOCIATION CONFLICT

Barbara A. Lee and James R. Chelius

Although not mentioned explicitly in the U.S. Constitution, the right of individuals to associate with other persons has been granted constitutional protection by courts interpreting the first amendment's free speech guarantees.[1] First Amendment law regarding associational freedom has permitted membership in subversive organizations,[2] association with individuals preaching racial and religious intolerance,[3] and association with "gangsters,"[4] as long as the association does not result in treason or criminal conduct. Although first developed in the context of associating for political purposes, the freedom of association doctrine has also been used to challenge laws requiring nondiscrimination in selecting members for social clubs,[5] laws regulating the number and relationship of people sharing a residence,[6] and laws regulating certain industries that have historically been subject to corruption.[7]

Lawmakers intent upon eliminating corruption in the solid waste,[8] longshoring,[9] and casino[10] industries have subjected these industries to close scrutiny through regulation by executive branch agencies. One characteristic

Advances in Industrial and Labor Relations, volume 5, pages 291-317.
Copyright © 1991 by JAI Press Inc.
All rights of reproduction in any form reserved.
ISBN: 0-89232-940-8

of this regulation is government scrutiny of the friends and business colleagues with whom important members of the industry—owners, managers, and labor union leaders—associate. Industry representatives who associate with individuals *suspected* of having ties to organized crime may, by law, be denied a license to operate a business, to work in the industry, or to act as a collective bargaining representative on behalf of industry workers.

Parallel to the concerns about corruption in these heavily regulated industries is concern about corruption in certain labor unions. Despite occasional public attention to particularly visible excesses, resulting legislation, and occasional flurries of enforcement, the problem of corruption is substantial (President's Commission 1986). While controlling crime in labor unions is an important matter of criminal justice, it takes on an even broader significance in the current environment of low and declining union membership. One of the key factors influencing a worker's decision about joining a union is the negative image of "big labor" (Brett 1980), and criminal activity is a part of that perception.[11] It would certainly help unions to reestablish themselves as an attractive option for workers if they could lessen the criminal influence on their organizations. Despite the legal and practical reasons for internal reform, however, very few unions have successfully taken on this challenge.[12]

While there is no systematic evidence that criminal activities in unions are any greater now than they have been (or that they are any greater in the labor movement than other parts of society), frustration with the lack of success using older statutes (Bellace and Berkowitz 1979; President's Commission 1986) has resulted in a new approach to eliminating corruption, and has resulted in increasingly vigorous enforcement by state and federal authorities. Certainly the most prominent of these efforts has been the U.S. Justice Department's use of the Racketeer Influenced and Corrupt Organizations (RICO) statute[13] to impose a court appointed administrator with independent authority over most internal affairs of the International Brotherhood of Teamsters (Raskin 1989). In addition, a Teamster local has been placed under a trustee by a federal district court judge in New Jersey,[14] and a roofers' local has met a similar fate in Pennsylvania.[15]

A central element in both the use of RICO and the close regulation of corruption-prone industries is the punishment of individuals who have not necessarily been convicted of crimes but rather have been found to associate with undesirable persons. Therefore, common to all of these is a conflict between constitutional guarantees of associational freedom and the goal of eliminating organized crime. Frequently, the criteria for receiving a license to work in the industry or to serve as a union officer for that industry's employees require the individual to demonstrate good moral character, and state that association with career criminals or other individuals of bad repute will disqualify the individual from licensure.

Among the cases addressing the constitutionality of these licensing criteria, the most thoroughly litigated is the challenge of Local 54 of the Hotel and Restaurant Employees and Bartenders International Union to New Jersey's Casino Control Act.[16] Two officers of this union have been required to resign as a condition of their local's being permitted to represent workers in the New Jersey casino industry. The case was litigated in both state and federal courts and reached the highest court in each system. Despite the extensive litigation in both fora, the courts gave relatively scant attention to the freedom of association claims raised.[17] However, given the continuing importance of the organized crime problem in unions, the increased use of RICO and similar statutes, and the presence of bills before both houses of Congress to modify this law (*New York Times,* June 27, 1989), it is timely to examine the fundamental conflict between associational freedom and reduction of crime in unions.

It is understandable, and certainly laudatory, that lawmakers and government regulations are attempting to eliminate the serious social and economic scourge of organized crime. It is not our purpose to argue on civil libertarian grounds that either organized crime or corrupt labor union officials should escape prosecution. Considering the labor movement's inability to eliminate corruption from certain unions (President's Commission 1986; Benson 1979), it is certainly appropriate for government to assume the responsibility. We are also not arguing that *all* association, whatever its intent or outcome, deserves constitutional protection. First Amendment law is replete with cases in which the Supreme Court has refused to extend protection to certain types of speech or expressive conduct (Van Alstyne 1984); clearly, there are examples of association that do not deserve protection as well.

But does the compelling nature of the problem of organized crime and its infiltration of industries and unions outweigh *any* colorable freedom of association interests that union officers may have? Society may support a requirement that paroled felons not associate with other felons because of the potential for recidivism. But should a similar prohibition on associating with persons linked to organized crime be a requirement for a union officer to represent employees in regulated industries, whether or not criminal conduct has occurred or is suspected? If no crime has been committed, the "harm" to be avoided by prohibiting association is the *appearance* of corruption, rather than corruption itself. Yet textbook First Amendment law—developed by scores of Supreme Court opinions—forbids laws that prohibit association that "appears" to be for criminal purposes when no crime has been committed or is planned.[18]

This paper will examine the criteria used by state and federal courts to evaluate the constitutionality of New Jersey's Casino Control Act in regard to its restrictions on the associational freedom of union officers. First, the development of the doctrine of freedom of association, primarily through decisions of the U.S. Supreme Court, will be surveyed. The complex and extensive litigation between Local 54 and the state of New Jersey over the constitutionality of the state's attempts to oust union leaders who had ties to an alleged organized crime figure will then be summarized. Next, the paper addresses the question of *whose* freedom of association is burdened when union officers are required to resign their office as a condition of the union's being permitted to represent employees in a state-regulated industry, and then discusses the claims of associational freedom made by the parties in the Local 54 case and the response of the courts. Finally, an analysis of the degree to which the courts considered the full spectrum of the associational interests of the various individuals and groups involved in the litigation, and the implications of this case for labor relations and public policy are considered in the conclusion.

THE FREEDOM OF ASSOCIATION DOCTRINE

An issue fundamental to the discussion of associational freedom is the determination of what "association" means. Because legal doctrines are developed on a case-by-case basis and are often narrowed or skewed by the facts of the case in which the doctrine was developed or interpreted, no clear definition of association, and no discrete categories of protected or unprotected association have been articulated by the courts. The results of case analysis, discussed below, demonstrate that the purpose for which the association is conducted affects the degree of protection the courts are willing to afford it. But the associational behaviors, the relationship among the parties (for example, friends, business associates), or the presence or absence of some outcome of the association are often either irrelevant or of minor significance to the court. This uncertainty about what kinds of association deserve constitutional protection made it difficult for the union in the Local 54 case (discussed in the next section of this paper) to articulate a compelling associational interest that the court should protect from state destruction.

One of the reasons for the late and incomplete development of the freedom of association doctrine is that the right to associate freely for a variety of private and public purposes is not addressed explicitly in the U.S. Constitution (Fellman 1963), nor has the U.S. Supreme Court recognized association as "an independent and unique right" (Raggi 1977). Instead, the doctrine was first developed in the context of state laws regulating the activities of members of subversive organizations, vagrancy, and criminal activity, while another group of cases applies the doctrine to situations where a law or regulation burdens an intimate relationship, such as marriage or parenthood.

The doctrine of associational freedom begins with the notion that "the right of individuals to associate or to refrain from association ought to be protected to the same extent, and for the same reason, as individual liberty is protected" (Emerson 1964, p. 4). Abernathy (1981, p. 174) describes the doctrine's historical development as "the addition and removal of restraints on free voluntary association, and the determination of the kinds of formal safeguards to the free exercise of the right of association." He chronicles the attempts of state and federal governments to restrict religious association and prohibitions on labor organizations (whose association was viewed as a criminal conspiracy until the passage of protective legislation in the twentieth century).[19] Attempts to restrict the activities of political parties were struck on associational freedom grounds,[20] as were efforts to prohibit individuals from associating with gangsters, prostitutes, and other "bad people."[21] Burdens placed upon membership in or support of subversive organizations (including loyalty oaths) and restrictions on associations formed to advance political ideas were also ruled invalid on associational grounds (Abernathy 1981, pp. 201-204; Fellman 1963, p. 173).

If, however, the association is not for purposes that are explicitly political, the courts have not applied such a strict test. State laws regulating the formation of group medical practices have been upheld under the "minimum rationality"[22] test because the regulation did not limit political or expressive action.[23] Tribe (1978, p. 701), an eminent constitutional scholar, has criticized, as unnecessarily limited, the Supreme Court's fashioning of associational freedom doctrine, saying:

> The Supreme Court has quite consistently regarded arguments about freedom of association as reducible not to the broad question of whether those who act in concert are merely seeking together a goal they would be privileged to seek separately, but to the much narrower question of whether the actors are seeking a goal independently protected by the First Amendment.

Thus, government regulation of economic or other nonpolitical association is subject to a lower level of scrutiny than that afforded association for political purposes.

While associational freedom was first developed around rights protected by the First Amendment, more recent protections for intimate association originated in Supreme Court opinions regarding privacy. First articulated in *Griswold* v. *Connecticut* (1965), the freedom of association given protection was rooted in the "penumbras" of the Constitution and in the fundamental right to privacy in the marital relationship.[24] Subsequent cases addressed governmental burdens on households of unrelated persons, although with inconsistent results.[25] Most recently, the right of intimate association has been discussed in challenges to the application of nondiscrimination laws to "private" groups such as law firms,[26] the Jaycees,[27] the Rotary Club,[28] the Kiwanis Club,[29] and single-sex social clubs.[30] These cases have asserted the right of the organizations' members *not* to associate with members of the opposite sex (in each case, women);[31] the court has ruled that the public interest in eradicating discrimination outweighs any colorable private interest in avoiding association with certain categories of persons.[32]

In a recent case in which associational freedom claims were addressed, Justice Brennan divided the doctrine into two categories: expressive and intimate associations. Expressive associations, he stated, were those "for the purpose of engaging in those activities protected by the First Amendment— speech, assembly, petition for the redress of grievances, and the exercise of religion." Freedom of intimate association, he wrote, protects "choices to enter into and maintain certain intimate human relationships."[33] Analysis of the cases in which freedom of association claims have been made suggests that this dichotomy is overly simplistic because it ignores the substantial overlap between the categories (Failinger 1987, p. 145) and is too narrow to encompass the spectrum of associations involved.

It is clear that the various categories of associational freedom are not discrete, and Justice O'Connor has, in fact, commented that some organizations have multiple associational purposes. She states that the courts must determine the nature of the activities that the organization "predominantly engage[s] in" in order to determine the degree of scrutiny to which the governmental burden on that association is subjected.[34] This threshold determination is imperative because the degree of judicial protection given associational freedom varies depending upon the purpose of the association. Failinger (1987, p. 149) describes a "spectrum" of associational freedom, with intimate association at one extreme, expressive political association at the opposite end (both of which receive substantial protection), and economic and social association in the middle (both of which receive less protection). The notion of a spectrum is a useful organizing device to analyze the degree of judicial protection for each type of association for which protection from governmental intrusions is urged.

Political Association

Associations for the purpose of furthering rights protected by the First Amendment were the first to receive judicial protection[35] and have been widely analyzed in the legal literature (Fellman 1963; Abernathy 1981; Emerson 1964; Rice 1962; Tribe 1978). In such cases, a state or federal law burdens association whose purpose is primarily political, such as the NAACP,[36] membership in the Communist party,[37] or political parties.[38] These cases have been litigated under equal protection and due process theories, with the resulting judicial standard of review that the state's "regulations [must be] adopted to serve compelling state interests, unrelated to the suppression of ideas, that cannot be achieved through means significantly less restrictive of associational freedoms"[39] in order to justify the substantial intrusion upon the political association at stake.

Economic Association

Although Tribe (1978, p. 948) warns that "it will not do to draw a bright line between 'economic' and 'civil' liberties ...," protection for association whose purpose is primarily economic or commercial is substantially weaker than the protection afforded political association.[40] The Supreme Court has been inconsistent in the standard of review applied to state and federal statutory burdens on the practice of professions,[41] commercial speech,[42] and membership in labor unions.[43] In some cases, such laws have been subjected to a "minimum rationality" standard of scrutiny and in others have had to satisfy a "substantial state interest test." Under the "minimum rationality" standard, the court determines whether the burden the government has placed upon association is rationally related to a legitimate state interest, while under the "substantial state interest" standard, the government must demonstrate that its regulation is "appropriately tailored" to effect the substantial interest.[44] Justice O'Connor has noted that "the State is free to impose any rational regulation on the commercial transaction itself. The Constitution does not guarantee a right to choose employees, customers, suppliers, or those with whom one engages in simple commercial transactions, without restraint from the State."[45]

Social Association

While this category has not been discussed explicitly by the courts, it could be argued that cases involving the right to join tenant associations,[46] the right of a gay college student organization to attain official recognition,[47] and the right to associate with "bad" persons[48] involve social association rather than political, economic, or intimate. Associations placed in this category could overlap with intimate association, on the one hand (depending, for example, on whether the association with the "bad" person involved a marital or other familial relationship) or could even overlap with the political category (if, for example, one of the purposes of the gay student group was political action on behalf of gay rights). Dating has been found to be a protected association,[49] as has loitering for innocent purposes with individuals suspected of drug possession or distribution.[50] In fact, it could be argued that association that has neither a political, economic, nor intimate purpose could, by default, be viewed as "social" association. Attendance at social events (parties, weddings, funerals) or spending time with another whose company one enjoys would be other examples of social association. While it would be difficult to argue that social association is as "important" or as deserving of constitutional protection as political, economic, or intimate association, it is also difficult to envision the harm that such association could cause—such that a state might wish to regulate it. While the category of social association is not as well developed as the others, for the purpose of examining the burdens placed on the association of union officers with organized crime figures, the category is a useful one.

Intimate Association

Karst (1980, p. 629) defines intimate association as "a close and familiar personal relationship with another that is in some significant way comparable to a marriage or family relationship." He does not confine his definition to marriage or family relationships, noting that "in principle the idea of intimate association also includes close friendship," although the Supreme Court has not determined whether or not friendship could be included in this category. Justice Brennan's definition of an intimate association would also include friendship. He wrote that such association is "distinguished by such attributes as relative smallness, a high degree of selectivity in decisions to begin and maintain the affiliation, and seclusion from others in critical aspects of the relationship."[51] While Justice Brennan may have been describing a marital or other familial relationship, close friendships, especially long-standing ones, appear to match his definition. Friendships are generally dyads—a small number. Friendships are voluntary (which some family relationships are not). Close friendships often involve the sharing of confidences, problems, or other private communications which would presumably occur in "seclusion from others."

Justice Powell, writing for a unanimous court in *Board of Directors of Rotary International* v. *Rotary Club,* noted that "we have not held that constitutional protection is restricted to relationships among family members."[52] Tribe, in criticizing the distinctions among types of intimate association afforded protection by the Supreme Court, has stated that an "enduring relationship" should qualify for protection as intimate association, even if there is no marital or family relationship involved.

> The embedding of a choice within a close human relationship or network of relationships should always be regarded as significantly increasing the burden of justification for those who would make the choice illegal or visit it with some deprivation.... [G]overnmental interference with *any* such relationship should be invalidated unless compellingly justified (Tribe 1978, pp. 989-990).

Tribe's criticism stems from the fact that the federal and state courts have been inconsistent in the standard of review applied to government burdens on intimate association. The Supreme Court has applied strict scrutiny and disallowed governmental restrictions on access to contraceptives for married couples and eligibility for food stamps for households of unrelated persons.[53] Conversely, the court applied the minimum rationality test to a claim that a zoning ordinance that forbade more than two unrelated persons from sharing a dwelling impinged on intimate association; the court denied that any associational interest existed.[54] A line of cases in which plantiffs have been deprived of their jobs because of intimate relationships have generally been subjected to the minimum rationality standard of review, presumably because the law does not outlaw the association but merely penalizes the individual for that association by depriving him or her of their livelihood.[55]

It thus appears that judicial protection for political association is stronger than for intimate association, and also that political association is defined more broadly than intimate association. It is further evident that government restrictions on economic and social association are much more difficult to invalidate than burdens on political or intimate association. This outcome has special significance in the context of a state law provision declaring union officers ineligible to hold office in unions that represent employees in regulated industries.

THE LOCAL 54 LITIGATION

The litigation by Local 54 of the Hotel and Restaurant Employees and Bartenders International Union challenging New Jersey's Casino Control Act is lengthy and complex. The associational freedom claim was only one of several theories under which the case was litigated; a brief synopsis of the case is necessary to set the context for the discussion of the associational freedom issues.

The Casino Control Act, passed in 1977, requires every employee working in casinos or casino hotels to be either registered with or licensed by the state's Casino Control Commission.[56] The act lists criteria for the denial of a license, among which are convictions for certain criminal acts or "identification ... as a career offender or a member of a career offender cartel *or an associate of a career offender or career offender cartel* in such a manner which creates a reasonable belief that the association is of such a nature as to be inimical to the policy of this act and to gaming operations."[57] The law requires that any union that represents employees of casinos or casino hotels register with the Casino Control Commission; "officers, agents and principal employees" must comply with the qualifications listed for employee licensure in order for the union to be permitted to register.[58]

In 1978, Local 54, which at the time represented approximately 14,000 individuals, most of whom were employed in the ten Atlantic City casinos and casino hotels,[59] filed its registration statement with the Casino Control Commission. The commission directed the Division of Gaming Enforcement (DGE) to investigate the backgrounds of the union officers.[60] After a lengthy investigation, officials of the Division of Gaming Enforcement reported to the commission that several officers of Local 54 were tied to Nicodemo Scarfo, the reputed head of the Philadelphia-based Bruno organized crime family. Specifically, the DGE accused Local 54's president, Frank Gerace, and a trustee, Frank Materio, as well as a union business agent, Karlos LaSane, of permitting Scarfo to influence the appointment or nomination of union officers, the allocation of union business, and the use of union funds for Scarfo's personal gain. The division asked the commission to hold a hearing on the suitability of these individuals to continue in union office, asserting that as a condition of Local 54's continued registration with the commission, Gerace, Materio, and LaSane should be required to resign their union offices.

Before the hearing was held, the union challenged the Casino Control Act under two theories. First, the union asserted that Section 7 of the National Labor Relations Act preempted state legislation that attempted to regulate labor-management relations.[61] Second, the union asserted a First Amendment challenge to the provision in Section 86 of the Casino Control Act prohibiting licensure of anyone who the commission identifies as "an associate of a career offender or career offender cartel."[62] The union's motion for a temporary restraining order was denied,[63] and although the union appealed that ruling, the commission proceeded with its hearing on the fitness of the union officers. The hearing lasted from June through September, 1982, and culminated in the commission issuing a decision disqualifying the officers on the basis of their ties to Scarfo, and requiring their removal. The commission further ordered that, in the event that any of the officers remained in office, Local 54 would be prohibited from collecting dues from any employee licensed or registered under the Casino Control Act.[64]

Local 54 sought relief in both state and federal courts. First, it asked for a stay of the commission's order in federal district court, which was granted pending the Third Circuit's ruling on the earlier denial of the injunction. Second, the union appealed the commission's order to the state's appellate court. While the state appeal was pending, the Third Circuit ruled that the act was preempted by the National Labor Relations Act.[65] Local 54 then asked the state appellate court to dismiss its appeal of the commission's order without prejudice, which was done.

The commission and Division of Gaming Enforcement appealed the Third Circuit's decision to the U.S. Supreme Court, arguing that the act was a legitimate use of the state's police power to reduce or eliminate the influence of organized crime. In a 4-3 decision, the Supreme Court ruled that the act's regulation of the qualifications of casino union officials did not conflict with Section 7 of the National Labor Relations Act (which guarantees to employees the right to freely elect their own bargaining agent and to select representatives of their own choosing).[66] The court relied on an earlier Supreme Court decision, *DeVeau* v. *Braisted*[67] in which the court had found that the NLRA did not preempt the New York-New Jersey waterfront compact that imposed restrictions on officials of the longshoremen's union in an attempt to reduce corruption in that union.[68] The court concluded that Congress had left areas within labor-management relations that states could permissibly regulate, and that "where the States were confronted with the 'public evils' of 'crime, corruption, and racketeering,' more stringent state regulation of the qualifications of union officials was not incompatible with the national labor policy as embodied in Section 7."[69]

Following the Supreme Court's decision, the Casino Control Commission issued a Supplemental Order in September, 1984 mandating that Gerace, Materio, and LaSane resign their offices by the end of the month.[70] The union and the officers immediately appealed the commission's order to the New Jersey Superior Court, Appellate Division, and also asked the federal court to stay the commission's order. The requested relief was denied;[71] the commission sought a court order to enforce its 1984 order, which was granted, and the three officials resigned their offices.[72]

The State Court Litigation

Both the union and two officials, Gerace and Materio, challenged the act as violating the associational rights of the officers and the union members.[73] Furthermore, they asserted that the language describing "career offenders" and "inimical to the purposes of the Act" was unconstitutionally vague, making illegal conduct that was never clearly defined.[74]

The officers argued several points with regard to the asserted First Amendment violations. First, they reminded the court that the commission had been able to find no evidence of illegal activity or other wrongdoing on the parts of Gerace or Materio. The officers had provided bail money for Scarfo when he was indicted for murder, and the commission had evidence of close business relationships between them and Scarfo, but no evidence of illegal conduct. The commission had disqualified the officers on the basis of evidence that Scarfo had influenced the appointment of union agents and was involved in union matters. But the officers denied that Scarfo had influenced union affairs. Absent influence, the ouster was based only on "guilt by association," which was prohibited by a long line of Supreme Court cases.[75]

The state argued that the association between the officers and Scarfo was "not innocent," and did not deserve First Amendment protection. In the event, however, that the court found the association deserving of constitutional protection, the state argued that a compelling state interest in the integrity of the gaming operations within the casinos outweighed whatever constitutional protections the association might expect to receive. Furthermore, whether or not actual illegal activity had occurred, the state argued that the appearance of a potentially corrupt relationship impugned the integrity of gaming, and that was a sufficient reason to disqualify the officers.[76]

Although the legal briefs filed by the officers contained impassioned pleas about freedom of association generally, the legal rationale for protecting the association between the officers and Scarfo was not presented clearly. The incompleteness of the associational freedom doctrine itself is probably a partial cause of this lack of clarity. But the officers did not distinguish carefully among the various categories of associational freedom. In their zeal to protect their associational freedom, the officers blurred the distinctions between political and intimate association and cited cases involving both types of association without clarifying how each applied to this particular relationship. Perhaps if the officers had distinguished more carefully among the various categories of association and buttressed their arguments with the precedents that supported each category, the court would have given more credence to their argument. Because it did not, the state was able to attack the officers' characterization of the *nature* of the relevant associational rights, and to argue that association for a purpose that was "not innocent" did not deserve constitutional protection.

As noted above, four types of association may be distinguished as deserving of constitutional protection: political, economic, social, and intimate. Although the officers characterized their association with Scarfo as "social," legal arguments made to buttress their constitutional challenge cite cases involving political and intimate association as well. The briefs did not differentiate these four types of association, nor did they question the state's assertion that association with Scarfo ipso facto meant influence by Scarfo. The officers' scrambling of the various categories of association gave the state the opportunity to select certain cases cited in the officers' brief and argue that they were not relevant (while, in fact, they were). It also permitted the state to minimize the importance of the officers' associational interest by arguing that it had no legitimate *business* purpose, even though social or intimate associations presumably are not entered for business purposes. Had the officers focused on intimate association, stemming from a long-time friendship begun as children, the support for their legal arguments would have been clearer and would have forced the court to confront the issue directly. Furthermore, the officers could have argued that, under the 1984 *Roberts* precedent, the state was required to demonstrate that it could not sufficiently protect the integrity of the casino industry through "means significantly less restrictive of associational freedom."[77] Considering the importance of the issue at stake, the officers' failure to argue fully the scope of associational protection and its pertinence to their particular situation contributed significantly to the courts' ability to deny that *any* associational interest merited protection from the application of the Casino Control Act.

Despite the fervor of their arguments, the union officers lost on all of their claims before the New Jersey Superior Court, Appellate Division. The court ruled that the act did not violate the officers' associational rights, for not every social relationship is protected by the Constitution, but only those involving "certain intimate human relationships" such as creating and sustaining a family, raising and educating children, and cohabiting with one's relatives." Even assuming that the relationship between the officers and Scarfo was protected, the court continued, the state had a compelling interest in protecting the integrity of the casino industry and fostering "public confidence and trust in the credibility and integrity of the regulatory process and of casino operations" which overrode any associational interests. The court remarked that "the operative question is not whether the associations between Gerace, Materio, and Scarfo are lawful or ethical, but rather what impact such associations have on the policies intended to be served by casino gaming regulation."[78] On appeal, the New Jersey Supreme Court denied review.[79]

While the outcome of this case may be attractive to most who want to reduce the influence of organized crime, it has troubling implications for individual liberty. Rather than define the exact nature of the officers' associational interest, the appellate court chose to assume, for the sake of argument, that "some" protected associational interest existed, but that the state's interest deserved greater protection.

This is not to say that, had the court defined the nature of the associational interest, it would have been forced to rule in favor of the officers. The court had found, using the strict scrutiny standard, that the state's interest in the appearance of integrity was compelling. Had the legal issues been presented more clearly, the court would have had to characterize the relationship as intimate, economic, political, or perhaps as social. That characterization would then have required the court to state specifically *why* the state's interest justified a burden on that association, and also to demonstrate that there were no equally satisfactory alternatives that imposed a lesser burden on association. The lack of attention to this issue by the parties permitted the court to sidestep it as well, leaving us with an opinion that neither specifies the *kind* of association that must defer to the state's compelling interest nor requires the state to demonstrate that alternative methods of preventing corruption in the casino industry that posed less of a burden on association were less effective.

The Federal Court Litigation

The union, independent from the officers, then pressed its own freedom of association claims in federal court. Here again, the union could not persuade the court that either the act's registration requirement or its exclusionary language violated the associational rights of the union or its members.

The union argued that its members had a First Amendment right to associate with the officers, stemming from their right to elect representatives of their own choosing under Section 7 of the National Labor Relations Act. The union stated that, even if the court disregarded the asserted associational rights of

Gerace and Materio, the associational rights of the local's membership were being trampled by the state's insistence that the officers remove themselves from leadership of the local.[80] The state disagreed, asserting that nowhere in First Amendment law did a right exist for union members to be represented by particular individuals, and arguing that Gerace and Materio had not been required to cease associating with Local 54 members, but had merely been required to surrender their union offices. While the state admitted that a government directive to stop associating with the local and its members would be a direct violation of the officers' First Amendment rights, such a directive had not been given.[81]

The union had asserted that the act infringed the rights of the union as an institution, acting on behalf of its members. The court disagreed, stating that the union could still carry on its collective bargaining and other representational activities, despite the absence of Gerace and Materio, and that the state's interest in combatting corruption clearly outweighed any interest the union might have in retaining the services of its officers.[82] On appeal, the Third Circuit upheld the trial court in all respects.[83] The union decided not to appeal to the U.S. Supreme Court, so the lengthy litigation finally came to an end.

It is possible, however, that litigation will ensue in the future if Gerace or Materio reapply to the commission under the act's provision for allowing "rehabilitated" individuals to overcome their previous exclusion under the act.[84] It remains to be determined whether legal theories of the significance of those used in the recent litigation will be able to be raised to challenge any commission reluctance to declare Gerace and/or Materio rehabilitated.

WHAT ASSOCIATIONAL FREEDOMS ARE AT STAKE?

When the associational freedom framework developed in the first section of this paper is applied to the facts and theories of the Local 54 litigation, it seems clear that neither the parties nor the courts addressed the issue thoroughly. Each of the three types of association recognized by the Supreme Court, as well as the fourth category of social association suggested in our framework could be alleged here, and protections for three distinct associational interests could have been analyzed. Instead, the parties blurred the distinctions among the categories of association, and the courts did not go beyond the arguments of the parties to clarify the interests at stake and the degree to which those interests deserved constitutional protection.

The Association Between the Officers and Scarfo

Throughout the litigation, Gerace and Materio admitted their former association with Scarfo, but insisted that it was a social relationship based upon friendship. Furthermore, the officers argued the commission had conceded that it had no clear evidence that either officer had committed a criminal act with Scarfo or on his behalf; thus, they had been deprived of their offices on the basis of guilt by association where the association was a purely social one, protected by the Constitution.[85] The plaintiffs complained that the statute's prohibition on association with career offenders was overbroad, for

> no distinction is made between associations which have a specific intent to further criminal activity and those that do not but which are merely expressions of legitimate First Amendment activities ... [N]o distinction is made between associations formed and conducted within the context of labor and representational activities within the Casino and Casino Hotel Industry and those which are formed and conducted outside of the purview of the Commission's jurisdiction and regulatory powers.[86]

The state, on the other hand, denied that the relationship between the officers and Scarfo was a social one. The courts agreed, saying that the association involved "more than innocent social contacts and less than knowing involvement in criminal acts." The federal district court conceded that social association deserved constitutional protection, but only when its purposes were innocent; and here, the court felt, the association was "not innocent."[87] At best, the court concluded, the officers' association with Scarfo was an economic one, of mutual benefit, with criminal overtones. The state had argued that the association with Scarfo had no legitimate purpose, and thus no constitutional protection. Furthermore, the state argued, the commission found that Scarfo influenced the selection of union leaders, participated in union business decisions, and wielded other forms of influence over Local 54, which made the association an economic one, not a social one.[88] The courts agreed, and found no constitutional protection for the association.

The type of association at stake here is important because it determines the standard of judicial review. Economic association would require only the minimum rationality standard, while intimate association would require the court to apply strict scrutiny. Although five federal and state court opinions addressed the associational freedom of the union officers, none addressed explicitly whether the standard of review should be minimum rationality or strict scrutiny.[89] Three of the opinions, however, included an analysis of whether the state's interest in the integrity of the gaming industry was compelling (applying strict scrutiny without stating so specifically), deciding that whatever associational protections the officers might have enjoyed for their relationship with Scarfo, the state's interest outweighed those protections.[90]

It appears that the associational interests asserted by the plaintiffs were limited to social association with Scarfo. Although they attempted to import the standard of review for intimate association from *Roberts,*[91] they characterized the relationship as social rather than as intimate. Given that intimate association could plausibly be viewed as encompassing an "enduring" friendship, Gerace and Materio could have argued that their association with Scarfo, based on its longevity and its ties to their families, was intimate association rather than social, which would have made it arguably more difficult for the courts to deny that the association was a protected one.

It is unlikely that the result would have changed, however, even if Gerace and Materio had been able to convince the courts that their association with Scarfo was an "intimate" one. Only rarely have individuals denied jobs on the basis of an intimate relationship challenged that denial successfully.[92] Furthermore, the courts emphasized that where such a denial was viewed as unduly burdensome, the relationship had been found to be innocent: even if the relationship had been truly "intimate," the relationship in this case could not be said to be innocent, the courts said.[93]

We are not arguing against the court's use of strict scrutiny in these cases; if the interests at stake are intimate association, as we believe they may be, then strict scrutiny is the correct standard. What *is* troubling, however, is the burden on association, imposed by the state and sanctioned by the courts, without a more careful articulation of the nature of the association, its relative importance in constitutional terms to other forms of association, and the consideration of less restrictive alternatives to accomplish the state's interest in the integrity of the casino industry.

The Association Between the Officers and the Union

A second associational interest alleged by the plaintiffs was the association between the union as an organization and the officers. The union asserted a First Amendment right to choose its own officers and to take group action to further the interests of union members through the activities of those officers.[94] It asserted that the very requirement of registration with the commission infringed upon these protected associational interests. It also argued that depriving Local 54 of Gerace and Materio's services would cripple the union's ability to represent its members effectively.

The state scoffed at the allegation that only Gerace and Materio could conduct union business effectively, and the courts agreed. The registration requirement did not prevent the union from performing its functions as a collective bargaining agent,[95] and other officers were knowledgeable and presumably capable of conducting union business. Claims that "Gerace is the only one who can competently run the union are implausible," asserted federal district court judge Brotman.[96] Although the union had argued that "[t]he issue here is that of protecting the union's fundamental First Amendment rights, not whether the Union can survive an improper intrusion into those rights,"[97] the appellate court declared "We do not find that the union's right of free association extends so far as to include a right to elect particular union officers."[98]

Although the union made a claim late in the litigation that forcing the officers to resign burdened a "quasi political" association,[99] the court said "we do not find that the state's disqualification provision impermissibly burdens the union's expressive activity. Rather, the restriction...is akin to a reasonable regulation of a manner of expression and only incidentally affects the union's expressive activity."[100] What the court appears to be saying is that the casino law merely limits the union's choice of a spokesperson for its political activities, rather than limiting those activities altogether. While legal precedent has dealt with situations where membership in organizations was burdened, there is no Supreme Court precedent for a situation such as this, where the organization is told that a particular individual cannot speak for it, or represent it, at the risk of the organization's losing the majority of its financial resources.[101] The court could have reached the same result by conceding a protected political association but found that the state's compelling interest in the integrity of the casino regulatory system outweighed that interest. The court's refusal to acknowledge the burden on the union's expressive activity is troubling because it reduces protection for the expressive activities of unions, and puzzling because such a limitation on expressive activity was unnecessary to reach the end the court sought.

The Association Between the Officers and Union Members

The plaintiffs also asserted a third type of associational interest: that between the officers and individual union members. They argued that the law infringed upon the members' "First Amendment right" to choose their own bargaining representatives, guaranteed by Section 7 of the National Labor Relations Act.[102] The union argued that, "[t]he challenged statute is a draconian impediment to the union movement in that it gives the State an absolute veto power over whom the union members can choose as their leaders."[103]

The state, citing an earlier case in which legislation aimed at reducing corruption in labor unions was upheld, stated that "[f]reedom of association does not go so far as to guarantee union members the right to be represented by a particular individual no matter what the circumstances."[104] The courts agreed, noting that Gerace and Materio could still be union members, and, in fact, they could still serve as union officers, albeit not in a union affiliated with the casino industry.[105]

The plaintiffs did not specify which kind of association this alleged "freedom to choose" entailed. One could argue that the selection of representatives to bargain over terms and conditions of employment is economic, albeit with political overtones. Social association was not burdened, as the members could continue to associate with Gerace and Materio as co-members rather than as leaders. Even if the plaintiffs had argued a burden on economic association, the deferential standard of review for burdens on such association, combined with the judicial findings that the state's interest in burdening this association was compelling, would not have changed the outcome of the litigation.

IMPLICATIONS OF THE LOCAL 54 LITIGATION

Examining the approaches of the parties to the associational freedom claims demonstrates that none of the actors addressed the full spectrum of claims that could have been made, and that the courts have not produced a thorough nor comprehensive analysis. The precedent created by these opinions is troubling, for they deny the existence or the significance of associational freedom for union officers, union members, or unions themselves. The issue is important from a social policy perspective as well as a legal one. Although unions have been called "voluntary organizations" (Fellman 1963, p. 48), in many ways they differ sharply from voluntary organizations in terms of both the benefits and burdens under which they operate. In many respects, they have adapted in response to the laws established to partially shield them from the vagaries of the marketplace.

Unions enjoy a special legal status which includes some protection from the conspiracy and restraint-of-trade laws as well as limitations on the courts' use of injunctive relief. They also have the ability to sue, despite the fact that they are unincorporated associations (Rice 1962, pp. 91-92). Furthermore, the federal labor laws give the elected bargaining agent a monopoly in representing all the members of the bargaining unit, as long as a majority of the members voted for that union. In most states, union and agency shops, where individuals must join or at least make financial contributions whether or not they wish to, strengthen the power of the union while denying individuals the right not to associate with other bargaining unit members.[106] In addition, unions control huge pension and welfare funds, make sizable investments through these funds, and wield considerable political clout. Rice (1962, p. 92) asserts that "the legislature, in permitting compulsory unionism, is endowing the labor union with a governmental character ... [and this protection gives] semipublic status [to] the erstwhile private group."

But unions have substantial burdens that purely voluntary associations do not encounter. They are subject to the civil rights laws, and may not discriminate in admitting individuals to membership.[107] They have a judicially imposed duty of fair representation owed to every member of the bargaining unit, irrespective of whether the individual is a dues-paying member of the union.[108] Union officers and agents must report on their own financial assets and the financial operations of the union to the U.S. Department of Justice, and federal law governs some of the internal operations of unions.[109] Undoubtedly these restrictions have been placed upon unions as a result of misconduct by certain unions over the years, but the restrictions upon the operations of unions do not obviate the substantial political, economic, and social purposes of unions.

The foregoing argument is not meant to imply that government should reduce or cease its efforts to eliminate the influence of organized crime from industries and the unions linked to those industries. The regulatory scheme developed by New Jersey for the casino industry has withstood vigorous legal challenge, receiving the blessing of the highest state and federal courts. Because this regulatory effort will continue and likely increase (Manserus 1989), it is desirable to consider more explicitly the appropriate balance of crime fighting and the broad range of associational freedoms in this unique context.

In balancing these concerns, policymakers may wish to consider that, despite the breadth of New Jersey's insistence that individuals involved in the casino industry not associate with "career offenders," the statute has not been completely successful in eliminating the influence of union officers alleged to have ties to organized crime.[110] This lack of success, combined with the requirement that government burdens on association demonstrate that they are the least restrictive alternative, suggest that policymakers may wish to consider some regulatory alternatives. For example, the legislature might require the enforcement agencies to produce credible evidence that the association is for the purpose of, or has resulted in, some kind of criminal activity. Or perhaps the state might have to show some evidence that the "career offender" wielded influence, either directly or indirectly, in union affairs.[111] This latter "less restrictive alternative" would not have changed the outcome of the Local 54 case, but it would have resulted in a more tightly reasoned and limited opinion. While most individuals would agree that people with mob connections should not be union leaders, the courts' interpretation of New Jersey's regulatory approach yields a principle that may well be troublesome in other settings. This principle may, in fact, have the effect of virtually eliminating associational freedom for individuals connected with closely regulated industries.

ACKNOWLEDGMENTS

The authors are grateful to Gary Ehrlich, Deputy Attorney General, New Jersey Division of Gaming Enforcement and Eugene Schwartz, Assistant Attorney General and Deputy Director, Legal, New Jersey Division of Gaming Enforcement as well as to two anonymous reviewers for their comments on an earlier draft of this chapter.

NOTES

1. The First Amendment reads "Congress shall make no law respecting an establishment of religion, or prohibiting the free exercise thereof; or abridging the freedom of speech, or of the

press; or the right of the people peaceably to assemble, and to petition the Government for a redress of grievances." The Supreme Court ruled in *NAACP* v. *Alabama ex rel. Patterson*, 357 U.S. 449 (1958) that freedom of association derived from the explicitly-protected rights of speech and assembly, and thus itself was protected by the First Amendment.

2.   *U.S.* v. *Brown*, 318 U.S. 437 (1965) (struck as unconstitutional Sec. 504 of the Labor Management Reporting and Disclosure Act that made current or former members of the Communist party ineligible to hold office in or serve as a consultant to a labor union).

3.   *National Socialist Party* v. *Skokie*, 432 U.S. 43 (1977).

4.   *Lanzetta* v. *New Jersey*, 306 U.S. 451 (1939).

5.   *Roberts* v. *United States Jaycees*, 468 U.S. 609 (1984).

6.   *Village of Belle Terre* v. *Borass*, 416 U.S. 1 (1974).

7.   For a discussion of attempts to reduce corruption in certain industries through government regulation, see President's Commission on Organized Crime, 1986.

8.   See, for example, New Jersey Solid Waste Management Act, N.J.S.A. 13:1E-1 to 13:1E-135.

9.   New York Waterfront Act, N.Y. Unconsol. Laws (65) §9933.

10.   N.J.S.A. 5:12-1 et seq.

11.   In reporting on a series of polls about organized labor's image, Medoff (1984) noted that the honesty and ethical standards of labor leaders were found to be "very low or low" by 44 percent of the respondents. Among various occupations this was surpassed only by car salesmen at 55 percent. In another poll, 54 percent of the respondents agreed with the statement that "many union leaders have known ties with racketeers and organized crime."

12.   For a history of union efforts at self-reform, see Benson (1979, pp. 172-244).

13.   18 U.S.C. §1961 et. seq.

14.   *United States* v. *Local 560,* International Brotherhood of Teamsters, 581 F. Supp. 279 (D.N.J. 1984), aff'd, 780 F.2d 267 (3d Cir. 1985), cert. denied, 106 S. Ct. 2247 (1986). This case was brought under the civil RICO statute.

15.   *United States* v. *Roofers' Local* 30, 128 LRRM 2580 (E.D. Pa. 1988). The judge created a "decreeship" rather than a trusteeship, but the special master appointed under the "decreeship" appears to have powers similar to those of a trustee.

16.   *Hotel and Restaurant Employees and Bartenders International Union* v. *Danziger*, 536 F. Supp. 317 (D.N.J. 1982), rev'd, 709 F.2d 815 (3d Cir. 1983), rev'd and remanded sub nom *Brown* v. *Hotel and Restaurant Employees and Bartenders Union Local 54*, 468 U.S. 491 (1984), *Hotel and Restaurant Employees and Bartenders International Union* v. *Read*, 597 F. Supp. 1431 (D.N.J. 1984), aff'd mem. 772 F.2d 895 (3d Cir. 1985), 641 F. Supp. 757 (D.N.J. 1986), aff'd, 832 F.2d 263 (3d Cir. 1987); In re: Local 54, 203 N.J. Super. 297 (App. Div. 1985), certif. denied, 102 N.J. 352 (1985), cert. denied sub nom *Gerace* v. *New Jersey Casino Control Commission*, 106 S. Ct. 1467 (1986).

17.   Although the U.S. Supreme Court rendered an opinion in this case, it did not address the associational freedom issue, but decided the case on pre-emption grounds alone.

18.   See, for example, *Elfbrandt* v. *Russell*, 384 U.S. 11 (1966) (striking an Arizona law subjecting state employees to discharge for membership in the Communist party). See also *Shelton* v. *Tucker*, 364 U.S. 479 (1960) (holding unconstitutional an Arkansas law requiring public school teachers and college faculty to disclose every organization in which he or she was a member during the previous five years) and *Keyishian* v. *Board of Regents*, 385 U.S. 589 (1967) (invalidating a New York law that excluded from state employment anyone who was or had ever been a Communist).

19.   The first federal statute offering significant protection to unions in the private sector (excluding railroads, which received protection under the Railway Labor Act of 1926) was the Wagner Act, passed in 1935. 29 U.S.C. §141 et seq.

20.   *NAACP* v. *Alabama ex rel. Patterson*, 357 U.S. 449 (1958).

21. An example of such a law was New Jersey's Gangster Act that provided criminal sanctions for "any person not engaged in any lawful occupation, known to be a member of any gang…" The U.S. Supreme Court struck the law as unconstitutionally vague in *Lanzetta* v. *New Jersey,* 306 U.S. 451 (1939).

22. The minimum rationality test is described in the text accompanying Note 44 (p. 299).

23. *Garcia* v. *Texas State Board of Medical Examiners,* 384 F. Supp. 434 (W.D. Tex. 1974), aff'd mem. 421 U.S. 995 (1975).

24. 381 U.S. 479 (1965).

25. Compare *U.S. Dept. of Agriculture* v. *Moreno,* 413 U.S. 528 (1973) (law denying food stamps to households of "unrelated persons" struck; the court decided this case on equal protection grounds, but discussed the associational interests involved in dicta) with *Village of Belle Terre* v. *Borass,* 416 U.S. 1 (1974) (zoning ordinance forbidding more than two unrelated people from sharing a dwelling upheld under minimum rationality test; no protected associational interest found).

26. *Hishon* v. *King & Spaulding,* 467 U.S. 69 (1984).

27. *Roberts* v. *United States Jaycees,* 468 U.S. 609 (1984).

28. *Board of Directors of Rotary International* v. *Rotary Club,* 481 U.S. 537 (1987).

29. *Kiwanis International* v. *Ridgewood Kiwanis Club,* 627 F. Supp. 1381 (D.N.J. 1986).

30. *New York State Club Association* v. *New York City,* 108 S.Ct. 2225 (1988).

31. In each case, plaintiffs posed state or federal civil rights claims which the defendants countered with freedom of association claims; in each case, the courts determined that there were no protected intimate associations.

32. For a thoughtful discussion of the clash between equality and freedom of association, see Failinger (1987).

33. *Roberts* v. *United States Jaycees,* 468 U.S. 609, 618 (1984). See also *Board of Directors of Rotary International* v. *Rotary Club of Duarte,* 481 U.S. 537 (1987).

34. *Roberts* v. *United States Jaycees,* 468 U.S. 609, 634 (1984). (O'Connor concurrence).

35. For a thorough analysis of the historical development of the freedom of association doctrine through 1980, see Abernathy (1981).

36. *NAACP* v. *Alabama ex rel. Patterson,* 357 U.S. 449 (1958); *NAACP* v. *Button,* 371 U.S. 415 (1963).

37. *U.S.* v. *Robel,* 389 U.S. 258 (1967) (striking statute forbidding defense workers from membership in the Communist party); *Elfbrandt* v. *Russell,* 384 U.S. 11 (1966) (striking loyalty oath requiring that employee not be a member of the Communist party). But see *Cole* v. *Richardson,* 405 U.S. 676 (1972) (upholding oath that required employee to swear to uphold and defend the Constitution).

38. *Williams* v. *Rhodes,* 393 U.S. 23 (1968) (state law regulating ability of new political parties to be placed on ballot struck as unduly burdensome). See also *Cousins* v. *Wigoda,* 419 U.S. 477 (1975) (invalidating state law that nullified national political party rules regarding presidential convention delegate selection).

39. *Roberts* v. *United States Jaycees,* 468 U.S. 609, 623 (1984).

40. See, for example, *Roberts* v. *United States Jaycees,* 468 U.S. 609, 634-638 (1984) (O'Connor concurrence).

41. *Garcia* v. *Texas State Board of Medical Examiners,* 384 F. Supp. 434 (W.D. Tex. 1974), aff'd mem, 421 U.S. 995 (1975) (using minimal rationality standard to uphold Texas law requiring that health maintenance organizations be administered by medical doctors). Criteria for admission to professions have also been challenged as unconstitutionally vague, under a due process theory.

42. See, for example, *Zauderer* v. *Office of Disciplinary Counsel of Superior Court of Ohio,* 471 U.S. 626, 638 (1985) (determining that state could regulate lawyer advertising under the standard of a "substantial governmental interest" using means that "directly advance that interest") and *Central Hudson Gas and Electric Corporation* v. *Public Service Commission of New York,*

447 U.S. 557, 566 (1980) (determining that the regulation of commercial speech "may extend only as far as the interest it serves" and articulating a standard of review requiring the government to demonstrate that the law "directly advances a substantial government interest and is appropriately tailored to that purpose").

43.   *Railway Mail Association* v. *Corsi,* 326 U.S. 88 (1945); see also *Steele* v. *L & N Railroad,* 323 U.S. 192 (1944).

44.   *Central Hudson Gas and Electric Corp.* v. *Public Service Commission,* 447 U.S. 557 (1980).

45.   *Roberts* v. *United States Jaycees,* 468 U.S. 609, 634 (1984) (O'Connor concurrence). O'Connor apparently believes that the "substantial state interest" standard is insufficiently deferential for court review of burdens on economic or commercial association, and has deplored a recent opinion in which Justice Brennan applied that standard to invalidate a Kentucky bar association regulation prohibiting the use of truthful, nondeceptive letters by attorneys to solicit business. In a dissenting opinion, O'Connor wrote:

> We have never held ... that commercial speech has the same constitutional status as speech on matters of public policy, and the Court has consistently purported to review laws regulating commercial speech under a significantly more deferential standard of review.

Shapero v. *Kentucky Bar Association,* 56 U.S.L.W. 4532, 4537 (June 13, 1988). She cited an earlier case, *Ohralik* v. *Ohio State Bar Association,* 436 U.S. 447 (1978) in which the court upheld an Ohio law banning in-person solicitation by lawyers. In that opinion (pp. 455-456), Justice Powell wrote:

> To require a parity of constitutional protection for commercial and noncommercial speech alike could invite dilution ... of the force of the Amendment's guarantee with respect to the latter kind of speech ... we... have afforded commercial speech a limited measure of protection, commensurate with its subordinate position in the scale of First Amendment values, while allowing modes of regulation that might be impermissible in the realm of noncommercial expression.

46.   *Thorpe* v. *Housing Authority of City of Durham,* 386 U.S. 670 (1967) (tenant alleged she was evicted because she served as president of a tenants' organization; the court remanded for a statement of reasons for the eviction).

47.   *Healy* v. *James,* 408 U.S. 169 (1972) (college cannot use subject-matter test to determine whether to grant official recognition to campus group).

48.   See, for example, *Lanzetta* v. *New Jersey.* For an excellent discussion of state burdens on association with "bad" people and the courts' views of those laws, see Fellman (1963, pp. 77-86).

49.   *Wilson* v. *Taylor,* 733 F.2d 1539 (11th Cir. 1984) (Overturning, on freedom of association grounds, the dismissal of a police officer fired for dating the daughter of a reputed organized crime figure. The court noted that, had the city of Winter Park argued that the nature of police work justified the associational burden, the discharge might have been upheld.) Contra, *Baron* v. *Meloni,* 556 F. Supp. 796 (W.D. N.Y. 1983) (upholding discharge of deputy sheriff for associating with wife of suspected organized crime figure who was under surveillance by sheriff's office).

50.   *Sawyer* v. *Sandstrom,* 615 F.2d 311 (5th Cir. 1980).

51.   *Roberts* v. *United States Jaycees,* 468 U.S. 609, 620 (1984).

52.   *Board of Directors of Rotary International* v. *Rotary Club,* 481 U.S. 537 (1987).

53.   *Griswold* v. *Connecticut,* 381 U.S. 479 (1965) and *Department of Agriculture* v. *Moreno,* 413 U.S. 528 (1973).

54.   *Village of Belle Terre* v. *Borass,* 416 U.S. 1 (1974).

55. See, for example, *Horosko* v. *School District of Mt. Pleasant Township,* 6 A.2d 866 (Pa. 1939) (upholding dismissal of teacher for unprofessional conduct because she worked evenings as bartender in husband's bar); *Hollenbaugh* v. *Carnegie Free Library,* 436 F. Supp. 1328 (W.D. Pa. 1977), aff'd mem, 578 F.2d 1374 (3d Cir.), cert. denied, 439 U.S. 1052 (1978) (upholding discharge of library employees, one of whom was married to someone else, for living together and conceiving a child out of wedlock); *Ferguson* v. *Freedom Forge Corp.,* 604 F. Supp. 1157 (W.D. Pa. 1985) (upholding discharge of foreman for associating with former company president who had recently been fired). Also see *Wilson* v. *Taylor,* 733 F. 2d 1539 (11th Cir. 1984). The fact that the courts have refused to find a protected property right in one's job is an additional disincentive to the use of strict scrutiny in these cases. See, for example, Gordon and Lee (1990).

56. N.J.S.A. 5:12-1 et seq. For a discussion of the provisions of the Casino Control Act and the concerns it attempts to address, see Cohen (1982) and O'Brien and Flaherty (1985).

57. N.J.S.A. 5:12-86(f) (emphasis added).

58. N.J.S.A. 5:12-93; N.J.A.C. 19:41-12.8 (1982). If the union does not register, the law permits the Commission to order the casinos to transmit neither dues nor pension payments to the union. N.J.S.A. 5:12-93(b).

59. Brief on Behalf of Respondent, State of New Jersey, In re: Hotel and Restaurant Employees and Bartenders International Union Local 54, 203 N.J. Super. 297 (A.D. 1985). At the time of the litigation, ten casinos were in operation in Atlantic City.

60. The law permits, but does not require, the Commission to direct the Division of Gaming Enforcement to investigate the background of any applicant for registration or licensure under the Act. N.J.S.A. 5:12-76 and 94. In practice, however, the Division investigates every applicant. Interview with G. Henningson, Deputy Director, Operations, Divison of Gaming Enforcement, Department of Law and Public Safety, Trenton, N.J. (Aug. 27, 1987).

61. An earlier attempt by Florida to require union business agents to meet state licensing criteria had been overturned by the U.S. Supreme Court in *Hill* v. *Florida ex rel. Watson,* 325 U.S. 538 (1945) on the theory that Congress occupied the entire area of labor-management relations when it passed the National Labor Relations Act. Local 54's challenge to the New Jersey law relied heavily on the Hill precedent. The union also challenged a provision of the Casino Control Act that empowered the commission to order that the employees' dues and employer pension contributions be withheld from the union as a sanction for failure to register with (or a registration being disapproved by) the commission. This issue was not addressed by the Supreme Court on the grounds of ripeness, as the sanction had not yet been applied.

62. The union challenged this provision on overbreadth (denial of associational rights) and vagueness (denial of due process) theories.

63. The union had sought to enjoin the commission hearing pending its challenge to the law's constitutionality; an injunction was denied. *Hotel Employees and Bartenders International Union* v. *Danziger,* 536 F. Supp. 317 (D.N.J. 1982).

64. Opinion of the New Jersey Casino Control Commission in the Matter of Hotel and Restaurant Empoyees [sic] and Bartenders International Union Local 54, Docket No. 81-LO-1, Sept. 28, 1982.

65. *Hotel and Restaurant Employees and Bartenders International Union* v. *Danziger,* 709 F.2d 815 (3d Cir. 1983).

66. *Brown* v. *Hotel and Restaurant Employees and Bartenders International Union Local 54,* 468 U.S. 491 (1984). For a discussion of *Brown,* see Comment (1985).

67. 363 U.S. 144 (1960). *DeVeau* was not exactly on point, for the New York law in question disqualified union officers who had been convicted of crimes, not merely for associating with reputed organized crime figures.

68. For an account of the bistate efforts to reduce the influence of organized crime in the longshore industry, see *International Longshoremen's Organization* v. *Waterfront Commission*

of New York Harbor, 495 F. Supp. 1101 (S.D.N.Y. 1980), aff'd in part, 642 F.2d 666 (2d Cir. 1981), cert. denied, 454 U.S. 966 (1981).

69.   *Brown* v. *Hotel and Restaurant Employees,* p. 508. The holding in *Brown* was later incorporated into federal law in the Comprehensive Crime Control Act of 1984. The relevant provision states:

> Notwithstanding this or any other Act regulating labor-management relations, each State shall have the authority to enact and enforce, as part of a comprehensive statutory system to eliminate the threat of pervasive racketeering activity in an industry that is, or over time has been, affected by such activity, a provision of law that applies equally to employers, employees, and collective bargaining representatives, which provision of law governs service in any position in a local labor organization which acts or seeks to act in that State as a collective bargaining representative pursuant to the National Labor Relations Act, in the industry that is subject to that program.

28 U.S.C. §524(a) (West 1988 Supp.) The Supreme Court did not address the associational freedom claims originally included in the union's complaint because the Third Circuit had not reached these issues.

70.   Supplemental Order of the New Jersey Casino Control Commission in the Matter of Hotel Employees and Bartenders International Union Local 54, Docket No. 81-LO-1, September 12, 1984.

71.   *Hotel and Restaurant Employees and Bartenders International Union* v. *Danziger,* 597 F. Supp. 1431 (D.N.J. 1984).

72.   In re: Hotel and Restaurant Employees and Bartenders International Union Local 54, 203 N.J. Super. 297 (A.D. 1985).

73.   Although three union officers challenged the act under the pre-emption theory, only Gerace and Materio pursued freedom of association challenges. The third officer, Karlos LaSane, had been disqualified on the basis of a prior felony conviction. He did not pursue freedom of association claims, but did participate in the vagueness challenge.

74.   The vagueness claim, argued under a due process theory, was also unsuccessful in both state and federal courts.

75.   Brief of Appellants Gerace, Materio, and LaSane, In re: Hotel and Restaurant Employees and Bartenders Union Local 54, 203 N.J. Super. 297 (A.D. 1985).

76.   Brief of Defendants in Support of Cross Motion for Summary Judgment, In re: Hotel and Restaurant Employees and Bartenders Union Local 54, 203 NJ Super.297 (A.D. 1985).

77.   *Roberts* v. *United States Jaycees,* 468 U.S. 609, 623 (1984).

78.   203 N.J. Super. 297, 328 (A.D. 1985).

79.   102 N.J. 352 (1985), cert. denied sub nom *Gerace* v. *New Jersey Casino Control Commission,* 106 S. Ct. 1467 (1986). The officers had decided to press their claims in state court; therefore, their litigation had ended, but the union asserted protected associational interests independent of the officers' and chose to litigate those claims in federal court. Brief on Behalf of Respondent, p. 10.

80.   Brief in Support of Motion for Summary Judgment, Hotel and Restaurant Employees and Bartenders International Union Local 54 v. Read, 641 F. Supp. 757 (D.N.J. 1986).

81.   Brief on Behalf of Defendant Division of Gaming Enforcement, Hotel and Restaurant Employees and Bartenders International Union Local 54 v. Read, 641 F. Supp. 757 (D.N.J. 1986).

82.   *Hotel and Restaurant Employees and Bartenders International Union Local 54* v. *Read,* 641 F. Supp. 757, 765 (D.N.J. 1986).

83.   *Hotel and Restaurant Employees and Bartenders International Union Local 54* v. *Read,* 832 F.2d 263 (3d Cir. 1987).

84. Section 90(h) of the act describes the showing an individual must make to demonstrate rehabilitation sufficient to overcome the presumption of unfitness because of the individual's inability to meet the statutory criteria for licensure. N.J.S.A. 5:12-90(h).

85. Brief on Behalf of Appellants Gerace, Materio, and LaSane, p. 66.

86. Plaintiffs' Memorandum in Support of Motion for Preliminary Injunction, *Hotel and Restaurant Employees and Bartenders International Union Local 54* v. *Danziger,* 536 F. Supp. 317 (D.N.J. 1982), p. 14.

87. *Hotel and Restaurant Employees and Bartenders International Union Local 54* v. *Read,* 597 F. Supp. 1431, 1446 (D.N.J. 1985), aff'd mem, 772 F.2d 895 (3d Cir. 1985).

88. Brief [of Defendants] in Opposition to Application for Temporary Restraining Order, *Hotel and Restaurant Employees and Bartenders International Union Local 54* v. *Read,* 597 F. Supp. 1431 (D.N.J. 1985).

89. Three courts, although finding no burden on a constitutionally protected association, determined the state's interest to be compelling, presumably because "case law is somewhat unsettled on the freedom of association issue presented by plaintiffs," *Hotel and Restaurant Employees* v. *Read,* 597 F. Supp., p. 1448, and to reduce the potential for reversal by an appellate court.

90. In re: Hotel and Restaurant Employees and Bartenders International Union Local 54, 203 N.J. Super., p. 326; *Hotel and Restaurant Employees and Bartenders International Union Local 54* v. *Read,* 597 F. Supp., p. 1447; *Hotel and Restaurant Employees and Bartenders International Union Local 54* v. *Read,* 641 F. Supp., p. 765.

91. Brief on Behalf of Appellants Gerace, Materio, and LaSane, p. 66.

92. See, for example, *Wilson* v. *Taylor,* p. 1447. Also see *Baron* v. *Meloni,* 556 F. Supp. 796 (W.D.N.Y. 1983) and *Hollenbaugh* v. *Carnegie Free Library,* 436 F. Supp. 1328 (W.D. Pa. 1977), aff'd mem, 578 F.2d 1374 (3d Cir.).

93. *Hotel and Restaurant Employees and Bartenders International Union Local 54* v. *Read,* 597 F. Supp. 1431, 1446 (D.N.J. 1985), aff'd mem., 772 F.2d 895 (3d Cir. 1985).

94. Plaintiffs' Memorandum in Support of Motion for Preliminary Injunction, *Hotel and Restaurant Employees and Bartenders International Union Local 54* v. *Danziger,* 536 F. Supp. 317 (D.N.J. 1982).

95. Hotel and Restaurant Employees, 641 F. Supp., pp. 763-764.

96. Hotel and Restaurant Employees, 597 F. Supp., p. 1449.

97. Brief for Appellant, *Hotel and Restaurant Employees and Bartenders International Union Local 54* v. *Read,* 832 F. 2d 263 (3d Cir. 1987).

98. Hotel and Restaurant Employees, 832 F.2d, p. 267.

99. Reply Brief in Support of Plaintiffs' Motion for Summary Judgment, *Hotel and Restaurant Employees and Bartenders International Union Local 54* v. *Read,* 641 F. Supp. 757 (D.N.J. 1986).

100. Hotel and Restaurant Employees, 832 F.2d, p. 267.

101. The union was threatened with the cutoff of all dues paid by casino employees if the officers did not resign.

102. Brief in Support of Motion for Summary Judgment, *Hotel and Restaurant Employees and Bartenders International Union* v. *Read,* 641 F. Supp. 757 (D.N.J. 1986), p. 16.

103. Petition for a Writ of Certiorari, *Gerace* v. *N.J. Casino Control Commission,* 106 S. Ct. 1467 (1986), p. 39.

104. The cited language is from *International Longshoremen's Organization* v. *Waterfront Commission of New York Harbor,* 495 F. Supp. 1101, 1134 n. 44 (S.D.N.Y. 1980), aff'd in part, 642 F.2d 666 (2d Cir. 1981), cert. denied, 454 U.S. 966 (1981).

105. In re: Hotel and Restaurant Employees and Bartenders International Union Local 54, 203 N.J. Super. 297, 349 (A.D. 1985): *Hotel and Restaurant Employees and Bartenders International Union Local 54* v. *Read,* 597 F. Supp. 1431, 1449 (D.N.J. 1985).

106.   See, for example, *Railway Employees Department* v. *Hanson,* 351 U.S. 225 (1956). See also *Abood* v. *Detroit Board of Eduation,* 431 U.S. 209 (1977).

107.   Unions are subject to the provisions of Title VII of the Civil Rights Act of 1964, which forbids discrimination by unions in admission to membership or in selecting employees. 42 U.S.C. §2000e et seq.

108.   *Vaca* v. *Sipes,* 386 U.S. 171 (1967).

109.   Labor-Management Reporting and Disclosure Act of 1959, 29 U.S.C. §§401-531 (1973).

110.   A recent study of the impact of New Jersey's Casino Control Act has concluded that its restrictions on union officers have had little success in reducing the alleged influence of organized crime figures on Local 54. See Lee and Chelius (1989).

111.   The state had alleged that Scarfo influenced union matters, but the opinions do not address this issue explicitly.

REFERENCES

Abernathy, M.G. 1981. *The Right of Assembly and Association,* 2nd ed. Columbia: University of South Carolina Press.

Bellace, J. and A. Berkowitz. 1979. *The Landrum-Griffen Act: Twenty Years of Federal Protection of Union Members Rights,* No. 19. Philadelphia: Wharton School Labor Relations and Public Policy Series.

Benson, H.W. 1979. *Democratic Rights for Union Members.* New York: Association for Union Democracy.

Brett, J.M. 1980. Why Employees Want Unions. *Organizational Dynamics* (Spring):47-59.

Comment: Constitutional Law—Federal Preemption—New Jersey's Casino Control Act Not Preempted by NLRA—*Brown* v. *Hotel & Restaurant Employees International Union Local 54.* 1985. *Seton Hall Law Review* 15:656-684.

Cohen, R.B. 1982. The New Jersey Casino Control Act: Creation of a Regulatory System. *Seton Hall Legislative Journal* 6:1-20.

Emerson, T.I. 1964. Freedom of Association and Freedom of Expression. *Yale Law Journal* 74:1-35.

Failinger, M.A. 1987. Equality Versus the Right to Choose Associates: A Critique of Hannah Arendt's View of the Supreme Court's Dilemma. *University of Pittsburgh Law Review* 49:143-188.

Fellman, D. 1963. *The Constitutional Right of Association.* Chicago: University of Chicago Press.

Gordon, M.E. and B.A. Lee. 1990. Property Rights in Jobs: Workforce, Behavioral, and Legal Perspectives. Pp. 303-348 in *Research in Personnel and Human Resources Management,* edited by G. Ferris and K. Rowland. Greenwich, CT: JAI Press.

Hutchinson, J. 1972. *The Imperfect Union.* New York: E.P. Dutton & Co.

Karst, K.L. 1980. The Freedom of Intimate Association. *Yale Law Journal* 89:624-692.

Lee, B.A. and J.R. Chelius. 1989. Government Regulation of Union-Management Corruption: The Casino Industry Experience in New Jersey. *Industrial and Labor Relations Review* 42:536-548.

Manserus, L. 1989. As Racketeering Law Expands, So Does Pressure to Rein It In. *New York Times* (March 12), p. E-4.

Medoff, J. 1984. Study for the AFL-CIO on Public's Image of Unions. *Daily Labor Report,* 247 (December 24), pp. D1-D23.

New York State Organized Crime Task Force. 1988. *Corruption and Racketeering in the New York City Construction Industry.* Ithaca, NY: ILR Press.

New York Times. June 27, 1989. Broad Use of RICO is Upheld, pp. D1, D23.

O'Brien, T.R. and M.J. Flaherty. 1985. Regulation of the Atlantic City Casino Industry and Attempts to Control Its Infiltration by Organized Crime. *Rutgers Law Journal* 16:721-758.

President's Commission on Organized Crime. 1986. *The Edge: Organized Crime, Business, and Labor Unions*. Washington, DC: U.S. Government Printing Office.

Raggi, R. 1977. An Independent Right to Freedom of Association. *Harvard Civil Rights-Civil Liberty Law Review* 12:1-30.

Raskin, A.H. 1989. The Teamsters Take It On the Chin. *New York Times* (March 17), p. A35.

Rice, C. 1962. *Freedom of Association*. New York: New York University Press.

Tribe, L. 1978. *American Constitutional Law*. Mineola, NY: Foundation Press.

Van Alstyne, W.W. 1984. *Interpretations of the First Amendment*. Durham, NC: Duke University Press.

Advances in Industrial and Labor Relations

Edited by **David Lewin,** *Graduate School of Business, Columbia University,* **David B. Lipsky,** *New York State School of Industrial and Labor Relations, Cornell University* and **Donna Sockell,** *Graduate School of Business, Columbia University*

REVIEW: "Annual research volumes ideally should supplement the mission pursued by journals. They should provide an outlet for material that by some standard other than quality is precluded from accpetance by journals. The tricky part is choosing that standard. David Lipsky explicitly defines such a standard by selecting for this volume papers of two kinds: integrated reviews of the literature and theoretical works...
The papers in this volume are a useful contribution to the field."
— *Industrial and Labor Relations Review*

This series publishes major original research on all subjects within the field of industrial relations, including union behavior, structure, and government; collective bargaining, in both the private and public sectors; labor law and public policies affecting the employment relationships; the economics of collective bargaining; and international comparative labor movements. Reflecting the multi-disciplinary nature of industrial relations, its contributors include economists, sociologists, and other social scientists as well as lawyers and specialists in labor relations. Although there are now several journals that publish research on industrial relations, the space limitations of these journals preclude their publishing longer—and possibly more reflective—studies. Many industrial relations scholars have sought a forum for the publication of research that is too long for a journal article but not enough for a book or monograph.

Volume 1, 1983, 283 pp. $63.50
ISBN 0-89232-250-0

Edited by **David B. Lipsky,** *New York State School of Industrial and Labor Relations, Cornell University* and **Joel M. Douglas,** *National Center for the Study of Collective Bargaining in Higher Education, Baruch College.*

CONTENTS: Preface, *David B. Lipsky.* **Union Organizing in Manufacturing: 1973-76,** *Ronald Seeber, Cornell University.*

The Unionization Process: A Review of the Literature, *Richard Block and Steven L. Premack, Michigan State University.* **Unionization in Secondary Labor Markets: The Historical Case of Building Services Employees,** *Peter Doeringer, Boston University.* **The Relationship between Seniority, Ability, and the Promotion of Union and Nonunion Workers,** *Craig A. Olson and Chris J. Berger, State University of New York, Buffalo.* **The Effects of Civil Service Systems and Unionsim on Pay Outcomes in the Public Sector,** *David Lewin, Columbia University.* **Organizations and Expectations: Organizational Determinants of Union Membership Demands,** *Samuel Bacharach and Stephen M. Mitchell, Cornell University.* **Bargainers' Perceptions of Academic Bargaining Behavior,** *Robert Birnbaum, Columbia University.* **Towards a Theory of the Union's Role in an Enterprise,** *Donna Sockell, Columbia University.*

Volume 2, 1985, 377 pp. $63.50
ISBN 0-89232-444-9

Edited by **David B. Lipsky,** *New York State School of Industrial and Labor Relations, Cornell University*

CONTENTS: List of Contributors. Preface, *David B. Lipsky.* **Problem Solving in American Collective Bargaining: A Review and Assessment,** *Richard B. Peterson, University of Washington and Lane Tracy, Ohio University.* **Unions and Productivity: A Review of the Research,** *James B. Dworkin and Dennis A. Ahlburg, University of Minnesota.* **Labor Monopoly Models and the Marshallian Rules: An Institutional Appraisal,** *Lawrence Mishel, Cornell University.* **Unionism, Bargaining Spillovers, and Teacher Compensation,** *John Thomas Delaney, Columbia University.* **The Effectiveness of Public Sector Impasse Procedures,** *Paul F. Gerhart and John E. Drotning, Case Western Reserve University.* **Strategic Choice and Collective Action: Organizational Determinants of Teacher Militancy,** *Samuel B. Bacharach, Stephen M. Mitchell, Cornell University and Rose Malinowski, Organizational Analysis and Practice, Inc.* **Toward a General Theory of Industrial Relations,** *William N. Cooke, University of Michigan.* **Tactical Planning of Collective Bargaining: A Facet-Theoretic Approach,** *Arie Shirom, Tel-Aviv University.* **Toward a Contingency Theory of the Grievance-Arbitration System,** *Thomas R. Knight, University of British Columbia.* **Labor Relations and Class Conflict: A Critical Survey of the Contributions of John R. Commons,** *Michael Shalev, Hebrew University.*

JAI PRESS

Volume 3, 1986, 316 pp. $63.50
ISBN 0-89232-642-5

Edited by **David B. Lipsky,** *New York State School of Industrial and Labor Relations, Cornell University* and **David Lewin,** *Graduate School of Business, Columbia University.*

CONTENTS: List of Contributors. Current Research on Industrial Relations Regulation, Bargaining Theory, Progressive Discipline, and Occupational Influence on Unionism, *David Lewin, Columbia University and David B. Lipsky, Cornell University.* **Collective Bargaining in Regulated Industries,** *Wallace Hendricks, University of Illinois.* **Delay in the Union Election Campaign Revisited: A Theoretical and Empirical Analysis,** *Richard N. Block and Benjamin W. Wolkinson, Michigan State University.* **The Regulation of Bargaining Disputes: A Cost-Benefit Analysis of Interest Arbitration in the Public Sector,** *John Delaney, Columbia University, Peter Feuille, and Wallace Hendricks, University of Illinois.* **Unions, Turnover, and Employment Variation,** *Jonathan S. Leonard, University of California, Berkeley.* **A Model of Arbitration and the Incentive to Bargain,** *Frederic C. Champlin, University of Oklahoma, and Mario F. Bognanno, University of Minnesota.* **Power Dependence in Collective Bargaining,** *Edward J. Lawler, University of Iowa, and Samuel B. Bacharach, Cornell University.* **Progressive Discipline in American Industry: Its Origins, Development, and Consequences,** *Sanford M. Jacoby, University of California, Los Angeles.* **Job Conent, Job Status, and Unionism,** *Jack Fiorito and Daniel G. Gallagher, University of Iowa.*

Volume 4, 1987, 251 pp. $63.50
ISBN 0-89232-909-2

Edited by **David Lewin,** *Graduate School of Business, Columbia University,* **David B. Lipsky,** *New York State School of Industrial and Labor Relations, Cornell University* and **Donna Sockell,** *Graduate School of Business, Columbia University.*

CONTENTS: List of Contributors. Introduction, *David Lewin, Columbia University, David B. Lipsky, Cornell University, and Donna Sockell, Columbia University.* **The Characteristics of National Unions,** *Jack Fiorito, The University of Iowa and Wallace E. Hendricks, The University of Illinois.* **Toward a Model of Union Commitment,** *Clive Fullagar, The University of Witwatersrand, South Africa and Julian Barling, Queen's University.* **Labor Unions and the U.S. Congress: Pac Allocations and Legislative Voting,** *Marick F. Masters, The University of Pittsburgh and Asghar Zardkoohi, Texas A&M University.* **The UAW and the Committee for National Health**

Insurance: The Contours of Social Unionism, *David C. Jacobs, The American University.* **Toward a Ststematic Understanding of the Labor Mediation Process,** *Richard B. Peterson and Mark R. Peterson, The University of Washington.* **The Skill Distribution and Competitive Trade Advantage of High-Technology Industries,** *Ann P. Bartel and Frank R. Lichtenberg, Columbia University.* **Women in the Automated Office: Computers, Work, and Prospects for Unionization,** *Daniel B. Cornfield, Vanderbilt University.* **Management Issues Facing New-Product Teams in High-Technology Companies,** *Deborah Gladstein Ancona, Massachusetts Institute of Technology and David F. Caldwell, Santa Clara University.* **The Determinants of Bargaining Structure: A Case Study of AT&T,** *Marianne Koch, David Lewin, and Donna Sockell, Columbia University.*

Supplement 1 - Collective Bargaining in the Public Sector in the United States: A Time of Change
1990, 229 pp. $63.50
ISBN 1-55938-041-1

Edited by **Amarjit S. Sethi,** *University of Ottawa,* **Norman Metzger,** *Mount Sinai Medical Center and* **Stuart J. Dimmock,** *University of Maryland and Basildon & Thurrock Health Authority, England*

CONTENTS: Introduction, *Amarjit S. Sethi, Stuart J. Dimmock, and Norman Metzger.* **Collective Bargaining and Industrial Relation Theory,** *Amarjit S. Sethi, University of Ottawa, Stuart J. Dimmock, University of Maryland and Basildon & Thurrock Health Authority, England and Norman Metzger, The Mount Sinai Medical Center.* **The Status of Public Sector Bargaining Law,** *Eaton H. Conant and Gregory Hundley, University of Oregon.* **The Growth and Development of Public Sector Labor Movement,** *Mark Karper, LeMoyne College.* **Living with the Negotiated Agreement,** *Norman Metzger, The Mount Sinai Medical Center.* **Dispute Resolution,** *Norman Metzger, The Mount Sinai Medical Center.* **The Changing Environment of Public Sector Pay Determination,** *Philip K. Way, University of Cincinnati.* **Special Issues in Public Sector Industrial Relations: A North American Perspective,** *Morley Gunderson, University of Toronto.* **Information Technology: Strategic Choices for Management and Union,** *Amarjit S. Sethi, University of Ottawa.* **The Future of Public Sector Collective Bargaining,** *Amarjit S. Sethi, University of Ottawa, Norman Metzger, The Mount Sinai Medical Center, and Stuart J. Dimmock, University of Maryland and Basildon & Thurrock Health Authority, England*

Advances in the Economic Analysis of Participatory and Labor Managed Firms

Edited by **Derek C. Jones,** *Department of Economics, Hamilton College* and **Jan Svejnar,** *Department of Economics, University of Pittsburgh*

The series publishes theoretical, empirical and institutional analyses of the behavior of films, sectors and economics in which workers participate in decision making. While the emphasis is on economic analysis, studies from related disciplines (history, industrial relations, operations research, political science, psychology and sociology) are welcome. Quality of papers, as judged by independent referees, is the sole criterion for publication. Longer manuscripts, exceeding the usual journal format, are also welcome.

Volume 3, 1988, 400 pp. $63.50
ISBN 0-89232-769-3

CONTENTS: List of Contributors. Foreword, *Derek C. Jones and Jan Svejnar.* **I. THEORETICAL ADVANCES. Section A: General. Equity, Efficiency and Incentives in Cooperative Teams,** *Bentley McLeod, Queens University.* **Contract Curves and Slutsky Equations in a Theory of the Labor-Managed Firm,** *Hajime Miyazaki, Ohio State University.* **Some Consequences of Differential Shareholdings Among Members in a Labor-Managed and Labor Owned Firm,** *Jan Erik Askildsen, University of Oslo, Norman Ireland and Peter J. Law, University of Warwick.* **Increasing Alienation: The Work Environment and the Direction of Technical Progress Under Alternative Forms of Enterprise Organization,** *Roger A. McCain, Brooklyn College.* **Towards a Classical Reconstruction of the Economic Theory of Self-Management,** *Peter Lichtenstein, Boise State University.* **The Viability of Labor-Managed Firms with Cournot-Nash Workers in a Mixed Economy with Profit Maximizing Firms,** *Arnold Katz, University of Pittsburgh.* **Optimal Wage Rates and Profit Sharing in a Firm,** *John Bennett, University College, Cardiff.* **Section B: Share Economy. Codetermination, Profit Sharing and Full Employment,** *Domenico Mario Nuti, European University Institute.* **The Share Economy: Taxation Without Representation,** *John Bonin, Wesleyan University.* **Employment, Prices, and Money in the Share Economy: An Alternative Way,** *Michael Bradley and Stephen C. Smith, George Washington University.* **On Unemployment in Weitzman's Share Economy,** *Benedetto Gui, University of Trieste.* **Free Access vs. Revenue Sharing on**

Alternative Systems for Managing Employment Externalities, *F. Cugno and M. Ferrero, University of Turin.* II. EMPIRICAL AND INSTITUTIONAL ADVANCES. Economic Behavior of Yugoslav Enterprises, *Janez Prasnikar, University of Ljubljana and Jan Svejnar, University of Pittsburgh.* A Model and Measure of Employee Participation: Guttman Scale Tests of the Espinosa-Zimbalist Hypothesis, *John Cable, University of Warwick.* The New Hungarian Economic Reforms and Their Effect on Enterprise Behavior, *Laura D'Andrea Tyson and Steve Popper, University of California, Berkeley.*

Volume 4, In preparation, Summer 1991
ISBN 0-89232-977-6   Approx. $63.50

Also Available:
Volumes 1-2 (1985-1987) $63.50 each

JAI PRESS INC.
55 Old Post Road - No. 2
P.O. Box 1678
Greenwich, Connecticut 06836-1678
Tel: 203-661-7602

JAI PRESS

J A I   P R E S S

Industrial & Labor Relations Review
Cumulative Index, Volumes 1-39, 1947-1986

Compiled by **Brian Keeling** and **Wendy L. Campbell**

Prepared under the auspices of the New York State School for Industrial and Labor Relations, Cornell University

1986, 359 pp.   LC 87-29636 $125.00
ISBN 0-89232-640-9

Together, the 39 volumes of the *Industrial and Labor Relations Review* that were published as of July 1986 are perhaps the most complete existing encyclopedia of contemporary developments in industrial and labor relations. In the more than 1300 articles and 3000 book reviews published in the *Review* since mid-century, the field's foremost scholars have examined every major event and theoretical development in manpower development, labor economics, income security, collective bargaining, labor law, organizational behavior, labor history, and international and comparative industrial relations. It is no wonder that the *Review* is widely acknowledged as the leader in its field and has almost double the number of subscribers if the nearest competitor.

To date, there has been no easy way to locate articles on specific subjects or revies of specific books in the *ILRReview*. That will soon change, however, with the release of a cumulative index carrying articles both by subject and by authors' names, as well as an index of book reviews by book author, for volumes 1-39 (through the July 1986 issue). For the first time, the nearly four decades of research, analysis, and comment in the *ILR Review* will be available in a meaningful sense to students, researers, practitioners, and the merely curious.

JAI PRESS INC.
55 Old Post Road - No. 2
P.O. Box 1678
Greenwich, Connecticut 06836-1678
Tel: 203-661-7602